The underground economies

The underground economies

Tax evasion and information distortion

Edited by

Edgar L. Feige

UNIVERSITY OF WISCONSIN, MADISON

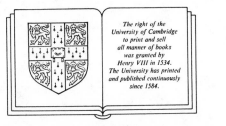

The right of the
University of Cambridge
to print and sell
all manner of books
was granted by
Henry VIII in 1534.
The University has printed
and published continuously
since 1584.

Cambridge University Press

Cambridge

New York   New Rochelle   Melbourne   Sydney

Published by the Press Syndicate of the University of Cambridge
The Pitt Building, Trumpington Street, Cambridge CB2 1RP
32 East 57th Street, New York, NY 10022, USA
10 Stamford Road, Oakleigh, Melbourne 3166, Australia

First published 1989

Printed in the United States of America

Library of Congress Cataloging-in-Publication Data
Feige, Edgar L.
The underground economies/Edgar L. Feige.
p.   cm.
Bibliography: p.
ISBN 0-521-26230-5
1. Informal sector (Economics)   I. Title.
HD2341.F45   1988
381–dc 19   88–4252
                                              CIP

British Library Cataloguing in Publication Data
Underground economies.
1. Black economy.
I. Feige, Edgar L.
339

ISBN 0 521 26230 5

For
Lara
David
Michelle

Contents

CONTENTS

Contributors

ROBERT R. ALFORD University of California, Santa Cruz

PHILIPPE BARTHELEMY Université de Droit, d'Economie et des Sciences d'Aix-Marseille

AMANDA S. BAYER Board of Governors of the Federal Reserve System, Washington, D.C.

G. A. A. M. BROESTERHUIZEN Central Bureau of Statistics, The Netherlands

BRUNO CONTINI Universita degli Studi di Torino

EDGAR L. FEIGE University of Wisconsin, Madison

F. J. M. FELDBRUGGE Leiden University

BRUNO FREY University of Zürich

ISTVAN R. GÁBOR Karl Marx University of Economics, Budapest

INGEMAR HANSSON National Economic Institute, University of Lund

ARNE JON ISACHSEN University of Oslo

ENNO LANGFELDT Institute für Weltwirtschaft an der Universität Kiel

ROBERT T. MCGEE Federal Reserve Bank of New York

ROLF MIRUS University of Alberta

MICHAEL O'HIGGINS University of Bath

RICHARD D. PORTER Board of Governors of the Federal Reserve System, Washington, D.C.

ROGER S. SMITH University of Alberta

STEINER STROM University of Oslo

Preface

Most of the essays in this volume are the outgrowth of the International Conference on the Unobserved Economy that was convened at the Netherlands Institute for Advanced Study in the Humanities and Social Sciences (NIAS) during the summer of 1982. The editor wishes to express a debt of gratitude to the Netherlands Institute for Advanced Study for its outstanding institutional support and to the Liberty Fund for its generous financial support for the conference. The Liberty Fund's executive director, Dr. Neil McLeod, helped with the planning of the conference program.

The success of the conference is owed to the support of its sponsors, the enthusiasm of the participants, and to competent and friendly help offered by secretarial, library, and administrative staff of the NIAS. Special thanks are due to Patty Schevy and Ton Hoenselaars for their supportive organizational and editorial efforts. The financial support of my own research by the Ford Foundation, the Alfred P. Sloan Foundation, and the Netherlands Institute for Advanced Study is gratefully acknowledged.

Introduction

EDGAR L. FEIGE

This volume explores the nature, meaning, measurement, and implications of the still largely uncharted domain of economic activity that has come to be known by the popular catchphrase the "underground economy." It is generally thought to consist of those economic activities and the incomes derived from them that circumvent or otherwise elude government regulation, taxation, or observation. This is a subject that arouses great curiosity, many anecdotes, and few admissions of involvement. The term has been used to cover a wide range of economic activities including but not limited to the traffic in drugs, prostitution, pornography, gambling, "off-the-books" employment, "skimming," "moonlighting," and tax evasion. What these disparate activities appear to have in common is the penchant of those who engage in them to conceal them from government and public scrutiny.

Public attention was drawn to the underground economy during World War II when higher tax rates, price controls, and rationing programs provided incentives for firms and individuals to participate in various "black market" activities. Black market transactions were typically effected by cash payments in order to eliminate a ready audit trail that could otherwise be used by tax authorities and other regulatory agencies for enforcement purposes. A major form of tax evasion was underreporting income to the Internal Revenue Service (IRS).

Although anecdotal evidence of black market activities and tax evasion were widespread, it was left to Cagan (1958) to devise a simple currency ratio method for obtaining a rough quantitative measure of the size of unreported income. He found that unreported income at the end of the war amounted to almost 23% of adjusted gross income reported to the IRS. The IRS employed its own audit control program in an effort to independently establish the amount of income not properly reported on tax forms, but Holland's (1959) research revealed that IRS audit procedures were only able to detect a fraction of the unreported income earned from interest and dividend payments. Pechman (1959) cited this latter evidence in a plea to Congress to initiate a tax reform that would extend automatic withholding to interest and dividend payments. The suggested reforms were rejected by Congress, and the issue of tax evasion faded from public view.

1

Interest in underground economic activity was revived when Gutmann (1977) employed Cagan's procedure to calculate a point estimate of $175 billion as the size of the "subterranean" economy in 1976, amounting to roughly 10% of gross national product (GNP). Feige's (1979, 1980) subsequent calculations, based on a modified currency ratio method and a newly developed transactions method, produced a series of temporal estimates suggesting that the "irregular," or "unobserved," economy had grown dramatically since the late 1960s and that its size was considerably larger than indicated by earlier estimates. Monetary statistics revealed that currency had grown relative to demand deposits despite widespread predictions of the advent of a "cashless society." The U.S. currency holdings per family were in excess of $2,000, and more than 40% of the value of the nation's cash was in the form of $100 bills.

These studies put forward the conjecture that rising tax rates, costly government regulation, and public disenchantment with the tax system had produced widespread noncompliance with the tax code. A major form of noncompliance was believed to be the underreporting of taxable income to the IRS. The IRS responded to this concern by criticizing estimates based on monetary methods and producing, in their place, audit-based estimates of unreported income and associated tax revenue losses. These initial estimates nevertheless acknowledged that in 1976 unreported incomes amounted to between $100 billion and $135 billion with a corresponding tax gap amounting to between $19 billion and $25 billion.

A corollary to the problem of unreported income is that efforts to evade taxes might also produce distortions in other bodies of government data. For example, the construction of National Income and Product Accounts (NIPA) depends upon tax source data. If tax source data is biased, the nation's basic macroeconomic information system is vulnerable to systematic distortions. This in turn suggests that some of the anomalies that plagued the economics profession during the decade of the 1970s might be explicable in terms of distorted official statistics rather than to explanations of ad hoc shocks to the system or macrotheory gone awry. Could the surprising stagflation experience of the decade and the unexplained declines in productivity be associated with a growing but hitherto unobserved economy? Representatives of government statistical agencies cast doubt on these suggestions by publicly expressing confidence in the reliability of official data sources.

These questions nevertheless attracted considerable public attention and controversy. The popular press dubbed the phenomenon the "underground economy," and the Joint Economic Committee of the

U.S. Congress described the underground economy as one of the most interesting and most disturbing subjects they had examined. Public attention focused on the troubling implications of growing noncompliance with tax laws. Was the government losing its ability to collect the revenues necessary to finance public expenditures? Did the tax code require fundamental reform in order to restore a high level of voluntary compliance? Moreover, was the veracity of the nation's macroeconomic data system being compromised as a result of economic incentives to distort information?

Much of the controversy concerning the underground economy focused on the various estimates of its size and growth. Critics of the currency ratio methods challenged the assumptions employed in the estimating procedures and pointed out that some of the evidence cited to substantiate the emergence of an underground economy was open to alternative interpretations. The transaction method, acknowledged to have avoided many of the conceptual shortcomings of other methods, could not be fully implemented because of missing data. Survey methods were suspect because of the problems of self-selection bias and the questionable veracity of recorded responses. The efficacy of audit procedures was questioned, particularly in the realm of uncovering unreported income where the burden of proof lay with the auditor rather than with the taxpayer. The ensuing discussions reflected a growing appreciation of the methodological difficulties entailed in all efforts to measure economic behaviors that individuals and firms were strenuously attempting to hide. It also became more evident that different empirical procedures were in fact measuring different components of underground activity and therefore could not be directly compared. These and other aspects of the underground economy hypothesis required further elaboration.

The classification of underground activities needed to be refined to reflect the substantive concerns of different investigators. The underground economy appeared to mean very different things to labor economists, criminologists, fiscal experts, macroeconomists, and national income accountants. The nature of underground activities in market-oriented systems was likely to be quite different from that of centrally planned systems and was also likely to depend upon the level of a country's development. It appeared that no single definition of the underground economy could serve all these diverse purposes. Alternative definitions would therefore have to be fashioned in light of the relevance that particular underground activities had to different areas of economic inquiry.

A taxonomic framework was required to clarify the interrelationship between prohibited illegal activities, tax evasion activities, and information-distorting activities, and empirical methods needed to be examined in order to determine precisely which components of underground activity were being measured by different techniques. Efforts to test the robustness of results under different assumptions and to replicate studies under different circumstances might also help to resolve outstanding disputes.

Economists cannot readily replicate empirical studies in a laboratory; they must rely on experiments thrown up by history. The historical experience of Europe provided a promising opportunity to extend the study of underground economic activities. Tax rates in many European nations exceeded those in the United States, as did the costliness of regulations in labor and capital markets. The economic incentives to engage in underground activities were clearly present in many European economies. Would similar methods applied to different countries yield similarly disturbing results? Were other methods of measurement available under different circumstances?

Informal inquiries among academic and government experts revealed that there was widespread interest on both sides of the Atlantic in the problems of tax evasion, unregistered labor, and the fiscal and macroeconomic implications of what was variously called the unobserved, hidden, and shadow economy. The conference on the unobserved economy was convened to provide an international forum for economists to consider these issues. Participants were requested to review and evaluate the literature in their respective countries and to undertake empirical studies that might be comparable to work already completed for the United States. They were also encouraged to critique existing work and to present new conceptual and empirical approaches to the subject.

The diverse nature of the activities that different researchers found important suggested that it was best to abandon the notion of a single underground economy and, instead, to identify the variety of underground economies that were germane to salient economic problems. Their boundaries would be delimited by the purposes and perspectives of substantive areas of investigation. The goals were to develop useful definitions for different underground economies; choose appropriate nomenclature to describe them; design, evaluate, and implement alternative measurement methods; and determine the relevance of the findings to other contemporary economic issues.

Chapter 1 presents a classification scheme of underground activities that reflects the substantive issues that have been raised in the United States. The chapter describes three interrelated underground economies

4

– the "illegal" economy, the "unreported" economy, and the "unrecorded" economy – whose incomes are respectively germane to the problems of economic crime, tax evasion, and the reliability of the nation's information system. Alternative estimation procedures that have been used in the United States are examined and evaluated with respect to their conceptual strengths and empirical robustness. The U.S. studies indicate that during the early 1980s unreported income was estimated to range between $280 billion and $420 billion, amounting to 16–24% of reported adjusted gross income. The corresponding implied tax losses are in excess of $100 billion. Surprisingly, the unreported income from illegal activities is estimated to be less than 15% of total unreported income. Time series estimates of unreported incomes suggest that tax evasion rose very dramatically during World War II and again during the past twenty years.

It is during this latter period that high growth rates of unreported income are suspected of having contributed to the problem of unrecorded income that could have distorted the nation's macroeconomic information system. Estimates of total unrecorded income are considerably larger, more variable, and less reliable than those of unreported income. The government has now acknowledged the problem of unrecorded income and has undertaken a historical revision of its NIPA statistics in order to reflect the effects of IRS estimates of misreporting on federal income tax returns.

The second chapter, by Alford and Feige, elaborates the thesis that social science information systems are highly vulnerable to the distorting effects produced by "observer–subject–policymaker feedback." They argue that information must be treated as an endogenous variable in social systems whenever there exist behavioral incentives and mechanisms to manipulate the information system. They show that the underground economy is one of many examples of information endogeneity in the social sciences. Whenever social indicators are used as triggers for policy, they cease to function as objective measures of system activity and become readily corrupted.

McGee and Feige (Chapter 3) develop a formal macroeconomic model to illustrate the economic consequences of rational policymaking undertaken with false information. They show how an initial "statistical illusion" of economic malaise brought on by growth in the unrecorded economy can lead well-intentioned government policies to destabilize the economy. Full-employment policies can create "stagflation" when the monetary authority unwittingly stimulates the observed economy at a time when total economic activity – recorded plus unrecorded – is near capacity output. This specification of the model corresponds closely to the situation that prevailed during the 1970s. Alternatively, when the government adopts an anti-inflation monetary policy, as it did in 1979, the model predicts that an increase in underground economy activity will lead to growing government deficits and high real rates of interest. The model essentially presents an alternative explanation of the economic events during the past two decades. It is an explanation that relies heavily upon the emergence of an unrecorded and hence unobserved sector of economic activity.

Chapter 4 raises the normative question of how large the underground economy should be. Some writers have praised the underground economy as a highly efficient entrepreneurial sector that serves as a constructive buffer against the inefficiencies brought on by taxes and regulations. Others view the underground economy as undermining the social fabric since it deprives legitimately constituted government of required revenues and illegally redistributes income from the honest to the dishonest citizen. Bruno Frey examines and evaluates a number of conceptual approaches to this dilemma and finds that none of them are capable of providing a satisfactory resolution to this normative issue.

The second part of the volume consists of specific country studies that present and evaluate evidence of underground activities in different nations. The first essay by Porter and Bayer (Chapter 5) was not part of the original conference but came to my attention after a decision had been reached to prepare the present volume. Their contribution represents a thorough and highly critical examination of alternative monetary methods that have been employed throughout the world to estimate underground activities. Porter and Bayer review these methods in depth, pointing out their relative strengths and vulnerabilities. They attempt to demonstrate that some of the monetary statistics that have been cited as evidence supporting the underground income hypothesis do not necessarily require an underground economy explanation. Their chapter emphasizes the limitations of monetary measurement tools and serves as a sobering counterweight to the sizable monetary estimates of underground activity in the United States, Canada, Germany, and the United Kingdom that are reported in other chapters.

Broesterhuizen's work on the Netherlands (Chapter 6) produces a sensible framework for analyzing the sensitivity of national accounts to distortion. By examining the detailed composition of NIPA and determining the extent to which particular sectors rely on tax source information, he is able to infer the aggregate impact on the reliability of the NIPA of different degrees of underreporting of income to tax authorities.

O'Higgins's essay (Chapter 7) reviews the various NIPA discrepancy methods that have been proposed as measures of the underground economy in the United Kingdom and finds these methods wanting. He also shows that unlike the experience in the United States, the U.K. ratio of currency to demand deposits fell as a result of the reduced costs of transacting with checks. A similar finding emerges from Langfeldt's chapter on Germany (Chapter 8). O'Higgins's review of the U.K. evidence reveals that different methods of estimation have produced wide differences in the quantitative estimates of the underground economy. As is the case in most of the countries studied, the monetary methods produce the largest estimates. O'Higgins employs the temporal estimates of the growth of underground activity to determine whether the underground economy exhibits a cyclical pattern. If the underground economy moves countercyclically, it will serve to dampen fluctuations in overall economic activity. If it moves cyclically, it reinforces fluctuations in the observed sector. The conceptual framework presented in Part I suggests that the underground economy is expected to behave countercyclically, but the scant evidence from the United Kingdom does not conform with this expectation.

Langfeldt's study of Germany employs many of the same methods that have been used in the United States and with surprisingly similar results. It appears that the unobserved sector in Germany is sizable and that it grew substantially during the decade of the 1970s as tax rates also increased. Mirus and Smith (Chapter 12) employ similar methods for Canada with broadly consistent results. Once again, measured fluctuations in the unobserved sector correspond with fluctuations in tax rates.

The Hansson study of Sweden (Chapter 9) comes to the surprising conclusion that tax evasion does not seem to have increased in a country that claims among the highest tax rates in Europe. His conclusions are however largely based on evidence from survey information and discrepancy measures that have been shown to be poor indicators of unobserved activity. Tax audit information for Sweden appears to be consistent with findings for the United States. Hansson also examines the issue of the optimal size of tax evasion and concludes that from the standpoint of allocative efficiency, some amount of tax evasion may be socially desirable but evasion also has distributive consequences.

Isachsen and Strom (Chapter 11) add evidence for Norway based on both a conventional monetary estimate and an innovative survey method designed in such a way as to provide data that correspond to the variables suggested by the formal theory of tax evasion under uncertainty. Since the theory is highly ambiguous with respect to expected signs of key derivatives, their approach provides a unique empirical basis for assessing the impact on evasion of changes in tax rates, perceived penalty rates, and detection probabilities.

Italy is popularly regarded as having a major unobserved economy, and Contini (Chapter 10) explains the basis for this perception. The Italian case is unusual insofar as its unobserved sector was initially detected as a result of a completely implausible decline in the observed labor force participation rate. By the mid-1970s less than 35% of the total population was registered as belonging to the labor force. Regional labor market surveys revealed off-the-books employment and National Income Accounts required upward revisions of close to 10% during two years in order to properly account for the productivity of workers in small-sized firms that had been artificially underrepresented in the accounting procedures.

Barthelemy (Chapter 13) reviews the French literature's concern with questions of definition and summarizes a number of empirical studies that estimate "black labor" and tax evasion. The French studies employ survey, audit, and monetary methods.

In the third part of the volume, Felbrugge and Gábor provide a unique glimpse into the meaning and importance of what is called the "second economy" in centrally planned systems. The second economy of socialist countries is even more difficult to define than the unobserved economy in market economies because of the complex manner in which the "second economy" is interwoven with the official economy.

Felbrugge (Chapter 14) takes us on a scholarly excursion into the second economy, exploring its legal, political, and economic implications in the USSR. On the surface there appears to be little relationship between the concepts that guide research on the unobserved economy and those that illuminate the significance of the second economy, but these initial impressions are dispelled by the illuminating insights offered by Feldbrugge and Gábor. By focusing the reader's attention on the issue of how the state obtains control of resources under the two systems, we come to recognize that noncompliance with tax laws in the West does in fact have its parallel under a centrally planned system. In the West, individuals earn incomes that are then taxed away. In the Soviet and Hungarian system, the resources are withheld (taxed) at the outset by the overall imposition of scarcity as dictated by the central plan. Feldbrugge points out that there are effectively no penalties for tax evasion in the Soviet Union, yet violations of rules for currency transactions or theft of socialist property carry maximum penalties of fifteen years of confinement or even death. Gábor (Chapter 15) points out that in the Western countries, control is based on the application of rules such as tax laws. In centrally planned systems, control is paradoxically based on the infringement of rules. The state's legal system is such that the conduct of normal activity typically involves the violation

8

of law. As such, each citizen experiences the "permanent general possibility of exposure and punishment by the state as an external power." It is the selective exercise of the laws that gives the state political control, and thus it needs to subtly encourage activity in the second economy. When the economy suffers from central plan inefficiencies, the second economy is there to act as a safety valve for political discontent in much the same way that noncompliance with tax laws increases income in the private sector and buffers declines in the official economy of Western countries. It is this shock absorber role that explains the symbiotic interwoven relationship between the official and the second economy.

The underground economies of both East and West, being sizable, contribute to the overall economic efficiency of their respective systems by virtue of the fact that they circumvent the inefficiencies introduced by taxation and restriction of market mechanisms. But these gains are achieved at the cost of undesired redistributions of income and degradations of information systems. Moreover, since the most important forms of underground activities are illegal, their growth invariably serves to unravel the social fabric of both societies. It is perhaps these realizations that have prompted politicians in both systems to consider fundamental structural changes that seek somehow to internalize the benefits of underground activities while inhibiting their corrosive effects. The United States has recently enacted a fundamental reform of its taxation system that reduces tax rates, eliminates tax loopholes, and strengthens noncompliance penalties. One of the major aims of the reform is to recoup tax revenues by lowering the benefits and increasing the costs of entry into the underground economy of tax evasion. The Soviet Union is now undergoing a fundamental restructuring of its economic life that implicitly seeks to incorporate the efficient second economy into the official sector. As allocative barriers of the central plan are relaxed to accommodate the second economy, income taxes must now be introduced as a means for the government to retain control over resources and their distribution. It appears that the universality of underground activities and the growing recognition of their consequences serves as a powerful catalyst for independent changes that draw East and West closer together.

PART I

The meaning, measurement, and policy implications of the underground economies

CHAPTER 1

The meaning and measurement of the underground economy

EDGAR L. FEIGE

If we are to believe official government statistics, the U.S. economy of the 1970's displayed symptoms of economic maladies that earlier generations of economists thought could not coexist. The decade was plagued with high rates of inflation, unacceptable levels of unemployment, slowed growth, and declining productivity. The simultaneous occurrence of inflation and recession baffled economic diagnosticians and precipitated what has been called a crisis in macroeconomic analysis. The inconsistency between the predictions of conventional macroeconomic theories and the "facts" of economic life have led to a re-examination of both the theories and the facts.

During the earlier decade of the 1960's, our theories and experience led us to believe that the economy was characterized by a stable downward-sloping Phillips curve, a menu of trade-offs between unemployment and inflation from which to choose the most socially desirable combination. Macroeconomic models provided relatively accurate forecasts of future economic activity. Policymakers pursued conventional Keynesian policies in efforts to fine tune the economy, working to stabilize it at full employment. The prevailing optimism of the time encouraged the belief that relatively low levels of unemployment could be attained while maintaining reasonable price stability and a healthy rate of economic growth. Since inflation was thought to have negligible economic consequences, full-employment policies could be pursued that would cyclically balance budgets, while providing the economic growth necessary to generate the government revenues required to finance the growing demands for social expenditure programs. These optimistic hopes were rudely shattered by the economic facts of the past fifteen years.

The forecasts of macromodels became increasingly wide of the mark. The Phillips curve began to spiral upward and outward, requiring the neologism "stagflation" to describe the joint occurrence of inflation and recession. As macroeconomic policy appeared increasingly impotent against this unusual malady, the term "economic crisis" was heard with greater frequency than during any period since the Great Depression.

13

The economics profession was confronted by a growing chasm between the world of theory and the world of observation. The theory was imaginatively modified to incorporate "supply side" and "rational expectation" effects to account for some of the observed anomalies in the economic system. Energy price shocks bore the burden of explaining the simultaneous occurrence of inflation and recession, while dynamic expectation theories attempted to account for their persistence and the government's inability to restore the economy to a stable equilibrium. Despite these theoretical innovations, a coherent and empirically plausible consensus on the causes of the stagflation experience still eludes our grasp, as does an adequate explanation for the dramatic growth in government deficits.

A complementary approach toward bridging the gap between theory and observation is suggested by the maxim, "if the facts don't fit the theory, check the facts." Is it possible that the facts of economic life have become systematically distorted as the result of our failure to notice the growth of an "unobserved," or "underground," sector of economic activity? The underground income hypothesis (UIH) represents an effort to reassess the veracity of the economic facts that are generated by official government agencies who collect and disseminate key economic indicators. Their information signals guide both analysis and policy. In brief, the hypothesis suggests that a large and growing segment of economic activity may escape the elaborate measurement system that government agencies have established to monitor economic activity. Since that measurement system relies to a major extent on tax information, the growth of non-compliance with tax laws can produce distortions in the information system that generates our observations on the progress of economic activity. The UIH raises a new set of questions to be asked and offers some tentative answers that might help to resolve several of the outstanding paradoxes in our midst. The questions deal with the adequacy of the information system on which individuals, firms, and governments rely for rational decision making. McGee and Feige (Chapter 3) demonstrate that a growing unobserved sector that flaws the information system can produce stagflation symptoms similar to those experienced during the 1970's when the government is committed to a full-employment policy. Alternatively, when the policy emphasis is on price stability, a growing unobserved sector can create budgetary deficits of the type we are presently experiencing.

The UIH suggests that some of the basic taxonomic distinctions embedded in both Keynesian and post-Keynesian conceptual frameworks require extension. The core of traditional macroeconomic doctrine focuses on the consequences of resource shifts between the private and the government sectors. The UIH suggests that attention must also be focused on the consequences of resource shifts between the observed and the unobserved sectors of the economic system.

When the substantive concern is the reliability of broad economic indicators such as those produced by the National Income and Product Accounts (NIPA), the observed, or "recorded," sector of the economy consists of those economic activities that are regularly caught in the net of our official statistical accounting mechanisms. This recorded sector furnishes us with our perceptions of the fundamental facts of macroeconomic life. Not only does it function as the basis for generating the questions that the economics profession seeks to answer, it also provides the fodder for our forecasting industry, our empirical tests, and our policy prescriptions. A growth of "unrecorded" economic activity that escapes the purview of the official NIPA creates systematic discrepancies between what is recorded in our information system and what is actually taking place in the economy. If the official information system becomes systematically biased, it will generate misguided questions, erroneous answers, and false information to both citizens and policymakers alike.

In the context of fiscal economics, the observed sector refers to the amount of income that is "reported" to the fiscal authority under our current system of voluntary tax reporting. Non-compliance with the tax code generates "unreported" income, namely, the difference between the amount of income that ought to be reported to the tax authority and the amount actually reported. A growth of unreported income reduces the ability of the fiscal authority to generate revenues and, ceteris paribus, generates budget deficits. Moreover, since the income recorded in the NIPA system relies on data reported to the tax authorities, a growth of unreported income can also lead to a growth of unrecorded income. In short, a large and growing unobserved sector reallocates resources away from the domain of observation and control. It affects our perceptions of economic reality and the reality itself. Its allocation and distribution consequences can have important implications for macroeconomic stabilization policy and tax policy.

The aim of this chapter is to develop a taxonomic framework of definitions and nomenclature for characterizing different types of underground activities and to review and evaluate alternative methods for estimating the size and growth of this elusive phenomenon. The taxonomic framework presented in what follows is germane to the institutional setting of developed Western nations, and the empirical investigation focuses on the major methods that have been employed to estimate the magnitude and temporal development of the unobserved sector in the United States.

The meaning of the unobserved economy

The literature produced by "underground economists" has generated a plethora of terms (underground, subterranean, shadow, informal, hidden, parallel, black, clandestine, second, household, etc.) to describe various aspects of the unobserved sector of the economy. This proliferation of concepts illustrates the fact that what is here termed the "unobserved sector" is in fact an amalgam of many diverse activities whose relevance to inquiry depends partly upon the problem at hand. Whereas each of these terms contributes something to our understanding of particular aspects of the subject, the multiplicity of concepts has tended to confuse rather than to clarify the important substantive issues raised by the discovery that potentially significant segments of economic activity may be imperfectly accounted for in the conventional data bases forming the very foundation of empirical inquiry in economics.

Alternative measures of the size of what is popularly called the "underground economy" have revealed a wide range of estimates of its magnitude. These apparent inconsistencies suggest not only the difficulty of attempting to estimate a phenomenon whose raison d'être is to defy detection, but more importantly, the fact that the different measures are incommensurable since they are estimates of different conceptual entities. To date, little effort has been devoted to the elaboration of useful conceptual distinctions of different notions of "underground income" and to the reconciliation of diverse empirical measures. What is required is a taxonomic framework that discriminates among different aspects of the phenomenon and provides empirical links between the various theoretical constructs and their real-world counterparts. One distinction that deserves greater attention is the difference between *economic* and *fiscal* concepts of income. All too often, the underrecording of income in the NIPA has been erroneously identified with the issue of tax evasion.

Total economic income

Macroeconomic theory defines income as the maximum amount of consumption that can be undertaken in a given period without altering the stock of wealth. In principle, this broad notion of total economic income makes no distinction between market and non-market consumption. Conceptually, consumption of goods and services includes all items that have positive market or shadow prices due to their relative scarcity. In U.S. practice, however, empirical measures of economic income are limited to the consumption of legally produced market goods and services (produced by labor, capital, and property) supplied by residents of the country during a specified time period. The conventional macroeconomic accounting practices that are embodied in the NIPA thus necessarily sacrifice conceptual completeness in order to reduce the cost and error of actual measurement. If we define recorded income as that component of total economic income empirically captured in the NIPA statistics, then "total unrecorded income" can be seen to consist of

1 income produced in prohibited economic activities deemed "illegal" by the law of the land,
2 income produced in non-market (bartered) legal activities, and
3 income produced in legal market activities (monetary) that for various reasons escapes NIPA measurement.

A simple taxonomic framework for total economic income and its components is displayed in Table 1.1.

In principle, total economic income includes all income produced in both the market and the non-market sectors. Precisely what determines the boundary (AB) between these two sectors is one of the major substantive issues of micro-labor-economics, with its emphasis on labor force participation rates. Development economics is largely concerned with the macrodeterminants of the (AB) boundary and the rapidity with which it shifts up over time. Some authors have referred to the output of the non-market sector as the "informal economy" (Skolka, 1985), whereas others have used the same term to describe market activities (Smith et al., 1982).

Both market and non-market income-producing activities can be further classified according to the societies' social conventions as embodied in legal statutes that distinguish between legal and illegal activities. The legal status distinction identifies those income-producing activities regarded as illegal under criminal law. Illegal income-producing activities are presently excluded from the U.S. NIPA, whereas the UN-OECD System of National Accounts (United Nations, 1953) makes no distinction between legal and illegal activities.

What is germane to the issue of the unobserved economy as it relates to economic income is the question of what is and what is not recorded in NIPA. As displayed in Table 1.1, recorded income[1] includes most

---

[1] Recorded income can be measured with different degrees of "grossness," thus giving rise to distinctions between gross national product and net national product (NNP). Estimates of national income are derived from NNP by subtracting indirect tax and non-tax liabilities, business transfer payments, and the statistical discrepancy and by adding subsidies less the current surplus of government enterprises. Finally, personal income is derived from national income by subtracting corporate profits with inventory

17

Table 1.1. *Taxonomic framework for economic income*

Theoretical construct	Market classification	Legal status activity	Reporting status	NIPA component
		Illegal activity C_____D	Unrecorded income	Monetary unobserved sector
	Market income		E_____F	G_____H
Total economic income		Legal activity	Recorded income	Estimated gross national product
	A_____B	A_____B	A_____B	
	Non-market income		Imputed income	
		Legal activity C_____D Illegal activity	E_____F Unrecorded income	G_____H Non-monetary unobserved sector

legal market income as well as minor imputations for particular components of legal non-market income.[2] Total unrecorded income thus includes illegal market and non-market activities. In addition, total unrecorded income includes legal market income that unwittingly escapes NIPA detection (the upper CD–EF boundary in Table 1.1) as well as legal non-market income (the lower CD–EF boundary), which is conventionally excluded from the NIPA due to the difficulties engendered in measuring the size of this component.

Unrecorded illegal income arises from the production and distribution of goods and services regarded as illegal by social convention. In the United States, such goods include drugs and pornographic materials; services include prostitution and value added in loan sharking. In practice, such illegal activities are excluded from the accounts, except to

valuation and capital consumption adjustments, net interest, contributions for social insurance, and wage accruals less disbursements and by adding government transfer payments to persons, personal interest income, personal dividend income, and business transfer payments.

[2] The Bureau of Economic Analysis makes imputations for food produced and consumed on farms and also includes imputations for non-monetary transactions such as rent for owner-occupied housing.

the extent that some illegally produced income might be "laundered" into data sources underlying the NIPA.

The final component of total economic income is unrecorded legal market income. Legally produced income can escape measurement in the NIPA as a result of deficiencies in NIPA estimation procedures and underlying data sources. Since illegal income and non-market income is excluded from the NIPA by convention rather than by inadvertent omission, we reserve the term "unrecorded income" to denote legal market income that ought (under current accounting conventions) to be included in the NIPA but is not.

Fiscal income

Fiscal income is defined by legislative tax statutes that identify those sources of "income" that are to be included in the nation's tax base. On the one hand, fiscal income is a broader concept than total economic income since it includes realizations of appreciated asset values in addition to income earned from currently produced goods and services. On the other hand, it is a narrower concept, since economic income includes categories of income explicitly excluded by the fiscal code. Most non-market household production is excluded from fiscal income although it is legitimately considered to be part of total economic income. It is also the case that fiscal income may exclude items specifically imputed in the NIPA.[3]

The components of fiscal income are determined by fiscal legislation rather than by the economic criterion of current production of scarce goods and services. As displayed in Table 1.2, a nation's potential income tax base (including total economic income and capital gains realizations) is legally subdivided into taxable and untaxed income. In the United States taxable income includes income earned from illegal activities.

The IJ lines in Table 1.2 define the tax avoidance boundary insofar as individuals have legal discretion to shift their activities between taxed and untaxed sectors. Taxable income from both legal and illegal activities is further subdivided into reported and unreported income components. Shifts from the reported taxable income sector into the unreported taxable income sector (crossing the KL line) constitute one form of tax evasion, namely, underreporting of legal and illegal sources of taxable

---

[3] An example would be food grown and consumed on a farm, which is excluded from fiscal income under U.S. tax law but is considered to be a segment of total economic income for which NIPA imputations are undertaken.

Table 1.2. *Taxonomic framework for fiscal income (personal income taxes)*

Potential tax base	Legal classification	Reporting status	Effective tax base	NIPA relationship
	Untaxed income	Legally non-reported income	Avoidance	
	I_____J	I_____J	I_____J	
		Unreported income		O_____P
		K_____L	Evasion	
			M_____N	
Total economic income	Taxable income	Reported income	Adjusted gross income	Personal income
				O_____P
			M_____N	
Capital gains and other		K_____L	Evasion	
		Unreported income		
	I_____J	I_____J	I_____J	
		Legally non-reported income	Avoidance	
	Untaxed income	income		

income. A second source of tax evasion arises from the overreporting of deductible adjustments to income. Fraudulent overstatement of these adjustments to income is strict tax evasion. On the other hand, tax-induced expenditures on goods or services that constitute allowable deductions are a legitimate form of tax avoidance. The fragility of this distinction has led to the introduction of yet another neologism, "aviosion," to describe questionable practices that raise adjustments to total reported income.

The effective tax base (before deductions) for the federal income tax is known as adjusted gross income (AGI). The AGI is the sum of all taxable income sources that have been reported on federal tax returns minus adjustments to income. Unobserved income in the fiscal context is simply "unreported income" measured as the difference between the income that should have been reported for federal income tax purposes had the fiscal code been adhered to and the income actually reported (areas IJKL in Table 1.2). A further caveat is required to take account of unreported incomes and expenditures that arise from underreporting on state and local taxes. Since virtually no research has been undertaken on the amount of underreporting of state and local taxes, the term "unreported income" is often used to refer to underreporting on the federal income tax.

From the foregoing discussion, it is evident that "total unreported income" is not synonymous with "tax evasion" since tax evasion also includes overstated tax deductions. Moreover, unreported income is a totally different concept than total unrecorded income. The former represents an empirical understatement of federal taxable income, whereas the latter reflects an underestimation of total economic income.

The relationship between the observed and unobserved sectors

When the observed sector is taken to constitute all the measured economic activity that is recorded in conventional national income accounting frameworks such as NIPA, its overwhelming corpus consists of income-producing market activities that utilize money as the medium of exchange.

The unobserved sector consists of two components: a market sector that utilizes money as a medium of exchange in the production and distribution of goods and services and a non-monetary sector in which real goods and services are produced but are either directly consumed by the producing unit (e.g., the household) or are informally exchanged by a bartering mechanism.

The monetary unobserved sector will include the output of illegal production of goods and services, since these are, by accounting conventions, excluded from the standard accounts. Much more significantly, this sector comprises a wide range of legitimate income-producing activities that for a variety of reasons are not appropriately captured in the social accounting mechanism. Such activities would include all incomes that are earned but not fully recorded in the national income accounts. To the extent that fiscal information is an important underlying source of NIPA data, income that is not reported to the fiscal authorities will consequently lead to an underestimation of economic income as well. The motives for non-reporting or misreporting of information are alleged to include tax evasion, regulatory evasion, avoidance of costs of compliance, or simply mistrust of government.

Ultimately, the accuracy and coverage of any social accounting system, regardless of the ingenuity of its design, will depend upon the cooperation and honesty of the reporting units. Whether such cooperation is eroded by the economic incentives inadvertently inherent in any system of governance or by a growing alienation from the articulated legal and social values of a society, the first casualty of reduced compliance is the social data base.

The non-monetary component of the unobserved sector comprises those vital economic activities of households, firms, and voluntary institutions that produce real outputs that are bartered and are by convention, or inadequate data, largely excluded from conventional income accounts.

The omission from economic analysis of both the monetary and non-monetary components of the unobserved economy has been rationalized in the prevailing, yet unsupported belief that the monetary component is relatively small and can therefore be ignored. The non-monetary component, while large, is assumed to remain a relatively stable fraction of observed income. However, if cyclical and secular shifts between the unobserved sector and the observed sector are sizable in comparison to shifts within the observed sector between government and private activities, then their conceptual omission will weaken the predictive power of any macroeconomic theory.

In order to illustrate the potential importance of the unobserved economy, it is useful to describe the secular relationship between the unobserved and the observed sectors of a hypothetical economy over time in its development from a subsistence economy to a modern welfare state. For simplicity, assume that the total private real income of the economy (observed and unobserved) grows at a constant rate over time, thereby abstracting for the moment from the intrusions of technological discoveries, natural or political calamities such as famines or wars, business cycles, countercyclical policies, and efficiency effects produced by resource shifts. Each of these factors can be reintroduced into the analysis, at the cost of simplicity.

The total private real income of this hypothetical society is represented in Figure 1.1 by T_0-T_5, which depicts the unperturbed growth of real income at a constant rate. The economy begins at t_0, when its total subsistence income is equal to T_0. During the time period t_0-t_1, the entire economy consists of an unobserved non-market, non-monetary sector. At time t_1, the simultaneous social contrivances of organized markets and a monetary medium of exchange are introduced. Given the inherent informational and allocation efficiencies of these key social innovations, we would expect a dramatic shifting of resources from the non-monetary to the monetary sector and thus a growth of the monetary sector (represented by M_1-M_2) that exceeds that of the total economy.

At time t_2, we introduce the social scientist, an observer, armed with a variety of procedures for measuring economic activity. The observer sets herself the task of measuring the legal component of the monetized

22

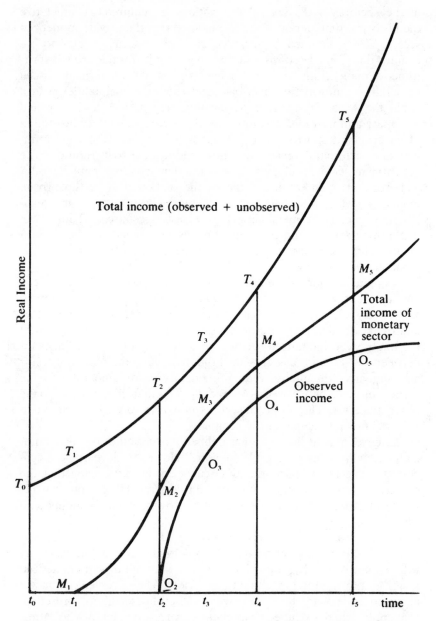

Figure 1.1. Hypothetical relationships between the observed and unobserved sectors.

market sector M_2–M_5. Several observations are required to characterize the historical time period t_2–t_3. We assume that the private monetized sector, having attained a particular state of maturity, begins to encounter diminishing returns and that therefore its former growth starts to decelerate. In time, this sector begins to produce externalities such as pollution, information overload, and economic inequalities, which strain the social fabric. It is during this time period that we would anticipate a more rapid development of the complementary institution of government, spurred on by demands for physical and legal infrastructure, external defense, education, and income redistribution. The government sector, seeking to satisfy the demands for "public goods" and working to internalize some of the externalities of the private monetary sector, will in turn resort increasingly to taxation and regulation as means of marshaling the requisite resources. Thus, both diminishing returns and the competing resource needs of the government sector will slacken the initial exuberant growth of the private monetary economy.

As greater resources are devoted to improve and broaden the social measurement system, we would expect the growth of the "observed sector" O_2–O_3 to exceed that of both the private monetized sector and of the total private sector. During this period, we would expect the unobserved monetized sector – measured by the vertical distance between O_2–O_3 and M_2–M_3 – to shrink relative to the observed sector and, similarly , the unobserved non-monetary sector – measured by the vertical distance between M_2–M_3 and T_2–T_3 – to decline relative to the observed sector. The observed sector will, conversely, grow relative to the total private income of the economy.

The development literature has dubbed this period of perceived dramatic growth as the period of "takeoff." However, development economists have been appropriately circumspect in recognizing that the perceived growth is in part a statistical illusion, reflecting improvements in the measurement system rather than growth of the economy as a whole.

In our hypothetical history the period t_3–t_4 is of particular interest since it is during this period that the observed sector of the economy will be approximately proportional both to the total private monetized sector and to the total income of the society. The observed sector will never coincide with the total private monetized sector as a result of conventions that exclude comprehensive measurement of the latter. More significantly, complete social measurement will be frustrated by the inherent limitations of any system that depends essentially on the honesty and reliability of voluntary reporting units. Since the hallmark of this period is the accurate characterization of total economic activity given by the observed sector, from the perspective of the social scientist, it is an ideal age for observation. It is during this period that well-conceived economic theories and models that are themselves rooted in empirical observation will have the highest chance of explaining and predicting economic behavior. In essence, predictions and explanations of macroeconomic events will be uncontaminated by the effects of substantial and unrecognized shifts between observed and unobserved economic activity. As long as the unobserved sector remains roughly proportional to the observed sector, government policies based on proportionally accurate information signals have the highest chance of achieving stabilization goals. Unfortunately, it is highly unlikely that this fortuitous nexus of observed facts and underlying reality will last indefinitely.

During the subsequent period (t_4-t_5), the hypothesized increase in unobserved activities creates a divergence between the growth rates of the unobserved and observed sectors. During this period, observers of highly developed societies will experience the mirror image of the problem that confronts the observer of developing economies. Namely, the unobserved sector will be growing relative to the observed sector.

In centrally planned economies, many official prices are artificially maintained below equilibrium prices, causing the official sector to develop the inevitable shortages that are characteristic of Eastern European countries. Many of these countries develop a "second," or "parallel," economy with market-determined prices and wages that are above those in the official sector. These price differentials provide the incentives that induce a shift of resources into the unobserved sector. Similarly, in market-oriented economies, where governments acquire resources both for the provision of public goods and for redistributions via taxation, tax incentives induce a shift of economic activity toward the unobserved sector. Taxation and regulation can be escaped legally by switching resources into the non-monetary unobserved sector. Here one would expect the development of "do-it-yourself" activities. One would also expect an increased incidence of illegal underreporting and non-reporting of taxable monetary income as parts of the economy go "off the books."

If it is the case that many highly developed economies have passed unknowingly into an era where the unobserved sectors of the economy are expanding relative to the observed sectors, what are the implications that follow? First and foremost, our conventional economic indicators will give an increasingly distorted picture of the true state of economic affairs. Official statistics will reveal a slowing rate of real output even when the total economy is growing at its normal pace. Official price statistics in centrally planned economies will understate the true price level, whereas market-oriented economies will produce official price indices that overstate the actual level of prices. If the unobserved sector grows rapidly, with employees in the observed sector searching for secondary jobs off the books, official productivity measures decline if output is understated more rapidly than inputs are reduced. Under social welfare systems with liberal unemployment benefits, official unemployment statistics may become temporarily bloated as people "out of work" find alternative jobs in the unobserved sector.

Macroeconomic forecasts would tend to become systematically biased, overpredicting real growth rates of output and underestimating prices. Finally, and perhaps most significantly, citizen and policymaker decisions, however rational, will be based on false economic signals, thus converting the perception of malaise into the reality of economic distress.

The relevance of these conjectures to our own economy depends critically on an empirical issue, namely, how large is the unobserved sector and how fast has it been growing? If the sector exists, how can it be measured? If it has been growing, what telltale traces will it leave in its wake?

Measuring the unobserved sector: methodological issues

Any attempt to measure a social phenomenon whose raison d'être is to defy observation is fraught with complex conceptual and empirical difficulties. All estimates of the size and growth of the unobserved sector are likely to contain substantial errors. It is therefore necessary to establish some methodological criteria for what investigators would regard as reasonable evidence that the phenomenon has been estimated within tolerable limits. Any research strategy must be sufficiently broad to encompass available evidence from diverse social sciences. The evidence may be qualitative, anecdotal, or quantitative. Since different methods are likely to measure different aspects of the unobserved sector, estimates must be reconciled in terms of the correspondence between different concepts of unobserved activity.

Three major classes of information are available to the researcher, and each has an important role in the analysis. First, there is the large and suggestive body of anecdotal information that is not easy to analyze by the systematic procedures of modern quantitative methods. Such "institutional" information is, however, highly relevant as a qualitative

26

guide to both the frequency and nature of the phenomenon under investigation. Anecdotal institutional information provides a necessary starting point for inquiry. It serves to raise many key questions and points the research in specific directions concerning both the sources and processes involved in unobserved economic activities.

A second class of information utilizes systematically collected micro-observations, be they from individual surveys, tax returns, unemployment records, or other similar sources. Microdata approaches are useful insofar as they yield disaggregated information that sheds light on distributional issues and can also be of value for administrative purposes such as tax enforcement. Microapproaches to estimation tend to be costly and typically yield point estimates of the size of unobserved activity rather than temporal estimates of the growth of the sector. The inability of microapproaches to track the temporal development of the unobserved sector may preclude their use in uncovering the temporal causes and consequences of the phenomenon. Another shortcoming of the microapproaches is that they typically rely on obtrusive methods of observation that may compromise the quality of the data collected. Incentives to conceal information jeopardize the veracity of the response given to the observer or data collector. Business and tax records may be falsified to avoid regulation or taxation. Survey studies may suffer from high rates of non-response and from self-selection biases.

The results of microinvestigations may also be sensitive to the method used to query respondents. An Internal Revenue Service (IRS, 1980) taxpayer opinion survey on tax evasion, which used both direct questions (with assurances of anonymity) and a randomized response technique, revealed that the randomized response yielded evasion estimates between 62 and 433% higher on some questions than the direct question approach.

An alternative approach to measurement relies upon macroeconomic data sources. An advantage of macroapproaches is that they employ published data sources that have been collected for purposes unrelated to the study of the unobserved economy. Because these are unobtrusive measures, they are not susceptible to willful distortion on the part of a respondent. Such approaches are typically less costly to undertake, and they provide estimates of both the size and growth of unobserved activities. All of the macroapproaches to be reviewed depend on monetary aggregates that are collected for purposes unrelated to unobserved activities. The macromethods require explicit counterfactual assumptions to produce estimates of the unobserved economy. The reliability of any particular macroapproach will therefore depend upon the reason-

27

ableness of the assumptions that underlie the estimation procedure and ultimately on the power of the estimates to explain other macroeconomic anomalies.

Given the difficulties inherent in any effort to quantify the unobserved sector, the various approaches to measurement are best viewed as complementary, yielding insights into different aspects of the issue.

Measuring the non-monetary unobserved sector

The empirical difficulty of deriving estimates of the non-monetary sector of the economy (comprised primarily of non-market production of goods and services in the household) has precluded the inclusion of this sector into the conventional NIPA. Time budget surveys have been employed in serveral countries to determine the time spent by family members in various forms of household production. Chadeau (1985) has surveyed various methods employed to estimate the monetary value of unpaid household production. The major problem in these studies is finding an appropriate method for valuation. The two most widely used valuation methods are opportunity cost and market costs. The opportunity cost approach attempts to measure the value of lost market income that results from production activities in the home, whereas the market cost approach values household production activities at corresponding market wage rates that would be paid if outside workers were hired to perform the productive activities. The resulting estimates are sensitive to the particular valuation method employed and the coverage of household activity. The overall estimates range between 20 and 50% of recorded gross national product (GNP), but this range is narrowed considerably when account is taken of the different coverage and different valuation methods employed by different studies. Murphy (1978, 1982) suggests that the non-market sector may range between 37 and 51% of the market economy in the United States. Inter-temporal estimates of the size of the household production have yet to produce conclusive evidence relating to the secular trend of household production. Murphy's studies of the United States suggest that the sector may have declined between 1960 and 1970 as a percentage of GNP but increased between 1970 and 1976.

Measuring the monetary unobserved sector

Various methods have been proposed to measure what is casually called the "underground economy." When the results of these different methods are indiscriminately lumped together, they give a misleading impression of a very wide range of estimates. A key difficulty in assessing the consistency of empirical evidence on the monetary unobserved sector is that different methods measure different components of unobserved activity. Often the studies are vague about what precisely is being measured, and surveys of the empirical literature on the subject have failed to clearly establish which particular facet of unobserved activity was measured by different techniques. Once proper account is taken of the fact that different methods measure different components of unobserved activity, the estimates produced by different methods are more consistent than appears at first blush. Some methods attempt to estimate unrecorded income, others measure unreported income, and some methods estimate unrecorded transactions. The complex conceptual and empirical interrelationships between various notions of unobserved income are discussed in detail in Carson (1984), Parker (1984), and Feige (1985a).

A second source of variance in reported estimates arises from the use of different assumptions required for different estimation procedures. The range of variation resulting from alternative assumptions can be examined by the use of sensitivity analysis. As different approaches to the estimation of monetary unobserved activities are reviewed, special attention is given to what is being measured and what assumptions are employed to derive particular estimates. Finally, some of the variation between estimates results from the use of different data sources and time periods.

Discrepancy methods

Discrepancy methods are widely used as a means for estimating particular components of unobserved income. The discrepancy approach is feasible whenever independent means exist to estimate the same conceptual entity. If one procedure for measuring a particular form of unobserved activity is believed to be relatively free of biases induced by that activity while another procedure is known to be affected by the activity, the discrepancy between the two can be used to measure the *net* effect of the unobserved activity. In practice, great care must be exercised in interpreting discrepancy measures. They are typically not measures of the size of the unobserved sector. The observed discrepancy between two measures often reflects conceptual differences in what the two measures purport to estimate. Moreover, if both procedures are directly or indirectly affected by the unobserved activity, then the discrepancy method simply measures the difference between the two approaches rather than the absolute magnitude of the unobserved

29

sector. The most common discrepancy approaches are reviewed separately in order to highlight the different aspects of unobserved activity that each measure captures.

National accounts discrepancies: unrecorded income

The income and expenditure sides of the national income accounts are typically estimated from different data sources. To the extent that the two sides of the accounts are measured by relatively independent methods, Macafee (1980) proposed that the discrepancy between an expenditure side estimate of national income and an income side estimate of national income might be used to estimate the size of the unrecorded sector. If individuals are less likely to misrepresent their expenditures than they are to misrepresent income, such a method would capture the net difference in misrepresentation on the two sides of the accounts. This difference should not be interpreted as a measure of the size of unrecorded income since both sides of the accounts may understate economic activity.

The raw initial discrepancies that may be discovered between the two sides of the accounts are rarely published. When sizable initial discrepancies do appear in practice, the accounts are usually revised to reduce the discrepancy (Chapter 7). The final reported discrepancy, known as the "statistical discrepancy," is of no value as an estimate of total unrecorded activity.

Frey and Pommerehne (1982, p. 9) display a table of unexplained differences in national income measures, which they represent as "estimates in terms of national income for the size of the underground economy" (p. 8). The range of the reported estimates is from 1 to 23.2% of GNP. The lower estimates are in fact discrepancies that arise from independent estimates of the two sides of the NIPA. At best, these estimates capture a fraction of unrecorded income. The high estimates refer to discrepancies between NIPA income measures and incomes reported on tax returns. The latter are partial estimates of unreported income. None of the reported estimates measure the size of the underground economy, and since each reported estimate measures a different income concept, they should not be lumped together.

As is shown in the next section, it is possible to construct a reconciliation between the NIPA measure of personal income and the IRS measure of taxable income declared on federal income tax returns, namely, AGI. The NIPA personal income measure must first be adjusted to account for all items included in personal income that need not be reported to the tax authority. It must furthermore be adjusted for all items that should be reported to the tax authority but are not included in personal income. The resulting figure reflects an NIPA-based estimate of the amount of AGI that should have been reported to the IRS. The difference between this NIPA estimate of AGI and the actual AGI reported to the IRS is known as the "AGI gap."

The AGI gap discrepancy measure: unreported income

The AGI gap represents a carefully constructed discrepancy measure that attempts to estimate unreported income. The AGI gap would be a conceptually appropriate estimate of unreported fiscal income under the following conditions:

1 Personal income (PI) was accurately measured, that is, there is no unrecorded income.
2 Correct adjustments are made for all conceptual differences between the economic income measure PI and the fiscal income measure AGI.[4]

Although the AGI gap is unlikely to yield an empirically exact measure of unreported fiscal income (due to the difficulties of measuring many of the large reconciliation items required to make PI and AGI conceptually compatible), it is nonetheless of interest since it highlights the conceptual similarities and differences between NIPA accounts and tax-based source information. These conceptual interdependencies are crucial for an understanding of how underreporting of tax source information will ultimately impact NIPA measures of GNP and PI.

The AGI gap measure is best interpreted as a rough measure of noncompliance in the reporting of income for the federal income tax. It understates total unreported income insofar as it takes no account of underreporting of other taxes nor does it capture unreported illegal income since the latter is not included in NIPA estimates of personal income. Moreover, to the extent that the NIPA measure of personal income is understated as a result of other unrecorded income, the AGI gap will correspondingly understate unreported income. The gap may overstate unreported income to the extent that personal income includes income earned by individuals whose income falls below the filing threshold.

Figure 1.2 displays the Bureau of Economic Analysis (BEA) original

---

[4] These include adjustments to personal income for imputations already made for underreporting on tax source information that goes into the construction of PI as well as adjustments for underreporting of capital gains income and illegal income that is taxable but not included in PI.

31

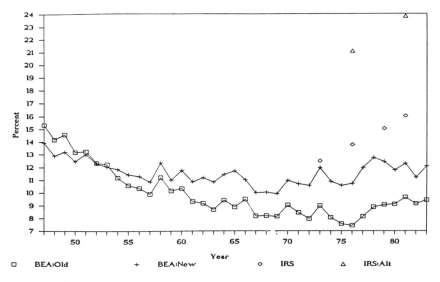

Figure 1.2. Unreported income as percentage of AGI. Alternative government estimates.

(BEA:Old) and revised AGI gap (BEA:New) as a percentage of re-ported AGI for the period 1947–83.[5] The original gap estimate sug-gested a secular decline in the percentage of unreported income from 1947 to 1976 and an upturn thereafter. The revised estimate suggests a secular decline in the percentage of unreported to reported income from 1947 to 1969 and a secular increase during the decade of the 1970's. The size of the AGI gap is revised upward by an average of 4% for the decade of the 1950's, 21% for the 1960's, and 36% for the decade of the 1970's. By 1983, the AGI gap had increased to $235.6 billion, suggesting that more than 12% of reported AGI was unreported in that year.

Figure 1.2 also displays the most recent IRS estimate (IRS) of total unreported income and an alternative measure (IRS:Alt) based on the IRS data employing an alternative set of assumptions to derive the estimate.[6] A review of the IRS method is presented next.

---

[5] The original "BEA gap" estimates (labeled BEA:Old) were prepared by the Bureau of Economic Statistics before the comprehensive revision of NIPA statistics in 1985. The revised series (labeled BEA:New) reflect the effect of the newly revised NIPA data.

[6] The BEA estimates and the IRS estimates are not strictly comparable because the IRS estimate includes unreported illegal source income whereas the BEA estimate does not.

The IRS discrepancy method: unreported income

In response to the publicity given to monetary estimates (Gutmann, 1977; Feige, 1979) that suggested a sizable unobserved sector, the IRS (1979) undertook its own massive investigation of the extent of under-reporting on federal income tax returns. Although the IRS refers to its methodology as a "direct" method, it is in fact an amalgam of discrepancy methods, survey methods, and various forms of imputation based on microdata. The methods employed by the IRS to obtain components of its final estimate of total unreported income include

1 audit studies to determine the unreported legal source income of filers,
2 exact match studies of social security numbers to determine the non-filer population and income imputations for non-filer income,
3 crime statistics to determine the amount of unreported illegal source income, and
4 survey information to determine unreported income of "informal suppliers."

The first two procedures are essentially discrepancy methods. In order to determine the unreported legal source income of filers, the IRS analyzed the discrepancy between the amount of reportable income as established by auditors on sample returns with the amount of income actually reported by the taxpayer. This difference was also used by the BEA to improve its estimates of NIPA income based on tax information sources.

The unreported incomes of non-filers is estimated by a three-step procedure. The IRS first attempts to match survey information from the current population survey with administrative records from the Social Security Administration on the basis of social security number matches. The matched survey records are then compared with social security numbers in the IRS master file of returns. Matched records produce a filer series while mismatches indicate that the survey record belongs to a pool of potential non-filers who are then classified as "delinquent non-filers" and "legitimate non-filers" on the basis of whether their imputed incomes exceed or fall short of the filing threshold. The estimate of total non-filer unreported income is imputed from the survey information for records of delinquent non-filers. In 1972, the IRS estimated a population of five million delinquent non-filers whose unreported income was assumed to be represented by their survey responses.

Unreported illegal incomes are imputed on the basis of estimates of consumption or sales of illegal goods and services that are in turn estimated from various crime statistics. Finally, the income of what the IRS calls "informal suppliers" is obtained from survey information.

The initial IRS (1979) study concluded that in 1976, between $75 billion and $100 billion of *legal source* income was not properly reported on the individual federal income tax return, with a resulting revenue loss of between $12.8 billion and $17.1 billion. Another $25.3 billion to $35.2 billion of *illegal source* income was estimated as unreported, with an added tax revenue loss of $6.3 billion to $8.8 billion. The subsequent IRS (1983) report raised the estimate of unreported 1976 legal source income to $131.6 billion and more than doubled its estimate of legal source lost revenues to $39.2 billion. On the other hand, the study slashed the estimate of illegal source income to $13.4 billion and reduced the corresponding estimate of lost revenue to $3.8 billion. The second IRS study concluded that, by 1981, total unreported income on the federal income tax amounted to $283 billion, or 16% of reported adjusted gross income.[7] The higher estimates of unreported income from the second IRS report necessitated a comprehensive revision of the NIPA by the BEA (1985). The NIPA revision raised the estimate of 1984 personal income by $100 billion. This revision reflected previously unrecorded income that resulted from misreporting on tax source information used by the BEA.

Each component of the IRS final estimate of total unreported income required a myriad of assumptions. The complexity of the IRS procedures and the confidential nature of some of their underlying data make it difficult to assess the reliability of their final result. There are however reasons to believe that the IRS estimates are biased downward and that the final estimates are highly sensitive to some key specifying assumptions.

The initial IRS (1979) study assumed that the amount of unreported income detected by intensive audits of sample returns reflected the correct amount of unreported legal source income. When this assumption was challenged, the IRS undertook to audit the reliability of its auditing procedures. Unreported income detected by auditors on specific returns was compared with data obtained from income payers who independently file information returns to the IRS. This procedure revealed that intensive audits on average detected only twenty-three cents of every dollar of unreported income uncovered by the information returns. On the basis of these findings, the IRS employed an arbitrary multiple of 3.5 to inflate its initial audit estimates for *all* categories of

---

[7] The IRS (1983) estimates are included in Figure 1.2 (labeled IRS).

income. A crucial step in the IRS procedure was their assumption that auditors were equally successful in detecting unreported income covered by information returns such as wages, salaries, interest, and dividends as they were in detecting non-covered incomes such as proprietor and small-business incomes. Since the auditors only detected twenty-two cents of every dollar of documented unreported income for the former group, it seems reasonable that they would have detected less in the latter group where taxpayers knew that the IRS had no separate information returns filed as a separate check on the accuracy of their returns.

A sensitivity analysis by Feige (1986a) reveals that if the IRS had employed its actual audit findings for incomes covered by information returns but had assumed that auditors could only detect ten cents of every dollar of unreported income of proprietors and small business not covered by information return requirements, this change in assumptions would have significantly increased the estimate of unreported income. As depicted in Figure 1.2, the alternative set of assumptions described in the preceding (labeled IRS:Alt) raised 1981 estimated unreported income as a percentage of AGI from 16% to almost 24%.

Similar problems plague other aspects of the IRS study. The incomes of non-filers are imputed from household survey information. The IRS (1983, p. 75) acknowledges that "it is quite possible that people who have not reported any of their income to the IRS will feel inhibited in reporting their income to persons who interview them on a household survey." Nevertheless, the IRS proceeds with the assumption that all incomes are correctly reported in household surveys, regardless of whether individuals did or did not report their incomes to the tax authority. Similarly, the IRS assumes that "informal suppliers" fully report their true incomes to survey interviewers.

The IRS estimates of illegal incomes also rely on detailed assumptions concerning such matters as the amount of marijuana used in the average cigarette, the purity of retail cocaine, and the effective retail price discount offered to heavy drug users. Small variations in these assumptions can cause substantial changes in the final estimates of illegal source incomes.

In short, what the IRS describes as a "direct" method for estimating unreported income, is in fact a circuitous method, involving a multitude of questionable assumptions. Sensitivity analysis reveals that plausible changes in some key assumptions can result in a doubling of the estimates actually reported by the IRS. The strength of the IRS study lies in its disaggregative approach, which is useful for the implementation of administrative policies concerning audit rates and penalty policies.

Summary of official government estimates

Figure 1.3 summarizes the various measures of the percentage of AGI estimated to be unreported in the United States for the year 1981. The range of estimates is between 12 and 24% of AGI, between $217 billion and $422 billion. The high estimate is based on an alternative set of assumptions regarding the IRS procedure for determining the amount of legal source unreported income from audit procedures. If all estimated unreported income had been properly declared to the IRS, the resulting tax revenues of between $70 billion and $135 billion would have eliminated the budget deficit for that year. These results suggest that non-compliance with tax laws may be a major factor in explaining the burgeoning budget deficits.

The estimates of unreported income are also germane to the issue of the veracity of the NIPA. To the extent that NIPA procedures for estimating recorded income are dependent on tax source information, higher estimates of unreported incomes will require further upward revisions of the NIPA.

The currency-ratio approaches

Interest in the monetary unobserved sector was initially stimulated by some apparent anomalies related to the amount of currency in circulation and its denominational structure. Although economists had predicted that the advent of credit cards and other financial innovations would ultimately bring about a "cashless society," per capita currency holdings grew rather than declined and by 1986 stood in excess of $950. Moreover, more than 40% of the value of the nation's currency supply is held in the form of $100 bills. The ratio of currency to demand deposits also showed considerable growth during the past two decades.

Currency is widely assumed to have a comparative advantage over checks for the payment of purchases of goods and services that individuals wish to conceal from the authorities. A rise in currency stocks and payments may therefore be taken as a rough indicator of the extent to which these transactions may not be reported to government authorities.

One of the most popular methods for estimating the monetary unobserved economy has been the simple currency-ratio method. This procedure was first used by Cagan (1958) in an effort to estimate unreported income during World War II. Cagan's method was later applied by Gutmann (1977), who estimated that the "subterranean" economy of the United States amounted to almost 10% of official GNP in 1976. This simple currency-ratio method (C/D) has now been applied

36

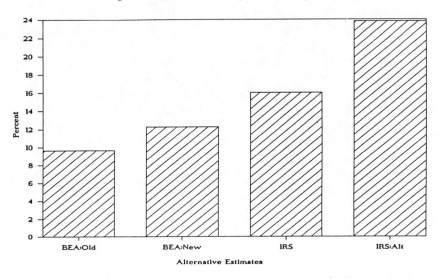

Figure 1.3. Unreported income as percentage of AGI. Government estimates for 1981.

in many countries as a first approximation of the size of the "under-ground" economy. A review of the currency method and the various results produced by this approach is undertaken in what follows. In order to examine the usefulness of the currency-ratio method, it is helpful to construct a general model, of which it can be shown that all currency-ratio methods used to date are special cases. Let

C = actual currency stock
D = actual stock of demand deposits
Y_o = observed income
u = subscript to denote unobserved sector
o = subscript to denote "observed" sector
k_o = ratio of currency to demand deposits in observed sector
k_u = ratio of currency to demand deposits in unobserved sector
v_u = unobserved sector income velocity
v_o = observed sector income velocity

When the object of analysis is to estimate unreported income on federal income tax returns, the appropriate empirical counterpart of observed income is adjusted gross income. When the object of the analysis is to estimate unrecorded income, the analysis should be based on a NIPA aggregate that is properly adjusted for non-monetary im-

37

putations and for imputations already included in the recorded aggregate that correct for omissions due to underreporting on tax source data. When a NIPA aggregate such as GNP is used as the proxy for reported income in the foregoing model, the results may not be interpreted as estimates of unreported income or of non-compliance with the tax code. Such an interpretation requires additional specifications of the complex changing relationship between the tax base and GNP.

The estimates reported in the following employ variants of the currency-ratio method to obtain estimates of unreported income. They therefore employ estimated AGI as the empirical counterpart to the observed sector. The use of AGI as the income variable allows a direct comparison between the currency-ratio estimates and the estimates of unreported income produced by government agencies.

A general currency-ratio model contains the following specifications:

$$C = C_u + C_o \tag{1}$$

$$D = D_u + D_o \tag{2}$$

$$k_o = C_o/D_o \tag{3}$$

$$k_u = C_u/D_u \tag{4}$$

$$v_o = Y_o/(C_o + D_o) \tag{5}$$

$$v_u = Y_u/(C_u + D_u) \tag{6}$$

$$\beta = v_o/v_u \tag{7}$$

Equations (1) and (2) decompose the actual stocks of currency and demand deposits[8] into their unreported and reported components. Equations (3) and (4) are definitions of the terms k_o and k_u, which can be viewed either as functions or constants. Similarly, equations (5) and (6) define income velocity in the two sectors. To solve the model for Y_u, we must evaluate (6) in terms of the model's observable variables, namely, C, D, and Y_o. Repeated substitution and rearrangement of terms yields the general solution for Y_u as

$$Y_u = \frac{1}{\beta} Y_o \frac{(k_u + 1)(C - k_o D)}{(k_o + 1)(k_u D - C)} \tag{8}$$

[8] It must be noted that although Cagan's original study examined the ratio of currency to the "total money supply," the appropriate definition of the "money supply" must be limited to those assets that directly function as media of exchange. In practice, currency and demand deposits and other checkable deposits comprise the final exchange media in the United States. The C/D method should therefore be applied with D defined as demand deposits plus other checkable deposits. This convention is followed in all following estimates of the unobserved monetary sector.

Equation (8) expresses the unreported sector as a function of the observable variables Y_o, C, and D and the three parameters or functions β, k_u, and k_o.

The simple currency-ratio method

The simple C/D method employs the following restrictive assumptions:

1 Currency is the exclusive medium of exchange in unreported transactions ($D_u \rightarrow 0$; $k_u \rightarrow \infty$).
2 The ratio of currency to demand deposits remains constant except for changes induced by the growth of unreported income (k_o is constant over time).
3 The amount of unreported income produced by a dollar of currency transacted in the unreported sector is the same as the amount of reported income produced by a dollar of currency transacted in the reported economy.

Assumption 1 implies that unreported transactions are never paid by check; therefore, k_u approaches infinity. Assumption 2 asserts that k_o is constant over time. Assumption 3 implies that $\beta = 1$. Imposing these restrictions on the general model presented as equation (8) produces the restrictive form

$$Y_u = Y_o \frac{(C - k_o D)}{(k_o + 1)D} \tag{9}$$

which is the mathematical representation of the simple currency-ratio method.

Equations (8) and (9) reveal the theoretical shortcoming of the C/D method when it is interpreted as a method for estimating unrecorded income. Any improvements in the measurement of observed income, such as imputations in GNP for unreported income in tax source data, will increase rather than decrease the estimated magnitude of the unrecorded sector and will leave the estimated ratio of unrecorded to recorded income unaffected by the improvement. This deficiency can in principle be eliminated by subtracting the amount of unrecorded income that is imputed in recorded income from both sides of equations (8) and (9).[9] The resulting magnitude would then represent an appropriate measure of unrecorded income. This problem does not arise when the

---

[9] The new U.S. NIPA estimates of national income include an adjustment of $147.5 billion for misreporting on income tax returns.

C/D method is used to estimate unreported income since no imputations for unreported income are made in the reported AGI series.

Empirical implementation of even the simple C/D method requires an estimate of k_o. Gutmann (1977) follows Cagan (1958) in assuming that k_o can be approximated by the actual ratio of currency to demand deposits in the period immediately preceding World War II. This approach is justified by the fact that prior to the introduction of the income tax, the incentives for unreported transactions were nil, and therefore, no unreported economy existed at this time. Under this assumption, k_o is approximated by

$$k_o = \left(\frac{C_o}{D_o}\right)_{1940} = \left(\frac{C}{D}\right)_{1940} \tag{10}$$

If we further assume that k_o is constant over time, it is possible to derive estimates of Y_u/Y_o for the period 1940–82 based on equations (9) and (10) and the following set of restrictions:

(i) $\qquad\qquad\qquad k_{ot} = k_{o(1940)}\quad$ for all t

(ii) $\qquad\qquad\qquad k_u \to \infty$

(iii) $\qquad\qquad\qquad \beta = 1 \tag{11}$

The resulting estimate is displayed in Figure 1.4 and is labeled $C{:}40$. This simplest estimate suggests that the ratio of unreported income to reported income rose dramatically during World War II, rising above 12% of reported income. Thereafter, Y_u/Y_o declined during the post-war period, reaching a low of about 3% in 1960. The ratio then grew gradually until 1973, after which it accelerated to its estimated 1984 level of 15.8%.

Sensitivity analysis of the currency-ratio method

Since each of the limiting assumptions employed by the simple currency-ratio method have been widely criticized, it is useful to examine the sensitivity of the final results to a relaxation of each of its underlying assumptions.

We first consider alternatives to assumption (11i), which utilizes 1940 as the benchmark year for estimating k_o. In principle, any year for which there exists an independent estimate α of Y_u/Y_o can serve as a base year for the currency-ratio method. Given any α_t, it is possible to solve equation (9) for k_{ot} and to employ the new benchmark to generate an alternative time path of unreported income:

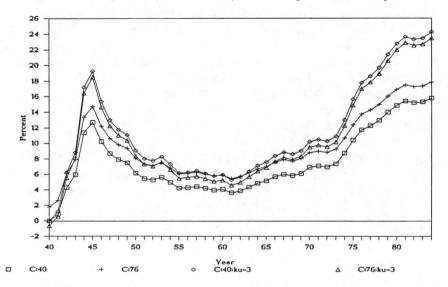

Figure 1.4. Unreported income as percentage of AGI. Simple currency ratio models.

$$k_{ot} = \frac{C_t - \alpha_t D_t}{\alpha_t D_t + D_t} \tag{12}$$

Figure 1.4 displays the estimated time path of unreported income (C:76) when the IRS estimate of α_{1976} is employed as the benchmark. The effect of this adjustment is to proportionally increase the simple estimate that assumes no unreported income in 1940.

A second modification of the simple method is to drop the assumption that currency is the exclusive medium of exchange for unreported transactions. Smith et al. (1982) surveyed "informal" suppliers and found that only 50% of informal purchases of home repairs and catering services were paid with cash and that approximately 25–30% of purchases of other informal services were effected by non-cash payments. The IRS (1979, p. 13) found that underreporting of interest and dividend payments suggest that "the unreported income problem extends beyond incomes paid in currency." The available evidence is insufficient to determine the exact proportion of unreported income that is transacted with currency, but it is reasonable to assume that 25–35% of such payments are in fact made with checks. The following calculations assume that roughly 75% of total unreported income is transacted with currency so that $k_u \approx 3$.[10] If currency payments account for only two-thirds of unreported income, then $k_u \approx 2$. For any given benchmark and any given value for k_u, equation (8) can be solved to determine the appropriate value for k_{ot}. The resulting expression will also contain the parameter β. The final estimates of unreported income will therefore depend upon the particular values chosen for these key parameters, and the general currency-ratio model can be employed to relax each of the restrictive assumptions contained in the simple framework.

Figure 1.4 displays the estimates that result when $k_u = 3$ for both the original 1940 benchmark (C:40: $k_u = 3$) and the IRS 1976 benchmark (C:76: $k_u = 3$). The relaxation of both the original benchmark assumption and the assumption that currency is the exclusive medium of exchange had the effect of raising estimated unreported income to almost 24% of reported income by 1984. Moreover, these latter specifications suggest that unreported income grew at a faster rate since 1960 than was evident from the more restrictive specifications.

The foregoing results retained the assumption that $\beta = 1$, namely, that the income velocities for reported and unreported income are identical. If unreported income is largely concentrated in the service sector, which requires fewer intermediate transactions, β is likely to be less than unity. On the other hand, a lower propensity to consume unreported income would imply $\beta > 1$. If $\beta < 1$, the foregoing estimates of unreported income are too low, and conversely, if $\beta > 1$, the estimates are too high.

The foregoing simulations of the currency-ratio model assume that the benchmark estimate for k_o is constant. In the spirit of Cagan's (1958) original investigation of the currency ratio, k_{ot} may alternatively be regarded as a stable function of other economic variables. The function can be estimated by conventional econometric methods. Tanzi (1982, 1983) employs a variant of this approach that relaxes the restriction that k_{ot} is a constant but reimposes the restriction that currency is the exclusive medium of exchange for unreported transactions, that is, that $D_u \rightarrow 0$. Under this latter assumption, the observed C/D is defined as

$$\frac{C}{D} = \frac{C_o}{D_o} + \frac{C_u}{D_o} = k_o + \frac{C_u}{D} = f_1(y, r, ws) + f_2(\tau) \tag{13}$$

where:

[10] Simulation experiments suggest that the final estimates of unreported income are quite sensitive to the particular value chosen for k_u. Closer scrutiny of the IRS estimates of unreported income by income class may provide a more precise estimate of k_u.

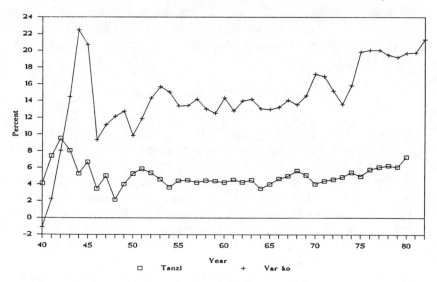

Figure 1.5. Unreported income as percentage of AGI. Econometric currency ratio models.

y = reported income
r = rate of interest
ws = income share of wages and salaries
τ = average effective marginal tax rate

Equation (13) can be estimated to obtain a forecast of C/D. A time series estimate of k_o is then obtained by setting tax rates equal to zero. Tanzi's procedure relies on the assumption that unreported income depends exclusively on the rate of taxation and requires an estimate of the amount of currency that would be held if tax rates were zero.

Figure 1.5 displays Tanzi's reported estimate of underground income as a percentage of AGI for the model that permits k_o to vary over time. Tanzi's reported estimates are considerably lower than those obtained by any of the previously described methods. Acharya (1984), Feige (1986c), and Porter and Bayer (Chapter 5) have each raised conceptual and econometric objections to Tanzi's procedure. Thomas (1986, p. 788) concludes "that the apparently significant results presented by Tanzi for 1930–80 are a statistical artifact constructed from a significant static relationship for 1930–45 and a non significant static misspecification of a dynamic relationship for 1946–80." Figure 1.5 displays the alternative estimate of unreported income obtained from dynamic forecasts of the

43

variable k_o model [Var k_o] that corrects the shortcomings of Tanzi's procedure.[11] The resulting estimates are almost three times higher than those reported by Tanzi and also exhibit a different inter-temporal pattern.

A comparison of alternative estimates

Table 1.3 presents a summary of alternative estimates of unreported income for 1981. The table also includes a rough estimate of the tax loss associated with each estimate of unreported income.[12]

Table 1.3 reveals that the range of estimates obtained by the currency-ratio models are surprisingly consistent with the range of estimates produced by entirely different means by government agencies. Excluding the early BEA estimate of the AGI gap and the flawed Tanzi estimate, the range of unreported income is estimated to be between $217 billion and $422 billion. The least restrictive currency-ratio models yield estimates of unreported income between $350 billion and $420 billion, which correspond closely to the estimates obtained with alternative assumptions employing the IRS procedure. These estimates suggest that more than 20% of AGI is unreported on federal income tax returns with resulting revenue losses in excess of $100 billion.

Estimating unrecorded income

The NIPA form the empirical foundation of macroeconomic analysis. Our ability to understand the workings of the macroeconomic system

---

[11] The estimate employs the BEA measure of AGI instead of Tanzi's GNP variable and replaces Tanzi's tax rates with estimates of the average effective marginal tax rate computed by Barro and Sahasakul (1983). The estimates are based on dynamic forecasts of the additive specification implied by equation (13) rather than on static forecasts of the multiplicative form used by Tanzi. The estimated equation is based on the post–World War II years in order to eliminate the spurious effects introduced into Tanzi's equations by the bank failures of the Great Depression, which produced a dramatic increase in the currency ratio totally unrelated to growth of unreported income. For higher estimates of unreported income based on the period 1940–80, see Feige (1986c). The ARMA estimates in Figure 1.5 are for the period 1947–80. The estimated equation is

$$C/M = \begin{array}{ccccc} 1.201 & + & 0.630\tau & - & 1.531(ws) & + & 0.049r & + & 0.00002y \\ (8.724) & & (4.953) & & (7.266) & & (.164) & & (2.340) \end{array}$$

[12] The estimated tax loss was calculated by multiplying the estimated unreported income by the IRS (1983) estimate of the ratio of the total tax gap per dollar of total unreported income. Since the IRS estimated tax gap measure includes the effects of overstated expenses and deductions, the estimates for the tax loss assume that the effects of these adjustments to total unreported income are the same for all methods. This assumption is weakest for the BEA estimate since illegal source income is largely excluded from the estimate of personal income.

44

The meaning and measurement of the underground economy

Table 1.3. *Summary of unreported income estimates, 1981*

Method	Notation	Unreported income (billions)	Percentage of AGI	Revenue loss (billions)
Discrepancy				
BEA–AGI gap original	BEA:Old	171.00	9.65	54.51
BEA–AGI gap revised	BEA:New	217.40	12.26	69.31
IRS reported results	IRS	283.88	16.01	90.50
IRS alternative assumptions	IRS:Alt	422.06	23.81	134.55
Currency ratio models				
Simple: 1940 base = 0	C:40	273.22	15.41	87.10
Simple: 1976 base (IRS)	C:76	309.63	17.47	98.70
General: 1940 base = 0: $k_u = 3$	C:40: $k_u = 3$	419.70	23.68	133.80
General: 1976 base (IRS): $k_u = 3$	C:76: $k_u = 3$	405.57	22.88	129.30
Tanzi reported 1930–1980[a]	Tanzi	117.99	7.31	37.61
General: variable k_o	C:Var k_o	350.72	19.79	111.80

[a] 1980 estimate.

and to make informed policy judgments is conditioned by the accuracy of the NIPA. The NIPA are constructed from a variety of data sources that may be contaminated directly and indirectly by the growth of an unobserved economy. One important underlying data source for the accounts is tax-based source information. When tax information is distorted, the NIPA must be appropriately adjusted to reflect such distortions. Parker (1984) suggests that the relationship between tax source information and final NIPA aggregates is highly complex. The task of investigating the implications of unreported income on unrecorded income is made more difficult by the fact that the last compendium describing NIPA data sources and uses was compiled more than thirty years ago.

Interest in the extent of underrecording of income in NIPA was revived during the past decade as a result of the currency-ratio estimates that suggested that unreported income was a significant and growing problem. In 1979, a representative of the BEA testified before the House Committee on Ways and Means (October 9, 1979) that "from $6 to $10 billion – or about one-half of one percent of total GNP is missing." After the IRS (1983) study, it became apparent that the NIPA required substantial revision to take account of the new IRS estimates of unreported income. At the end of 1985, the BEA (1985) published a comprehensive revision of the NIPA. The most significant single com-

45

ponent of the revision was the improved adjustment for misreporting on income tax returns. For the year 1984, charges against GNP were revised upward by 101.2 billion. The newly revised NIPA (BEA, 1985, p. 2) included total adjustments for national income amounting to $147.5 billion (4.85%) and for personal income to $117.3 billion (3.77%).

These new NIPA revisions exclusively reflect the higher IRS estimates of unreported income on tax source data. No effort has been made to measure the indirect effects of tax and regulatory incentives for firms and individuals to misreport information on surveys and other data sources used in the construction of NIPA.

The only independent estimates of total unrecorded income are those obtained from the use of currency-ratio models that employ a NIPA income concept. Feige's (1980) (C/D) estimates of total unrecorded income are replicated by Porter and Bayer (Chapter 5). The simple currency-ratio specification yields a 1981 estimate of total unrecorded income of some $427 billion, and the simulations from the general currency-ratio model suggest that total unrecorded income could be in excess of $750 billion.[13] In short, the currency-ratio methods of estimating total unrecorded income produce results that suggest that the recent NIPA revisions, which only take account of IRS estimates of misreporting on federal income tax returns, reflect only a portion of total unrecorded income.

The transactions method

Feige (1979) proposed an alternative approach for estimating the volume of unobserved monetary transactions and total monetary unrecorded income. The conceptual basis for this "transactions method" is rooted in Fisher's (1911) equation of exchange, which specifies the equality between the total volume of payments (MV) and the total volume of transactions (PT). In principle, if it were possible to obtain independent estimates of MV and of recorded PT, the difference between the two measures would represent an estimate of the total volume of unrecorded transactions. The Fisher payment–transaction identity can be employed as a check on the recorded volume of transactions in much the same way that the Keynesian income–expenditure identity is presently employed as the basic check on current NIPA estimates of

---

[13] The general currency-ratio model simulations reproduced by Porter and Bayer (Chapter 5) assume that $k_u = 2$ and $\beta = 0.9$ and employ a 1964 base period in which unrecorded income is assumed to be 5% of recorded income. These estimates fail to take proper account of imputations already included in GNP for previously unrecorded income.

aggregate income. Feige (1985b) employed the equation-of-exchange framework to estimate the total volume of unrecorded monetary transactions for Sweden.

In the absence of estimates of the total volume of transactions (recorded and unrecorded transactions), one can obtain estimates of the total volume of payments (MV), which in turn can be used to estimate the volume of unrecorded income. Let

$(py)^*$ = total income
$(py)_r$ = recorded income
$(py)_u$ = unrecorded income
  C = currency
  V_c = currency velocity
  D = checkable deposits
  V_d = checkable deposit velocity
PT = total transactions

Then

$$(py)^* = (py)_r + (py)_u \qquad (14)$$

and

$$CV_c + DV_d = PT \qquad (15)$$

If total transactions are assumed to be proportional to total income, then the equation of exchange implies that

$$(PT)/(py)^* = k^* = (CV_c + DV_d)/(py)^* \qquad (16)$$

and,

$$(py)_u = [(CV_c + DV_d)/k^*] - (py)_r = (py)^* - (py)_r \qquad (17)$$

Given estimates of total payments and recorded income, it is possible to obtain estimates of unrecorded income given the benchmark parameter k^*. An estimate of k^* can be obtained either by assuming that there exists some period during which all income is properly recorded or from an independent estimate of the proportion of total income that is unrecorded in any given year.

The transactions method for estimating unrecorded income differs from the currency-ratio approaches in several important respects. The currency-ratio approaches rely upon changes in the relative stock of currency to signal shifts to the unobserved sector. The transactions approach focuses on the total volume of payments that is not recorded in our current accounting systems. Implicit in the currency-ratio approach is the notion that the stock of circulating currency and the stock

47

of demand deposit balances are reasonable representations for the amount of work that money does in effecting exchange. However, the amount of work that money performs depends upon both the stock outstanding and the number of times per year that the stock is used to effect payments, that is, on the transactions velocity of money. Rather than assume constant transactions velocities for the exchange media, the transactions approach seeks to directly incorporate variable velocities into the analysis.

The transactions approach also avoids most of the other restrictive assumptions required by the currency-ratio models. No assumptions are required concerning the exclusive use of currency in transacting unrecorded income. No assumption is required that fixes the ratio of currency to check use in either recorded or unrecorded transactions, and no assumption is required concerning the relative size of the income velocities in the two sectors. Finally, as revealed by equation (17), any improvements in recorded income will be properly reflected in the estimate of unrecorded income. The method does however require a benchmark estimate for k^*.[14]

The transactions approach critically assumes a proportional relationship between total transactions and total income.[15] This assumption has been employed in monetary theory for decades. It is the implicit assumption that permits replacing transactions with income as the scale variable in money demand functions. It is also the assumption required to transform the equation of exchange into a theory of the demand for money. It therefore serves as a basis for deriving monetarist relationships between the money stock and key macroeconomic variables such as the price level and real output. Despite the long-standing and essentially unquestioned use of the assumption in traditional monetary theory, its use in deriving estimates of unrecorded income has been appropriately challenged as a result of the surprisingly high estimates of unrecorded income that Feige (1979) reported in applying an early version of the procedure.

Despite the conceptual advantages of the transactions method, its successful empirical implementation is severely constrained by present data limitations. The primary empirical limitation is that we cannot readily construct a time series comprising the total volume of gross

---

[14] In the empirical estimates presented in what follows, the benchmark is taken to be 1939. It is assumed that in 1939 the ratio of net transactions to private sector recorded monetary income equaled k^*.

[15] If the ratio of transactions to income is a stable function of observable variables, the transactions approach can be readily modified in exactly the same way as the C/D approach was modified to allow k_o to be a function rather than a constant.

transactions for the U.S. economy. This limitation is largely the result of accounting conventions adopted in the flow-of-funds accounts that report net transaction flows rather than gross flows. This data limitation is not inherent in the manner in which data are collected since virtually all data records refer to gross rather than net flows. Rather it is the result of accounting conventions designed to bring flow-of-funds accounts into greater conceptual conformity with current NIPA procedures.

In order to obtain an approximate estimate of gross transactions, we must rely on estimates of total payments obtained from data on both the stocks and turnover of the final exchange media. The resulting estimate of total payments must in turn be adjusted in two important respects. First, the estimated volume of payments must be related to a conceptually consistent income variable. Second, total payments need to be adjusted in order to eliminate those transaction components that are unlikely to be proportionally related to income over time.

Payments estimates are derived from measures of debits to demand deposits and other checkable deposits. The recorded debit statistics refer to debits made to accounts held by individuals, partnerships, corporations, and state and local governments. In short, the payments series excludes the transactions of the federal government. The monetary payments of the non-federal sector must be correspondingly related to the monetary income generated in the non-federal sector. Since GNP includes federal government expenditures and imputations for non-monetary transactions, both of these components must be subtracted from the relevant income concept. The resulting income aggregate refers to the monetary income of the non-federal government sector, which consists primarily of the monetized private economy. Since the unreported and unrecorded activities are presumably absent from the federal government sector, the foregoing income concept is germane to the problem at hand.

Total transactions can be usefully decomposed into (a) transactions associated with the production of final output, (b) transactions involving existing real or financial assets, and (c) pure transfer exchanges. Both transfer payments and financial transactions are likely to exhibit fluctuations that are not directly proportional to changes in total income. The former could result from changes in fiscal policy, the latter the result of financial innovation. As such, estimates of gross payments can be adjusted to net out major financial transactions and direct transfers. The resulting net transaction measure is more likely to satisfy the proportionality assumption.

The initial estimate of gross transactions is constructed from two components, total currency payments and debits to checkable deposits of individuals, corporations, partnerships, and state and local governments. A variety of turnover rates are reported for demand deposits, and we employ the turnover series that excludes large financial centers in order to net out to the greatest extent possible what Copeland (1952) refers to as "financial fluff."[16] Total currency payments are derived from Feige's (1986b) time series estimates of currency velocity.[17] The estimate of gross payments is further adjusted to eliminate financial asset transactions and transfer payments in order to arrive at a net transactions total.[18]

Given an estimate of net transactions and private-sector monetary income, equation (17) is employed to derive an estimate of "total monetary unrecorded income." In principle, this magnitude represents an estimate of all private-sector incomes effected by monetary payments that are omitted from GNP. As such, the measure includes all illegal incomes that are consciously excluded from the NIPA as well as legal income that is inadvertently excluded as a result of inadequate adjustments for underreporting of income in tax source data and survey data and non-reporting of income from activities that are completely off the books. Total monetary unrecorded income is a broader concept than the unreported income on federal income tax returns. It includes incomes that fall below the federal filing threshold as well as incomes that go unreported to fiscal agencies other than the IRS. It is broader than unrecorded income insofar as it includes incomes (illegally earned) that would not be counted in GNP under current accounting conventions. In short, the estimate produced by the transactions method should not be directly compared to those estimates reported in earlier sections of this chapter because the underlying income concepts are incommensurate. Nevertheless, the concept has important economic meaning. The sum of total unrecorded monetary income and recorded monetary income represents a measure of the total income produced in the economy that is paid for with cash or checks.

Figure 1.6 displays two transactions method estimates of total

---

[16] The historical series on debits and turnover have been periodically revised and therefore require splicing for periods during which changes in definitions and sample sizes have taken place. A historical series is obtained by proportional adjustments based on overlapping years for which both the old and the new series are available.

[17] This new currency velocity series employs a 1984 Federal Reserve benchmark estimate derived from the survey of currency usage.

[18] The specific adjustments discussed in detail in Feige (1980) include the removal of stock and bond sales recorded on major exchanges, estimated debits arising from transfers to other checkable deposits and cash withdrawals, estimated debits arising from transactions in repurchase agreements, time and savings deposits, money market funds, overnight Eurodollars, imports and capital outflows, and private-sector transfer payments to the government.

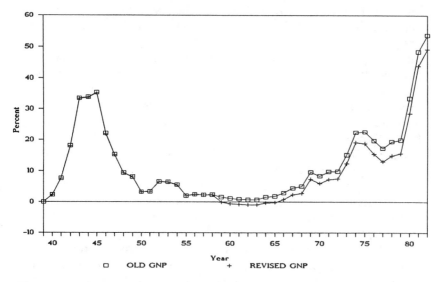

Figure 1.6. Estimated percentage of GNP unrecorded. Transactions method estimate for 1939 to 1940.

unrecorded monetary income as a percentage of recorded GNP. The series labeled old GNP is based on pre-1985 GNP estimates that did not include the latest revisions for misreporting on the federal income tax. The revised GNP series is based on the most recent revised estimates of GNP. The vertical gap between the two series represents the reduction in total unrecorded income brought about by the latest GNP revision. The vertical distance between the horizonal axis and the revised GNP series represents the transaction method estimate of total monetary income that is still omitted from the GNP accounts in percentage terms.

After the dramatic increase in unrecorded activity during World War II and the subsequent post-war reabsorption of the unrecorded sector into the recorded economy, the unrecorded sector remained negligible until the latter half of the 1960's. During this period official estimates of nominal GNP growth adequately reflected the growth of total nominal income. The estimates suggest that nominal unrecorded income began to rise during the latter half of the 1960's and reached a temporary peak in excess of 25% of official GNP by 1975. During this period official estimates of GNP growth may have systematically understated the growth of total economic activity. The percentage of unrecorded income appears to have temporarily declined in 1976 and 1977 but rose dramatically from 1979 to 1982. By 1982, the estimates suggest that total

51

unrecorded income was 49% of GNP.[19] The results for the years 1980–2 appear highly improbable as they suggest a huge sudden increase in total unreported activity. Closer analysis of the underlying data reveal that this unexpected rise is primarily due to a dramatic acceleration in demand deposit turnover that is not offset by financial adjustments to the debit series. A recent change in the manner of estimating the turnover series may be partially responsible, but the more likely cause is an incomplete adjustment for purely financial transactions resulting from innovations in cash management methods. Until this empirical issue is resolved, the estimates for the most recent years must be viewed with considerable caution.

The temporal path of unrecorded income as estimated by the transactions method exhibits a U-shaped pattern similar to that estimated by alternative methods for the post–World War II period. Regardless of the particular unobserved income concept being measured, the different methods suggest a growth of unobserved activity during World War II, a subsequent decline, a period of relative stability, and then an upturn during the latter half of the 1960's. This temporal consistency is remarkable insofar as the different methods measure different components of unobserved activity and rely on very different indicators of such activity. The currency-ratio approaches rely on the relative growth in currency stocks to obtain their results. The transactions approach yields a similar temporal pattern despite the fact that cash payments as a fraction of total payments have steadily declined since the end of World War II.

Figure 1.7 displays the growth rate of nominal GNP and of nominal total income (GNP plus total monetary unrecorded income). The estimate displayed in Figure 1.7 suggests a strong growth of unrecorded income during the World War II period and a subsequent decline in the post-war years. It appears as if nominal economic growth during the war years was much stronger than that suggested by official statistics, whereas the immediate post-war years were not as robust as indicated by official estimates. During the decade of the 1950's and the first half of the 1960's, official GNP growth rate estimates adequately reflected the movements in nominal total activity. However, since the late 1960's, the observed growth rate was generally below the overall rate of growth.

---

[19] Porter and Bayer (Chapter 5) attempt to replicate the transactions approach and arrive at an estimate of 59.8% for the year 1981 using a 1939 benchmark. The Porter–Bayer attempted replications incorrectly add government payments to net transactions (Table 5.2, footnote j) and fail to adjust the GNP measure for imputed income and government expenditures. Other minor differences in the results arise from the use of Federal Reserve benchmarked currency velocity estimates in this chapter.

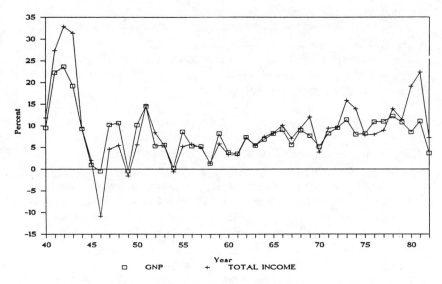

Figure 1.7. Nominal growth: GNP and total income. Transactions method estimate.

The foregoing empirical results broadly conform with a necessary condition for accepting the unobserved income hypothesis; namely, they appear to show that during the last two decades, the unobserved sector grew relative to the observed sector. The results from the transaction method must however be viewed with caution, particularly in light of the remarkably high estimates of unrecorded income obtained for the last three years of the study. It is very likely that the results are affected by the rapid financial innovations that took place during this period, which would have the effect of raising the ratio of transactions to income for reasons unrelated to the growth of unrecorded income.

One troubling implication of the results of the transactions method is that the widely used assumption of a proportional relationship between total transactions and income may be incorrect. If this assumption is violated, it not only suggests that the foregoing transactions estimates of unrecorded income are too high, but more significantly, it also calls into question the implicit use of this assumption in other areas of monetary and macroeconomic theory. The violation of the proportionality assumption may explain the predictive failure of many money demand functions. It also suggests that monetary influences on macroeconomic activity will not be well represented by changes in the stocks of monetary aggregates. If the work money does in the economy does not

53

depend upon the money stock but rather on the changing intensity with which money is used to effect transactions, then money supply definitions must be modified to take explicit account of the turnover of money balances. In short, considerable attention needs to be focused on the causes and consequences of the changing relationship between total transactions (PT) and total income (py).

Summary and conclusions

The phenomenon popularly known by the metaphorical term "underground economy" consists of a variety of economic activities, or more properly, the incomes from those activities, that escape or are concealed from the society's current techniques for monitoring economic activity. This characterization, while all-inclusive of the activities we seek to study, is nevertheless too broad to be analytically useful. When the focus turns toward the theoretical elaboration of the implications of the "unobserved" or "underground" economy or to a concern with its empirical estimation, more refined concepts are required. The particular definitions chosen to characterize the activities we wish to study must be tailored to the specific problem under investigation. Two central issues emerge from the literature on the unobserved economy. The first deals with the problem of non-compliance with the fiscal code, the second deals with the veracity and reliability of our major indicators of economic activity. A key measure of the degree of non-compliance with the tax system is the amount of unreported income, namely, the difference between the amount of income that ought to be reported to the tax authority and the amount actually reported. A measure of the reliability of our economic indicators is the amount of income that is not properly recorded in conventional NIPA, namely, unrecorded income. The interconnection between unreported and unrecorded income depends upon the extent to which indicators of economic activity rely on tax source information for their construction.

A variety of methods have been proposed to measure unreported income. All existing estimates suggest that compliance has deteriorated, and the recent upward revisions of official IRS estimates have helped to narrow the gap between competing measures of unreported income. The empirical results presented in this chapter suggest that unreported income in the United States is estimated to range between $280 billion and $420 billion, amounting to 16–24% of reported adjusted gross income in 1981. There appears to be little doubt that the non-compliance problem is of major proportions and has increased significantly during the past two decades. There does however remain a significant absolute difference between official IRS estimates and independent estimates employing alternative methods. This author's analysis suggests that the higher range estimates are more likely to be correct. The implied revenue losses from non-compliance appear to be a major factor in explaining the growth of budget deficits in the United States.

The well-documented growth of unreported income has important implications for unrecorded income and hence for the issue of the veracity of the nation's information system. Growing non-compliance with the tax code has both direct and indirect effects on the NIPA. The direct effects arise from the specific use of tax source information in the construction of the NIPA. Once we know the full extent of misreporting on tax source information, we can calculate the amount of income that is not properly recorded in the NIPA. This adjustment reflects the direct effect of misreporting on underlying tax source information. The recent major revisions in the U.S. NIPA now reflect an estimate of this direct effect. The reliability of the revision is of course conditioned on the reliability of the IRS estimates of unreported income. If the latter are understated, then the currernt NIPA revisions also understate the direct effect of misreporting. The more difficult problem arises from the indirect effects of the growth of non-compliance on unrecorded income. Individuals and firms that misreport tax information are unlikely to respond candidly to requests for other types of information that are employed in the construction of NIPA. The consequences of the insidious contamination of other data sources is much more difficult to estimate, and no attempt has been made to adjust the official NIPA for these indirect effects.

The monetary measures that purport to estimate the size of unrecorded income suggest that, since the late 1960's, a growing percentage of total economic activity has eluded capture in our official NIPA data. Part of the problem may be related to the growth of illegal income captured in the monetary methods but excluded from NIPA by accounting conventions. The larger component is likely to be related to legal source incomes that may be unwittingly excluded from NIPA because they are either off the books or are not properly recorded in non-tax data sources employed in the construction of the NIPA.

The temporal pattern of estimates of unrecorded income is broadly consistent with the hypothesis that the economic malaise experienced during the past two decades may be in part a statistical artifact, resulting from a systematic deterioration in the reliability of our economic indicators. This suspicion has recently been reenforced by the remarkable finding by the Federal Reserve Board (Avery et al., 1984) that roughly 88% of the nation's currency supply is "missing." Surveys of currency usage of U.S. households find that these households admit to holding a mere 12% of the nation's currency in circulation outside of financial institutions. The volume of currency payments supported by this 12% of the circulating currency supply accounts for 40% of recorded personal consumption expenditures. Since check payments are known to be the dominant form of payment in the United States, it appears that official estimates of recorded incomes and expenditures considerably underestimate true economic activity.

The UIH suggests that an explanation of many of the events that have puzzled the economics profession during the past two decades may reside in the closer examination of the "facts" of economic life. Our professional tendency is to modify theories so that they conform more closely to the official facts produced by our current measurement apparatus. If that apparatus has gone awry as a result of a growing unobserved economy, we will be better served by fixing the social information system than by modifying theory to conform to erroneous facts.

CHAPTER 2

Information distortions in social systems: the underground economy and other observer–subject–policymaker feedbacks

ROBERT R. ALFORD and EDGAR L. FEIGE

Social indicators are historically important as part of the general effort to quantify information into data usable for the social sciences. This development has fundamentally changed the character of every such field of inquiry. The earlier qualitative and philosophical approach to the study of human behavior has given way to quantitative and formal attempts to mimic the natural sciences by emphasizing statistical inference and experimental design. Specialization grew dramatically not only between disciplines but also within them. Political economy became political science and economics. Economics split into macro- and micro-specialties.

Although major gains have resulted from the tendency to quantify and specialize, there have also been major costs, and every discipline debates the relative costs and benefits of these developments.[1] In those social sciences concerned with the relations between institutions and individual behavior, the problem is not limited to the scientific issues of the validity of experiments and the appropriate objects of statistical hypotheses. Enormously complex social phenomena have been telescoped into aggregate measures usable as an input into public policy. A vast array of information about economic activity, political behavior, and social trends are summarized into quantitative symbols, sometimes a single number such as the gross national product (GNP). Because of their apparent objectivity, simplicity, and universality, these measures are used as a basis for both scientific investigations and public policy. In complex social systems, social indicators have become crucial informational inputs for both private and public decision making.

---

[1] Psychologists have come closest to replicating the natural sciences, but even psychology is embroiled in a fundamental debate between "authenticity" and a holistic approach vs. "accuracy" and a scientific approach. See Gibbs (1979). The dominant issue in the debate is how, and whether, discoveries based on experimental data can be useful in real-world situations.

This development has raised a new set of issues about the reliability of the indicators, which have typically been dealt with from the narrower methodological perspective of the problem of measurement error (Morgenstern, 1963). Our concern is with the more complex interaction between the "subject" reporting data, the "observer" collecting and aggregating those reports into social indicators, and the "policymaker" who utilizes the indicators in the decision-making process.[2] Recent research on the unobserved economy provides an important exemplar of the complex interactive system we shall call "observer–subject–policymaker feedback." We believe that this phenomenon has critical implications for both social science and public policy.

The importance of social indicators

The social indicators – national census, surveys of public opinion, national income data, voting records, crime statistics, time series data for all kinds of social records and archives – are a product of the age of industrialization par excellence. It has been argued that the expansion of a centralized state apparatus made systematic data gathering both necessary and possible. Both socialist and capitalist economies require data for planning the allocation and distribution of society's resources. Increasingly, the basic economic data necessary for both economic and political decisions are gathered by the state. Data gathering and aggregation have become professionalized. The specialized social sciences are both based upon and help generate certain types of data: demography based on the census; macro- and microeconomics use national income accounts and surveys; political science and sociology use voting statistics and public opinion surveys.

The reliability and validity of social measurements are important. Accurate data provide the empirical foundation for developing social policy, informing public opinion, and conducting social research. In the case of highly policy-oriented disciplines such as economics, the policy, opinion, and research functions of social indicators merge.

---

[2] See Feige (1982b). Our thesis is an extension of the important argument of Kenneth Boulding, who has repeatedly asserted that knowledge of the social system is an integral part of the system's dynamic behavior. See Boulding (1971). More specifically, Campbell (1974) cited several instances of what he calls "the corrupting effects of quantitative indicators" in the context of evaluation research. The implications of their important ideas have not yet been incorporated into the corpus of social science inquiry nor have they been adequately recognized by policymakers. See also Campbell et al. (1965).

Recent indicators of system "crisis"

An alarming coincidence of signals from various indicators suggest that fundamental changes have occurred during the past decade. Disciplinary specialization has allowed certain trends to be observed, but there has been all too little interdisciplinary concern with what they may mean from a societal perspective.

Sociologists have drawn attention to a classic theme in their discipline, "social organization," which conventionally includes indicators of divorce, crime, and industrial strife. Divorce rates in both the United States and Europe have shown dramatic increase, almost doubling between 1965 and 1975 in the United States and more than tripling in countries such as the United Kingdom and the Netherlands during the same period. A recent study of crime in the United States revealed that it "has grown at a rapid rate in all U.S. cities regardless of their size, location, minority populations or whether they are gaining or losing population."[3] Crime statistics in European countries reveal similar trends, nearly doubling during the decade of the 1970's. The first half of the 1970's also "saw a general increase of labor disputes everywhere... across the whole of Europe" (Flora, 1981, p. 379).

Political scientists have independently expressed a growing concern with the problem of society's "ungovernability" and the emergence of new forms of political participation. Indices of "trust in government" have plummeted over the past fifteen years. As Table 2.1 indicates, survey response indexes reflecting trust in the U.S. federal government fell from a value of 55 in 1964 to a value of −39 in 1978.[4] Similarly, indicators representing the perception of citizens' perception of honesty in government declined dramatically, while there was a growing perception that the government was run by "big interests" rather than for the benefit of the public as a whole.

European indicators tell a similar story. Governing majorities in most European democracies dwindled steadily during the 1970's. From 1949 to 1972, the average share of parliamentary seats held by the governing coalition in twelve European countries was 59 percent and never fell below 55 percent. Yet from 1972 to 1976, the average share fell just below 50 percent (Flora, 1981).

---

[3] A report in the *International Herald Tribune* (March 3, 1982) of a study by Herbert Jacob and Robert L. Lineberry of Northwestern University. Ten cities were studied in depth, and 396 cities over 50,000 were studied for selected variables.

[4] *American National Election Studies Sourcebook 1952–78*, University of Michigan Survey Research Center: Ann Arbor, Michigan.

Table 2.1. *Trust in federal government index*

Year	PDI[a]
1958	50
1964	55
1966	34
1968	25
1970	9
1972	8
1974	−26
1976	−30
1978	−39

[a] PDI refers to the proportion answering "always or most of the time" minus the proportion answering "some or none of the time" to the question relating to trust in the federal government.
Source: American National Election Studies Data Sourcebook, 1952–78 (University of Michigan Survey Research Center), p. 257. For a detailed review of many surveys reporting the same general trend, see Lipset and Schneider (1983).

Similar patterns of widespread malaise in Western democracies have been reflected in economic indicators: slowed growth rates in real income, declining trends in productivity, substantially higher levels of unemployment, and inexplicably high rates of inflation. These signals have encouraged a general concern with an "economic crisis." Simultaneously, and we believe not unrelated, there is evidence of declining compliance with existing tax regulations, a growth in what has been described as the "underground," or "unobserved," economy (Feige, 1980) and the associated development of alternative forms of economic organization.

Each of the disciplines has separately voiced apprehension about the apparent disintegration of the institutions it monitors, as indicated by the trends just summarized. Do these signals represent evidence of some more fundamental underlying process? Are they perhaps evidence of the manner in which economic events affect political and social behaviors and vice versa? Are we observing an explosive social system, which violates our usual assumptions of equilibrium and homeostasis? If the indicators are not objective measures of the social activities under study but are rather themselves outcomes of the system, the process that generates the indicators requires description.

Models of social systems and the role of information flows

Social systems are inherently so complex that any attempt to model them requires a high degree of simplification and abstraction. Disciplinary specialization has resulted in the development of models of separate components of the social system's building blocks. Thus, economists have constructed sub-system models that purport to explain economic outcomes such as income growth, inflation, and unemployment. Political scientists have modeled voting behaviors and bureaucratic decision making. Only recently have serious efforts been made to capture the critical linkages between the economy and the policy. A typical schema for a simplified political–economic system model is presented in Figure 2.1. Almost every casual arrow or feedback loop in such models assumes accurate information, whether coming to or from voters, economic policymakers, other government officials, or firms (Hibbs and Fassbinder, 1981).

Systems of the type displayed in Figure 2.1 are equilibrium models incorporating the fundamental notion of homeostasis, namely, the maintenance of critical variables within a tolerable range of limits. In such models, external shocks to the system activate either economic or political responses that return the system to an equilibrium state. Such models therefore require various control mechanisms that receive, interpret, and respond to information signals. The information signals are typically conveyed by the symbols of social indicators. Thus, in the model described in the preceding, information concerning the economy is conveyed through the indicator system of national income accounts and price and unemployment indices. These signals, insofar as they affect mass political support, will be transformed into other information signals representing voter preferences that are again captured in the symbols of social indicators that influence the decisions and policies of government.[5]

Virtually all policy implementation assumes that the signals from the information network operate effectively, providing social indicators that contain approximately correct information. Our contention is that this latter assumption is likely to be incorrect under a wide range of circumstances. Indeed, we wish to argue that the information content of social indicators is likely to become distorted by the very operation of

---

[5] In some instances, economic indicators immediately trigger policy reactions, as in the case of "automatic stabilizers." Here, pre-existing rules short cut the discretionary government decision network in order to eliminate the lagged response of the political process. Indexation of wages and salaries to price indexes, nominal tax schedules, unemployment benefits, and indexed social payments are obvious examples.

61

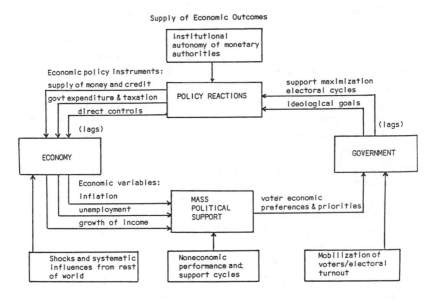

Figure 2.1. Typical model of political–economic system. (*Source:* Hibbs and Fassbinder, 1981, p. 4.)

the economic, social, and political institutions they seek to describe. We shall argue that the more important a social indicator becomes as a signaling device for public policy responses, the more likely it is that the indicator itself will degenerate as a descriptive measure of the behavior of the social system. Moreover if this degeneration of information content is not perceived by decision makers, or if they are unable to do anything about it, the social system itself may become highly unstable.[6]

Observer–subject–policymaker feedback

In order to gain insight into the nature of an information system that relies on social indicators, we must first examine the institutional requirements for the production of social indicators. First, there is the primary information source, the subject. A subject is typically an individual, firm, or government agency furnishing information in the form of records, or responses to questionnaires or through self-reporting.

[6] See McGee and Feige (1982). See also Feige (1981). See Gordon (1981) for a critique of one important social indicator as unreliable but for different reasons.

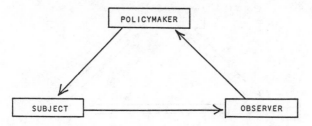

Figure 2.2. Simple information system.

Second, an institutional entity collects and aggregates the basic data reported by (or the behavior exhibited by) the subject. We call this actor the observer. Third, some institutional entity, or the policymaker, must exist to interpret and apply the data to some social policies that are relevant to specific interests.

Informational integrity of a system assumes that each of the three actors' interests and perceptions have a significant degree of autonomy such that informational transfers between the actors in the system will be relatively accurate and unbiased. This assumption justifies the dual claim of social indicators to objectivity and of public policy to rationality. Direct unbiased information flows can thus be represented by the diagram displayed in Figure 2.2.

What types of informational disturbances can induce dysfunction of such a control system? At the most trivial level, there may be a changed relationship between the underlying social phenomenon we wish to measure and the measurement instrument, which generate continual adjustments and redefinitions of social indicators such as GNP, price indices, unemployment statistics, and various survey indices. Such "improvements" in measurement often take the form of changing the domain of observation and thus change the meanings attached to former values of the indicators. If it becomes difficult to distinguish between changes in the indicators due to changes in measurement techniques and changes in the actual phenomenon being measured, appropriate interpretation and "recalibration" can become a severe problem. In developing economies, for example, improvements in the economic reporting mechanism that increase the domain of economic observation can easily be misinterpreted as representing a period of unusual growth, or takeoff.

In Figure 2.3 we represent various types of possible feedbacks between the subject, the observer, and the policymaker that are, we believe, a more accurate representation of the actual workings of the

63

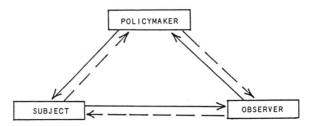

Figure 2.3. Information system with feedback loops.

information system, including the significant probability of systematic information distortion.

First, the very fact of being observed and the potential use of that information by policymakers may change both the reporting and the actual behavior of the subject. Consider, for example, the interaction between the subject and the observer. In social systems where the subject is a human being, the presence of an observer can have a major effect on both the reporting of the subject and the subject's actual behavior.[7]

The subject, the observer, and the policymaker interact in diverse ways, with multiple feedbacks of various kinds and intensities. Figure 2.3 represents a simple taxonomy of feedback possibilities. Different social indicators may be quite differently affected depending upon the source, motivation, and intensity of the feedback effect. Each feedback loop is complicated by different economic, bureaucratic, or political interests that create varying intensities of feedbacks. The degree of the feedback will be intensified where each actor has special interests in the indicator and a stake in the continuation of the feedback system itself.

Various observer–subject–policymaker feedbacks take place in different contexts. The first type of feedback takes place in a context in which the observer and policymaker are perceived by the subject as being closely interrelated. The most obvious example is reporting on tax information, where the subjects readily understand that their self-reported activities will have immediate and predictable consequences

---

[7] Such effects have been recognized in particular disciplines, and research techniques have been developed to reduce specific impacts of such feedbacks. Medical experiments consider the "placebo effect," and the important contributions of the evaluation research literature attempt to design measurement systems that minimize the corruption of the measurement instrument (Campbell, 1974). Sociology and psychology concern themselves with "unobtrusive measures" designed to minimize the effect of the observer on the subject.

for them. Underreporting of income, even though subject to penalties, also holds the possibility of reduced tax liabilities.

The second type of feedback arises when the roles of the subject and observer fuse, as in the case of bureaucratic performance. Here the policymaker attempts to derive information on the subject–observer with the intent of measuring performance standards. When such measures are perceived by the bureaucracy being studied as inputs to policy decisions affecting the bureaucracy itself, strong incentives arise for the falsification or non-reporting of critical information. The stronger the perceived negative consequences of accurately and completely reporting various types of information, the more likely is the possibility of false and misleading information being produced.

Relatively little attention has been directed to the implication of these feedback effects on the specification and operation of social information systems. The problem of feedback of social indicators on the system itself arises because of the simultaneous increase in both the necessity and the capacity to measure social, economic, and political behavior by economic and political institutions. Recent dramatic feedback effects may be due to the rapid development of the information system coupled with a growing awareness on the part of subjects of the consequences of their own reporting activities. Information is disseminated so rapidly and acted upon so directly that subjects, observers, and policymakers perceive their own interests are directly affected not simply by the quality of the information transmitted but by the nature of the information itself. As policymakers exercise greater control over both subjects and observers, the informational inputs required for that control are increasingly likely to be contaminated.

System effects: the unobserved economy

Although separate examples of policy feedback have been noticed in each discipline, their full social implications have not been realized, partly because of disciplinary specialization itself, partly because of the absence of a significant exemplar. Our concern is to show the pervasive character of information and policy feedbacks using the example of the growth of the unobserved economy as a way of justifying a call for interdisciplinary methodological and theoretical work.

Economists in the 1960's believed that they could control the economy with automatic stabilizers and "fine tuning," but the turbulent decade of the 1970's witnessed the failure of central predictions of macroeconomic models. The growing disparity between the theoretical predictions of economics and actual macroeconomic trends constitute a series of anomalies the theoretical models of economics cannot adequately explain. Ad hoc explanations range from "supply shocks" (Peruvian anchovy harvest failures and the formation of the OPEC oil cartel) to the failure of central banks to implement the policies of monetarists. It is ironic that at the time when information systems may have become most vulnerable to distortion, economic theorists have explained away the impotence of government policies with "rational expectations" hypotheses.

Statistics used to measure and explain these trends are informational inputs for both discretionary government policies and the "thermostatic" controls for the fiscal systems linked to policy. They require accuracy, yet reflect only the activities in the observed sector of the economy: income, consumption, investment and savings, prices, and unemployment. Any systematic discrepancy between the social indicators and the economic activity they purport to measure will generate serious errors of policy. Recent research suggests that systematic biases associated with a large and growing sector of unrecorded economy activity have been introduced into the system of social indicators.[8] The unobserved sector escapes the social measurement apparatus because of accounting conventions, non-reporting, or underreporting. It includes both market and non-market exchanges that utilize money and also barter in both legal and illegal economic activities.

The observer–subject–policymaker feedback mechanism can be illustrated in the context of the unobserved economy by regarding government data collection as the *observer* and individuals and firms as the *subjects* who volunteer information through the vehicles of surveys, or self-reporting. Subjects perceive the observer as an agent of a government that taxes, regulates, subsidizes, and transfers resources, thereby creating both disincentives to report honestly and incentives to underreport incomes, expenditures, and employment. Potential exposure or detection is reduced by "skimming," false invoicing, and going off the books. Subjects are also likely to shift from taxed and regulated activities toward non-market and "do-it-yourself" activities, enhancing eligibility for subsidies and transfer payments.

The policy consequences may be drastic. Consider an economy whose total economic activity grows at some normal rate, whatever that might be, but whose unobserved sector grows faster than the observed sector due to shifts from the latter to the former. The causes for such shifts may

---

[8] For example, the Bureau of Economic Analysis (Parker, 1984) has recently incorporated an improved adjustment for tax source misreporting in 1977 amounting to $81.5 billion for charges against GNP and a $69.3 billion adjustment for personal income.

be increased tax burdens, increased costs of regulatory compliance, or simply a general erosion of trust in government. As the observed sector activity becomes a smaller fraction of total economic activity, income statistics will display a reduced growth, falsely signalling the onset of a recession. This impression will be reinforced as unemployment figures are bloated by workers who shift to off-the-books activities but claim unemployment insurance benefits. At the same time, consumer price indices will *overstate* the true price level. Price statistics are gathered exclusively from the observed sector. They do not reflect the lower prices potentially available in the unobserved sector.

Lower growth, higher unemployment, and lower productivity induce both direct and indirect governmental actions that stimulate expenditures and transfers. Higher price indices via indexation induce higher wages, social security benefits, and retirement pay. They also stimulate inflationary expectations that themselves bring on real inflation. Thus, traditional economic theory and common sense tell us that what may begin as a statistical illusion is soon transformed into an unpleasant reality. Nor does the story end here. Higher prices push people into higher marginal tax brackets, thereby increasing real tax burdens. This in turn will induce further shifts into the unobserved sector, and the cycle begins anew. When the tax base shrinks at the very time that government expenditures increase, government deficits grow, requiring higher interest rates to attract funds to finance the deficit and to compensate lenders for higher expected inflation. In market economies, exchange rates will be affected as well as the balance of payments. As citizens begin to perceive that governmental actions are exacerbating the economic disturbances, trust in government declines and compliance is further reduced. This feedback process has no invisible hand to wave it back to stability because the corrective mechanisms are flawed.

This picture is one of a growing economy that exhibits symptoms of stagflation solely as a result of a statistical artifact. The economic patient is healthy, but the social thermometer has gone awry.

This analysis is supported by empirical evidence that there is, in fact, a substantial and growing unobserved sector. Studies of the United States, Canada, Italy, Germany, and the United Kingdom suggest that the monetary unobserved economy ranges between 5 and 25 percent of the observed income.

As illustrated by Figure 2.4, the unobserved sector in the United States and United Kingdom has grown dramatically during the 1970's, a growth corresponding to the onset of major perceived economic difficulties.

The usefulness of the unobserved economy exemplar is that it con-

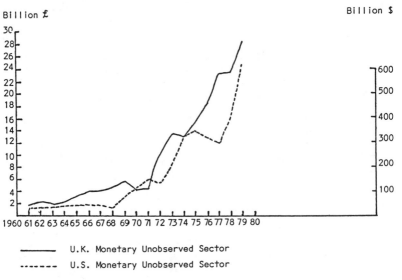

Figure 2.4. Estimates of the U.K. and U.S. unobserved monetary sector, 1960–79. (*Source:* Adapted from Feige, 1981.)

ceptually illustrates the various types of information feedbacks displayed in Figure 2.3. Conventional models of the political–economic process allow for one set of important interactions between the political and economic systems, but such models are incorrectly predicated on the assumption that information flows are unaffected by these interactions. The unobserved economy example illustrates how the *information system* itself can become contaminated in such a way as to produce misleading social indicators and, consequently, misguided actions on the part of citizens and policymakers alike.

Political implications of the unobserved income hypothesis

. The hypothesis that there exists a large and growing unobserved economy partially explains some of the paradoxical anomalies that confront the economics profession. It might equally serve to shed light on some of the empirical anomalies in the political science literature. Citing the Michigan Survey Research Center findings, McCracken (1973) has noted: The striking feature of responses, however, is the extent to which there is substantially more optimism reflected in people's view generally about their own economic situation than in their views about the economic and political environment. If individual participation in unobserved economic activities is not reflected in broad social indicators of economic activity, this presents a possible explanation for the discrepancy between the perception of the general economic situation and the individual's personal economic situation. What is particularly paradoxical, however, is that aggregate economic indicators appear to affect political popularity to a much greater extent than individuals' perceptions of their own economic situation. Fiorina reveals that "previous micro level research has found weak and inconsistent effects of personally experienced economic conditions" (1981). Whereas Frey claims that "actual data on economic conditions as collected and published by statistical offices perform very well in popularity functions...Among perceived economic indicators, those referring to general economic conditions perform better than those referring to the respondent's own economic conditions" (Frey and Schneider, 1981).

The empirical findings suggest that individuals evaluate their own economic conditions more optimistically than they do general economic conditions but rely on economic indicators rather than their personal experiences in their voting decisions. But the publicity given to economic indicators may override individually perceived economic conditions as a factor influencing political responses.[9] This possibility suggests not only that social indicators produce wrong signals but more ominously that citizens use false information in their political and economic decision making. This hypothesis would help to explain the decline in trust in government and unduly pessimistic economic expectations. If political and economic behaviors are shaped not by individual life cycle experience (Wilensky, 1981) but more importantly by social indicators signalling information at odds with individual experience, then we must seriously reassess the foundations of "rational" decision making in both the economic and political domains.[10]

The observer: professional and bureaucratic performance

The simple information model assumes that both the observer and the policymaker are separate and disinterested actors. In fact, both are

[9] Lipset and Schneider (1983) summarize recent research that found "people's assessment of their own personal well-being remains high, even while their confidence in institutions and their optimism about the country as a whole is deteriorating" (p. 402). Lipset and Schneider, however, accept the basic validity of economic indicators of unemployment, inflation, and productivity, using them to interpret survey data on the steady loss of popular confidence in American institutions (p. 407).

[10] The standard economics view is expressed well by Arrow (1951), who assumes that "individual values are taken as data and are not capable of being altered by the nature of the decision process itself." He asserts that this is a "standard view" in economic theory. Clearly, that assumption must be questioned.

diverse and have interests of their own that affect the measurement of social indicators and their translation into public policy. For example, attempts by observers (professional bureaucrats, social scientists, and government agencies responsible for gathering and aggregating data,) to measure bureaucratic performance may distort the behavior of the subject. Attempts to gather information at the "top" of an organization about the performance of subordinate officials changes the behavior and activities of those below. Subordinates try to evade observation and to shift behavior toward creditable and rewarded activities. Similarly, bureaucratic units either shift their behavior toward measurable activities that create the appearance of serving organizational goals or face immediate sanctions: budget and personnel cuts, denial of necessary resources, reorganization, or even termination.

Moreover, "hard" indicators of performance (dollars spent, buildings built, employees hired) may only be imperfectly related to the legitimate goal of the agency. This behavior is reinforced by value-added measures of government production that assume dollars spent is an indication of contribution to social welfare by the state.[11]

Another instance of feedback in measures of bureaucratic performance is the innovation of plea bargaining in courts. This was an organizational adaptation by police departments to the bureaucratic and political requirement of increasing their ratio of solved to unsolved crimes: the "clearance rate." This measure provided an incentive to change the behavior of subjects – criminals and the police. Criminals who confessed to more crimes got leverage with the police to recommend a lower sentence. As a result, the clearance rates were themselves affected. Public policy dealing with the causes of crime and the management of the courts could be affected by the fictitious inflation of the proportion of "solved" crimes, resulting from the creation of a performance indicator (Skolnick, 1966, Chapter 8).

None of these examples question the integrity of bureaucratic officials. On the contrary, our argument rests on the assumption that officials are professionals who act neutrally to further organizational goals, among which is the valid purpose of protecting the jurisdictions set up by legitimate legislative decisions. Public programs and agencies are given organizational autonomy in order to allow accountability, in-

---

[11] A pertinent discussion of the problem of "contaminated" data in the reports of bureaucratic agencies, particular data likely to be used in assessing performance in budgetary review, appears in Hood and Dunsire (1981, pp. 28–36). Although they do not let the ambiguities of the data interfere with systematic empirical analysis, one of their main points is that there is almost no way in which even to define a "department" because information on staffing, budgets, jurisdictions, programs, and legal authority are almost impossible to discover and correlate with each other.

cluding the capacity to measure effective performance. If officials were given less autonomy, measurable indicators of performance would be even more difficult to devise because the organizational boundaries of accountable behavior could not be defined clearly, either for legal or political surveillance. This is an intrinsic dilemma in the development of social indicators of organizational performance. The basic point is that the internal incentives within bureaucracies are not likely to lead to a search for the best economic indicators.

Many of the features of the actor we have called the observer are analyzed in the literature called "evaluation research." Crime statistics and plea bargaining are only two examples of topics upon which evaluation research has been conducted. Whereas many works of this type have real value, they are still subject to the distortions inherent in disciplinary specialization and dependence upon quantitative indicators. For example, with the shift in educational resources toward the hard sciences and away from the social sciences and humanities, social scientists increasingly feel the need to publish articles that have some kind of quantitative data and statistical techniques of analysis. Looking too deeply into the presuppositions underlying the generation of the data will result in delay at best or at worst in failure to be able to publish at all.[12] Considerable incentives are created to accept readily available "databank" sources of information and to analyze them in a manner that generates statistically significant results (Feige, 1975).

The policymaker: elite responses to political participation

Analogous processes of observer–subject–policymaker feedback in both political institutions and public bureaucracies exacerbate the difficulties of dealing with the consequences of a large and growing unobserved economy. The incentives governing the behavior of bureaucrats and legislators make it difficult for them to discover and to act upon the deficiencies of core economic indicators. The conventional indicators used by policymakers to assess public opinion and preferences tend to be either surveys or elections results. Both are likely to be afflicted with the equivalent of non-response and sampling biases, which reduce both

---

[12] A recent example from some of the best and most careful work in political science shows that the assumption that the basic data on national income, employment, and the size of the public sector are basically accurate is simply taken for granted and does not even require discussion. If the bias introduced by observer–subject–policymaker feedback varies systematically with some of the dependent and independent variables, the conclusions may be seriously affected, but it is beyond our scope to speculate on how. See Cameron (1978, pp. 1243–61).

the adequacy of the data and the potential capacity for recognizing the biases.[13]

The assumption of the simple information model is that policymakers want objective data from the bureaucracy, want objective feedback, and have no interests of their own except to register public preferences and produce effective public policy that will maintain social order and further economic growth. But here, again, the simple element we have labeled the policymaker is in fact a complex coalition of political and administrative elites with their own electoral and career interests. In some cases political elites do not want accurate data. Having direct and documented access to the "facts" closes the escape hatch of "plausible deniability" so popular in the Nixon administration and with corporate executives who did not want to know, for example, about the bribery of officials in foreign countries.

Similarly, the process of establishing a program or agency by a legislature or other policymaking body is not a disinterested act. Frequently, politicians create programs and their bureaucracies as a symbolic response to public pressure but do not give those programs enough resources and authority to do their mandated job. They can argue in the electoral arena that they have been responsive and responsible by creating a program and deserve to be rewarded in the next election. By establishing the bureaucracy, politicians have simultaneously escaped responsibility, since inefficiencies can be blamed on an agency outside their control, but they have earned political credit as responsible policymakers.

The relevant point here is that neither professional politicians nor bureaucrats have a stake in accurate social indicators. The multiple feedbacks that generate the consequences we have outlined are a system problem. No individual and no political or governmental institution is in a position to correct them because of *their* own structural interests.

The non-response problem

Political elites normally assume that the non-respondents to surveys are not significant. Interested citizens will respond, and a lack of response is tantamount to satisfaction or to an inability or unwillingness to act. In either case there is no political threat.

---

[13] A pioneer sociological essay defending the possibility of rational social policy based on valid "social indicators" (Bell, 1973) contains absolutely no discussion of the validity of the data or the possibility of contamination and distortion of the fundamental information by observer–subject feedback. Yet the entire argument assumes without any question the possibility of gathering valid data about social and economic trends.

The problem is analogous both for elites and for social science estimates of the probable attitudes and behavior of non-respondents. In many economic surveys in the United States and in Europe, the non-response rate is 25–40 percent on survey questions. Typically, the way this is handled is to assume that the responses of non-respondents would have been the same as those of respondents with the same demographic characteristics.

In more refined work, respondents' demographic characteristics are compared to known population values in order to assign more informed values to the imputations required for non-respondents. However, this solution is insufficient when there is reason to believe that non-respondents with typical demographic characteristics nevertheless engage in fundamentally different behavior than respondents. In the case of illegal or quasi-legal activity, this presumption seems highly plausible. To date, there is no solution to this problem, but recognizing its existence explains in part the discrepancy between estimates of unobserved activities based on survey methods as opposed to indirect macromethods since the survey suffers more from the non-response bias.

However, if the non-response is not an accident but a volitional act, then any particular non-respondent is likely to be someone who has something at stake, necessarily disqualifying them as "uninterested" citizens. Traditional methods of dealing with omitted information of this type are flawed. They are incapable of accounting for the self-selection of non-respondents, nor can they assess the degree of bias in the answers of respondents.[14]

Similar problems plague the construction of other economic indicators, most notably national accounts, which rely on survey data for estimates of income and expenditures.[15] In each case, non-respondence is at least partly a result of observer–subject–policymaker feedback. Non-response and underreporting of incomes and expenditures represent biases introduced into social indicators as a direct result of actions by subjects motivated by their perception that observers and policymakers can regulate, tax, or otherwise influence their behavior as a consequence of reporting requirements.

[14] The problem of non-response has become one of the major issues in recent econometric literature, and some important new techniques are being developed to deal with the problem. See Heckman (1979). The issue is important not only for voting behavior, but is perhaps even more salient for research being undertaken to measure the size of the unobserved economy by survey methods. In general, survey techniques yield estimates of unobserved economic activity well below those derived from indirect macromethods.

[15] For example, in the current population survey data base, family non-response rates on questions pertaining to income increased from 14 percent in 1970 to 26 percent by 1976. See Feige (1980, p. 35).

Information – behavior feedback

In political science it is recognized that public opinion polls change opinion both at the point of reporting opinion and after the feedback to the public about what "most people think." People tend to give what they think will be the most effective or the most legitimate response. In the case of political party support, if a party is rising in the polls, it will attract more support because it is perceived as a potential winner. If it is seen as losing (other things being equal, of course), the process of decline will be accelerated. Thus, the observation and reporting of public opinion feeds back on public opinion itself. The reporting of public opinion on whether a party is likely to win or a program is popular also affects decisions of political leaders concerning strategy, media reporting, and policy. In turn, their actions either reinforce or undermine the actions of key opinion-making elites. This phenomenon has assumed greater importance with the highly visible actions of political leaders and the practically instant feedback of public opinion measures back to the public itself.[16]

However, political institutions function as if public opinion is a valid measure of what people want and how they are likely to behave in elections. Institutional arrangements only allow public opinion to be expressed and responded to in certain ways. Expressions of preferences and political demands are channeled through interest groups and parties. In a political context in which parties have become weakened both because of loss of a solid base in party identification and because of the increasing power of interest groups to maintain direct access to policy-makers, quicker feedback of opinion via the media may reduce the capacity of public opinion to discipline political leaders *if* it is seen by leaders as subject to manipulation.[17] However, regardless of the direction of causality, if public opinion is shaped by erroneous economic

---

[16] In partial response to this problem, France allows no polling one week prior to the election.

[17] Key, a political scientist, in his seminal study of American public opinion (1961), discussed "linkages" and "feedback" but did not consider the possibility of observer–subject feedback. Basically, his concept of feedback consisted of the idea of the mutual influence of political leaders attempting to "mold public opinion toward support of (government) programs and politics" (p. 422) and of the "flow of influence to as well as from the government" by public preferences (p. 423). Key's subtle analysis of the multiple and interrelated impacts of government decisions upon public opinion is an elaborate version of a mechanical control model of information. He says, for example, that "the opinion context...may be regarded as a negative factor; it fixes the limitations within which action may be taken but does not assure that action will be taken" (p. 424).

74

indicators, whatever impact it has upon governmental decision making will be distorted.

"Unobserved politics": social movements

Another example is a political analog to the economy. Political elites, similar to economic elites, "measure" political activity by yardsticks drawn from conventional institutionalized procedures. Just as economic activity is reported by surveys and various direct measures of economic activity, so political activity is "reported" via voting and related legitimate mechanisms of political participation. Policy is based on the assumption that the entire electorate is "counted" in the composition and policies of the coalition constituting the government at any given time. Just as the measure of GNP assumes that all significant economic activity has been measured, so reports of voting behavior assume that all significant political opinion and activity is ultimately registered in the ballot box.

The formation of an effective governing coalition fails if the main reason for a large amount of non-voting is alienation, not satisfaction, and if non-voters have a capacity and a readiness to re-enter the political system in non-institutionalized forms of social movements that are not "registered" except as illegal and disruptive behavior.

The political analog to the unobserved economy is therefore the development of unobserved politics, the unhinging of individual political participation from the traditional apparatus of democratic representation: elections, parties, and legislatures. Temporary one-issue movements, social movements around new issues – recently feminism, environmentalism, anti-abortion, the nuclear freeze – become the expression of political consciousness. Such movements are based upon fluid political identities and do not rely upon traditional political symbolism to generate support. Traditional symbols of party loyalty (i.e., Democrat and Republican) no longer tie an individual to a party or even to a government identified with a stable political ideology and policy commitments. The prevalence of incremental policies attempting to remove the ideological, Left–Right dimension from politics has reduced the proportion of the electorate identifying with a party viewed as representing their interests.

The greater interdependence of economic and political institutions is not matched by an integration of the bulk of the population into those institutions. On the contrary, just as an increasing fraction of economic activity is not accurately measured by the indicators that shape policy, an increasing fraction of political activity is not taken into account by the

75

institutionalized measures of participation. Whether some of this non-institutionalized political behavior is a response to the perceived "costs" of conventional reported behavior is an important question, as is the issue of the extent to which the general loss of trust in social and political institutions leads to unobserved political movements. Or, political behavior that is not "measured" by established political institutions may simply make it more difficult for policymakers to deal with the consequences of the unobserved economy.

Failure of disciplinary specialization and institutional interdependence

The consequences of observer–subject–policymaker feedback are further exacerbated by the difficulty of an integrated theoretical and empirical attack upon the problem. Specialization in the social sciences is based upon the assumption that there are relatively autonomous clusters of causes and consequences conventionally labeled the "economy," the "political system," the "social structure," or the "culture." The fundamental assumption about the nature of modernizing societies within which these disciplines developed and that justified the specialization in the first place is that institutions become differentiated to serve specialized functions. It is assumed that causal sub-systems define a scientific object (a "field") and become the focus for disciplines studying the economic, political, or social factors, behaviors, and institutions.[18]

Such overall differentiation was historically seen as a positive and progressive trend linked to economic growth, individual freedom, increasing education, and social mobility, increasing political participation. "Dysfunctions" were indeed recognized – the decline of traditional bases of social solidarity and the loss of older forms of social control over behavior – but these dysfunctions were seen as temporary, as lags, as problems to be solved, partly with the aid of the specialized social sciences. If they were confined within a given institutional realm, they could be compensated for, either by further differentiation to mute the structural strains or by one institution "stepping in" to restore equilibrium resulting from the malfunctioning of another.

"Slack" in the total system was seen as allowing a considerable

---

[18] Conventional work both in political science and in Marxist political economy take the rational capacity of the state to make policy, and specifically its capacity to gather accurate economic data, simply for granted. A critique of this literature from a philosophic standpoint is Connolly (1981), who argues that both Marxist economists and mainstream political scientists "underplay...the extent to which citizens... quietly obstruct the performance of the political economy." (p. 136).

amount of "error" in any one institution or sub-system. Public opinion would act as a corrective mechanism, disciplining political leaders. The economy could function with minimum regulation. The state would mainly protect the institutions of markets and production and mediate social conflicts. Communities and families would be subject to the impact of economic growth and decline, but the state would step in if necessary to provide basic welfare subsistence. Each social science field assumed that the institutions in the intellectual jurisdiction of the *other* fields functioned normally and did not have to be considered in their own specialized analyses.

The consequences of information distortion

Even in some theoretical monographs that consider feedback as a system problem, the consequences for the accuracy of data are not considered.[19] The examples we have given are separate illustrations of observer–subject–policymaker feedback in economic activity, public opinion, and bureaucratic performances. Their combined effects are impossible to understand within any single disciplinary perspective.

This point must be stressed. Each institution involved with the social measurement of economic activity, public opinion, and bureaucratic performance must rely upon, must assume, and is even a *product* of social measurement. These institutions are based upon the premise that there are (within reasonable ranges of error) objective ways of measuring how much income people earn, whether they are working, and what they want from government. If multiple feedbacks exist, then the problem of valid social measurement and the search for an analytic framework that can comprehend them is compounded.

Observer–subject–policymaker feedback in the realms of public opinion, organizational performance, and economic activity are closely related. Analyses of them cannot assume that they are independent. If social indicators of public opinion, the performance capacity of state agencies, and GNP are simultaneously distorted in ways that are connected, obviously some serious problems exist. These problems are hardly even recognized by social science analysts and policymakers alike because they are perceived within specialized disciplinary frameworks and not captured by the established machinery of social measurement.

Some might argue that the unobserved economy constitutes a safety

---

[19] Despite the importance of the concept of feedback in the pioneering work by Deutsch (1966), he does not consider the possibility of systematic contamination of the basic data by the processes we have defined as observer–subject–policymaker feedback.

valve. People can opt out of the observed economy to find employment in the unobserved one, and this provides flexibility and increased options. But this view takes no account of the cumulative social psychology of this behavior. If people begin to act in ways that are contrary to law or are no longer subject to social constraints, even if the economic implications in the short run are healthy, in the longer run the bases of social order may be eroded. Although the sheer burden of taxes and regulation may partly explain the growth of the unobserved economy, as most economists would argue, the erosion of "trust in government" is also important (Feige, 1980). Political and social alienation is becoming apparent with the decline of party identification and the erosion of governing majorities. When political alienation interacts with economic incentives, threshold tolerances of social cohesion may be reached.

State policymakers are under multiple pressures from powerful interests groups, from the general need to keep the economy productive, and from the need to legitimize the system by democratic procedures that allow mass participation. One important manifestation of breakdown may be an inability to develop internally rational procedures for gathering accurate social measurements.

Conclusions

Because part of our argument is based upon data derived from social indicators and another part is a critique of their validity, we have to be especially clear about what is real and what is not. Not all of the social indicators that have exploded in the 1970's are illusory fictions. On the contrary, the expansion of the unobserved economy may indeed be linked to larger political problems of "social disorganization" and "political ungovernability" as conventionally described. The indicators behind those labels refer to real trends. Crime and divorce rates have climbed in Western societies. Identification with major parties has indeed dropped, as has the stability of ruling political coalitions. The trends are real, although their meaning, causes, and consequences remain obscure. The reality of these trends may be linked to the growth of the unobserved economy. The conceptual elaboration of the problem of observer–subject–policymaker feedback is intended to point toward a general hypothesis about the apparent anomalies in the key empirical indicators central to the social sciences.

One result of observer–subject–policymaker feedback is to distort the social indicators and instead signal the onset of economic crisis. What is ominous about this possibility is that the empirical evidence from political science appears to support the view that the distorted social indicators also influence political decision making. If true, an initial statistical illusion will become actual political and economic malaise. *Rational individuals* are basing decisions on *irrational information*. Thus, the evidence of economic, social, and political "crises" may well reflect in part a flaw in the information system, which itself is structurally generated.

The introduction of quantitative data and the statistical techniques has given rise to cliometrics, sociometrics, and econometrics. The *T*-statistics, regression analyses, and path analyses replaced literary and qualitative descriptions of social behavior and institutions, embodied in the quantitatively unsupported theories of Marx, Adam Smith, Weber, and de Tocqueville. It is time to ask new questions about the quality of our quantitative evidence as opposed to simply further manipulating the same kind of evidence. In economics, this means making inquiries into the implications of rational behavior based on "irrational" information. The question can be extended to the other specialized social science disciplines with particular ramifications for both public policy and research design, especially evaluation research.

What is required is a reevaluation of our fundamental data bases in the light of an assumption of observer–subject–policymaker feedback. The concept of a society as a whole composed of sub-systems with feedbacks would broaden the scope of theoretical conceptions of problems and the relevant data. We wish to restore the role of the generalist as legitimate and thus the importance of multiple types of legitimate information and evidence without denying the role of the specialist. In fact, the immediate and dramatic exemplar of the unobserved economy suggests the possibility that specialists in different areas may resolve to pursue these issues in their own disciplines and develop interdisciplinary strategies to understand them. Our rough effort to put together pieces of an interdisciplinary puzzle has relied upon the insights and the data developed by the specialized disciplines. Separately, these pieces are necessary but not sufficient to analyze the increasingly complex social system in which rapid changes are generating forms of economic, social, and political behaviors that escape traditional modes of measurement. Information is central to an understanding of complex social systems. With equal force, we must come to recognize that knowledge of the social system is required for the understanding of our own information base.

CHAPTER 3

Policy illusion, macroeconomic instability, and the unrecorded economy

ROBERT T. MCGEE and EDGAR L. FEIGE

During the decade of the 1970's, many Western economies unexpectedly suffered through periods of high unemployment, slowed economic growth, and high rates of inflation. In the 1980's, the major problem has become high interest rates and massive government deficits. The discrepancy between the factual observations of macroeconomic phenomena and the traditional theories that sought to explain them has created disillusion with the economics profession and the perception that macroeconomics in particular is in a state of crisis. Ad hoc modifications of conventional theories and innovative alternative explanations of stagflation and rising deficits have provided economists with a host of doctrinal issues to dispute. However, the absence of any consensus on the underlying causes and cures for these economic maladies has left the economics profession and policymakers in a state of great uncertainty as they confront a deteriorating situation. It is now apparent that the professional optimism that characterized the decade of the 1960's was shattered by the economic record of the 1970's. The prospects for the present decade will depend upon our ability to correctly diagnose what went wrong in the last one.

In the decade of the 1960's, the U.S. economy enjoyed an average rate of inflation of 2.8% combined with an average rate of unemployment of 4.7%, whereas during the 1970's, the economy experienced inflation at 6.6% and unemployment at 6.2%. The enthusiastic profession of the 1960's believed that it was possible to fine tune an economy that was thought to be characterized by a trade-off between inflation and unemployment. The disillusioned economists of the 1970's sought explanations for the unprecedented increases in both inflation and unemployment in ad hoc supply shocks such as the formation of the OPEC cartel. Rational expectations and natural rate of unemployment theories were elaborately specified to explain the emasculation of economic policy and the predictive failures of large-scale econometric models. Monetarists sought refuge in the claim that their recommendations had not adequately been put in practice, whereas Keynesian economists blamed the spread of monetarist doctrines. Neoclassical economists placed stringent rationality and market-clearing constraints on their models even as neo-Keynesians sought out market imperfections and behavioral irrationalities as the explanation of stagflation. The long-standing tradition of demand-oriented macrotheory reluctantly, but precipitously, embraced the promises of supply side economics. Amidst this intellectual pandemonium, economic facts stubbornly defied the most creative efforts to reconstruct an apparently failing theory.

Recently, yet another hypothesis has been advanced by Feige (1980; see also Chapter 1) as a possible explanation of the widening gap between observed economic facts and received economic theory. The unrecorded income hypothesis suggests that perhaps it is the economic facts that require scrutiny rather than the economic theories. According to this perspective, the growth of an unrecorded economy has distorted the official information system that is sending the current signals of economic malaise. As economic activity shifts from the recorded to the unrecorded sector, some basic economic indicators such as real growth rates, employment, and productivity may become understated. As false reporting and non-reporting becomes endemic among individuals and firms as a result of growing incentives and preferences to avoid the scrutiny of governmental data collection agencies, social indicators become contaminated by the process Alford and Feige (Chapter 2) describe as "observer–subject feedback." A growing body of empirical evidence suggests that the unrecorded economy is of substantial magnitude and has grown during the decade of the 1970's in many of the world's most highly developed economies.

The promise of the unrecorded income hypothesis is that it offers an alternative perspective on the current state of economic malaise. By shifting the emphasis away from a restructuring of received theory toward an investigation of the reliability of economic "facts," the perspective raises an entirely different set of questions to be asked and seeks answers that may at once be consistent with traditional theory and the facts of economic life.

If it is the case that social indicators are themselves corruptible and can produce misleading information to both the public and policymakers, then we must inquire into the nature and magnitude of such distortions and examine the implications of an information system capable of producing systematically false signals. We may well be in a position to retain the assumption of behavioral rationality on which so much of our theory is based once we realize that rational individuals and policymakers will nevertheless produce irrational outcomes if the information basis for their decisions is systematically distorted.

The macroeconomics of unrecorded income

Dynamic descriptions of economic systems require specifications of expectation formation behavior. Rather than replace the powerful assumption that expectations are conditioned by available information in a rational manner, with alternatives based on asymmetric illusions, we seek to investigate the consequences of rational expectation formation based on irrational information. The fundamental illusion that may exist within the economy, and among those who study it, is the assumption that the economic facts that motivate behavior are accurate or at least unbiased. The unrecorded income hypothesis provides a conceptual challenge to this deep-seated belief. It offers an alternative characterization of a dynamic social mechanism that tends to distort the information base established to describe the system itself.

As a result of high marginal tax rates and other costly government regulations, individuals and firms have economic incentives to hide their activities from governmental data collection agencies. Whereas individual economic actors may still have relatively accurate information concerning their own economic circumstances, they nevertheless rely on broad social indicators for gauging the general economic situation. Survey results suggest that individuals appear to be much more optimistic about their personal economic situation than about the general economic situation. This is precisely what would be expected when aggregate data based on false reporting produce the statistical illusion of economic malaise. If policymakers and citizens respond to false information signals, this can produce genuine economic malaise. What is required then is the formulation of a macroeconomic model that takes explicit account of a growing unrecorded economy and traces the implications of such a phenomenon on the dynamics of the economic system.

Feige (1980, p. 57) presented some suggestions concerning the formulation of such a model:

Such a model would incorporate the various incentives and costs relevant to inter-sectorial shifts of resources...The model would specify the dynamic behavior of individuals, firms, and governments as they respond to official information that is systematically biased in directions previously described. Such a model would be capable of demonstrating formally that an exogenous shock to the system, such as supply shocks, higher taxes, or political disillusionment, could induce major shifts between the recorded and the unrecorded sectors. Such shifts in turn would affect official statistics in such a way as to induce the appearance of stagflation symptoms, which, in their turn, could lead to economic behaviors that transform the illusion of stagflation into the reality of stagflation. Such a model would depart from conventional equilibrium assumptions and would seek instead to define the necessary and sufficient conditions under which the hypothesized dynamic instability would occur.

This chapter is a preliminary attempt to formally introduce some of these ideas into a standard macroeconomic model. Our major concern is with the effects of "policy illusion," namely, the process whereby policymakers react to observed economic information without regard to the existence of the unrecorded economy. We will demonstrate that under a wide range of plausible conditions, well-intentioned policy action based on information gathered solely from the recorded sector will lead to stagflation in the recorded economy. The growth of the unrecorded sector will produce symptoms of economic decline that are transformed into actual stagflation as a direct result of policy illusion.

Our aim in this chapter is not to enter into the current disputes of the theoretical literature of macroeconomics but rather to show how the phenomenon of an unrecorded sector can be incorporated into existing macromodels to gain alternative insights into macrodynamics. To this end, we present in the text a simple graphical description of the consequences of both exogenous and endogenous growth in the unrecorded economy, focusing attention on the consequences of policy reactions to misinformation. The technical model that underlies the graphical analysis is presented in the Appendix. The basic model that describes the economy is adapted from McGee (1982) and extended to include both recorded and unrecorded sectors. The basic model is an aggregate dynamic model of income determination that is rich enough to permit both the monetary neutrality results of rational expectations and natural rate models and the non-neutrality results stemming from Tobin-type asset effects and tax-induced supply side effects. The model is therefore capable of examining the consequences of both monetary and fiscal policies under conditions of downward sloping, upward sloping, and vertical Phillips curves.

The nature of the problem

The theoretical issues posed by macroeconomists in the last decades have clearly been motivated by their observations of the facts of economic life. Just as Keynes's general theory was fundamentally shaped by the factual experience of the Great Depression, so has recent theoretical inquiry been molded by the economic record of the past two decades. The record is based on official government statistics and is most easily summarized in the changing relationship between the rate of inflation and the level of unemployment. As Figure 3.1 reveals, unemployment rates steadily declined with only modest increases in the rate of inflation during the decade of the 1960's. The subsequent decade was charac-

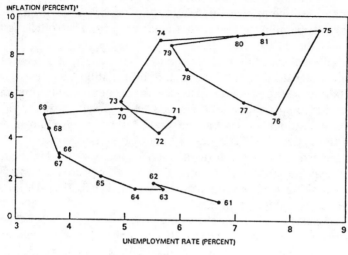

PERCENT CHANGE IN GNP IMPLICIT PRICE DEFLATOR.
SOURCES: DEPARTMENT OF COMMERCE AND DEPARTMENT OF LABOR.

Figure 3.1. Inflation and unemployment rate.

terized by a drift toward higher inflation rates and higher levels of unemployment.

The economists of the 1960's attributed the salutary economic record to their own subtle manipulations of policy control variables, whereas the economists of the 1970's sought to blame structural economic change and policy blunders for the dismal record. In neither decade was the record itself challenged.

Feige (Chapter 1, Figure 1.6) estimated the relative growth of the monetary unrecorded economy in the United States during the decades of the 1960's and 1970's. What is startling about these estimates is the dramatic growth displayed in the unrecorded sector beginning in 1966 and continuing with two temporary reversals during the decade of the 1970's. The estimates suggest that the unrecorded sector remained essentially a fixed proportion of the recorded sector during much of the 1950's and 1960's. On the other hand, the rapid relative growth of the unrecorded sector in the 1970's may have introduced systematic distortions in more recent official government statistics. These statistics serve as the fundamental information base for government policy. We therefore entertain the possibility that at least a part of the instability of the inflation–unemployment relationship described in the preceding may be attributable to false signals emanating from the official government statistics.

The rational expectation literature raised the question of what restriction must be placed on the formation of information-based expectations such that expectations be consistent with a general equilibrium model. Our aim is to entertain a different question; namely, how will the properties of a rational expectation general equilibrium system be modified when the system itself is shocked by an exogenous growth in the unrecorded economy that distorts the information basis used in the formation of expectations? Furthermore, what are the properties of a system in which shifts from recorded to unrecorded activities are an endogenous part of the system itself?

The general equilibrium model employed throughout this chapter is described in detail in the technical Appendix. In the text we present simplified graphical expositions of the system's dynamics under alternative sets of assumptions.

The vertical Phillips curve and full-employment policy

The first regime we consider is an economy with a vertical Phillips curve. The monetary authority is charged with the activist responsibility of maintaining full employment. Figure 3.2 illustrates an initially stable economy with a zero inflation–full employment equilibrium point at A. The model is constructed to conform to the prevailing rational expectation–natural rate view where stability occurs when monetary growth $\dot{m}$ equals the rate of growth of real income $\dot{y}$. The initial full employment–zero inflation equilibrium A is maintained so long as $\dot{m} = \dot{y}$. Any attempt to push the unemployment rate U below its natural rate U_n will induce movements along the vertical Phillips curve, raising inflation without producing any lasting effect on the unemployment rate U_n.

Consider the consequences of an exogenous once-and-for-all increase in the unrecorded economy. An external shock to public confidence in government such as the Vietnam War or the Watergate episode could trigger a shift from the recorded to the unrecorded economy. Income and employment shift off the books, and individuals previously employed in the recorded sector shift to unrecorded jobs, declaring themselves unemployed. Since recorded unemployment increases for all inflation rates, the observed Phillips curve shifts to the right. The new observed unemployment rate is U_1^o, and this in turn induces a monetary expansion to $\dot{m}_1$. The monetary authorities' reaction is pictured in the

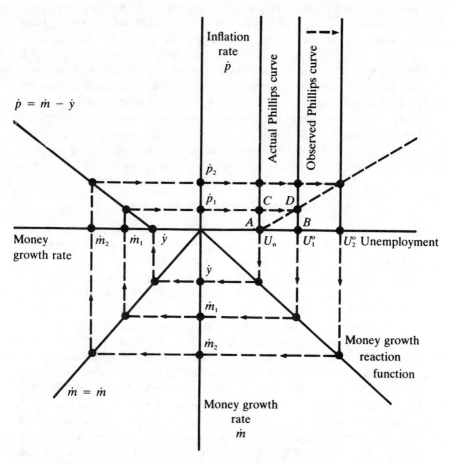

Figure 3.2. Effect of exogenous shift to unrecorded sector where long-run Phillips curve is vertical and monetary policy is counter cyclical.

lower right quadrant and represents an activist counter cyclical policy. The higher growth rate in the money supply in turn raises the inflation rate to $\dot{p}_1$ since money growth now exceeds the growth rate of real income. A new equilibrium is established with actual unemployment at its former level U_n, observed unemployment at U_1^o, and a higher inflation $\dot{p}_1$. Thus, the effect of a once-and-for-all shift in the composition of total employment from observed to unrecorded employment will move the economy from an observed position A to the illusionary position D, which will be maintained. The result is the appearance of stagflation. Although there has been no change in actual unemployment, observed unemployment is higher, and there has been an actual increase in the rate of inflation. If the external shocks to public trust continue or if the public disillusionment with government policy provokes further shifts to the right in the observed Phillips curve, the process will be repeated. Observed unemployment rates will increase, and higher inflation moves the economy to a new observed point such as E. Every exogenous increase in unrecorded activity will stimulate another round of actual inflation and observed higher unemployment. Hence, stagflation will be observed as an upward sloping Phillips curve along points ADE even though the actual economy is structurally characterized by a vertical Phillips curve through point A.

An upward sloping Phillips curve

An additional complication is added for policymakers if the rising inflation rates in Figure 3.2 are accompanied by higher real tax rates due to insufficient indexation of the tax system. If higher tax rates reduce output and employment because of negative supply side effects, then the long-run Phillips curve will slope to the right, reflecting higher unemployment as inflation rises. An economy with inflation-induced tax increases can be characterized by an upward sloping Phillips curve as shown in Figure 3.3. As before, we characterize a position of zero inflation equilibrium at point A, with unemployment at its natural rate U_n, and $\dot{m} = \dot{y}$. An exogenous increase in the unrecorded economy will produce an observed rightward shift in the Phillips curve. At the prevailing zero inflation rate, the unemployment rate observed is U_0^o at point B. As the monetary authorities respond to the higher observed unemployment rate with higher money growth, the inflation rate is pushed up to $\dot{p}_1$. Since the real tax rate is assumed to rise as a result of inflation-induced bracket creep, real supply side effects raise actual unemployment to point C and observed unemployment to U_1^o at point D. The higher observed unemployment again induces a "countercyclical" policy response that has the unintended consequence of producing both actual and observed stagflation. So long as the monetary authority maintains its "full-employment" policy objective, it paradoxically initiates a real as well as an observed stagflation spiral. If external shocks to the system bring on further shifts toward the unrecorded sector, this tendency toward an explosive system will become even more exaggerated as the observed Phillips curve continues to shift rightward.

We have demonstrated that an initial illusion in the information system induced by a once-and-for-all increase in the unrecorded economy can transform an otherwise stable equilibrium into an unstable

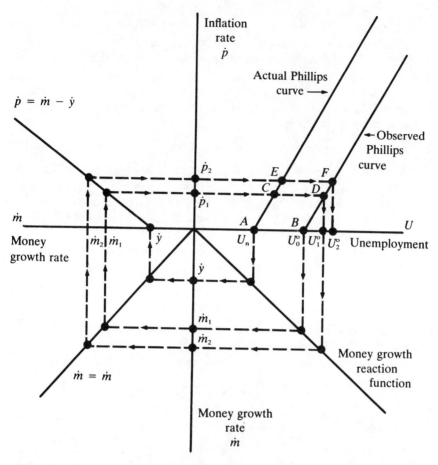

Figure 3.3. Effect of exogenous shift to unrecorded sector where long-run Phillips curve is upward sloping and monetary policy is counter cyclical.

system characterized by a real stagflation explosion. The mere illusion of economic malaise is translated into the reality of economic chaos.

A further complication arises if the tax increases induced by inflation stimulated in turn endogenous increases in the unrecorded sector. Until now, we have treated the unrecorded sector as if it was exogenously determined entirely by citizens' attitudes toward government. If attitudes toward government remain unchanged, it is still possible that the unrecorded economy will increase solely due to economic incentives to hide more income in response to higher taxes.

To illustrate this endogeneity, we consider the simple model of the unrecorded sector presented in Feige and McGee (1983). We assume that the unrecorded economy is structured similarly to the observed economy. Thus, for the moment we ignore efficiency and productivity differences between the observed and unrecorded economy.

We assume that the representative household's preferences for unrecorded versus observed sector output can be represented by the Cobb–Douglas utility function:

$$U = cY_o^\lambda Y_u^{1-\lambda} \tag{3.1}$$

Output produced in the unrecorded sector Y_u is priced below output in the observed sector Y_o. The price discount is simply the tax rate θ. This price differential is assured by the assumption that competition in the unrecorded sector forces prices to correspond to the lower input costs of production made possible by evaded taxes.

The amount of income the representative household decides not to disclose is determined by maximizing equation (3.1) subject to the income constraint:

$$I - Y_o - (1 - \theta)Y_u = 0 \tag{3.2}$$

Observed sector output is taken as the numeraire good, and unrecorded sector output is therefore priced at $1 - \theta$.

The first-order condition for utility maximization requires that

$$\frac{\lambda}{1 - \lambda} = \frac{Y_o}{1 - \theta} Y_u \tag{3.3}$$

Since total output is constrained by

$$Y = Y_o + Y_u \tag{3.4}$$

where $Y_o = \gamma Y$ and $Y_u = (1 - \gamma)Y$, we can rewrite (3.3) as

$$\gamma = \frac{\lambda(1 - \theta)}{1 - \lambda\theta} \tag{3.5}$$

where γ is the share of actual output observed.

From (3.5), we note that the observed sector's share of total output decreases as tax rates rise and increases as preferences for observed sector output (λ) increase. This preference parameter (λ) reflects a myriad of social and political attitudes toward government that include trust and public morality. Its explicit inclusion as a parameter of the utility function permits the introduction of non-economic qualitative effects that are typically not considered in economics since preferences are taken as given and fixed.

Equation (3.5) provides the necessary linkage between tax policy and the unrecorded sector. As inflation increases in a regime with progressive taxation and inadequate indexation, real tax rates will rise. The impact of this endogenous increase in tax rates on the allocation of income between the observed and unrecorded sector is in addition to the more conventional supply side effects of higher taxes in reducing labor and capital supply and hence the tax base.

Figure 3.4 illustrates the consequences of introducing an endogenous shift to the unrecorded sector as a result of inflation-induced tax rate increases. As before, we begin the analysis with a zero inflation–full employment equilibrium at A and disturb the system with a once-and-for-all exogenous shift toward unrecorded activity. The Phillips curve is observed as being displaced to the right with observed unemployment at U_0^o. In response to higher observed levels of unemployment, the monetary authority (committed to a full-employment policy) raises the money growth rate with its consequent effect on inflation. At the higher inflation rate $\dot{p}_1$, bracket creep pushes individuals into higher tax brackets, increasing the effective real tax rate. The consequence of the induced higher tax rate can be partitioned into two separate effects. The first represents a pure supply side effect that moves the economy along the actual Phillips curve from A to C and along the observed Phillips curve from B to D.

Both actual and observed unemployment are higher as factors reduce their supplies in response to the higher tax wedge. In addition to this pure supply effect, there is an induced shift of activity from the observed to the unrecorded sector as a result of the higher incentive to under-report income. This endogenous shift to the unrecorded sector is displayed as a rightward rotation of the observed Phillips curve along a trajectory BEH. The higher observed unemployment represented by U_2^o can be decomposed into an illusionary rise in unemployment caused by the original exogenous shift to the unrecorded sector $U_0^o - U_n$; the real increase in unemployment reflected in the movement from point B to D, which reflects an induced supply side contraction; and a further illusionary increase in unemployment that results from the tax-induced shift to the unrecorded sector $(D-E)$. The combined effect is to raise observed unemployment to U_1^o, which in turn stimulates monetary expansion. As displayed in Figure 3.4, the continued adherence to a full-employment activist monetary policy produces a stagflation spiral, raising inflation rates as well as actual and observed unemployment. The endogenous shifts to the unrecorded sector are seen to further the dynamic instability of the model.

Three factors contribute to the problem we have described. First and

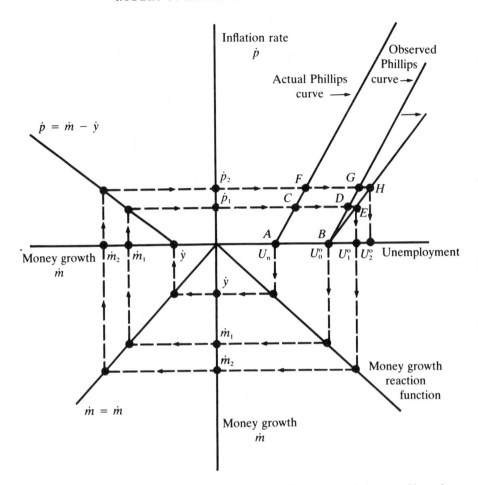

Figure 3.4. Effect of exogenous and endogenous shifts to unrecorded sector. Upward sloping Phillips curve and countercyclical monetary policy.

foremost is the distorted information produced by a shift to unrecorded activity. Second is the continued adherence to an activist countercyclical policy that itself is triggered by false information. Third, we have the effect of bracket creep. The identification of the problems suggests some possible solutions. The first requirement is to find methods for distinguishing between real and imaginary changes in the social indicators that trigger government policies. Once known, policy thermostats can be recalibrated to account for illusionary unemployment increases. Furthermore, tax systems can be indexed so as to eliminate the rise in real taxes induced by inflation. This latter suggestion has been incorporated into the Reagan administration tax program but is presently being threatened by political pressure for higher non-legislated taxes. Finally, the illustration makes clear the dangers of strict adherence to activist countercyclical monetary policy, particularly when that policy appears to fail in its objective. These exercises illustrate the possibility that a healthy economy directed by well-intentioned policymakers can be driven into the reality of an explosive stagflation situation as the result of an unrecognized shift from observed to unrecorded activity.

One apparent solution to the problem of dynamic stagflation is to abandon the countercyclical monetary policy and adopt in its place a fixed money growth rule. This policy change can be represented in Figure 3.4 by a counterclockwise rotation of the money growth reaction function that brings it parallel to the horizontal axis at a selected fixed growth rate of the money supply. The new policy would reverse the upward spiral in inflations and thus reverse the growth in unrecorded sector activity induced by bracket creep. However, as we shall see in the following section, it would be premature to conclude that indexation of the tax system and abandonment of the full-employment monetary policy represent costless solutions to the problems created by the growth of unrecorded activities.

Price stability targets and fiscal automatic stabilizers

In the previous sections, we analyzed the consequences of shifts to the unrecorded sector in an economy where the monetary authority was committed to an activist countercyclical policy. In such an economy, monetary policy typically operates to stabilize interest rates while permitting larger swings in money growth rates. To the extent that private credit demands are accommodated and government deficits are partially monetized, real interest rates will tend to be relatively low even when nominal interest rates rise pari passu with inflation. Such was the case during the 1970's as monetary policy accommodated rising credit demand.

In October 1979, the Federal Reserve adopted a new policy of stricter control of the growth of monetary aggregates with a view toward utilizing monetary control as the primary weapon against inflation. Interest rate stabilization and full-employment goals for monetary policy were abandoned in favor of the monetarist recommendations for stricter control of monetary growth in order to reduce inflation. One consequence of this policy change was the rise in real interest rates that became a major source of contention between the United States and Europe.

Our aim in this section is to consider the consequences of a shift to the unrecorded sector, in an economy where the monetary authorities are strictly committed to price stability via a fixed rule for monetary growth. In such a regime, monetary policy can no longer serve to accommodate public credit demands through monetary expansion, and thus fiscal deficits must be financed through heavier borrowing from the public. Since monetary policy is now aimed at a price stability target, the burden of income and employment stabilization falls more heavily on fiscal policy. We shall assume that the fiscal authorities rely primarily on automatic stabilizers that act to increase expenditures during periods of unemployment. Similarly, tax revenues will tend to shrink during periods of recession as the tax base contracts in the face of a fixed tax rate schedule.

Figure 3.5 illustrates the consequences of an exogenous shift to the unrecorded sector in an economy with a monetary price stability target and fiscal policy based on automatic stabilizers. We assume that the monetary authorities succeed in fixing a money growth rule with the effect of stabilizing the rate of inflation at some low level. As such, the rate of inflation can be ignored in the subsequent analysis.

Line *ACE* in the upper right quadrant of Figure 3.5 represents the locus of values of real interest rates and the unemployment rate consistent with equilibrium in the model. Higher real interest rates are associated with higher rates of unemployment since the economy's capacity declines with higher real interest rates. As real interest rates rise, previous economically feasible investment opportunities are eliminated, with a resulting fall in the economy's capital stock and a consequent decline in the demand for labor.

The lower right quadrant represents the endogenous relationship between the level of unemployment and the level of real government debt per capita. As unemployment rises, tax revenues fall as the income tax base shrinks at the very time that government expenditures rise to meet the higher need for unemployment benefits and other recession-linked social payments. Since monetary growth is fixed, the revenue shortfalls must be financed by public borrowing, which increases pressure on interest rates. We have represented the locus of equilibrium unemployment and government debt as a simple linear function; however, it is possible that as a result of higher interest payments on the existing debt, the curve may actually be non-linear, with government borrowing growing in greater proportion to increases in unemployment. This effect will simply strengthen the results that follow.

The upper left quadrant of Figure 3.5 shows the equilibrium relationship between the government's debt and the real rate of interest. This

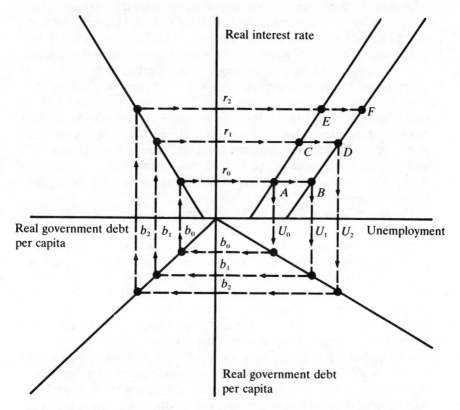

Figure 3.5. Effect of exogenous shift to unrecorded sector where monetary policy pursues price stability target and fiscal policy relies on automatic stabilizers.

equilibrium locus is also upward sloping as increased borrowing raises real interest rates. Point A displays an initial equilibrium with unemployment at U_0 and real interest rates at r_0. The borrowing b_0 required to finance outstanding government debt is consistent with the existing real rate of interest, and thus the entire economy is at an equilibrium, with monetary growth maintaining some fixed rate of inflation.

As before, we now consider the consequences of an exogenous shift to the unrecorded economy. The effect of such a shift is to produce a rightward movement in ACE to BDF since for every rate of interest, we now observe a higher level of unemployment. The higher observed unemployment level is illusionary and thus has no independent effect on the real values of the system; however, fiscal policy, which is calibrated

95

to observed unemployment, will automatically produce a larger deficit at U_1. The increase in government borrowing to b_1 will force the interest rate to r_1, which in turn produces a real supply side increase in both actual unemployment to point C and observed unemployment to U_2. As long as automatic stabilizers are triggered by the higher observed unemployment rates, government borrowing will increase, forcing the economy along an unstable path of higher interest rates and higher unemployment. Equilibrium inflation is unaffected, but the mere illusion of higher unemployment has created the reality of higher interest rates and higher real unemployment. Further shocks that produce additional rightward shifts in the interest rate unemployment locus will worsen the instability, as would any endogenous increase in unrecorded activities due to declining trust in government.

The model suggests that the most promising escape from the predicted worsening cycle of higher real interest rates and recession is to cut the links that permit debt increases to be automatically triggered by false unemployment signals. If the problem is correctly diagnosed as being caused by distorted information, it can be corrected by obtaining independent measures of the extent to which official data are contaminated by shifts into the unrecorded sector. Once the extent of information distortion is correctly measured, policy rules can be recalibrated to eliminate the previously described dynamic instabilities.

Alternatively, if the underlying information distortions go unnoticed and the problem is incorrectly viewed as being caused by rising debt, policies may be recommended to abandon and perhaps even to reverse conventional automatic stabilization rules. Political opposition to direct calls for greater taxation and reduced government expenditures during apparent recessions will all but eliminate this policy option. What remains is to impose arbitrary limitations on debt expansion that are unaffected by either the actual or the perceived state of the economy. The deficit reduction targets embodied in the recently enacted Gramm–Rudman–Hollings Act represent such a policy. It subverts the salutary stabilization effects of automatic stabilizers while ignoring the problem of false signals.

The fundamental problem that must be redressed is the deterioration in the information system that precipitates the predicted instabilities. Either we must find economic and political means to re-establish voluntary compliance with both the tax code and the data collection agencies of government (i.e., to restore all activity to the observed sector) or we must acknowledge the existence of the distorting information effects of the unrecorded economy and recalibrate policy instruments to properly account for the effects of the unrecorded sector.

The macroeconomics of unrecorded income

Summary and conclusions

It is now widely acknowledged that something important occurred during the decade of the 1970's that produced a period of economic malaise and policy ineffectiveness. The stagflation issue rose to the forefront of economic and political debate among policymakers and academics. The severity of the perceived economic crisis intensified the search for explanations and remedies. New theories have been advanced and major policy changes have been undertaken. Most significant among these has been a shift from a full-employment monetary target to a price stability target. The models we have examined suggest that such a shift in policy in the face of growing unrecorded activity can alleviate the problem of stagflation at the cost of high interest rates and burgeoning deficits.

The unrecorded income hypothesis suggests that many of the questions previously posed may be wide of the mark because the problem may lie with the facts themselves rather than with the theories that seek to explain the facts. The foregoing analysis is a first step in the direction of attempting to formalize some of the intuitions that follow from posing a different set of questions. We have examined the implications of the possibility that the information system that guides policy has become distorted as a result of observer–subject–policymaker feedback. We have shown that both activist countercyclical monetary policy and fiscal policy based on traditional automatic stabilizers can produce destabilizing rather than the intended stabilizing effects whenever such policies are based on systematically faulty information. Observer–subject–policymaker feedback describes a general mechanism that could systematically distort social indicators. Empirical evidence on the growth of the unrecorded economy suggests that such a mechanism appears to have been at work during the decade of the 1970's in the United States.

Although we have only scratched the surface of exploring the full implications of this process as it affects both expectations and real economic and political behavior, we believe we have at least established a simple mechanism capable of transforming an initial statistical illusion into the reality of economic instability. We have shown, moreover, that the doctrinal arguments over monetarist policies may be deflecting our attention from a more fundamental issue that will not go away even if monetarist arguments are correct and their policies are implemented. We believe that future policy questions must contain a serious examination of the issue of the growth of the unrecorded sector and its consequences for macroeconomic stabilization. Such a discussion can take the form of normative debate on the benefits and costs of a shift toward the unrecorded sector and the design of policies to either encourage or discourage the growth of the sector. Such a debate among economists will focus on issues of tax enforcement, tax reform, and optimal tax rates. Political scientists and sociologists may be more concerned with the implications of the erosion of public morality and the growth of alienation from governing institutions. The model presented here attempts to allow for both economic incentives and political and social attitudes.

What does seem clear is that regardless of one's normative perspective, there exists a positive problem for the social scientist that relates to the accurate measurement and appropriate interpretation of social indicators. A greater scientific understanding of the extent to which our current facts are distorted represents the greatest hope for the elimination of information errors that we have shown can have important destabilizing consequences. Policy illusion can be avoided either by eliminating the unrecorded sector so that the reliability of the information system is restored or by measuring correctly the magnitude of the existing distortion and recalibrating policy instruments to account for it accurately. Both approaches raise a new set of complex issues we hope will gain further attention.

What we have attempted to demonstrate is that distorted information can radically affect the stability of the economic system as it is presently constituted. When monetary policy is targeted on full employment, the outcome with distorted information is accelerating stagflation. When monetary policy is targeted on price stability while fiscal policy is geared to automatic stabilization of income, the outcome may well be higher deficits and higher interest rates. The root problem however does not seem to lie in defective theory or necessarily in defective policy prescriptions, for under both regimes we have described, policy can successfully attain stabilizing results so long as the social thermometer works accurately to produce correct information. However, a distorted information system can destabilize an otherwise stable economic system, and the predicted consequences of such distortions are broadly consistent with what we increasingly observe in our present-day economies.

APPENDIX
A MODEL TO ILLUSTRATE THE GRAPHICAL RESULTS

Model specification

The model consists of two parts. First, equations (3.1)–(3.5) in the main part of this chapter determine the division of total economic activity into its observed and unobserved parts. Equations (A.1)–(A.10) presented in this appendix determine the total levels of output and other economic variable values. Equation (A.1) makes output Y, at time t, depend on a Cobb–Douglas production technology. Equations (A.2) and (A.3) relate gross real factor returns to the respective marginal products implied by the production function. These equations determine labor and capital demand, respectively.

Equation (A.4) makes the non-money assets that wealth holders desire to accumulate for the next period dependent upon the after-tax anticipated real return and the anticipated inflation rate. Total non-money assets A_{t+1} are shown to be comprised of real bonds b_{t+1} and real capital K_{t+1} in equation (A.10). For ease of exposition, rather than introducing a separate bond demand function and the possibility of different real rates of return on bonds and capital, we regard bonds and capital as perfect substitutes. This implies that the after-tax real return to bonds and capital is the same. Thus, bonds and capital are added together into total non-money assets. Equation (A.4) is a kind of savings function that shows how non-money asset accumulation varies with the net of tax real return and inflation rates.

Equations

$$Y_t = K_t^a N_t^{1-a} \tag{A.1}$$

$$R_t = a Y_t K_t^{-1} \tag{A.2}$$

$$W_t = (1 - a) Y_t N_t^{-1} \tag{A.3}$$

$$A_{t+1} = B_0[(1 - \theta_k) {}_t R_{t+1}]^{\beta_1} ({}_t P_{t+1}/P_t)^{\beta_2} Y_t \tag{A.4}$$

$$M_t/P_t = C_0[(1 - \theta_k) {}_t R_{t+1}]^{-\alpha_1} ({}_t P_{t+1}/P_t)^{-\alpha_2} Y_t \tag{A.5}$$

$$N_t = N_0 \exp^{nt}[(1 - \theta_L) W_t/W_f]^{\delta} \quad \text{for } (1 - \theta_L) W_t \leqslant W_F \tag{A.6}$$

$$N_t = N_0 \exp^{nt} \quad \text{for } (1 - \theta_L) W_t \geqslant W_F \tag{A.7}$$

$$M_t = m(\pi D_t) \tag{A.8}$$

$$b_t = (1 - \pi) d_t \tag{A.9}$$

$$A_{t+1} = b_{t+1} + K_{t+1} \tag{A.10}$$

Model variables

t = time index
Y_t = total real output at time t
K_t = real physical capital stock at time t

N_t = employment
R_t = real rate of return before taxes on capital and bonds
W_t = real wage
P_t = price level of output in terms of money at time t
$_tP_{t+1}$ = price level anticipated at time t for next period
A_{t+1} = real bonds and capital wealth holders wish to hold until next period
M_t = nominal money supply
b_t = real bond supply to public
D_t = accumulated nominal fiscal debt
d_t = accumulated real fiscal debt

Model parameters

n = growth rate of labor force
N_0 = initial-period labor force
θ_L = tax rate on labor income
θ_K = tax rate on asset income (i.e., bonds and capital)
W_F = real wage at which labor supply is fully employed
m = money multiplier
π = share of deficit monetized by central bank
β_1 = elasticity of non-money asset demand with respect to anticipated real after tax return
β_2 = elasticity of non-money asset demand with respect to anticipated inflation
α_1 = elasticity of money demand with respect to anticipated real after tax return on non-money assets
α_2 = elasticity of money demand with respect to anticipated inflation
δ = labor supply elasticity with respect to after-tax real wage
a = Cobb–Douglas coefficient for capital
$1 - a$ = Cobb–Douglas coefficient for labor
$\exp$ = number with natural logarithm 1

A rise in the anticipated inflation rate makes interest-bearing assets preferable to non-interest-bearing money, which suffers a negative real return that rises with the inflation rate. This substitution away from money as an asset when inflation rises is a source that Fisher (1979) calls the "Tobin effect." It provides a potential mechanism for anticipated inflation to raise real levels of output and employment by stimulating capital formation.

Equation (A.5) is a demand function for real balances that depends negatively on the anticipated real return advantage on alternative assets, that is, bonds and capital. In addition, equations (A.4) and (A.5) make total asset accumulation vary positively with the level of real income.

Equations (A.6) and (A.7) specify the labor supply function. Labor supply is assumed to depend positively on the after-tax return to labor $(1 - \theta_L)W_t$. To capture the limits on labor supply inherent in the finite size of the labor force, a real wage rate W_F is postulated beyond which the entire labor force is willing to work. In other words, there is some wage rate at which the total supply of labor will be forthcoming. We assume in subsequent analysis that the economy operates in the region where the actual net of tax return to labor is less than W_F; that is, a rise in the wage rate will induce more labor supply. The sensitivity of labor supply to the net wage is captured in the parameter δ. If δ is zero, the labor supply is inelastic so that the entire labor supply will work at any wage rate.

Equation (A.8) is the money supply function. The monetary base πD_t is the share π of total government debt D_t monetized, that is, purchased by the central bank. This is assumed to be multiplied through the banking system's deposit creation powers by a factor of m.

Equation (A.9) shows the residual part $1 - \pi$ of the government's accumulated debt in real terms as the supply of bonds available to the public. The government deficit is either monetized by central bank open market operations or sold to the public as bonds.

To determine the model, it is necessary to specify the money growth rate and the government debt growth rate. We will refer to the setting of the money growth rate as monetary policy and the setting of the deficit as fiscal policy. The graphical analysis in the text of this chapter can be illustrated by examining the effects of the policy behavior we described there in the context of the algebraic model we have just outlined.

The Phillips curve and monetary policy

A steady-state equilibrium in the model is characterized by fixed relative prices, tax rates, and per capita real income and assets. The model is dynamic in the sense that a steady-state equilibrium can involve growing real levels of income, capital, bonds, money, and the labor force. The growth rate of the labor force determines the necessary steady-state growth rate of income and assets. If the labor force is not growing ($n = 0$), then steady-state equilibrium is at a stationary state solution where real values of all variables are fixed; but nominal values will change according to the money growth rate.

When the labor force grows, per capita real asset stocks and income are fixed in equilibrium; but this requires real income and asset stocks to grow pari passu with the labor force. Thus, a steady-state equilibrium with labor force growth requires the real government debt to grow with the labor force. If the labor force is fixed in size, then this condition requires that the real government debt is fixed. However, the nominal government debt must grow with the money supply to provide the monetary base and to maintain portfolio balance among the public real holdings of bonds, capital, and money.

A long-term Phillips curve relating the employment rate and the steady-state inflation rate is implicit in the model. This Phillips curve is linked directly to monetary policy because the steady-state inflation rate is equal to the money growth rate minus the growth rate of real income. Short-run responses and the effect of unanticipated transient impulses in money growth could also be analyzed.

To derive the steady-state equilibrium relationship between unemployment and inflation, which is presumed to be fully anticipated in the steady state, we substitute (A.1) into (A.2) for Y_t and take the current period expectation for next period's rate of return. This yields

$$_tR_{t+1} = a(K_{t+1}/N_{t+1})^{a-1} \tag{A.11}$$

Substituting (A.11) into (A.4) for $_tR_{t+1}$ and (A.1) into (A.4) for Y_t yields

$$A_{t+1} = \beta_0[(1 - \theta_K)a(K_{t+1}/N_{t+1})^{a-1}]^{\beta_1}(_tP_{t+1}/P_t)^{\beta_2}K_t^a N_t^{1-a} \tag{A.12}$$

In a steady-state equilibrium, $K_{t+1}/N_{t+1} = K_t/N_t$ and $N_{t+1} = (1 + n)N_t$.

Therefore,

$$\frac{A_{t+1}}{N_{t+1}} = \frac{\beta_0}{1+n}\left[(1 - \theta_K)a\left(\frac{K_{t+1}}{N_{t+1}}\right)^{a-1}\right]^{\beta_1}\left(\frac{_tP_{t+1}}{P_t}\right)^{\beta_2}\left(\frac{K_t}{N_t}\right)^a \tag{A.13}$$

Taking the natural logarithm of (A.13) and solving for the equilibrium capital–labor ratio, we have

$$\ln\frac{K}{N} = \frac{1}{(1 + \beta_1)(1 - a)}\{\ln\beta_0 - \ln(1 + n) + \beta_1[\ln(1 - \theta_K) + \ln a] + \beta_2\mu - \varepsilon\} \tag{A.14}$$

where μ is the steady-state inflation rate proxy variable, $\mu = \ln(_tP_{t+1}/P_t)$ and $\varepsilon = \ln(1 + b/K)$. The ε term in (A.14) represents the effect of the government debt alternative to capital accumulation as a form of saving. Other things being equal, a larger real government debt outstanding implies a lower level of per capita capital accumulation.

The employment rate is given by re-writing (A.6) as

$$E_t = \frac{N_t}{N_o \exp^{nt}} = \left(\frac{(1-a)(K_t/N_t)^a(1-\theta_L)}{W_F}\right)^\delta \quad \text{(A.15)}$$

where we have substituted (A.1) for (Y) in (A.3) and used the resulting expression for (A.3) in (A.6) for W_t to get (A.15). To express employment as a rate, we have divided (A.6) by the size of the labor force.

Taking the logarithm of (A.15), we obtain

$$e = \delta[\ln(1-a) + \ln(1-\theta_L) - \ln W_F] + \delta a \ln\frac{K}{N} \quad \text{(A.16)}$$

where e is the logarithm of the steady-state employment rate.

Using (A.14) in (A.16) for $\ln K/N$, we have the long-run Phillips relation (A.17) between inflation μ and the employment rate e:

$$e = \delta[\ln(1-a) + \ln(1-\theta_L) - \ln W_F] + \frac{\delta a}{(1+\beta_1)(1-a)}[\ln\beta_0$$
$$- \ln(1+n) + \beta_1[\ln(1-\theta_K) + \ln a] + \beta_2\mu - \varepsilon] \quad \text{(A.17)}$$

The derivative of (A.17) with respect to μ, the steady-state inflation rate, is

$$\frac{de}{d\mu} = -\left[\frac{\delta}{1-\theta_L}\frac{d\theta_L}{d\mu} + \frac{\delta a \beta_1}{(1-\theta_K)(1-a)(1+\beta_1)}\frac{d\theta_K}{d\mu}\right]$$
$$+ \frac{\delta a \beta_2}{(1+\beta_1)(1-a)} - \frac{\delta a}{(1+\beta_1)(1-a)}\frac{d\varepsilon}{d\mu} \quad \text{(A.18)}$$

Equation (A.18) gives the model formula for the slope of the Phillips curve.

If $de/d\mu > 0$, then a higher inflation rate results in a higher employment (lower unemployment) rate. This is the case of the traditional Phillips curve trade-off between inflation and unemployment. If $de/d\mu < 0$, then a higher inflation rate results in a lower employment (higher unemployment) rate. This is the case of steady-state stagflation. Finally, if $de/d\mu = 0$, the natural rate of unemployment hypothesis is verified, that is, the long-run Phillips curve is vertical.

Figure 3.2 assumes the vertical Phillips curve. Figure 3.3 assumes the stagflation Phillips curve. We did not treat the traditional Phillips curve possibility. Which curve is the appropriate curve depends on the sign of (A.18). The sign of (A.18) depends on two effects.

First there is the effect of inflation that can raise real tax rates in an inadequately indexed tax system. Higher tax rates will reduce the labor and capital stocks if the respective supply elasticities δ and β_1 are positive. This reduces employment for two reasons: (1) Less labor is forthcoming at lower real after-tax wage rates and (2) less labor is demanded at any given wage rate when capital is reduced by higher tax rates because the marginal product of labor is reduced. These effects are embodied in the first term of equation (A.18).

The second term of (A.18) is the positive Tobin effect of inflation on capital accumulation. This occurs because higher inflation makes cash balances less attractive relative to physical capital as an asset form for wealth holders. If this effect outweighs the negative tax effects of inflation, then employment rises with inflation. If the tax effect dominates, then the employment rate falls with inflation. If the two effects just offset each other, the long-run Phillips curve becomes vertical. McGee (1982) describes the conditions under which one effect will dominate the other.

The final term of equation (A.18) affects the magnitude but not the sign of the Phillips curve slope. This follows because

$$\frac{d\varepsilon}{d\mu} = \frac{d}{d\mu}\ln\frac{1+b}{K} = \frac{1}{1+b/K}\frac{1}{K^2}\left(K\frac{db}{d\mu} - b\frac{dK}{d\mu}\right)$$

Since our implicit fiscal policy assumption implies $db/d\mu = 0$, the sign of $d\varepsilon/d\mu$ depends on the sign of $dK/d\mu$, which is positive if the Tobin effect dominates and negative if the tax effects of inflation dominate.

For example, if the tax effect dominates, capital declines with inflation, and the ratio b/K rises. Government debt becomes a higher proportion of asset holdings. Since the decline in K is associated with a decline in Y, total asset holdings will be reduced. If ε stayed fixed, this would require an equal fall in b and K. Since b is fixed by fiscal policy, a greater fall in K is necessary to balance asset demands. In essence, this is a crowding-out effect. The employment loss from higher inflation is greater when government debt does not decline in line with the economy.

On the other hand, if the Tobin effect dominates, K will rise with inflation. In this case, the growth of asset demand with income requires a larger increase in K than would be necessary if government debt grew in line with the income level. There will be more employment in this case than would occur if b/K stayed the same. In summary, the third term of (A.18) reinforces the more dominant of the two basic effects of inflation in our model. In the case of a vertical Phillips curve this effect is neutralized.

These observations apply to the underlying actual Phillips curve for an economy characterized by our model specification. If there is an unobserved economic sector, then we might observe something quite different from the actual Phillips curve. We can combine the actual Phillips curve of equation (A.17) together with the composition of economic activity as it is divided between the observed and unobserved sectors to obtain the observed Phillips curve implied by equations (3.1)–(3.5) and (A.1)–(A.10).

The observed Phillips curve will differ depending on the size of the unobserved sector and how the unobserved sector reacts to inflation-induced tax increases. The observed steady-state employment rate is $E^o = \gamma E$. Taking logarithms yields

$$e^o = e + \ln \gamma \qquad (A.19)$$

where e is the logarithm of the actual employment rate, e^o is the logarithm of the observed employment rate, and γ is the equilibrium proportion of actual economic activity, which is observed.

Equation (3.5) determines γ as a function of individual preferences and the tax rate. For simplicity, we assume the tax rates θ on labor and capital are equal. Using (3.5) in (A.19) for γ, we have

$$e^o = e + \ln \lambda + \ln(1 - \theta) - \ln(1 - \lambda\theta) \qquad (A.20)$$

Given an actual employment rate, the observed employment rate will rise with the preference for observed sector output and fall with the tax rate.

The slope of the observed Phillips curve is

$$\frac{de^o}{d\mu} = \frac{de}{d\mu} - \frac{1 - \lambda}{(1 - \theta)(1 - \lambda\theta)} \frac{d\theta}{d\mu} \qquad (A.21)$$

If tax rates rise with inflation $(d\theta/d\mu > 0)$, the slope of the observed Phillips curve will be less than the slope of the actual Phillips curve. Thus, if the actual Phillips curve is upward sloping, it will appear to be worse when there is an unobserved sector. If the real Phillips curve is vertical, we may still observe an upward sloping Phillips curve because, despite the vertical slope of the real curve, equation (A.21) shows the observed curve can have a positive slope due to the induced effect of higher tax rates on the unobserved sector. It is even possible that the actual Phillips curve could be like the traditional curve, but the shrinkage of the observed economy as taxes rise creates the illusion of a stagflationary curve.

If the unobserved sector is exogenous with respect to tax rates, then (A.21) reduces to

$$\frac{de^o}{d\mu} = \frac{de}{d\mu}$$

and the unobserved sector just causes a parallel shift difference between the actual and observed Phillips curve.

Figures 3.2 and 3.3 assume such an exogenous unobserved sector, and $de/d\mu = 0$ and $de/d\mu < 0$, respectively. Figure 3.4 assumes $de/d\mu < 0$ and an endogenous component to the slope of the Phillips curve due to the endogenous response of the unobserved sector to inflation-induced tax rises.

The inflation–employment relation is based on the effect of monetary policy taking fiscal policy as a given. We turn next to the effects of fiscal policy in the model when we take monetary policy as given.

Fiscal policy and the unobserved economy

When monetary policy is fixed on an inflation rate target, the effect of an exogenous increase in the unobserved sector will be to create a gap between government spending and tax revenues. This deficit will necessitate an increase in the bond supply to the public in order to finance the loss of tax revenues to the unobserved sector. To the extent that this creates a crowding-out effect and raises interest rates, there will be a reduction in the equilibrium level of capital that will reduce the demand for labor and increase the unemployment rate. If government spending increases to compensate the unemployed, there will be an additional increase in the deficit that will add to the overall tightness in the credit markets.

Suppose therefore that government spending consists of exogenous expenditure $\bar{G}$, unemployment compensation at the rate ϕ of wages, and interest on the government debt. Then total government spending is given by

$$G_t = \bar{G} + \phi W_T(N_L - N_t) + R_t b_t$$

where N_L is the total labor force and $N_L - N_t$ is the unemployed labor supply.

Total tax revenues (without an unobserved sector) are given by

$$T_t = \theta Y_t$$

Steady-state equilibrium in the model requires that the government budget be balanced in a stationary state with a fixed labor force: Or in the case of a growing labor force, the amount of real outstanding government debt can grow pari passu with the labor force. For simplicity, we will treat the stationary state case to illustrate the effect of the unobserved economy on the unemployment rate.

Suppose the economy is initially in an equilibrium with a balanced

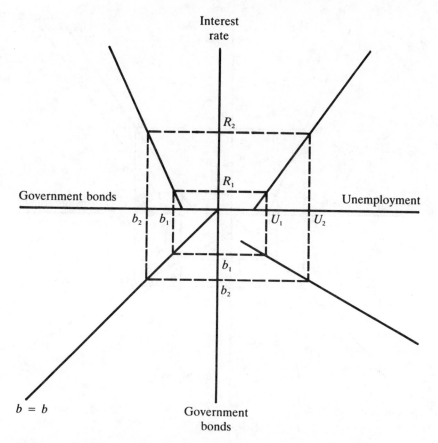

Figure 3.6. Equilibrium relations between government debt, interest rate, and unemployment.

budget and outstanding government debt b_1. Assume monetary policy is targeted on zero inflation, which in conjunction with the zero labor force growth rate implies the money supply is fixed. The equilibrium government budget constraint is then

$$G - T = 0 \quad \text{or} \quad \bar{G} + \phi W_1(N_L - N_1) + R_1 b_1 = \theta Y_1$$

Figure 3.6 illustrates such a stationary state equilibrium. Given this publicly held stock of government debt, there is an interest rate R_1 determined in the asset market. This corresponds to a particular level of the capital stock that together with the other relations in the model determines an unemployment rate U_1. The relations in Figure 3.6 are

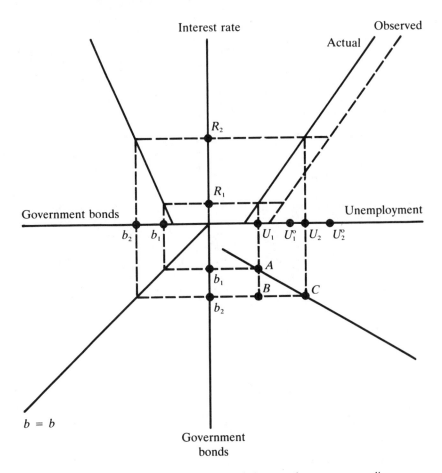

Figure 3.7. Effect of exogenous shift to unrecorded sector where monetary policy pursues price stability and fiscal policy includes automatic stabilizers.

drawn to illustrate the fact that increasingly high levels of government debt that are not monetized will raise the real interest rate and the unemployment level. For example, if the government's debt is b_2 instead of b_1, both the real interest rate and the unemployment rate will be higher at R_2 and U_2, respectively.

Figure 3.7 introduces the unobserved economy. The unobserved economy creates a discrepancy between the actual and the observed unemployment rate at each interest rate. This will disturb the government's budget constraint given monetary policy and exogenous government spending. We now have

108

$$G - T > 0 \quad \text{or} \quad G + \phi W_1(N_L - N_1) + R_1 b_1 > \theta Y_1$$

We assume taxes are only paid on observed income, and unemployment compensation is based on observed unemployment. Since $Y_1^o < Y_1$ and $U_1^o > U_1$, the right side of the budget constraint is reduced and the left side is increased, implying a fiscal deficit.

This fiscal deficit, which will not be financed by money expansion in our example, raises the stock of government debt held by the public to b_2.

Figure 3.7 shows that the deficit $b_2 - b_1$, which moves the bond supply from point A to point B, creates a disequilibrium in the asset market, which requires a rise in the interest rate to R_2 as more savings are accumulated as bonds and less are left for capital. This reduces income and employment.

A new equilibrium can be established at points R_2, b_2, U_2 if exogenous government expenditure $\bar{G}$ is reduced sufficiently to balance the budget at C. Observed unemployment would then be U_2^o. The unobserved sector would then have raised both interest rates and unemployment because of its effect on the government's accumulated debt.

If government expenditures are not reduced sufficiently to balance the budget at C, then the supply of bonds will continue to increase, further raising the interest rate and unemployment. This possibility results in the kind of deteriorating spiral depicted in Figure 3.4.

The effect of the deficit induced by the unobserved economy on the employment rate can be obtained by differentiating equation (A.17) with respect to the bond supply:

$$\frac{de}{db} = \frac{-\delta a}{(1 - a)(1 + \beta_1)} \frac{d\varepsilon}{db} < 0 \quad \text{since} \quad \frac{d\varepsilon}{db} = \frac{1}{K + b}[1 - n_{Kb}] > 0$$

where n_{Kb} is the elasticity of the capital stock with respect to the government bond supply, which is negative. Since the employment rate falls as the government's debt rises, the unemployment rate must rise.

CHAPTER 4

How large (or small) should the
underground economy be?

BRUNO FREY

The existence and growth of the unobserved economy entail both advantages and disadvantages. One of the major benefits is often considered to be the fact that it is one of the most productive and enterprising sectors of the economy, without which the population would be materially much worse off. An Italian author (Martino 1980, p. 2) states, for instance: "The so-called underground economy in Italy[is] a masterpiece of my countrymen's ingenuity, a second Italian miracle which has saved the country from bankruptcy." According to this view, the problem is not that people are active in the unobserved sector (they are simply responding rationally to the heavy burdens imposed upon them in the official economy) but rather the fact that the official economy is badly managed.

The major disadvantage is then thought to be that (a large part of) the unobserved economy is illegal and that its toleration would erode tax morality, leading to a general breakdown of law and order. Also, the falling revenue due to tax evasion is taken to create serious problems for the financing of those goods and services the population desires to have publicly provided. To compare the private as well as the social benefits and costs and to derive therefrom "social optimal" conditions has always been one of the main contributions of economics. Indeed, the theory of quantitative economic policy as developed in particular by Tinbergen (1952) and Theil (1968) provides a well-developed formal apparatus to deal with such comparisons at a macroeconomic level. An aggregate welfare function specifies the value "society" attributes to alternative states of the world, thus enabling a comparison between benefits and costs. This social welfare function is maximized subject to the restrictions imposed by economic scarcity and more specifically by the model of the economy within which the optimal state is sought. The result indicates how the available instruments should be set to secure optimal success. This aggregate maximizing approach can also be used to determine the socially optimal size of the unobserved economy.

In the first section a model is sketched in which the socially optimal use of the marginal tax rate in the official economy, the penalties and

111

the probability of detection in the unobserved economy, and therewith the socially optimal size of the unobserved economy are determined by using a special variant of the theory of quantitative economic policy, namely, that of optimal taxation. The following section shows that this social-welfare-maximizing approach is open to criticism and that an alternative approach is required. The theory of democratic economic policy is then presented as an alternative framework that is applied to the problem of the unobserved economy.

The socially optimal size of the unobserved economy

The theoretical background

Two branches of economic theory are relevant for determining how large or how small the unobserved economy should be from the point of view of society as a whole.

The first branch is the theory of optimal taxation. It is used to determine that tax rate (usually within a given tax structure such as linear taxation) that maximizes economic well-being as described by a social welfare function, taking into account the effect taxes have on the supply of labor and on the production of goods as well as on the distribution of income. This approach was first developed by Ramsay (1927) and has recently received a great deal of attention in the area of neoclassical public finance, particularly in the *Journal of Public Economics*.[1]

The second branch is the economics of crime as championed by Becker (1976), who studies the possibilities for controlling illegitimate activities, looking both at the supply of and the demand for (i.e., the partial neglect of protecting oneself against) offenses.[2]

These two branches of modern economic theory have been brought together only very recently. The first theoretical studies on tax evasion (such as Allingham and Sandmo 1972, Srinivasan 1973, or Singh 1973) are almost exclusively devoted to how individuals react to given tax rates, and choose to declare some part of it, depending on the subjectively expected probability of being caught and fined. Kolm (1973) rightly observes that such studies are primarily concerned with the behavior of the individual. The broader social aspect is only introduced when the public policy issue of how the tax rates should be optimally set is addressed, remembering that the individuals have an incentive to evade taxes and to become active in the unobserved economy.

---

[1] For surveys see, e.g., Sandmo (1976) or Bradford and Rosen (1976).
[2] This aspect has been particularly explored by Ehrlich (1973) using econometric analyses.

Application to the unobserved economy

In an important article, Sandmo (1981) develops a model in which the socially optimal use of the policy instruments and therewith the socially optimal size of the unobserved economy are derived for individuals who have the choice of working either in the official (taxed) or in the unobserved (untaxed) sectors of the economy. The model aptly conveys the basic philosophy of the social-welfare-maximizing approach as applied to the unobserved economy, and it is therefore worthwhile to present its basic features and main result. In order to make his model tractable, Sandmo confines himself to the labor market and to the taxation of personal income. Moreover, the demand side of the labor market receives a very stylized treatment by assuming constant marginal productivities. The incidence of tax evasion on the relative prices of consumer goods is completely disregarded.[3]

The analysis proceeds in two steps. First, the behavior of the non-evaders and evaders is considered. The labor supply of non-evaders proceeds along standard lines: An individual utility function $U^n = U(C^n, L^n)$ is maximized subject to the budget constraint $C^n = w^n L^n (1 - t) + a$, where U is utility, C is consumption, L is labor supply in the official (taxed) sector, w is the wage rate, t is the tax rate, and a is lump-sum income transfer. The superscript n indicates that the variables refer to the (identical) non-evaders.

The evaders maximize expected utility because they have to reckon with their illegal activity being discovered and punished. They have to consider two types of predicament. They may not be caught, in which case their consumption will be

$$C_1^e = w^e L^e (1 - t) + a + w^e E$$

where E is the labor supplied in the unobserved economy and the superscript e indicate that the variables refer to the evaders. Conversely, they are caught, in which case their consumption is

$$C_2^e = w^e L^e (1 - t) + a - b + w^e E (1 - \theta)$$

where θ is the penalty rate and b is a lump-sum fine imposed when evasion has been detected. These two equations constitute the budget constraints belonging to the expected utility

---

[3] Other simplifying assumptions are that the relative shares of the non-evaders and evaders are fixed and that the individuals within a group are identical. Across groups the utility function is the same.

$$U^e = (1 - p)U(C_1^e, L^e + E) + pU(C_2^e, L^e + E)$$

where p is the subjectively estimated probability of detection. Solving this constrained maximization problem yields the following qualitative results. The compensated substitution effects $\partial L^e/\partial t$ and $\partial E/\partial \theta$ are negative as expected; but without additional assumptions, it is not possible to derive the direction of the effect of increasing the probability of detection and of increasing the tax rate on the supply of labor in the unobserved economy ($\partial E/\partial p$, $\partial E/\partial t \gtrless 0$). As usual, the assumptions on the utility functions do not allow to sign the income effects, but for convenience Sandmo assumes that an increase in lump-sum income reduces labor input ($\partial L^e/\partial a$, $\partial E/\partial a < 0$).

Having analyzed the behavior of the two groups of individuals with respect to given instruments (t, θ, a, b, p), the second step consists of deriving the socially optimal policy. Sandmo takes it as a matter of course that such a policy is undertaken by the government, thus assuming that the society's and the government's optimization problems are identical. Before embarking on the formal social welfare maximization task, it must first be decided whether the preferences for illegal activities should be allowed to count in the social welfare function. Sandmo follows the utilitarian route, assuming that the positive association between the utility of the individual and of society (Pareto principle) is extended to individuals who violate the law. Counting, therefore, the utility of the evaders along with that of the non-evaders, the social welfare function is

$$W = N^n \gamma^n U^n + N^e \gamma^e [(1 - p)U(C_1^e, L^e + E) + pU(C_2^e, L^e + E)]$$

where γ^n and γ^e are the weights accorded to the utilities of the two groups. The government chooses tax rates t, penalties (θ, $-b$), and the probability of detection to maximize this utilitarian social welfare function on the condition that an exogenous revenue requirement R^* is met. Moreover, tax receipts must cover the cost of detecting invaders C, which is taken to be an increasing function of the probability of detection and of the number of evaders: $C = f(p, N^e)$. The government's budget constraint is thus $R(t, \theta, a, b, p) = R^* + f(p, N^e)$, indicating that tax revenue depends on the use of the policy instruments t, θ, a, b, p.

As Sandmo himself stresses,[4] it is difficult to obtain definite results

---

[4] "It should be stressed at the outset…that the problems raised are not of the kind which can be resolved unambiguously: the contribution that formal theory can make is primarily to create a framework within which the policy issues can be discussed in a logically consistent manner" (p. 267), and "models of optimum income taxation typically yield few results of general validity" (p. 279).

within the theory of optimal taxation, and even less so when tax evasion and the unobserved economy are added. Nevertheless, he is able to establish the following results for the use of policy instruments:

1 The marginal tax rate should have positive marginal tax revenue ($\partial R/\partial t > 0$) because otherwise revenue could be increased by lowering the tax, and a distortion could be reduced without cost. That it is not optimal to be on the downward sloping part of a Laffer curve is a rather obvious result.
2 There should (also) be a positive marginal revenue from raising either the penalty rate, the fine $-b$, and the probability of detection ($\partial R/\partial\theta$, $\partial R/\partial(-b)$, $\partial R/\partial p > 0$). In the extreme case in which the welfare of the evaders does not count in the social welfare function ($\gamma^e = 0$), the three policy instruments used to control evasion should be set so as to generate maximum tax revenue (the preceding inequalities then become equalities). This result follows as collecting money from the evaders can be used to alleviate the tax burden of the non-evaders, thereby increasing social welfare.

The results of this rather complicated constrained social welfare maximization are rather obvious as Sandmo himself admits (p. 278). Nevertheless, the socially optimal size of the evaders and therewith of (this part of) the unobserved economy is determined implicitly only through the social-welfare-maximizing values of the instruments, in particular the tax rate, penalties, and probability of detection when active in the unobserved economy. In order to highlight in which way the existence of an unobserved sector affects the results, Sandmo compares them to a situation where tax evasion is ignored, as in Dixit and Sandmo (1977). In this case, a paradoxical result follows: When tax evasion is present, the marginal tax rate should, contrary to the commonly held view, not necessarily be lowered. The reason is that the unobserved sector is also distorted by the penalties imposed, which lead to a suboptimal supply of labor to this sector. Thus, if an increase in the tax rate in the official economy induces people to offer more labor in the unobserved economy, this, ceteris paribus, suggests that taxation should be higher (Sandmo 1981, p. 281).

Critique of the welfare-maximizing approach

Sandmo himself is not all too confident about the specific results he produced or even about the general approach he adopts. He makes three reservations (pp. 284–7).

The first is that the determination of taxes and public expenditures are completely divorced from each other, a shortcoming that has already been criticized by Buchanan (1976) for the case of the general theory of optimal taxation. Recently, Lindbeck (1980) has convincingly shown that the effects of public expenditures on the incentives to supply labor are of crucial importance. Failing to consider one side of the fiscal account strongly distorts the picture, which puts the results reached by Sandmo (and others) into serious doubt.

Sandmo's second reservation rests on the fact that the utilitarian approach used (in accordance with traditional economic welfare theory) is strictly consequentialist; that is, the policies are to be judged exclusively in terms of the consequences of allocation achievements that follow.[5] It may well be, however, that the judgment is also based on the rules under which the economic system operates.

Third, Sandmo is uneasy about the implicit assumption that the individuals adjust passively to the tax rates and other instruments imposed by the government. An approach that models the interaction between the taxpayers and the authorities would be more realistic because the taxpayers (in a democracy at least) are able to influence tax rates by voting and other means. Sandmo admits, "This might yield an interesting new perspective on the descriptive theory of tax evasion although a normative theory would also be needed to tackle the question of optimal policy choice" (p. 286).

As I will point out in the following section, the three reservations made by Sandmo only scratch the surface, whereas the social-welfare-maximizing approach deserves to be criticized much more severely. Even the reservations made by Sandmo himself are of much greater consequence than he seems to admit. If these reservations and criticisms are taken at all seriously, the whole social-welfare-maximizing approach must be discarded and a new approach to the policy problem chosen.

The main criticism[6] of the social-welfare-maximizing approach for determining the size of the unobserved economy centers on three issues, and these will be discussed next.

---

[5] For this term and its interpretation see Sen and Williams (1982).

[6] Further criticisms against the standard approach (as exemplified by Sandmo) could be raised. Thus, the model of expected utility maximization used to describe the behavior of the evaders must seriously be questioned. There is a mass of real-life and experimental evidence that expected utility is not acceptable as a positive model of human behavior under uncertainty. A well-balanced survey is given in Schoemaker (1982). No discussion of this aspect is, however, intended in this chapter.

The aggregation problem

Since Arrow's (1951) pioneer study,[7] it is common knowledge that it is in general not possible to construct a social welfare function that meets a set of reasonable criteria on the properties of (1) the individuals' welfare functions and (2) the process of aggregation.[8] This impossibility theorem has been the subject of intensive research, but the basic result has remained the same: The social welfare function cannot in general be constructed on the basis of individual utilities except when extremely restrictive assumptions are made such as near identity of individuals (in which case the aggregation problem is, of course, trivial). A logically consistent preference aggregation becomes practically impossible as soon as multidimensional issues and conflicts between individuals or groups are considered, an aspect of life especially prominent where the conflicting interests of those employed in the official economy as compared to those who are in the unobserved economy are concerned.

The problem of empirical operationalization

Even if it were logically possible to establish a consistent social welfare function, the concept is far from being operational. It seems to be quite impossible, and has indeed rarely been attempted, to attach empirical values to the parameters of a social welfare function. In order to use the results of the social-welfare-maximizing approach to determine the optimal size of the unobserved sector for policy purposes, a rather precise knowledge of the parameter values is required. To circumvent the difficulty of empirically determining the parameters of the social welfare function, the adherents of this approach have sometimes resorted to simulations, inserting numbers they personally think appropriate. Although such a procedure may be useful to test the robustness of the model, it is of course not a satisfactory substitute for determining the parameters empirically.

---

[7] There are forerunners in the eighteenth and nineteenth centuries who have, in particular, shown that aggregation by simple majority voting may lead to logical inconsistencies, the best known being the Marquis de Condorcet and Charles Dodgson (under the pseudonym Lewis Carroll, the author of *Alice in Wonderland*). For an account see Black (1958).

[8] See the excellent survey book by Sen (1970) and in particular the studies by Plott (1976) and Kramer (1973).

The presumed existence of a benevolent dictator

The most important reason why the social-welfare-maximizing approach must be rejected is that it assumes the existence of a benevolent dictator turning the instrument variables as their socially optimal values. The crucial importance of this assumption has been stressed by Buchanan (1975, 1977) and long before him by Wicksell (1896). It can also be seen as a consequence of the utilitarian welfare approach, which "assumes a public agent, some supreme body which chooses general states of affairs for the society as a whole" (Sen and Williams 1982, p. 2). In reality, actors have neither the incentive nor the possibility to maximize the (unknown) social good or joint social welfare function. They simply pursue their own utility. The course of the economy and society should thus be interpreted to be the result of the interaction of decision makers who pursue their own ends. Sandmo (1981, p. 286) devotes three sentences to gaming interdependence of actors but does not draw the necessary conclusion that this prohibits the use of a social welfare function to be maximized.

As has also been pointed out, the theory of optimal taxation applied to determining the size of the unobserved economy assumes as a matter of course that the government is interested in and capable of maximizing the social welfare function. In Sandmo's words, "Given taxpayer behavior the government chooses tax rates, penalties and the probability of detection to maximize a utilitarian social welfare function" (1981, p. 265). There is no reason at all to assume that the politicians in power even try to behave in this way, even if they had the appropriate information. It is much more sensible to assume that politicians behave like everybody else in pursuing their own utility[9]. Indeed, within political–economic modeling there is ample econometric evidence that government behavior can well be explained by self-interest. In the case of politicians, this comprises the desire to achieve ideological ends and to stay in power.[10]

The main conclusion of our critical discussion of the social-welfare-maximizing approach is that government is not an exogenous actor in the political–economic system free to pursue the social good but is dependent on other decision makers, particularly on the support of voters and interest groups. Government sets the instruments at its disposal so as to reach its own goals as well as possible, taking into account

[9] This is, of course, the view propounded by public choice. For surveys see, e.g., Mueller (1979) and Frey (1978).

[10] Examples are Frey and Schneider (1978a,b) for the United Kingdom and the United States.

the reaction of the other actors, especially with respect to its re-election chance. Both sides of the fiscal account, that is, taxes and public expenditures, are used for this purpose. The procedure of the theory of optimal taxation that takes the tax revenue to be exogenously determined is therefore quite inappropriate.

The basic critical observations raised against the social-welfare-maximizing approach are accepted by a considerable number of economists, even by some leading specialists in the field of optimal taxation. The standard reaction, however, is that although the constrained maximization of a collective welfare function is deficient, it is the only approach available at present.[11] In the next section I shall argue that a viable alternative does exist that may act as a more satisfactory alternative to economic policymaking. This approach may be called the theory of democratic economic policy.[12] It is only in its formative stage and has never been applied to problems of the unobserved economy.

The unobserved economy and democratic economic policy

Process and outcome

In a system of decision makers each of which pursues his own utility, the size of the official as well as that of the unobserved economy is the unintended outcome of their actions. The government, in combination with an elected parliament, sets the policy instruments, in particular the tax rate, the penalties, and the probability of detecting tax evasion, taking its goals (e.g., its ideology) into account and the financial and re-election constraints it is subject to as well as the rules and institutions existing at a particular time and in a particular society. The individuals (and firms) react by choosing on the market that combination of work in the official and unobserved economies they find most advantageous for themselves. They also react, however, as citizens. At election time they tend to support the party that, ceteris paribus, is likely to put into effect the policy, with respect to the unobserved economy, that they prefer. The citizens' reactions again take place within the rules and institutions existing in the particular society. The political–economic system is thus closed in the sense that the government's actions influence the (potential and actual) taxpayers and voters, and their action in turn influences the government's behavior. It follows immediately that the process is the decisive factor; the size of the unobserved sector is only a consequence. The economic advisers who endeavor to influence the outcome of this

---

[11] Joseph Stiglitz, private communication, Zurich, March 1982.
[12] See Buchanan (1977), Brennan and Buchanan (1980), and Frey (1983).

political–economic interaction are therefore forced to analyze the political–economic process that brings about the outcome, in this case the size of the unobserved sector. In a liberal and democratic society, the criterion with which to evaluate how well the process functions is how far it satisfies individual preferences. This means that the economic policy analysis moves from an outcome-oriented to a process-oriented view.[13]

The economic policy advisers may in general influence the political–economic process in two different ways. First, they can analyze whether the existing rules (and institutions) that regulate the workings of the political–economic system function adequately, so that the political suppliers (government and public bureaucracy) are forced to comply with the individual's preferences. The economic advisers can suggest how the existing rules may be improved upon and how new rules could be devised and introduced.

Second, given the rules, the economic advisers can analyze how far the current political–economic process is able to cater for the individual's preferences and how far there are systematic and significant distortions. On the basis of such an analysis, suggestions can be made of how to overcome the distortions.

The two points of approach are now discussed with an eye to the problem at hand, namely, the existence and growth of the unobserved economy.

Influencing the rules

When the rules and institutional arrangements within which the current political–economic process takes place are changed, a different outcome may be expected. There are two main areas in which it is possible to change the existing rules or to devise new rules in order to bring about a combination of the official and unofficial economy that corresponds more closely to the preferences of the individuals then present.

The first possibility is to put more effective restrictions on the political suppliers, that is, on government and public bureaucracy. Since there is considerable evidence that taxpayers feel overburdened by taxes and government regulations relative to what they receive from public activity (taxpayer revolution),[14] the most important restriction would be to

---

[13] As has been mentioned in the preceding, this is closely connected to moving away from an exclusively consequentialist utilitarian, economic welfare theory point of view. Simon (1978) argues that process orientation is indicated whenever the interaction is complex; this is surely the case for the political–economic system as a whole.

[14] See e.g., Lowery and Sigelman (1981).

impose limits on the extent to which the political suppliers may impose taxes and regulations. This would restrict the amount of taxation and regulation the individuals have to bear above the level they would voluntarily consent to in exchange for the publicly provided goods and services. This particular type of excess burden on the individuals lies in the interest of government and bureaucracy, thereby increasing their material well-being and power.[15] Imposing a limit on amount of taxes and on the number and intensity of regulations would reduce the individual's incentives to become active in the unobserved economy, as has been shown by both theoretical and empirical research.[16]

The tax burden can be directly restricted by fixing the maximum share of taxes in national income or by assigning a limited tax base to the public sector. This will ensure that political suppliers do not increase tax revenue beyond a given sum.[17]

It is more difficult to devise rules that put a limit to the regulations imposed on firms and individuals operating in the official economy. There are four different ways in which the burden of regulations can in principle be controlled.[18] The most effective way is to limit the effects of those regulations issued to benefit the administration but damage individuals and firms in the official economy. Whereas this type of control would be ideal, it is difficult or even practically impossible to monitor. Second, the number of regulations issued is restricted. Whereas this type of control is more practical, it could be easily circumvented by issuing fewer, though more comprehensive, regulations. Third, the administrative process, that is, the way the regulatory decisions are taken, is monitored. If the administrative production function were known exactly, this would be equally effective by controlling the administration's output. However, it is one of the public administration's intrinsic characteristics that this production function is not well known. Nevertheless, in most cases, fixing the rules to be observed in administrative decision making is the only control practically possible and is indeed widely used despite its shortcomings. Finally, the inputs going into the administrative process can be controlled, for example, by limit-

---

[15] The drive of governments to expend more than the citizens desire has been one of the major themes of the economic theory of government (see footnote 9). It is the central point of the paper by Brennan and Buchanan (1980). So far, no well-developed macrotheory of bureaucracy exists within public choice, though Niskanen's (1971) hypothesis of budget maximization could well be generalized from a particular bureau to the bureaucracy as a whole.

[16] See Feige (1982a), Tanzi (1980), or Weck and Frey (1982).

[17] See Brennan and Buchanan (1980).

[18] See also Majone (1981/82), who distinguishes between output, process, and input control.

ing the number of public administrators and/or the financial budget allocated to them. Despite the obvious shortcomings of this control technique, rules restricting the input side of the regulatory process are again in wide use because such rules are relatively easy to design and to monitor.

The second possibility to bring about a more desirable combination of the official and unobserved economy is to force political suppliers to take the individuals' preferences more fully into consideration. If the appropriate rules can be set, an important motive for moving into the unobserved economy is discarded. Research by experimental psychologists suggests[19] that individuals are more inclined to pay the taxes and to observe the public regulations and thus to stay in the official economy if they are more satisfied with the level and structure of public expenditures. One possibility is to shift additional decision-making power to local communities to which the individuals are more closely attached.[20] Such a lively federalism need not stop at the level of communes but can extend down to city precincts or even blocks. Another possibility to make public expenditures and activities more accordant with the population's desires is to create or to extend the institution of popular referenda and initiatives. Thus, economic advisers have many possibilities to suggest rules for creating a balance between the official and unobserved economy, which is better attuned to the individuals' preferences.

Influencing the current political–economic process

Given the rules and institutions, all decision makers pursue their own utility in the day-to-day political–economic process. They will only undertake those actions they think will be to their benefit. For this reason, the advisers have little possibility of influencing the economic policy process. However, the decision makers are incompletely informed and are therefore ready to accept advice that helps them reach their own goals. Such informational advice can be addressed to two different kinds of decision makers, the political demanders (the individuals) and the political suppliers (government and public administration).

The information available to political demanders (individuals) about the benefits and costs of the unobserved economy will be systematically and significantly biased for various reasons. The main reason is that the individuals (and firms) who (which) are active in the unobserved economy are not well organized. The advantages of having an unobserved

---

[19] See, e.g., Scott and Grasmick (1981) or Spicer and Lundstedt (1976).
[20] See Buchanan (1977) and Frey (1983).

sector will therefore not be publicized to any great extent. The demands of the official economy, on the other hand, are better organized and therefore have a better chance of being heard and followed in the political–economic process. In particular, the interests of those working in the unobserved sector are not represented by any trade union. Most individuals work only part time in the unobserved sector and not in their own profession, for which reasons they have little incentive to join the respective trade unions. The existing workers' organizations rightly fear that they lose members when the unobserved sector grows. They have good reason to fight against the existence and further growth of the unobserved economy and to stress its disadvantages and dangers. For similar reasons, the interests of the producers in the unobserved sector will be represented much worse than in the taxed economy. The official producers' organizations actively oppose economic activity moving into the unobserved sector; the firms in the official economy (which finance these organizations) fear cost disadvantages and a reduction in sales due to the competition from the untaxed sector. It may thus be said quite generally that the organizations working in and being financed by the official economy strongly fight the unobserved economy because they lose influence and income by its existence.

On the other hand, the interests of those active in the unobserved economy are badly represented in the political–economic process. On the demand side there is thus a systematic distortion of the political–economic process in favor of the official economy and to the disadvantage of the unobserved economy. Taking this bias into account, the economic policy advisers may try to establish a counteracting influence by (1) informing the population on the advantages of an unobserved economy; (2) improving the possibilities of having the interests of the unobserved economy heard and observed in the political process; and (3) pointing out to political parties that they can win new members and additional votes by people active in the unobserved economy if they care for their interests. Such possibilities exist not only for parties outside the established spectrum such as the "Alternatives" or the "Greens" but also for parties fighting against state intervention. The economic policy advisers therewith have various possibilities at hand to work against the systematic distortion of information and the tendency to neglect the interests of those engaged in the unobserved economy.

The economic advisers may also affect the combination of the official and unobserved economies within the current political–economic process by providing information to political suppliers. Government is not necessarily opposed to the unobserved economy for ideological reasons. Every government has, however, a strong incentive to fight the unobserved economy for financial reasons. The larger the untaxed sector, the larger will be the loss of tax revenue. These financial repercussions are so important that they are most likely not compensated by any possible gain in support from the votes of those active in the unobserved sector. The government has a strong interest in using the instruments available to reduce the untaxed economy. The economic advisers have to accept this clearly defined interest; they know that the government will simply disregard any advice pointing in a different direction.

The public administration is even more strongly motivated to oppose the unobserved economy: It loses power and influence when a sector expands in which the workers and firms do not pay taxes and in which its regulations are disregarded.

The analysis makes clear that the economy policy advisers have little possibility of influencing the government's and the public administration's position with respect to the unobserved economy. They are only able to influence the way the policy instruments are applied. The political suppliers will listen to the economic advice given when it helps them to fight the unobserved economy most effectively. At this point the economic advisers have a chance of making their expertise felt so that the policy decisions taken conform as much as possible to the preferences of the individuals.

The government and public administration fight the unobserved economy in three different ways.

The first measure is to increase punishment for activities in the (untaxed) unobserved economy. This policy approach is rather obvious, so it is to be expected that the political suppliers will rely most heavily on it. The economic advisers can inform the government, politicians, and public administrators on the problems connected with using that instrument. They can in particular point out that providing severe punishment of activities in the unobserved economy makes the application of the laws difficult, since both the accused and the courts find such punishment to be illegitimate. An all too high degree of punishment would also reduce or eliminate marginal deterrence: If people are heavily punished already for a small amount of black work, they have little reason not to increase their engagement in the unobserved economy, as the punishment will not be (much) higher. Severely punishing activities in the unobserved sector does not only harm the individuals affected but also hinders the achievement of the goals the political suppliers wish to achieve.

The second policy measure is to reduce the level of tax rates and the number and intensity of public regulations, diminishing the incentive to switch to the unobserved sector. The policy advisers can ensure that

124

tax rates are not at such a high level that the maximum tax revenue is surpassed. Setting high tax rates is disadvantageous for both political suppliers and demanders because the tax receipts are smaller and the individuals are unnecessarily burdened.[21] Similarly, economic advice is possible with respect to regulations. In order to find the maximum level of regulations, it is necessary to distinguish between the intensity of regulations and the size of the domain regulated. The political suppliers (especially the public administration) benefit from an increase in both, but if the intensity of regulation is raised, the size of the domain regulated is diminished because the individuals and firms are induced to move to the unobserved sector. The economic advisers can therefore warn the political suppliers not to go too far with the intensity of the regulations because otherwise they would damage themselves by shrinking the domain of regulation.

The third policy measure the political suppliers use to fight the unobserved economy is to make public appeals and to apply moral persuasion in an attempt to increase the sense of guilt for working in the (illegal) unobserved economy. This amounts to an effort to improve tax morality (in the widest sense). So far, little is known about the way in which the preferences of individuals can be influenced. Economists in general are rather skeptical about this approach. Psychological experiments[22] suggest that there may even be a counterproductive effect. The fact that an appeal is made to act morally, that is, not to cheat on taxes, may be taken by individuals as a sign that tax morality is no longer the rule. This may even induce honest taxpayers to join the ranks of the others and to cheat on taxes too. The economic policy advisers can point out the possibility of such counterproductive effects to the government and public administration and can suggest that they therefore should use this policy instrument with care if they want to reach their goals. Tax morality will only improve consistently if the (potential) taxpayers can be convinced that the public expenditures financed by their taxes do in fact yield higher utility to them.

The discussion shows that the economic policy advisers have only a limited set of possibilities to influence the current political–economic

---

[21] To determine the maximum-yield taxrates beyond which it is harmful for all to go, the theoretical model by Sandmo (1981) discussed previously (as far as it relates to the behavior of non-evaders and evaders) is clearly relevant, as are the empirical estimates of the Laffer curve, such as by Stuart (1981) and Feige and McGee (1983) for Sweden or Feige and McGee (1982) for the United Kingdom. Buchanan and Lee (1982) have shown that it is important to distinguish between a short-run and a long-run view of the Laffer curve. Government acting within a legislative period tends to adopt a shorter run view than public bureaucracy, which is not subject to the re-election constraint.

[22] See Title and Rowe (1973).

process and, in particular, the combination between the official and unobserved economy because, on the political level, the actors have well-defined, personal interests they pursue. Nevertheless, the advisers can offer useful information with respect to the use of economic policy instruments. This advice raises the individuals' utility when it is possible to make suggestions that are in the interest of both political suppliers and political demanders.

Concluding remarks

The approach to the policy problem of the unobserved economy that presupposes a benevolent dictator able to determine what society's interests are and who would also act accordingly has up to now been the standard one. Evidence of this are the theories of quantitative economic policy and optimal taxation. The basic weaknesses of this kind of view have been discussed, and the alternative view of a democratic economic policy has been sketched and applied to the problem of the unobserved economy. The idea of an exogenous superplanner is given up in favor of a view of the political–economic system in which the decision makers, in particular the government, are endogenous. Within this framework, nobody can a priori say which size of the unobserved economy is socially optimal. Rather, the size of the official and unobserved economies are the outcome of the interactions of self-interested decision makers. This outcome may be influenced and may be made to correspond better to the preferences of the individuals by economic advisers, who can help the decision makers find a consensus on the most appropriate rules for governing the interactions as well as offer advice to the individual decision makers in the current political–economic process.

Acknowledgments

I am grateful to the participants at the Netherlands Institute for Advanced Studies Conference on the Unobserved Economy for useful suggestions for improvement, particularly to the organizer, Edgar Feige. The support of the Swiss National Science Foundation, grant no. 1.430-0.81 on Empirische Erfassung der Schattenwirtschaft in der Schweiz, is also gratefully acknowledged.

PART II

The underground economy in Western developed nations: measurement in different laboratories

CHAPTER 5

Monetary perspective on underground economic activity in the United States

RICHARD D. PORTER
and
AMANDA S. BAYER

There are widespread reports of a growing underground, or unobserved, economy in the United States and in other countries. The unobserved economy seems to develop principally from efforts to evade taxes and government regulation. Although no single definition of such activity has been universally accepted, the term generally refers to activity – whether legal or illegal – generating income that either is underreported or not reported at all (see Chapter 1 in this volume). Some authors narrow the definition to cover income produced in legal activity that is not set down in the recorded national income statistics.[1]

Recent discussion of underground economic activity was stimulated by publication of two estimates, one by Gutmann (1977) and the other by Feige (1979), of the size of the underground economy in the United States; these estimates were derived from aggregate monetary statistics. In the ensuing years, numerous other estimates have been made of the underground economy in the United States and in other countries. The magnitude of some of these estimates has prompted congressional hearings and various government studies. In 1979, the Internal Revenue Service (IRS, 1979) estimated that, for 1976, individuals failed to report between $75 billion and $100 billion in income from legal sources and another $25 billion to $35 billion from three types of illegal activity – drugs, gambling, and prostitution. In a more recent study, the IRS estimated that unreported income from legal sources rose from $93.9 billion in 1973 to $249.7 billion in 1981 whereas unreported income from these same three illegal activities rose from $9.3 billion to $34 billion (IRS, 1983). To estimate unreported legal source income, the IRS mainly used individual taxpayer data from its Taxpayer Compliance Measurement Program – which audits a sample of income tax returns – and data from its Information Returns Program – which utilizes information from the

---

[1] By convention, the national income accounts do not include illegal activities such as loan sharking or trafficking in illicit drugs.

129

payers of income. Estimates of unreported income from legal sources for individuals not filing returns were developed from cross-checking information from two nationwide household surveys against the records of the Social Security Administration and the IRS. Estimates of unreported income associated with illegal activity were based on survey data and arrest records.

Proponents of the monetary statistics approach question the accuracy of estimates derived from such sources as administrative records and surveys, with the assertion that the methods employed are likely to lead to an understatement of actual unreported income. They believe that monetary statistics provide a better source for gaging underground activity. Gutmann (1977), for example, postulates that currency is the sole medium of exchange in the underground economy, and thus an increase in activity in that sector would be evidenced by an increase in the ratio of currency to checkable deposits. Feige (1980), on the other hand, hypothesizes that activity in the underground economy is likely to be recorded in measures of total transactions but excluded from recorded income. Thus, changes in the ratio of transactions to income are evidence of changes in the relative size of the underground economy. These two "monetary statistics approaches" can be described as the currency-ratio method and the transactions-ratio method, respectively.

This chapter presents estimates of underground activity based on these approaches and some extensions; it points out advantages and potential drawbacks associated with each. In addition, the chapter also examines some of the reasons for the growth of per capita currency holdings, particularly in the form of larger denominations – another observation cited as evidence of underground activity.

Simple currency-ratio method

The first approach to estimating underground economic activity using monetary statistics is based on movements in the ratio of currency to checkable deposits – more simply, the currency ratio.[2] Three assump-

---

[2] The method was originally suggested by Cagan (1958) to evaluate the upward movements in the currency ratio in World War II. The method was later adopted by Gutmann (1977). The initial estimates of underground GNP made by Gutmann and by Feige covered a period when the levels of deposits in other checkable accounts such as ATS, NOW, and Super NOW accounts were small; they thus ignored these accounts in their work and used the ratio of currency to demand deposits. In the last few years these new accounts have grown rapidly and have tended to substitute for demand deposits rather than for currency; as a consequence, the ratio of currency to demand deposits has risen for reasons totally unrelated to underground activity. Thus, in this chapter, the currency-ratio estimates are based on the ratio of currency to checkable deposits.

Table 5.1. *Computed underground GNP using alternative methods for selected years[a] (in billions)*

Year	Simple currency ratio	Modified currency ratio	Econometric model of currency to M2		Transactions, 1939 base	Transactions, 1964 base[b]
			TW	T		
1950	15.9	21.5	14.5	9.4	27.6	43.1
1955	14.7	15.6	12.8	10.9	1.7	21.6
1960	17.3	17.1	20.7	13.2	−3.4	21.5
1965	31.6	38.6	26.3	17.1	9.6	44.3
1970	62.4	88.6	45.6	25.3	101.0	155.2
1975	150.8	246.0	77.0	46.6	467.3	567.1
1978	226.1	460.2	114.2	80.9	551.1	685.6
1979	317.8	558.5	130.7	88.6	628.4	779.2
1980	372.8	666.9	159.9	116.9	1095.6	1280.1
1981	427.1	767.6	n.a.	n.a.	1765.6	1999.2
1982	449.7	810.5	n.a.	n.a.	n.a.	n.a.
As ratio to record GNP (%)						
1950	5.6	7.5	5.1	3.3	9.6	15.1
1955	3.7	3.9	3.2	2.7	0.4	5.4
1960	3.4	3.4	4.1	2.6	−0.7	4.2
1965	4.6	5.6	3.8	2.5	1.4	6.4
1970	6.3	8.9	4.6	2.6	10.2	15.6
1975	9.7	15.9	5.0	3.0	30.2	36.6
1978	12.3	21.3	5.3	3.7	25.5	31.7
1979	13.1	23.1	5.4	3.7	26.0	32.2
1980	14.2	25.3	6.1	4.4	41.6	48.6
1981	14.5	26.0	n.a.	n.a.	59.8	67.7
1982	14.6	26.4	n.a.	n.a.	n.a.	n.a.

[a] For a description of each method see the text.
[b] In 1964 it is assumed that underground GNP equals 5 percent of observed GNP.

tions underlie this technique: (1) All underground transactions involve currency exclusively; (2) above-ground activity has a currency ratio that is constant over time; and (3) the underground income velocity of underground currency (i.e., the underground income supported by a dollar of underground currency) is the same as the above-ground currency holdings in that year. The estimated size of underground economic activity can then be derived as the product of underground currency (actual currency less that held in the above-ground sector) and the income velocity of above-ground M1. Table 5.1 lists the resulting estimates of underground gross national product (GNP) under the assumption that the benchmark currency ratio is 0.217.[3] The estimated size of the underground economy grows over time but remains roughly constant as a percentage of recorded GNP until the 1970's; that proportion then increases sharply, reaching a sizable 14.6 percent in 1982.

General currency-ratio method

Another monetary method that was subsequently developed by Feige (1980) generalizes the currency-ratio method. Feige argues that some firms and households use checks in underground transactions because they perceive that the ease of using checks outweighs the costs of leaving a "paper" audit trail; and to the extent that activity in the underground sector is service oriented, income velocity (the ratio of income to money holdings) may be higher in this sector than in the above-ground economy because fewer intermediate transactions occur in producing services. Specifically, Feige makes the following assumptions: (1) The currency ratio in the underground sector is 2; that is, for every two dollars underground participants hold in currency, they hold one dollar in demand deposit balances; (2) the underground income velocity of underground M1 (the sum of currency and checkable deposits) is 10 percent higher than its above-ground counterpart; and (3) in 1964, the base year, underground GNP equaled 5 percent of recorded GNP.[4] The modified currency-ratio estimates of underground GNP for selected years are shown, based on annual averages of the relevant data, in the second column of Table 5.1. In the mid-1960's, this currency-ratio method gives higher estimates of underground GNP than does Gutmann's simple currency-ratio method; beginning in the 1970's the gap between the two estimates widens greatly, and by 1982 the modified currency-ratio estimate of underground GNP, at 26.4 percent of above-ground GNP, is almost twice the estimate derived from the simple currency-ratio approach.

A further variant of the currency-ratio method:
Tanzi's model

Another variant of the currency-ratio method (Tanzi, 1983) can be used to estimate underground activity. Tanzi explicitly incorporates the effects

---

[3] This is the value that Gutmann (1977) estimated for the 1937–41 period; it was assumed that the underground economy did not exist at this time because tax evasion incentives were limited.

[4] For a discussion of the evidence supporting these assumptions, see Feige (1980). In the first chapter of this volume Feige examines the sensitivity of the general currency-ratio model to alternative parametric specifications.

of taxation on the currency ratio. He assumes that the demand for currency relative to M2 rises whenever real per capita income or the rate of interest on time deposits (which are included in M2) falls. The share of wages and salaries in national income, also included in the model, is assumed to have a positive effect on the ratio of currency to M2 to reflect changes in payment practices that have grown to involve greater use of checks. The ratio of currency to M2 is also assumed to be positively related to taxes. The latter assumption reflects the presumed pecuniary advantage of engaging in underground activity as taxes increase and there is an associated induced increase in the demand for currency for underground transactions relative to the other components of M2.

The empirical implementation of the model uses two alternative tax measures: a weighted average tax rate on interest income (TW) and the ratio of total net tax payments to adjusted gross income (T). The model (detailed in Appendix A) is estimated from annual data for the years 1930–80 using the pre-1981 definition of M2. Tanzi defines currency associated with underground activity as the difference between the model's predicted value of currency using the historical values of all explanatory variables (including taxes) and the predicted value if taxes were held constant at zero (i.e., if there were no taxes). As in the simple currency-ratio method, he assumes that the income velocities of underground and above-ground money balances are identical; underground GNP is then the product of underground currency balances and the above-ground income velocity of above-ground M1 balances. Table 5.1 presents the estimated size of underground activity based on the two different tax measures. In sharp contrast to the previous estimates, both of the estimates derived from the tax-driven model tend to stay in a relatively narrow range, around 5 percent of recorded GNP.

The transactions-ratio method

Feige (1979, 1980) also developed an alternative monetary statistics method of estimating underground activity based on the ratio of total monetary transactions to GNP. Instead of using *stocks* of currency and checkable balances, Feige focused on the *flow* of monetary services provided by the stock of M1, namely, the total dollar value of transactions in M1 balances.[5] The key assumption in this approach is that

---

[5] More precisely, Feige estimates total transactions on the basis of estimated transactions in currency and checkable deposits but chooses to omit transactions in traveler's checks since they must be purchased with either currency or checks.

total transcations are proportional to total economic activity ("total" here means the sum of above-ground and underground activity). Within this framework, transactions can be broken down into three components involving the production of final output, the exchange of existing real or financial assets, and direct transfer payments. Feige recognized that transfer payments exhibit a changing pattern over time and that purely financial transactions associated with asset exchanges probably have increased dramatically in response to various financial innovations. Thus, to derive a transactions measure appropriate for estimating underground activity, Feige deducted a number of major financial transactions and direct transfers from gross transactions to arrive at a net transaction measure; the theory is then reformulated in terms of the proportionality between net transactions and total income.

Table 5.2 depicts the way in which a net transactions series is constructed from the various underlying financial and nonfinancial series. Gross transactions in the table are the sum of estimated currency transactions and total debits to checkable deposits.[6] Three types of financial transactions are then subtracted from this measure of gross transactions: estimated debits to demand deposits for cash withdrawals and withdrawals to other checkable deposits; debits to demand deposits for the purchase of various money market instruments (repurchase agreements, overnight Eurodollars, time and savings deposits, and money market funds); and estimated transactions in the stock and bond market. Finally, several additional adjustments are made to make the net transactions and income series comparable.

---

[6] We are indebted to Professor Feige for providing these estimates. Feige (1979) initially used Laurent's (1970) method to estimate currency turnover. To illustrate the method, consider a representative economy with $100 in total currency. Every year $10 worth of currency is replaced (redeemed) by the Treasury because it is unfit to circulate any longer. Under these conditions, the average circulation of a given bill is ten years. Laurent assumed that each bill that was redeemed underwent G lifetime transactions while each bill that was still in circulation had undergone only $\frac{1}{2} G$ transactions. Using differential redemption rates by denomination, he computed the cumulative number of times each denomination was used in a transaction and the associated total cash payment per year as a function G. He then chose the value of G that maximized the correlation between total transactions (demand deposits plus currency transactions) and nominal GNP over the period 1861–1967.

In applying Laurent's method to the post-war period, Feige discovered that the transactions velocity of currency declined sharply, from 60 turnovers per year in 1940 to only 17 per year in 1944, principally because of lowering the quality of the currency in circulation to conserve labor and material during the war. Following Irving Fisher's suggestion that currency use patterns change slowly, Feige fit a simple nonlinear time trend to Laurent's data. Groups of large negative or positive residuals from this regression were then matched with archival records indicating administrative decisions to alter the quality of the currency. The fitted values from the regression formed the basis for the turnover estimates used in this method (Feige, 1980, pp. 26–29).

134

Table 5.2. *Consolidated data underlying transactions approach for selected years (billions of dollars of transactions, annual averages)[a]*

| | Gross transactions | | | Adjustments to gross transactions | | | | | Net transactions[j] |
| | Currency[b] (A) | Checkable deposits[c] (B) | Debits to demand deposits arising from cash withdrawals and transfers to other checkable deposits[d] (C) | Other financial transfers[e] (D) | Stock and bond transactions[f] (E) | Foreign transactions[g] (F) | Government payments[h] (G) | Taxes[i] (H) | (I) |
Period									
1939	396.3	443.2	198.1	41.8	13.0	4.8	11.2	1.8	591.3
1975	4127.4	13747.6	2068.5	427.6	167.0	180.7	353.6	176.3	13112.3
1980	6639.1	31406.6	3522.9	9524.9	523.0	449.5	557.9	346.2	24237.1
1981	7168.8	40858.5	4416.5	12099.1	533.0	507.3	621.6	402.7	30690.3

[a] Data underlying table compiled and adjusted from various underlying sources by Professor Edgar Feige, Department of Economics, University of Wisconsin, Madison.

[b] Based on *estimated* currency turnover rate using Laurent's method as adjusted by nonlinear time trend regression for purported changes in currency quality.

[c] The sum of other checkable and demand deposit transactions. Demand deposit transactions based on turnover concept exclusive of selected financial centers series spliced together between current reporting basis and various earlier concepts; turnover rate for other checkable deposits is set to equal its value in 1978 for 1963–77.

[d] *Estimated* for currency and demand deposits.

[e] Sum of *estimated* debits to demand deposits due to transactions in repurchase agreements, overnight Eurodollars, time and savings deposits, and money market funds.

[f] *Source:* Statistical Abstract of the United States, various years.

[g] Sum of imports and adjusted capital outflows.

[h] Sum of federal transfer payments and wages and salaries of government workers.

[i] Sum of personal contributions to social security and personal income taxes.

[j] Sum of columns A, B, and G less sum of columns C, D, E, F, and H.

Given the net transactions series, the calculation of underground GNP proceeds in much the same fashion as in the currency-ratio method. The proportionality hypothesis between adjusted transactions and income is invoked to estimate underground GNP: above-ground transactions are determined by multiplying the ratio of transactions to GNP in the benchmark period (which is assumed free of underground activity) times recorded GNP in some year. The excess of actual transactions over above-ground transactions in that year represents underground transactions; lastly, applying the benchmark ratio of transactions to income to the underground sector, the underground income supported by the estimated underground transactions can be inferred.

In addition, Feige argues that the above-ground service sector requires fewer transactions per unit of output than do sectors that use more intermediate inputs. Because the service sector has grown relative to the rest of the economy, he expects that in the absence of an underground sector, the ratio of net transactions to income would tend to decline. He argues that basing an estimate of underground GNP on the constancy of this ratio would likely result in understatements of such activity.

Table 5.1 lists alternative transactions-ratio estimates of underground GNP. The estimates in column 5 assume that there were no underground transactions in a 1939 base period whereas those in column 6 use a 1964 base period and the assumption that underground GNP equaled 5 percent of observed GNP in that year. The transactions-ratio estimates of the size of underground activity are even larger than those estimated from the currency-ratio methods, rising from approximately 10 or 15 percent of reported GNP in 1970 to much higher levels in recent years: by 1981 underground GNP is estimated to have equaled more than 60 percent of recorded GNP.[7]

Implied income velocity estimates for the monetary statistics methods

Except for those derived from Tanzi's model, all the estimates based on monetary statistics yield, since the late 1960's, increasing ratios of underground GNP to above-ground GNP, with the acceleration in these

---

[7] Editor's note: In the transaction method estimates presented in Table 5.1, Porter and Bayer inadvertently added government expenditures to total transactions rather than subtracted them from income. The effect of this error is to raise the estimates of unrecorded income. A corrected series of estimates employing the 1939 benchmark is displayed in Chapter 1, Figure 1.6.

Table 5.3. *Implied total income velocity of money using alternative methods to estimate underground activity and recorded velocity*[a]

Year	Alternative currency-ratio methods		Transactions-ratio method		
	Simple currency ratio	Modified currency ratio	1939 base	1964 base	Recorded M1
1950	2.700	2.750	2.804	2.943	—
1955	3.144	3.151	3.045	3.196	—
1960	3.705	3.704	3.559	3.745	3.583
1965	4.378	4.420	4.245	4.455	4.186
1970	4.996	5.120	5.180	5.436	4.701
1975	5.967	6.301	7.077	7.428	5.436
1978	6.929	7.483	7.742	8.125	6.168
1979	7.242	7.879	8.064	8.463	6.400
1980	7.487	8.220	9.288	9.748	6.558
1981	7.864	8.656	10.977	11.520	6.870
1982	7.691	8.479	n.a.	n.a.	6.711
	Average annual growth of implied velocity				
1950–70	3.1	3.4	3.3	3.1	3.5
1975–81	4.7	5.4	7.6	7.6	4.0
1975–82	3.7	4.3	n.a.	n.a.	3.1

[a] Velocity is measured as ratio of sum of above-ground or recorded GNP plus underground GNP to M1 measure.

ratios becoming particularly evident since 1975.[8] For example, the rate of growth of underground GNP derived from the modified currency-ratio approach increased at an 18.6 percent annual rate from 1975 to 1982, almost twice as fast as the above-ground GNP growth rate. An implication of this acceleration in the growth rates of underground activity is a sharp increase in the total income velocity of M1.

Table 5.3 displays the implied level of total GNP velocity – the ratio of the sum of above-ground and underground GNP to the level of M1 – for the alternative monetary statistics methods for the same years reported in Table 5.1; the lower panel displays velocity growth rates over selected periods. As the table indicates, both implied total and recorded

[8] However, as described in what follows, Tanzi's model produces sizable estimates of underground activity when the equation is simulated dynamically rather than statically.

velocity grew about 3 percent from 1950 to 1970. From 1975 onward, the estimated growth rate of implied total income velocity accelerated relative to that of recorded income velocity, with the latter staying close to its long-run historical trends. Consider, for example, the implied total velocity of the transactions-ratio method with a 1939 base period, given in the third column of Table 5.3. From 1950 to 1970 its implied total income velocity grew at a 3.3 percent annual rate; then this growth more than doubled to 7.6 percent per year from 1975 to 1981. That is, taking this estimate of total GNP at face value, it implies that growth in velocity as measured by the ratio of recorded GNP to M1 considerably understates true velocity growth. If sharp changes in velocity over short time intervals are considered unlikely, the estimates of underground economic activity in Table 5.1 are also called into question.

An econometric evaluation of the currency-ratio method

Whereas the underground economy may influence the currency ratio, other, probably more important factors clearly are omitted from consideration by the users of this approach. The conventional macroeconomic approach to analyzing these ratios involves a model based on either an above-ground transactions or an above-ground portfolio theory of the demand for money. The behavior of currency relative to checkable deposits or to M2 can, in fact, be explained with some degree of accuracy by standard econometric demand equations without reference to underground economic activity. Figures 5.1 and 5.2 display the actual and predicted values of the alternative ratios from simulations using the Board staff's quarterly econometric model; the simulations start in the third quarter of 1974 and extend through the third quarter of 1983.[9]

The present demand equations for these components are estimated over various sample periods, all of which ended in the last quarter of 1981. Thus, only the last seven quarters of the simulations represent the out-of-sample period. Accordingly, the close correspondence between the actual and simulated values of these ratios over the entire period does not represent a strong test of the explanatory power of the board model. Over much of this period, particularly the two-and-one-half-year period from 1974, third quarter, to 1976, fourth quarter, checkable deposits – in particular the demand deposit component of checkable

---

[9] In these dynamic simulations the determinants of the ratios – interest rates, real income, and so forth – took on their historical values. Appendix A presents a brief explanation of their structure.

138

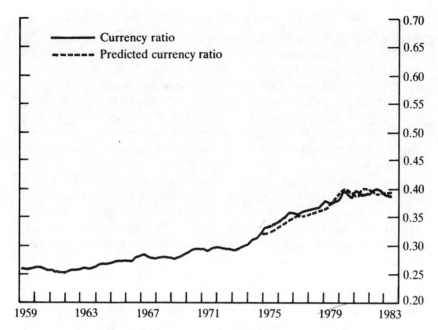

Figure 5.1. Actual and predicted currency ratios.

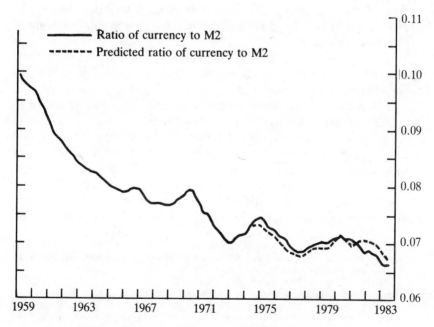

Figure 5.2. Actual and predicted currency-to-M2 ratio.

139

deposits – grew much less than predicted by a standard equation. To account for this episode, the present equation for demand deposits includes a shift variable (SHIFT) for this period. When it is removed, the model, as do most conventional demand equations, overpredicts demand deposits. The result of this overprediction of demand deposits is an implied underprediction of the ratio of currency to checkable deposits. Some might identify this resulting unexplained spurt in the currency ratio as an argument for the existence of an active underground economy.

Several factors, however, deny this underground economy explanation. First, the board model (Porter and Thurman, 1979) and other models (Garcia, 1978) provide no evidence of unexplained strength in currency itself during this period. Thus, the shortfall in predicting the currency ratio stems principally from the unexplained weakness in demand deposits. Second, this weakness has been examined in depth, and none of the proposed explanations rely on the underground economy.[10] Instead, it appears that in the presence of persistently high opportunity costs of holding demand deposits, deposit holders sought to improve their money management techniques. This quest was aided by improvements in computer and telecommunications technology, by the development of various cash management procedures such as cash concentration accounts and remote disbursement facilities, and by the growing use of new financial instruments that complemented many of these new techniques.

Figure 5.2 indicates that the board money demand models fairly accurately predict the currency-to-M2 ratio. However, since Tanzi's econometric demand model also tracks this ratio fairly accurately, a more detailed analysis of his model is needed.[11] As an alternative to standard models such as the Board model that assume only above-ground transactions and portfolio motives for holding currency and deposits, Tanzi attempts to recognize the presence of the underground economy by including an explicit tax term in his demand equation. The resulting estimates of the size of the underground activity depend importantly on the proper specification and estimation of the tax effect. Taking Tanzi's equation as specified,[12] inspection of the data for the

---

[10] The mid-1970's episode of demand deposit weakness has been intensively studied by a number of researchers: Judd and Scadding (1982); Porter, Simpson, and Mauskopf (1979); and Enzler, Johnson, and Paulus (1976).

[11] Recall that Tanzi used the older definition of M2.

[12] The Tanzi specification should be viewed as a reduced-form specification. To see this, consider equations for currency holdings of the underground and above-ground sectors. Let t^a be the tax rate on reported income in the above-ground sector and t^u the expected tax rate on underground income. Then in long-run equilibrium, real per

regression reveals that the dominant source of the positive relationship between the ratio of currency to M2 and taxes resides in the data for the period from 1930 to 1945.[13] Indeed, when the estimation period for the regression is restricted to the post-war years 1946–80, the tax variable either enters the equation with the incorrect sign – using T, the ratio of total net tax payments to income – or is not statistically significant – using TW, the weighted average tax rate on interest income (Appendix A). This specification also appears to produce very different estimates of the size of the underground economy depending on how the model is simulated. The Table 5.1 estimates follow Tanzi's work and simulate the equations statically, that is, the simulations are done taking into account the autocorrelation correction term that depends on the actual simulation error made in the previous period. However, a dynamic simulation of Tanzi's model – in which only the error at the beginning of the sample period is taken into account – produces an estimate of underground GNP that is about 18.5 percent of reported GNP in 1980, or about three times larger than that obtained using the static simulation of the equation.[14] Owing to the sensitivity of the estimated tax effects both to the sample period and to the manner in which the simulations are carried out, Tanzi's estimates of the underground economy must be viewed as highly uncertain.

Benchmark, velocity, and recorded GNP assumptions in the currency-ratio methods

The different currency-ratio estimates of the size of the underground economy depend on several critical underlying assumptions. As has been shown, the currency-ratio method produces large estimated increases in

---

capita currency holdings (C) will be functionally related to real per capita output in the two sectors (y^a and y^u), and the after-tax opportunity cost of holding currency in the two sectors, $r(1 - t^a)$ and $r(1 - t^u)$. Thus,

$$C = C^a[y^a, r(1 - t^a)] + C^u[y^u, r(1 - t^u)]$$

where underground output presumably depends positively on tax rates in the above-ground economy:

$$y^u = f(t^a)$$

Observe that tax rates enter the structural equation in several ways. Changes in enforcement of the tax laws, e.g. that affect t^u, would also alter the relationship between overall currency holdings and the above-ground tax rate.

[13] Even for the period before 1946, the specification can be questioned since it does not take into account the introduction of deposit insurance.

[14] Feige's (1986c) critique of Tanzi's procedure points out why the dynamic simulation is the appropriate procedure. The results of the dynamic simulation for the post-war years are displayed in Chapter 1, Figure 1.5.

both GNP and implied income velocity during recent periods. However, a small change in assumptions, particularly regarding the magnitude of the currency ratio in the above-ground sector, the so-called benchmark assumption, can drastically change the estimated size of the underground economy. For example, underground GNP can take on negative values whenever the actual currency ratio becomes smaller than the benchmark ratio. The comparable example in Tanzi's model concerns the threshold level of taxes whereby he assumes that underground activity arises as soon as any tax is placed on output. It would perhaps be more plausible to define a normal level of taxation and to associate growth in the underground economy only with tax increases in excess of the normal level. In any case, a more systematic treatment of these benchmarking problems is required.[15] Another important assumption involves the relationship between the GNP velocities of above-ground and of underground money balances. In the modified currency-ratio method the service orientation of the underground sector leads to a higher assumed velocity for this sector relative to the above-ground sector; in the other currency-ratio methods the two velocities are assumed to be equal. The larger negative time trend of demand deposits relative to currency, as has been estimated in the board's quarterly model, suggests that it is more difficult to economize on currency relative to demand deposits. Additional difficulties might also be experienced by underground holders because the transaction costs of converting currency to deposits are larger as a result of the required banking reports associated with large cash deposits or withdrawals. Consequently, quite apart from the service aspect of the underground economy, the income supported by a dollar of underground currency may be lower than the income supported by a dollar in the above-ground sector.

Although the benchmark and velocity assumptions play key roles in the approach, there is a more troublesome assumption that is implicit in the currency-ratio method: Currency-ratio estimates of the ratio of unrecorded GNP to recorded GNP are invariant to the method of estimating recorded GNP. Imagine two different numerical estimates of recorded GNP for a particular year. No matter which estimate was taken as recorded GNP, the currency-ratio estimate of the ratio of unrecorded GNP to recorded GNP would be the same. Thus, it follows

---

[15] Perhaps they can be related to independent estimates, such as produced by the IRS or the Bureau of Economic Analysis, of the size of the underground economy in various periods – as Feige (1980; Chapter 1 of this volume) has done in some of his papers. However, this solution is not fully satisfactory if these independent estimates are themselves suspect.

that any improvements in the estimate of recorded GNP by the Bureau of Economic Analysis would not change the currency-ratio estimate of the ratio of total GNP (recorded and unrecorded activity) to recorded GNP.

To summarize, without a more definitive treatment of the underlying velocity and benchmark assumptions, it is difficult to assess the final results of the alternative currency-ratio procedures. In addition, the currency-ratio estimates are not sensitive at all to changes in recorded GNP estimates. Presumably, improved estimates of recorded GNP should alter the estimated ratio of unrecorded to recorded GNP, but the available currency-ratio procedures do not allow for this possibility.

An evaluation of the transactions-ratio method

Econometric issues

It is more difficult to provide an econometric evaluation of Feige's transactions-ratio method since there is no established theory of total transactions, as there is for income velocity, which depends on the demand for money. However, casual inspection of the ratio of transactions to income suggests that it has moved positively with interest rates over much of this period. In a recent paper, Porter and Offenbacher (1984) offer a partial explanation for such movements based on an inventory model of money holdings under uncertainty. They show that debits to demand deposits for business firms should be positively related to both interest rates and a scale variable (which serves as a proxy for the size of the firm) and negatively related to the costs of making transactions.[16] Figure A5.1 in Appendix A shows predicted values from this model for the ratio of total demand deposit transactions outside of New York to nominal GNP from this model together with actual values of the ratio. As the figure indicates, some of the major movements in this debits-to-GNP ratio can be explained without reference to factors associated with the underground economy. However, this evidence should be regarded as highly tentative because no theory of total transactions is well established and the simulation results shown in Figure A5.1 are merely within-sample predictions. Until more experience with out-of-sample predictions is obtained, the apparent good fit of the Porter–Offenbacher model should be viewed skeptically.

---

[16] The particular proxy used for transaction costs is described in Simpson and Porter (1980). Also, for simplicity, the scale variable is taken to be recorded GNP.

Other issues

In comparison with the various currency-ratio methods, the transactions method has several distinct advantages, at least in theory. The method does not require any assumption concerning the relative income velocity in the above-ground and underground sectors. Nor does it require an assumption that currency is the exclusive medium of exchange in the underground sector or that currency and deposits are used in a given ratio in these sectors; it treats currency and deposits in a symmetric fashion. Moreover, improved estimates of recorded GNP can modify the estimate of the ratio of underground GNP to recorded GNP in the proper direction; that is, an increase (decrease) in recorded GNP would lower (raise) this ratio.

On the other hand, this method does require the specification of a transactions ratio in the above-ground sector, and similar to the other methods, the benchmark ratio that is chosen is a critical assumption. In practice, however, data limitations are the single most important problem in implementing the transactions method: Many assumptions must be made to develop the estimates of the necessary data series from existing data sources. As was indicated earlier, measurements of the turnover of the currency stock do not exist, resulting in the need to use an indirect estimation procedure. The problems of estimating currency turnover are relatively minor, however, compared to those associated with netting financial and real asset transactions from gross transactions.[17]

The portion of gross checkable transactions associated with demand deposits is not split into financial and nonfinancial transactions. Currently, the only data directly bearing on such a split exist for major New York City banks.[18] These data represent gross transactions that are almost exclusively financial given that these banks represent many of the nation's leading money center banks. In addition to removing the major New York City banks from his transaction series, Feige also uses an older historical series on debits at selected financial centers to eliminate some additional transactions that are also likely to be dominated by financial movements. But since this older series is no longer collected,

---

[17] Because there are no reliable data to indicate what portion of the currency stock is held abroad, any inference about domestic currency transactions could be overstated.

[18] In August 1983, demand deposit debits to all insured banks were $111.5 trillion at an annual rate; of this total, $48.4 trillion were transacted at these major New York City banks.

the relationship between it and any current series cannot be benchmarked from the existing data sources. There are also significant problems in netting out demand deposit debits involving the purchase of other financial claims. For example, comprehensive measures of the volume of activity on many types of security markets do not exist, nor are there direct estimates on the turnover rate of several important money market instruments such as repurchase agreements. In addition, improvements in money management techniques, particularly the use of cash concentration accounts by nonfinancial firms, result in debits to demand deposits that are purely financial in nature. These debits are not necessarily eliminated by the netting procedures used in the transactions-ratio method because they involve an increase in transactions among the demand deposit accounts held by nonfinancial corporations at different banks and not the purchase or sale of a money market instrument (Carlson, 1982). Some corporations apparently have been very efficient in reducing their holdings of M1 by using such methods.[19]

In examining the recent estimates from the transactions methods, it appears that increases in the transactions ratio are largely due to checkable deposits, not currency. For example, the estimated ratio of net transactions to recorded GNP increased from 8.46 in 1975 to 10.03 in 1981; but if the proportion of currency transactions was held fixed at its 1975 level, the transactions ratio would still have risen to a value of 9.54. Thus, the major explanation for the increase in the ratio lies in transactions involving deposits, not currency. Since the likelihood of being "caught" is probably higher when checkable deposits rather than currency are used in the underground economy, it would seem counterintuitive to associate all the increase in the income implied by this increase in the transactions ratio with underground transactions. Instead, it is more likely that at least part of the observed increase in the transaction ratio was related to purely financial transactions. This interpretation seems to be confirmed from an examination of the transactions-ratio method's growth of implied GNP velocity from 1980 to 1981 (Table 5.3). The resulting 18.1 percent annual rate of velocity growth in 1982 is about four times faster than recorded velocity growth for that year. Such a large increase appears unlikely and suggests that some financial component of the transactions has not been properly netted out in the recent estimates.

---

[19] Based on Board's flow-of-funds data, the share of M1 held by nonfinancial businesses fell from 34.2 percent in the first quarter of 1959 to 18.6 percent at the end of the third quarter of 1983, with the largest part of this decline taking place in the 1970's.

Summary of monetary statistics approach

There are a number of estimates of underground activity based on the monetary statistics methods. Nearly all of these estimates imply a relative rise in underground activity and in the total income velocity of money since 1970. The simple and modified currency-ratio estimates depend on a number of tenuous assumptions – the most critical being that (1) the currency ratio, the ratio of currency to checkable deposits, in the above-ground sector is constant despite changes in economic determinants such as interest rates and the own rate of return on NOW/ATS balances; (2) the ratio of underground to above-ground or recorded GNP is invariant to the way in which recorded GNP is measured; and (3) currency and checkable deposits are used in given proportions in the underground sector. The transactions-ratio method avoids these problems but does not appear to produce credible estimates in recent periods, owing to presumed difficulties in separating out purely financial transactions from other transactions.

Finally, there is the explicit econometric model of the ratio of currency to M2, which represents the underground economy indirectly through the use of tax variables. Unlike the other estimates, this method does not indicate any relative increase in the underground sector relative to total economic activity. However, this method does not also appear to be reliable: It makes the same invariance assumption as the other currency-ratio procedures; it does not allow for any use of checks in the underground economy; and it fails to estimate the tax effects very precisely in the post-war period.

An evaluation of the currency data

For many, the most compelling evidence concerning the existence of the underground economy involves the remarkable level of per capita currency holdings. At the end of 1982, currency holdings, including vault cash, stood at $675 per capita with just under 40 percent in $100 bills. These figures seem to contradict everyday experience. However, since there are no reliable estimates to take account of the portion of the currency stock held abroad, the holding of currency by domestic residents is clearly overstated.

Despite the high level of per capita currency balances, Figures 5.2 and 5.3 show that on-balance aggregate currency over the past twenty years has been declining, not rising, relative to M2, traveler's checks, domestic nonfinancial credit, nominal measured GNP, and nominal measured personal consumption expenditures. In the case of M2, this movement

146

should not be altogether unexpected since the nominal rate of return on M2 has moved up sharply over this period as a result of deregulation and higher nominal interest rates while the nominal return on currency has remained at zero. More striking is the fact that a similar declining pattern is apparent, at least through the mid-1970's, for the ratio of currency to traveler's checks even though traveler's checks, similar to currency, bear no nominal rate of return and, unlike currency, leave a paper trail (Figure 5.3). Finally, currency movements over the past years have been highly predictable in models such as the Board model, where no reference to the underground economy is made (Figure 5.4).

Nonetheless, some suggest that the accurate prediction of currency balances by econometric models may be fortuitous. Since currency holdings are the sum of above-ground and underground holdings, a relative decline in currency holdings in the above-ground sector due to changes in payment practices may offset a relative increase in underground currency holdings, thereby leaving the sum unaffected. More frequently, use of credit cards is perhaps one method by which above-ground currency holders may have economized on currency; however, credit card use represents only a small proportion of the estimated volume of total currency transactions – just over 2 percent in 1981 based on the currency transaction estimates in Table 5.2. A second suggested factor in the possible decrease of above-ground currency use is that an increasing fraction of individuals are paid by check rather than with currency. This factor is not accounted for in the standard currency demand specification; however, when this effect is captured with a series similar to the one used by Tanzi, the predictions of the Board currency equation are not materially altered.

On the other hand, it might be argued that since the mid-1950's aggregate currency balances (including vault cash) have only about kept pace with inflation so that real per capita currency holdings have been almost unchanged (Figure 5.5). Thus, if real per capita instead of total currency holdings were used in the monetary statistics approach, the relative size of the underground economy would be approximately unchanged from the early post-war period until now.[20]

As mentioned earlier, those who assert that there is a growing underground economy sometimes point to the rising proportion of $100 bills

---

[20] Because the total economy has grown over this period, the fact that real per capita currency holdings are relatively constant would imply, other things equal, that the underground economy has declined relative to the above-ground economy. However, the increase in the opportunity cost of holding currency and autonomous improvements in managing currency have apparently offset the increased level of transactions, leaving real per capita currency holdings about unchanged.

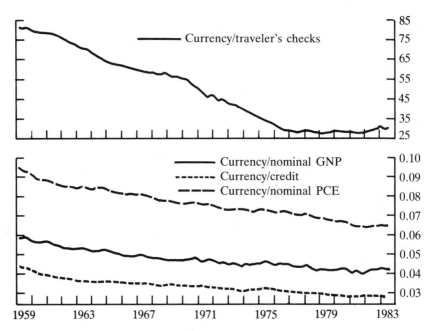

Figure 5.3. Ratios of currency to traveler's checks, GNP, credit, and prices.

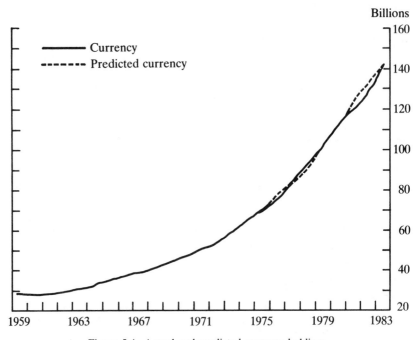

Figure 5.4. Actual and predicted currency holdings.

148

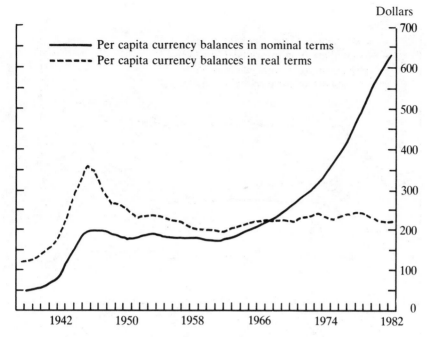

Figure 5.5. Per capita currency balances.

in the currency stock (see Figure 5.6). Even in real terms, the proportion of $100 bills is striking (Figure 5.7). Either this is evidence of increased underground economic activity or it reflects the desired behavior of above-ground transactors.

Focusing on the latter explanation, it should be noted that since 1969 the $100 bill has been the largest denomination issued.[21] Thus, increases in the price level that tend to increase the dollar size of transactions should lead to greater proportionate use of $100 bills, other things equal. This "convenience" aspect of $100 bills is not shared by other denominations. By drawing upon a model recently proposed by Cramer (1983), the precise importance of hundreds in the mix of denominations can be determined. Cramer assumed that economic agents attempt to minimize the number of physical units of currency used in an exchange of a given transaction size. Table 5.4 presents the results of applying Cramer's model to the various bill denominations in the United States for various transaction size ranges.[22] The estimates were constructed

---

[21] Denominations larger than $100 have not been printed since 1946. The use of these denominations had declined sharply over the years, and in 1969, there appeared to be no need to resume printing of the larger denominations – $500, $1,000, $5,000, and $10,000 bills.

[22] We are indebted to Gary Anderson of the Board staff for his technical assistance in putting together this table.

149

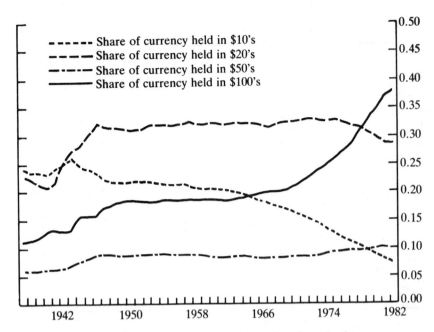

Figure 5.6. Shares of currency held in various denominations.

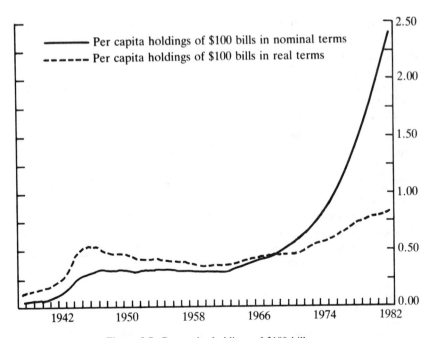

Figure 5.7. Per capita holdings of $100 bills.

150

Table 5.4. *Relationship between average transaction size and share of currency held in selected denominations*

β Parameter	Average size of transactions ($)	Share of $100 bills in optimal mix of denominations (%)	Share of $50 bills in optimal mix of denominations (%)	Share of $20 bills in optimal mix of denominations (%)
10	12.69	12	13	22
20	25.38	19	20	33
30	38.08	25	28	29
40	50.77	31	32	23
50	63.46	37	34	18
60	76.15	43	32	14
70	88.85	49	29	13
80	101.54	56	25	12
90	114.23	62	21	10
100	126.92	66	19	9

under the assumption that all transactions up to a certain size (β) were equally likely to occur (i.e., followed a uniform distribution) and that transactions larger than that size were assumed to follow a Pareto distribution, so that each successive transaction size beyond β was a little less likely to take place than the preceding transactions size.[23] Although it is difficult to compare the model's predictions with the actual mix of denominations in the United States, the table indicates that as the dollar size of individual transactions increases, the proportion of hundreds in the optimal mix of denominations rises. Thus, for example, as the average transaction goes from a little over $25 ($\beta = 20$) to a little over $100 ($\beta = 80$), the proportion of $100 bills goes from a 19 percent share to a 56 percent share.

From this perspective, changes over time in the share of currency held in various denominations are not too surprising (Figure 5.6). In 1978 the share of currency in $100 bills surpassed the share in $20 bills. The figure

[23] That is, the distribution function for transactions of size x was

$$f(x) = \begin{cases} c & \text{if } x \le \beta \\ c\left(\dfrac{\beta}{x}\right)^{\alpha+1} & \text{if } x \ge \beta \end{cases}$$

where $c = \alpha/\beta(\alpha + 1)$ and β is the upper limit of the uniform portion of the distribution. The Pareto parameter α was set equal to 1.65. This is the approximate value estimated for a variant of this model used to explain per capita holdings of $100 bills.

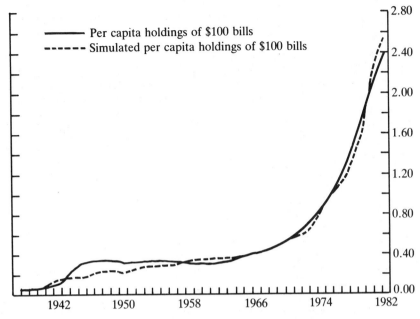

Figure 5.8. Actual and predicted per capita holdings of $100 bills.

shows that the last time a similar event occurred was in 1942, when the amount of money represented by the $20 denomination became larger than the amount held in $10 bills. Over the period from 1942 to 1970, per capita consumption expenditures grew from $605 to $6,048. Thus, whereas per capita consumption expenditures increased by a factor of 10, the size of the denomination in which the largest proportion of currency was outstanding increased only by a factor of 5.

Another way of evaluating the proposition that the growth of $100 bills may have an above-ground explanation is shown by the model developed in Appendix B, which focuses on hundreds exclusively. The model is derived from the following assumptions: (1) For transactions above a given size, the distribution of transactions follows a Pareto distribution; (2) over time, changes in the price level shift the size distribution proportionally; and (3) the number of $100 bills an individual holds is proportional to the probability that he or she will enter a transaction that involves at least a certain size. Under these assumptions, the model explains per capita holdings of $100 bills as a function of the price level. As Figure 5.8 indicates, the regression equation implied by the model performs quite adequately in the out-of-sample period, explaining a substantial part of the recent increase of per capita holdings of $100 bills. Thus, these theoretical and empirical results suggest that the growth of $100 bills may principally be related to economic and institutional forces at work in the above-ground economy.

Although the amount and form of currency holdings may appear suspect at first glance, the increase of per capita currency and $100 bill holdings can be explained without reference to underground activity. Increases in the price level as well as the available denominations of currency can account for patterns of currency holdings.

Conclusions

The analysis of monetary statistics has not progressed to the point where it can provide reliable estimates of underground economic activity. This data source does not provide firm support for the hypothesis that the share of the underground economy in the total U.S. economy has grown over time.

At present, the currency-ratio and modified currency-ratio methods rely on assumptions made solely for technical convenience rather than for consistency with either underlying economic theory or other empirical regularities. The presumed constancy of the currency ratio in the above-ground economy, despite ongoing changes in important economic determinants such as interest rates, is an assumption of convenience that underlies this approach. Although Tanzi has attempted to address this problem through the use of taxes in an explicit regression model, his work does not resolve the size of the estimated tax effects. All of these currency approaches implicitly make the questionable assumption that the ratio of above-ground GNP to recorded GNP is invariant to changes in the estimate of recorded GNP. The transactions-ratio method, on the other hand, treats checkable deposits and currency symmetrically and also avoids the invariance assumption of the various currency-ratio methods. Because it is hard to separate out purely financial transactions from gross transactions, however, implementing this technique in the United States is exceedingly difficult with present data sources. Perhaps as a result of this problem, the transactions-ratio estimates of underground activity for recent periods seem too high.

Despite these problems, the issues raised in evaluating underground economic activity pose some challenging questions regarding the use of currency and deposits as transactions media in the total economy. Perhaps as more satisfactory data sources and methodology are created, better answers to these questions can be found.

APPENDIX A

Empirical financial equations

Equations in the Federal Reserve Board (FRB) model

The demand equations for the components of M1 – currency (including traveler's checks), demand deposits, and other checkable deposits – as they currently appear in the Board's quarterly econometric model (Brayton and Mauskopf, 1985) are available on request from the author. Briefly, the equations for demand deposits and other checkable deposits are based on the same theoretical transactions model and, therefore, are estimated simultaneously and have similar empirical specifications. The per capita demand for deposits is a function of per capita income and the opportunity cost of holding the deposit, the difference between some market rate of interest and the own rate of deposits. In the case demand deposits, the own rate is zero, whereas for other checkables the own rate is R_{now}, the rate of interest earned on NOW accounts. Also worth noting is the fact that the interest rate term in these equations appears in a nonlinear fashion, thus allowing the interest rate elasticity of demand to change with the level of interest rates.

Mnemonics for equations

C = currency (Tanzi)
GNP = nominal GNP
N = population
PCE = personal consumption deflator (1972 = 100)
R = rate of interest paid on time deposits
RATCHET = cash management ratchet
RFF = federal funds rate
T = ratio of total income tax payments to income (Tanzi)
TW = weighted average tax rate (Tanzi)
U = error term for autocorrelation correction
WS/NI = ratio of wages and salaries in national income (Tanzi)
Y = real per capita income (Tanzi)

Tanzi's estimation results[24]

The sample period is 1930–80. Using the weighted average tax rate,

---

[24] Tanzi's equations were corrected for serial correlation with a first-order Cochrane–Orcutt correction. The values of these rhos, however, were not available.

$$\ln C/M2 = -5.0262 + 0.2479\ln(1 + \text{TW}) + 1.7303\ln(\text{WS/NI})$$
$$[-3.61] \quad\quad [5.81] \quad\quad\quad\quad\quad [5.33]$$
$$-0.1554\ln(R) - 0.2026\ln(Y) + \varrho_1 U_{-1} + e$$
$$R^2 = 0.950 \quad\quad \text{DW} = 1.576$$

Using the average tax rate,

$$\ln C/M2 = -4.2005 + 0.3096\ln(1 + T) + 1.5791\ln(\text{WS/NI})$$
$$[2.93] \quad\quad [5.26] \quad\quad\quad\quad [4.76]$$
$$-0.1603\ln(R) - 0.2804\ln(Y) + \varrho_2 U_{-1} + e$$
$$[3.37] \quad\quad\quad\quad [2.22]$$
$$R^2 = 0.947 \quad\quad \text{DW} = 1.677$$

Best reproduction of Tanzi's results[25]

The sample period is 1930–80. Using the weighted average tax rate,

$$\ln C/M2 = -5.0276 + 0.24791\ln(1 + \text{TW}) + 1.7304\ln(\text{WS/NI})$$
$$[-3.60] \quad\quad [5.78] \quad\quad\quad\quad\quad [5.32]$$
$$-0.15583\ln(R) - 0.20178\ln(Y) + 0.75189 U_{-1} + e$$
$$[-3.66] \quad\quad\quad\quad [-1.87] \quad\quad\quad [8.14]$$
$$R^2 = 0.951 \quad\quad \text{DW} = 1.574$$

Using the average tax rate,

$$\ln C/M2 = -4.219 + 0.30913\ln(1 + T) + 1.5827\ln(\text{WS/NI})$$
$$[-2.93] \quad\quad [5.23] \quad\quad\quad\quad [4.75]$$
$$- 0.1611\ln(R) - 0.27712\ln(Y) + 0.83188 U_{-1} + e$$
$$[-3.38] \quad\quad\quad\quad [-2.18]$$
$$R^2 = 0.948 \quad \text{DW} = 1.680 \quad \text{residual standard error} = 0.046788$$

Post-war estimation results using Tanzi's specification

The sample period is 1946–80. Using the weighted average tax rate,

$$\ln C/M2 = -0.40611 + 0.018224\ln(1 + \text{TW}) + 0.49337\ln(\text{WS/NI})$$
$$[-0.45] \quad\quad [0.29] \quad\quad\quad\quad\quad [2.22]$$
$$-0.016408\ln(R) - 0.095747\ln(Y) + 0.92868 U_{-1} + e$$
$$[-0.48] \quad\quad\quad\quad .[-1.23]$$
$$R^2 = 0.989 \quad \text{DW} = 2.10 \quad \text{residual standard error} = 0.018345$$

Using the average tax rate,

[25] Although Tanzi provided his data and estimation results, we were not able to reproduce his estimates exactly.

$$\ln C/M2 = 0.1753 - 0.049305 \ln(1 + T) + .57418 \ln(WS/NI)$$
$$[0.19] \qquad [-0.84] \qquad\qquad\qquad [2.57]$$
$$-0.051654 \ln(Y) + 0.93041\, U_{-1} + e$$
$$[-0.62] \qquad\qquad [15.02]$$

$$R^2 = 0.990 \quad DW = 1.97 \quad \text{residual standard error} = 0.018114$$

Debits equation

The sample period is 1962:1–1983:2.

$$\ln \frac{debits}{GNP} = -0.91548 + \sum_{i=0}^{3} a_i \ln(RFF)_{-i} + \sum_{i=0}^{3} b_i \ln(GNP)_{-i}$$
$$[-2.02]$$
$$+ \sum_{i=0}^{3} c_i (RATCHET)_{-i} + 0.8175\, U_{-1} + e$$
$$[13.16]$$

$a_0 = 0.012462$	$b_0 = 0.29977$	$c_0 = 0.0018843$
$a_1 = 0.034339$	$b_1 = 0.073013$	$c_1 = 0.0023097$
$a_2 = 0.032759$	$b_2 = 0.016727$	$c_2 = 0.001296$
$a_3 = 0.0077217$	$b_3 = 0.030554$	$c_3 = 0.0089329$
$\Sigma a_i = 0.087281$	$\Sigma b_i = 0.38661$	$\Sigma c_i = 0.006035$
$[2.15]$	$[5.26]$	$[3.13]$

$$R^2 = 0.99613 \qquad DW = 2.30 \qquad \text{residual standard error} = 0.020932$$

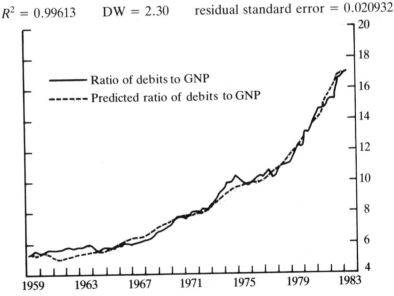

Figure A5.1. Actual and predicted transaction ratios.

United States

APPENDIX B: ASSUMPTIONS FOR
MODEL OF $100 NOTES

1. In 1967, when the consumer price index (CPI) was 1, the distribution of the sizes of currency transactions that were larger than some dollar amount a_0 was Pareto with parameter α:

$$f_0(x|x > a_0) = \alpha a_0^\alpha / x^{\alpha+1} \qquad x > a_0$$

2. The transactions that took place in later years were identical to those that occurred in 1967 except that each one involved P_t times as much money as its 1967 counterpart, where P_i is the CPI index in year t.

3. The number n_t of $100 bills a person holds in year t is proportional to the probability he will enter a transaction that involves at least τ dollars, say, $n_t = k \Pr(x_t > \tau)$.

4. The measured number of $100 bills per person is the product of n_t and u_t, where $\ln u_t$ has mean 0 and variance σ^2:

$$\bar{n}_t = n_t u_t$$

Given these assumptions, it is easy to show that (1) the probability that a transaction exceeds τ is proportional to the conditional probability that it exceeds τ given that it exceeds that year's threshold $P_t a_0$, (2) transactions in later years that exceed $P_t a_0$ are also Pareto distributed with parameter α; and (3)

$$\ln n_t = \alpha \ln(kca_0/\tau) + \alpha \ln P_t + \ln u_t$$

It follows that we can estimate α by regressing the logarithm of per capita holdings of $100, $\ln n$, on the logarithm of the price level, but we cannot distinguish among the remaining parameters of the model, k, c, a_0, and τ. Using a serially correlated error structure, estimates of this equation are (sample period, 1955–75)

$$\begin{aligned}
\ln n = \ \ &0.83864 \ + \ 1.6797 \ \ln(\text{CPI}) \\
&[-41.75] \quad\ \ [18.67] \\
&+ \ 1.4858 \, U_{-1} - 0.69338 \, U_{-2} + e \\
&\ \ [9.97] \qquad\qquad [-5.07]
\end{aligned}$$

$R^2 = 0.997 \ \ \text{DW} = 1.80 \ \ \text{residual standard error} = 0.01896$

157

The unrecorded economy and the national income accounts in the Netherlands: a sensitivity analysis

G. A. A. M. BROESTERHUIZEN

During the second half of the 1970's there has been a growing concern about the influence of unrecorded activities and fraud on the economy. This chapter examines the consequences of fraud on the reliability of macroeconomic statistics as a basis for economic policy making.

For policy making one needs statistics. When these statistics are biased because of a large and growing unrecorded sector, policy actions might miss their intended targets and may at times produce adverse macroeconomic effects. Feige and McGee (1988, Chapter 3) give some examples of what might go wrong because of distorted information. Distorted information and its consequences for public policy are also studied by Alford and Feige (1988, Chapter 2). This chapter studies the influence of fraud on macroeconomic statistics, particularly the gross domestic product (GDP). We use the term "fraud" to mean the non-reporting or underreporting of income to the tax authorities. Thus, income generated by illegal activities but known to the tax authorities (as is sometimes the case with prostitution) is not considered as fraud here. The chapter does not investigate what GDP would have been if everybody would have behaved in accordance with the law.

In an investigation of the influence of fraud on macroeconomic statistics it is of great importance that clear terminology is used. Following Heertje and Cohen (1980), the Central Bureau of Statistics (CBS) attaches the adjective "unofficial" to all flows of goods, services, and income that are not included in the national accounts. These flows are regarded as being in the "unofficial circuit." An understanding of the results of this investigation requires that one understands the difference between fraud and the unofficial circuit. We therefore devote the first section of this chapter to a more detailed explanation of the differences between these concepts. The section is concluded with a schema depicting a classification of productive activities. The decomposition of productive activities reveals why total GDP is only partly distorted by fraud.

The second section contains a sensitivity analysis of the possible effects of fraud on official GDP estimates. To this end, the components of GDP are grouped into six categories depending on either the estimation methods used or the sector of origin of the data. For each category of components, we indicate plausible ranges of distortions introduced by fraud. By combining categories, it is then possible to obtain a plausible upper bound for the distortion of GDP by fraud. The conclusion of this analysis is that it is very unlikely that overall GDP will be distorted by more than 5%.

The same type of analysis is applicable to an investigation of the consequences of fraud on the growth rates of GDP. Growth rates are used more intensively for the formulation of macroeconomic policy than are the levels of the variables. Discussions about the unofficial circuit should, therefore, also focus on the growth rate issue. The conclusion of the analysis is that growth rates of GDP are very unlikely to be biased by more than 0.5%.

The influence of fraud on the national accounts

It is a widely held belief that fraud always distorts the national accounts estimates. In this section we will argue that this is certainly not the case. Several methods described by Algera et al. (1982) are available in order to produce estimates of the national accounts and particularly GDP. The method of estimation employed by the CBS is known as the production method. The production method employs data supplied by producers of goods and services. Ideally, producers provide necessary information about their production and intermediary inputs. The method is used in order to construct an annual input–output table. This has the advantage that information from different sources can be compared and hence be used to reveal sources of distortion (Van Eck, 1983). The input–output table serves as an intermediary product in the process of forming the national accounts estimates.[1]

There are, however, instances where the production method cannot be directly employed. Statistical information is not always available for the production of all goods and services. Hence, in some cases, the national accounting agency must rely on other methods in order to obtain missing information. The "indirect" methods thus deviate from the ideal production method. If one imagines the economic process as a circular flow of goods and services, it is sometimes possible to estimate the production and intermediary inputs of some sectors by gathering

---

[1] The input–output tables are of course useful in their own right for various types of inter-industry analyses.

Table 6.1. *Classification of productive activities*[a]

| | Official | Unofficial | |
		To be included in national accounts	Need not be included in national accounts
1 Activities in which no fraud is involved	1.1 Production recorded in official files	1.2 Statistical undercoverage of legal activities	1.3 Do-it-yourself activities; household chores
2 Activities that involve fraud	2.1 Trading activities not reported to tax authority	2.2 Dabbling in construction sector	2.3 Clandestine subletting of rooms by private individuals

[a] Cells provide illustrative examples of types of activities.

data at different points in the circular flow. One example would be the production of the trade sector. Trade sector production is estimated by multiplying the value of goods, which is derived from surveys, by a trade margin that varies with each type of good. Some components of the agricultural sector also need to be estimated by indirect methods.

Estimates derived by indirect methods are likely to contain statistical errors. However, those components of the production process that are estimated by indirect means are not subject to the particular systematic distortions of the type introduced when fraud by producers is involved. Whenever information does not originate from the producers themselves, fraud by these producers does not distort the estimates based on indirect methods. This does not, however, imply that indirect estimates are free of all bias.

Thus, when the discussion is limited to statistical errors and distortions due to producer fraud, we may conclude that fraud will not always lead to distortion in the national accounts estimates since the estimation procedures used by the CBS involve the use of indirect methods of estimation that are more likely to be insensitive to these systematic distortions.

The relation between the unofficial circuit and fraudulent activities can be pictured in the matrix displayed in Table 6.1.[2] The matrix is meant to be a classification of productive activities.

[2] A more elaborate version of the matrix is found in Van Tuinen (1981), Blokland (1982), and Van Eck (1983).

Fraud consists of activities of the type classified in cells 2.1, 2.2, and 2.3. Some of these activities (e.g., 2.3) cannot distort the national accounts estimates because they should not be included in GDP according to the present definitions. This does not deny the fact that the growth of activities outside the production boundary is very important both for policy making and for the development of the national accounts in the future. As a consequence of the use of indirect estimation methods, some fraudulent activities (e.g., 2.1) are included in the estimates of GDP. In these cases we speak of fraud, implicitly included in the estimates. This is the gross value added that is included in GDP but is generated by activities not reported to the tax authorities. The sensitivity analysis carried out in the next section is concerned with a possible bias in the GDP estimate because of fraud. Hence, this analysis is concerned with the activities of cell 2.2.

Sensitivity analysis of the level of distortion

The sensitivity analysis of the national accounts estimates is based on a detailed investigation of the method used to produce particular components of the accounts and the relationship of each of these components to overall economic activity. The analysis examines in detail the composition of GDP, taken as the sum of the gross value added of the sectors of the economy. Components of the accounts are divided into six categories according to the estimation method employed or the sector of origin of the production. Some estimates originate in sectors that are almost free of distortion due to fraud. In other cases, estimates are formed by methods that are insensitive to fraud.[3] Before the sensitivity analysis can proceed, the GDP is divided into six specific categories.

The first category consists of those components of GDP that are estimated by the use of *indirect methods*. This category contains the gross value added of all sectors and branches of industry that are estimated by means of indirect methods. The following are included:

Agriculture (excluding horticulture), except for the value added generated by the production of agricultural seeds. The production is measured by multiplying the yield by the prevailing market prices. The yield is obtained by independent observers who estimate the acreage of crop and the average yield per acre.

Crude petroleum and natural gas production and exploration. Al-

---

[3] This sensitivity analysis of the national accounts estimates is inspired by comments made by Van Tuinen (1980) in public discussions about the unofficial circuit.

though the information about quantities originate with the producers, numerous independent checks are made. For example, it is impossible to sell considerable quantities of gas via the existing net of pipelines without any control. The importance of this sector for the Dutch economy implies that there is stringent control by the government. This would provide a strong argument for classifying this value added in category 2. Such a choice would not affect the conclusions of this chapter.

Petroleum industry. The gross value added is almost completely dependent on imported and exported crude petroleum and petroleum and coal products. These quantities and values are determined from customs declarations.

Operating of real estate. The production value is the total rent of rented houses plus the rental value of owner-occupied houses. This production is estimated by multiplying an average rent (or rental value) with the total number of rented houses (or owner-occupied houses).

The feature common to the methods used to form the preceding estimates is that the information is not systematically distorted by fraud, either by the producers themselves or by others. This means that whatever may be the percentage of fraud in these major groups, this percentage equals the percentage of fraud implicitly included in the estimates. Hence, the percentage of fraud by which the official estimates may be systematically biased is zero.

The second category represents government production. This category includes the gross value added of the government sector and that of state enterprises and firms subject to detailed government supervision. The following are included:

General government. The gross value added is the sum of compensation of employees, consumption of fixed capital, and indirect taxes paid by the government.

Value-added tax. This estimate is equal to the figure for the tax receipts on a cash basis of the Ministry of Finance minus the value-added tax on the intermediary inputs of some major groups (communication, banking, insurance, real estate operations, and health services) (CSB, 1982).

Public utilities. These are under detailed government supervision.

Railways. These are organized in a corporate enterprise of which the state is the only shareholder.

Tramways and regular bus services and subsidized motor coach services. These are subsidized and hence are subject to detailed supervision.

Communication. This is organized in a state enterprise.

163

Banking and insurance. The production value is the commission for services plus the interest margin (banking) or the net receipts of premiums minus indemnities (insurance). These are under the control of either the central bank (although it does not have control of all activities of banks, such as holding deposits of "black money") or the so-called Verzekeringskamer (Chamber of Insurance). By definition, the interest margin of banks does not contribute to GDP and will thus be subtracted.

Hospitals, mental homes, and nursing homes. These are financed by the government.

Subsidized welfare services, social-cultural and cultural institutions, and corporate business organs. These are mostly subsidized. They all keep to regulations concerning bookkeeping, staffing, and salary policy that are analogous to government regulations.

The estimates in this category are assumed to be unbiased by fraud since these sectors of the economy are not characterized by the type of fraudulent practices that cause GDP distortions.

The third category consists of large firms, and the fourth category consists of the production of small firms.

The estimates in these categories are reported to the CBS by the economic subjects themselves. In order to explain the contents of categories 3 and 4 we have to digress and explain in more detail the process of data collection and processing. Although these categories also contain estimates of such sectors as horticulture, fishery, and part of the service sector, the exposition is only concerned with industry.

The gross value added of the industry groups involved is estimated as follows. Enquiries are sent out yearly to the firms classified in these groups. In some groups only firms employing 10 or more persons are questioned; in other groups all firms are involved in the survey. The estimates obtained from these surveys will be raised, if necessary, in order to account for the gross value added generated by firms not covered by the surveys (firms employing less than 10 persons and own-account workers and non-paid family workers). This is mostly done (in the case of production) by multiplying production per worker (as obtained from survey data) by the number of persons in the uncovered group of firms. This number is derived from social security fund records and related institutions and from labor force census data for the own-account workers. These methods produce estimates of the gross value added per industry group.

Recently the CBS (1983) has carried out an investigation with the purpose of disaggregating these estimates into two parts: (1) the gross value added by firms employing more than 100 persons and (2) firms employing fewer than 100 persons.[4]

The fifth category contains the estimates of production for "uncovered firms," namely, those not included in the surveys. These estimates are derived by blowing up the estimates of the covered firms by an amount necessary to reflect uncovered firms. The sensitivity analysis treats the data of large and small firms differently for the following reasons:

a fraud by a large firm is likely to involve the knowledge of many individuals, particularly if the fraud continues for some years;

b in the Netherlands, firms employing at least 100 persons and for which the balance sheet fulfills some requirements are obliged to submit for approval their working account and balance sheet to a detailed control by a certified accountant; and

c large firms have more and better means to take advantage of all possibilities offered by fiscal regulations.

Hence, in these cases, tax avoidance probably plays a more important role than tax evasion.

This method of estimation is at least partially insensitive to fraud.

---

[4] The results of this investigation are used to form categories 3 and 4. Category 3 contains the gross value added of firms employing more than 100 persons in groups of industry where data originate from the producers and are not contained in categories 1 and 2. Category 4 contains the gross value added generated in firms employing less than 100 persons in the same groups of firms as are involved in category 3 (the data must originate from questionnaires filled out by the producers and are not contained in categories 1 and 2). This category also contains the value added generated by horticulture, fishery, and the production of agricultural seeds. Some additional clarifications concerning categories 3 and 4 are in order.

1 Category 4 also contains the gross value added generated by horticulture and by the production of agricultural seeds. In this sector the production is mainly determined by measuring the quantities that come up for auction. This information does not originate with the producers themselves but with the auctioneers. Although this represents a departure from the method of estimation used in this category, the resemblance is close enough to justify its inclusion in this category.

2 Data relating to firms in the service sector are not divided into two parts. In these cases the gross value added is assigned to category 4. This is done because the estimation methods differ completely from those used in the manufacturing sector, thus making a distinction by size very difficult. Moreover, the percentage of the gross value added of the service sector generated by large, non-governmental institutions, for which data originate with these institutions themselves, is rather small.

The estimation methods described are not insensitive to fraud. Underreporting by producers affects the figures. Ignoring the possibility that producers report higher production and gross value added to the CBS than to the tax office, we may conclude that there is no fraud implicitly included in the estimates.

Consider, for example, estimates of the value of production. Given an estimated production per worker in very small firms derived from the production per worker in the firms of the survey sample, the implicit fraud distortion is the same in both categories. In reality, the average fraudulent production per worker in very small firms may be higher than in large firms. Although some fraud is already included in the estimates, the total fraud not included (as a percentage of the gross value added) is obtained by adding the relative fraud among the number of working people (i.e., the difference between the actual number of working people and the number in the official estimates).

The final category (category 6) consists of value-added estimates that are derived from fiscal data.[5] The information on which the estimates in this category are based is derived from tax files and hence originates with the producers themselves. Thus, there is no fraud implicitly included in the figures.

The estimation of the production of the trade sector requires special mention. The production value of the trade sector is equal to the sum of the following items:

a Trade margins on goods dealt in, as obtained by multiplying the value of goods available for trade with a certain percentage. These margins can be divided into margins on imported goods and margins on domestic products.

b Autonomously determined margins on certain categories of goods, such as second-hand goods and gold for industrial use. Also the production of home and estate agents is included in the production value of the trade sector. This category is of minor importance.

c Indirect taxes paid on imported goods (excise taxes, import duties).

In order to allocate the gross value added of the trade sector among the six categories, the production value and intermediary inputs were divided proportionally. The allocation of the production value of the trade sector proceeded as follows:

1 The margins mentioned under b were omitted, as they are of minor importance; this implies that they are divided proportionally into the other margins.

2 The indirect taxes paid on imported goods were assigned to category 2.

---

[5] It includes own-account workers in the following groups: part of hotels, restaurants, cafes, repair of consumer goods, business services, renting of machinery and other movables, health and veterinary services, social-cultural institutions, and private households with wage-earning staff.

3 The trade margins on imported goods were assigned to category 1, since the value of these goods is obtained from customs declarations.
4 The trade margins on domestic products were divided according to the procedure described in what follows.

Let there be N groups of industry and let g_i be the margins on goods of group i, and

$$g = \sum_{i=1}^{N} g_i \qquad (6.1)$$

Let $A = \{a_{ij}\}, i = 1, \cdots, N, j = 1, \cdots, 6$, be a matrix such that a_{ij} is the proportion of the production of group i that belongs to category j. Then g (being the total of trade margins on domestic products) is divided into six parts $g^j (j = 1, \cdots, 6)$ such that

$$g^j = \sum_{i=1}^{N} g_i a_{ij} \quad \text{for } j = 1, \cdots, 6 \qquad (6.2)$$

By following the foregoing procedures, the GDP can be decomposed into each of the six categories for analysis. The lowest numbered categories are believed to be those least susceptible to distortion through fraud, whereas the highest numbered categories are believed to be most susceptible. The empirical estimates presented here are based on national accounts estimates for the year 1979. The final allocations of GDP into each of the categories is presented in Table 6.2 (a more detailed representation is found in Table 6.3). On the basis of these calculations, 53.7% of GDP is allocated to the first and second categories that are believed to be either estimated by indirect methods or represent sectors that do not lend themselves to fraud that distorts GDP.

In order to obtain estimates of a plausible range for the distortion caused by fraud on GDP, it is necessary to postulate several alternative scenarios concerning the percentage of each category that could be af-

Table 6.2. *Decomposition of GDP*[a]

	Categories						
	1	2	3	4	5	6	Total
GDP (billions of guilders)	65.2	104.6	61.3	54.0	11.3	19.7	315.9
Percent	20.6	33.1	19.3	17.1	3.6	6.2	100

[a] Market prices, billions of guilders.

Table 6.3. *Decomposition of GDP, 1979 (billion guilders)*[a]

First digit(s) of major group[b]	Category						Total
	1	2	3	4	5	6	
0	8.5	—	—	2.8	—	—	11.35
1[c]	0.5	—	—	—	—	—	0.5
2/3[d]	19.9	—	38.3	12.1	3.9	—	74.2
4	—	6.6	—	—	—	—	6.6
5	—	—	7.3	8.1	6.1	—	21.5
61/66	21.0	2.9	10.4	5.9	0.9	0.0	41.1
67/68	—	—	0.7	6.4	0.4	0.7	8.2
7	—	7.6	4.4	8.4	—	—	20.4
8	15.3	15.0	—	0.8	—	12.8	43.9
9	—	17.4	—	9.5	—	6.2	33.1
Government	—	44.4	—	—	—	—	44.4
Value-added tax on final expenditures	—	21.3	—	—	—	—	21.3
Interest margin of banks	—	-/-10.6	—	—	—	—	-/-10.6
Total	65.2	104.6	61.1	54.0	11.3	19.7	315.9
Percentage of total groups	20.6	33.1	19.3	17.1	3.6	6.2	100

[a] Numbers may differ slightly from national accounts estimates due to rounding.

[b] First digits of major groups: 0, agriculture and fishing; 1, mining and quarrying; 2/3, manufacturing except construction; 4, public utilities; 5, construction; 61/66, trade; 67/68, hotels, cafes, restaurants, and repair of consumer goods; 7, transport, storage, and communication; 8, banking, insurance, and business services; 9, other services. The reader is referred to CBS (1974) and CBS (1982) for further details.

[c] Excluding oil and gas production.

[d] Including oil and gas production.

fected by fraud. A sensitivity analysis of the vulnerability of GDP to fraud is conducted by applying five possible scenarios of fraud percentages for each category. The alternative fraud scenarios are presented in Table 6.4. Scenarios I–IV range from low degrees of fraud to very high degrees of fraud. The fifth scenario is regarded as a reasonable upper bound for possible distortions.[6]

[6] Considering the percentages presented in these alternative scenarios, it is important to recall that the construction of an input–output table permits numerous checks on the plausibility and reliability of the data. For example, data on the production of goods and services that have an intermediary use cannot be distorted to a large extent because although incentives for underreporting might exist for the producer, they most likely do not exist for the users. This supports our opinion that the percentages presented in Table 6.4 are certainly not too low.

Table 6.4. *Alternative scenarios representing possible fraud: percentage of gross value added*

Scheme	Category					
	1	2	3	4	5	6
I	0	0	1	5	10	20
II	0	0	2	10	15	30
III	0	1	3	15	20	50
IV	0	1	5	20	40	60
V	0	0	2	10	30	40

Table 6.5. *Absolute and relative estimates of GDP distortions due to fraud, 1979*

	Scheme				
	I	II	III	IV	V
Billions of guilders	5.8	11.6	20.5	28.6	15.3
Percentage of GDP	1.8	3.1	6.5	9.1	4.8

By applying the percentages of each scenario to the appropriate category, it is possible to arrive at estimates of the absolute and relative percentage of GDP distortion implied by each of the scenarios presented in Table 6.4. The results presented in Table 6.5 suggest a range of possible distortion from 1.8% of GDP to 9.1%. To the extent that scenario V is accepted as representing a plausible upper bound, we conclude that GDP is unlikely to be distorted by more than 5% as a result of fraud.

Analysis of the growth of GDP

The foregoing analysis has dealt with an examination of the possible size of the unofficial circuit and its consequences for distorting the level of GDP. The more important issue, to which we now turn, is the effect of fraud on measured growth rates of GDP. If the unofficial circuit distorts observed growth rates of GDP, this is likely to have even more serious consequences for macroeconomic policy, as has been described by Feige and McGee (Chapter 3). Growth rates of GDP are used more intensively than levels in the construction of macroeconomic models, implying that distorted growth rates will have serious implications for the predictive power of macroeconomic models. This section contains a sensitivity analysis analogous to the one presented in the last section, but here it is modified to focus on the issue of growth rates. Our point of departure is the division of GDP into six categories. The criteria for allocating the components of GDP into distinct categories involve grouping together components that have been constructed by methods that treat year-to-year changes in the same manner or by grouping components on the basis of the sector of origin of the source data.

The first category chosen in order to analyze year-to-year changes groups together those components of GDP based on "indirect" methods of estimation. The second category combines "government" components of the accounts. Since the yearly estimates in these two categories are believed to be free of bias from fraud, the year-to-year changes in the estimates will also be unaffected by fraud.

Categories 3 and 4 represent the components for large and small firms, respectively. Data classified in these categories originate with the producers themselves. Hence, growth of fraud, exceeding reported growth, distorts the year-to-year change in the official estimates. In the scenarios of the preceding section, we assumed that fraud in the small-firm category is greater than in the large-firm category. In our "growth rate" scenarios we also will assume that fraud in the small-firm category 4 grows faster than in the large-firm category 3.

The yearly change of the estimates of the fifth category, comprising "very small firms," is partially insensitive to fraud. The estimates in this category are formed by multiplying indicators (such as production per worker) with the appropriate factor (number of workers). Hence, the overall relative change is equal to the relative change of the indicator plus the relative change in the factor. The systematic bias in the estimates of this category is therefore equal to the systematic bias in the indicators as computed for category 4 plus the systematic bias in the factor. Therefore, the differences between the growth of the estimates in this category and the actual growth is the bias of category 4 plus a bias caused by fraud in the growth of the number of working people.

The final category 6 groups components whose estimates are based on fiscal source data. For 1977 the estimates were based on fiscal data, which were raised in order to account for fraud. For the years after 1977 the production and intermediary inputs per own-account worker are multiplied by indices that reflect the development of the prices, number of own-account workers, and productivity. These indices, which are numerous and are different for different sub-groups, are determined from several sources of information about salaries (wage indices), prices (e.g., price regulations of the government), and costs. However rough

170

these indices may be, they are based on information that is independent of producer reported data and, thus, are not systematically biased by fraud. Hence, the index of the change of the value added per man is determined in a way that is insensitive to fraud. The growth of the gross value added, being approximated indirectly, is not influenced by a possible growth of the percentage of fraud by own-account workers. What remains is a possible systematic bias in the growth of the number of own-account workers. Hence, the argument is similar to that which applies for category 5.

In our calculations we will use the following notation:

N = GDP as officially measured
N_i = gross value added classified in category i, $i = 1, \cdots, 6$
T = GDP as it really is.
T_i = gross value added classified in category i when everything that
    should be measured would indeed be measured, $i = 1, \cdots, 6$
F = absolute size of distortion of GDP by fraud
F_i = distortion of N_i by fraud, $i = 1, \cdots, 6$

We will use the following definitions:

$$f_i = N_i/N \qquad i = 1, \cdots, 6 \tag{6.3}$$

$$f_i^* = T_i/T \qquad i = 1, \cdots, 6 \tag{6.4}$$

$$a_i = (T_i - N_i)/N_i \qquad i = 1, \cdots, 6 \tag{6.5}$$

$$a = (T - N)/N \tag{6.6}$$

Relative changes of a variable are indicated by a tilde. The first observation we make is

$$\tilde{T} - \tilde{N} = a(\tilde{F} - \tilde{N}) \tag{6.7}$$

The distortion of the officially measured growth is dependent on the difference in growth between fraud and the official estimates $(\tilde{F} - \tilde{N})$ and on the relative size of the distortion (a). It is clear that the rapid growth of fraud affects the official estimates more when the amount of fraud is large than when it is small.

Thus, the foregoing analysis suggests that a sensitivity analysis of growth estimates can only be carried out in combination with analysis of levels. This enforces the cogency of the argument because a great distortion of official growth estimates is possible only in the case of the implausibly rapid growth of fraud when the existing level of fraud is already very extensive.

From the preceding definitions and equalities, we infer the following:

$$\tilde{T} - \tilde{N} = \sum_i f_i^*(\tilde{T}_i - \tilde{N}_i) + \sum_i (f_i^* - f_i)\tilde{N}_i \qquad (6.8)$$

It can be argued that the second term of the right side probably is negative. Indeed, for the scenarios presented earlier we have

$$f_i^* \leq f_i \quad \text{for } i = 1, 2, 3 \qquad (6.9)$$

Moreover, in the 1970's the highest growth figures have been realized in the first three categories. So, most probably,

$$\sum_i (f_i^* - f_i)\tilde{N}_i \leq 0 \qquad (6.10)$$

Given the size of this term and its coefficient, it is plausible to neglect this term entirely.

For scheme V, $f_i^* - f_i$ ranges from -0.0097 to 0.0209. Thus, in the rest of our calculations we use the term $\Sigma_i f_i^*(\tilde{T}_i - \tilde{N}_i)$ as an approximation from the foregoing for $\tilde{T} - \tilde{N}$.

Rewriting this expression yields

$$\tilde{T} - \tilde{N} \leq \frac{\sum_i (1 + a_i)}{(1 + a)a_i f_i(\tilde{F}_i - \tilde{N}_i)} \qquad (6.11)$$

where $\leq$ means is approximated from above.

Table 6.6 presents five scenarios representing alternative assumptions concerning the growth percentages $\tilde{F}_i - \tilde{N}_i$ for $i = 1, \cdots, 6$. Every percentage $\tilde{F}_i - \tilde{N}_i$ indicates the excess growth of the distortion of the official estimates. In each scenario, $\tilde{F}_1 - \tilde{N}_1 = \tilde{F}_2 - \tilde{N}_2 = 0$ because the official estimates are virtually unbiased by fraud.

The terms $\tilde{F}_3 - \tilde{N}_3$ and $\tilde{F}_4 - \tilde{N}_4$ indicate the excess growth of fraud in large and small firms, respectively. This excess growth is fully reflected in the distortion of the official estimates. The term $\tilde{F}_5 - \tilde{N}_5$ can be decomposed into two parts. The first component is the excess growth of fraud per worker in category 4, the second represents the excess growth of the number of unregistered working people (in terms of man years). Hence, the difference between $\tilde{F}_5 - \tilde{N}_5$ and $\tilde{F}_4 - \tilde{N}_4$ is at most the excess growth of the total employment in category 5 above the official estimates. Finally, $\tilde{F}_6 - \tilde{N}_6$ is equal to the excess growth of the total employment in this category above the official estimates.

When the preceding percentages are compared with the 6.3% rate of officially measured growth of GDP between 1979 and 1980, it appears that the assumed values for the growth of the unofficial circuit is rela-

Table 6.6. *Excess growth of fraud*

Scheme	Category					
	$\tilde{F}_1 - \tilde{N}_1$	$\tilde{F}_2 - \tilde{N}_2$	$\tilde{F}_3 - \tilde{N}_3$	$\tilde{F}_4 - \tilde{N}_4$	$\tilde{F}_5 - \tilde{N}_5$	$\tilde{F}_6 - \tilde{N}_6$
A	0	0	2	5	10	0
B	0	0	5	10	10	5
C	0	0	5	10	15	10
D	0	0	10	15	25	10
E	0	0	5	10	20	5

tively high, particularly for the scenarios represented by C, D, and E. Scheme E is used to provide a "high" scenario, which we consider to represent a reasonable upper bound for the excess growth percentages.

The influence of these schemes on the official growth estimates can only be measured if one knows the size of the unofficial circuit. Hence, we combined these "growth scenarios" with the "level scenarios" of the earlier section. For each combination we may compute the approximation of the bias in the officially measured growth.

The percentage rates of bias presented in Table 6.7 are computed without regard to the explicit fraud estimates in each particular category. However, the total explicit fraud estimation is taken into account and exerts a downward influence on the estimated growth bias. Taking time into account would lower the percentages in Table 6.7 by no more than 0.1%.

In our presentation of the scenarios I–V and A–E we stressed the magnitude of the percentages of scenarios III–V and C–E. Although we presented scenarios V and E as reasonable upper bounds for the level scenarios and growth scenarios, respectively, we may not conclude that the combination of V and E yields a reasonable upper bound for the distortion of the growth figures. We must take into account the low likelihood that such a combination of rather high percentages would actually occur. Over longer periods, it is more likely that a combination of scenarios II and B would be representative. It follows that a bias of more than 0.5% is only possible in the unlikely event that either the excess growth of fraud or the magnitude of the relative distortion of the official GDP estimates exceeds reasonable upper bounds. We therefore may draw the conclusion that a bias in the growth because of excess growth of fraud is most likely below 0.5%. Higher percentages are improbable.

173

Table 6.7. *Predicted bias in officially measured growth rates*[a]

Level of fraud	Excess growth of fraud				
	A	B	C	D	E
I	0.1	0.2	0.3	0.4	0.2
II	0.2	0.4	0.5	0.7	0.4
III	0.2	0.6	0.9	1.1	0.7
IV	0.4	0.9	1.2	1.7	1.1
V	0.2	0.5	0.7	1.0	0.6

[a] Predicted biases are calculated for given relative size of fraud (I, ⋯, V) and excess growth of fraud (A, ⋯, E). Biases are expressed in percentages.

Conclusions

In this chapter we presented a sensitivity analysis of the national accounts estimates in the Netherlands. The analysis concentrates on the bias introduced by fraud in GDP and its rate of growth. The bias in GDP is investigated by allocating specific components of GDP into categories such that the components in any category have a similar likelihood of being affected by fraud. The criteria for the allocation is determined by the sources and methods used to construct each component and the economic sector that each component represents.

In some categories fraud is implicitly included in the estimates. In other categories, the estimates relate to parts of the economy that do not readily lend themselves to fraudulent practices. Finally, in some categories of fraud, which are not implicitly included in the estimates, we obtain an indication of the size of the distortion of GDP. Our conclusion is that a bias in GDP that amounts to more than 5% is very unlikely.

In the second part of our analysis we concentrate on estimates of growth rates. A bias in the relative change of GDP can only be quantified if one knows both the excess growth of fraud (not already implicitly included in the estimates) above official growth and the relative amount of fraud that distorts the official estimates of GDP. By combining some scenarios of excess growth of fraud with the scenarios of relative distortion of GDP, it is possible to obtain some plausible estimates of the possible distortions contained in official estimates of the growth of GDP. Our conclusion is that a bias of more than 0.5% in the growth of GDP is only possible in the unlikely event of a very great distortion in the level of GDP or of improbably high percentages of excess growth of fraud.

CHAPTER 7

Assessing the underground economy in the United Kingdom

MICHAEL O'HIGGINS

In a cautious review of the evidence and measurement methodologies used in assessing the magnitude of the hidden economy in the United Kingdom, I argued that whereas "any conclusion is a matter of faith rather than hard facts...the effect of all the data taken together makes it difficult to believe in a figure of less than five per cent" (O'Higgins 1980, p. 36). Since then the official authorities – the Inland Revenue (IR) and the Central Statistical Office (CSO) – have discussed the question openly; IR compliance enforcement activity has shifted as a consequence of a new perception of where tax evasion is most prevalent – and most controllable; a working group of the Economics Committee of the Social Science Research Council (SSRC) has discussed and reported on the research questions relevant to the theory and measurement of the hidden economy; and studies have appeared with estimates of the unobserved economy that range from 2 to 15% of official national income at the end of the 1970's. What I want to investigate here is whether this profusion of material has reduced confusion about the magnitude and trend of the U.K. unobserved economy.

The essential conclusions of this chapter are that although monetary measures indicate unobserved economies of the order of 10–15% and other methods produce estimates in the range 3–8%, there is some suggestive evidence that the relative growth of the unobserved economy was checked and perhaps slightly reversed in the mid-1970's. This would accord with the intuitive suggestion that the scope and demand for unobserved activities is greatest in boom years when the formal economy is tight. If this were indeed the case, it would run counter to those theories that suggest that the recession is in part a statistical artifact arising from a failure to include the growing hidden economy in conventional measures of national income.

Defining the unobserved economy

Definitions of the unobserved economy in the United Kingdom are divided between those concerned with tax losses and those that focus

175

on national accounts measurement defects. Not surprisingly the Board of Inland Revenue chose the former type: "We...define the black economy as economic activity generating incomes which are concealed from the revenue-collecting authorities with the (specific) intention of evading tax" (BIR, 1981, p. 24).[1] This definition is also adopted by the SSRC Working Group (SSRC, 1981, paragraph 6.2), which rejects wider definitions as loose and unhelpful. For example, after quoting Stuart Henry's statement that the hidden economy "has been taken to refer to the criminal end of a range of activities that are more generally described as the informal economy and informal institutions," the SSRC comments: "Other definitions are similarly vague. It is, then, little wonder that qualitative, anthropological and often impressionistic research has prevailed over more quantitative and systematic work" (SSRC, 1981). The broader definition suggested by the CSO (Macafee, 1980, p. 81) is "the economic activity generating factor incomes which cannot be estimated from the regular statistical sources used to compile the income measures of gross domestic product." This is close to Feige's (1981, p. 205) definition of the unobserved economy: "all economic activity which, because of accounting conventions, non-reporting or under-reporting, escapes the social measurement apparatus, most notably the G.N.P. [gross national product] accounts." However, the slight difference of wording between the two raises the question implicit in Henry's definition: How does one identify the boundary between the unobserved and the informal or household sector of the economy? The examples are obvious enough: When does the friendly, if formalized, exchange of neighborhood services, such as the baby-sitting club where each member has income (twenty tokens) and faces a common price schedule (one token per hour pre-midnight, two per hour thereafter), move from being part of the household to part of the unobserved economy? Baby-sitting may be safely in the household economy, but if the formalized neighborhood exchange were of trade and professional services (plumbing, electrical work, legal or medical advice), would the same apply? These exchanges would fall outside definitions of the hidden economy that are based on concealed factor incomes (as both the IR and the CSO definitions are) but might be thought to come within Feige's definition, which focuses on unmeasured activity rather than unmeasured income. The question of how to treat such exchange activi-

---

[1] This source does not use the word "specific," but it has been used by the combined taxing authorities (the Inland Revenue and the Customs and Excise) in a definition contained in a note submitted to the Keith Committee on Enforcement Powers, February 1981.

ties acquires extra importance in the light of Gershuny and Pahl's (1980) arguments that the growth of the self-service economy will facilitate the "domestication" of the many production activities that might previously have taken place in the formal economy.

One manner to distinguish "barter exchanges" from "neighborly assistance" would be to define as economic activity any activity that draws upon an individual's primary employment skills and takes place or confers a benefit outside his or her own household. This definition captures the logic of regarding barter activities as income substitutes but would pose problems of measurement and of tax compliance enforcement. More particularly, it would capture neither the exchange activities of those with multiple skills nor unskilled activities.

In the longer run it would seem preferable to focus hidden economy definitions and measurement on concealed incomes and expenditures, with non-monetary exchange activities being assessed through measures of the social or household economy such as time use surveys.

The CSO and discrepancy measures of the hidden economy

Although the CSO adopts the broader definition of the hidden economy, their estimate of its size is less than half that of the IR. The CSO measure is based on discrepancies between the income and expenditure measures of national income and puts the hidden economy at 2–3% of gross domestic product (GDP), whereas the IR, making "plausible guesstimates" of the amount of tax evasion by self-employed and employed individuals, suggested a figure of 7.5%, which has been more recently modified to a range of 6–8%. This and the following sections set out and examine the basis of each of these assessments.

Income estimates of national income are generally lower than expenditure estimates, and this discrepancy is conventionally held to reflect the fact that although some income may be unreported or unrecorded, much of the expenditure it generates will show up in official statistics. Although the CSO have always accordingly increased the income measure by including an estimate of unreported income, it is only since recent controversies about the size of the hidden economy that they acknowledged this adjustment and published some details about it. The CSO view is that "the expenditure estimate of G.D.P. is regarded as an unbiased estimate of the value of all transactions apart from some illegal, immoral or sensitive items...In contrast, the income measure is dependent to a large extent on income data supplied to the Inland Revenue and it is possible that the levels of reported income may fall short of true income level" (Macafee, 1980, p. 85).

The crude income–expenditure discrepancy, known as the initial residual difference, is divided into three elements by the CSO:

1 underreporting of factor incomes,
2 timing errors that arise when transactions are recorded in different time periods by the different parties to the transactions, and
3 other estimating errors.

After the adjustment for the underreporting of factor incomes is made, the latter two errors are together termed the residual error. Table 7.1 sets out the magnitude of the initial residual difference since 1969 as well as the amount assumed to be unrecorded incomes and residual errors.

The results are surprising. In six of the twelve years for which data are given, the crude discrepancy (the initial residual difference) is less than 1% of GDP, and only from 1974 to 1976 does it rise over 2%. In absolute and relative terms it has fallen annually since the peak of 3.5% in 1976. It is clear from the data that the initial residual difference is partitioned between unrecorded income and residual error in such a way as to leave a fairly constant trend estimate of unrecorded income, with residual error picking up the variations about the trend. The CSO are assuming that in the 1960's and early 1970's unrecorded incomes grew up to around 2% of national income but have remained at that level since then.

The SSRC Working Group (1981, paragraph 2.1) expressed considerable skepticism about discrepancy measures of the hidden economy, and these data support that skepticism since they are quite different from previous, even quite recent, discrepancy-based measures of unrecorded income. The residual errors shown for 1978–80 in Table 7.1 are one and a quarter times the size of those published in the national accounts a few months ago; the new residual error for 1978 is a negative £887 million compared to the positive figure of £1,240 million that I cited two years ago (O'Higgins, 1980, Table 1). Nor is the variability of estimates a new phenomenon. I previously recorded (O'Higgins, 1980, p. 9) three different estimates given by the CSO in the space of six months. The variation in the estimates clouds any attempt to use the discrepancy even as a rough indicator of growth or contraction in the relative size of the hidden economy. Two years ago the data suggested rapid growth in the hidden economy during the 1970's, from less than 1% of national income in 1971 to almost 3% in 1978; the new data, as noted in the preceding, give a much more static impression. It is difficult to say whether this reflects the wisdom of hindsight or a statistician's tendency to prefer smooth data series!

Although the adjustment for unrecorded income is based largely on

Table 7.1. *The hidden economy and the income–expenditure discrepancy in the national accounts*

Year	GDP (E) £m	Initial residual difference £m	Initial residual difference Percentage of GDP	Unrecorded income £m	Unrecorded income Percentage of GDP	Residual error £m	Residual error Percentage of GDP
1969	39,667	150	0.38	466	1.17	−316	−0.80
1970	43,574	40	0.09	537	1.23	−497	−1.14
1971	49,490	1,010	2.04	578	1.17	432	0.87
1972	55,347	200	0.36	924	1.67	−724	−1.31
1973	64,347	160	0.25	1,236	1.92	−1,076	−1.67
1974	74,661	1,670	2.24	1,407	1.88	263	0.35
1975	94,475	2,550	2.70	1,830	1.94	720	0.76
1976	111,585	3,920	3.51	2,215	1.99	1,705	1.53
1977	126,943	2,530	1.99	2,496	1.97	34	0.03
1978	145,304	2,360	1.62	3,247	2.23	−887	−0.61
1979	166,464	1,330	0.80	3,754	2.26	−2,424	−1.46
1980	193,488	1,040	0.54	3,652	1.89	−2,612	−1.35

Source: GDP from *National Income and Expenditure, 1981 edition* (HMSO, 1981), Table 1.2. Other data from CSO, telephone conversation, April 1982.

the trend size of the initial residual difference, "advice from other government departments, such as the Inland Revenue, and evidence from production accounts also contribute to the estimation of missing factor incomes" (Macafee, 1980, p. 85). In fact, the CSO, in conjunction with the IR, makes educated guesstimates of unrecorded income by type of earner each year. Examples of this sectorial breakdown of unrecorded income are given for a number of recent years in Table 7.2.

The data indicate that over three-quarters of unrecorded income is assumed to arise in self-employment compared to one-fifth from employment income (or "moonlighting").

Within the categories of the self-employed, the construction industry, as might be expected, is assumed to harbor the highest levels of evasion. It accounts for approximately one-quarter of the total estimate of unrecorded income, which implies that hidden income is over one-third the size of recorded income in that industry. It may be noted that this estimate, unlike the others, is partly based on a production account for the industry and may therefore be rather more accurate than usual.

Overall, therefore, the discrepancy method does not produce any confident or consistent estimate of unrecorded income. Even if con-

179

Table 7.2. *Estimates of unrecorded income by type of earner*

	1971	1974	1977
	As percentage of total unrecorded income		
Self-employment income			
Forestry and fishing	0.2	0.4	0.3
Manufacturing	2.9	3.5	4.7
Construction	27.0	18.1	20.4
Transport and communication	2.0	1.7	3.7
Distribution	8.8	6.5	12.1
Insurance, banking, etc.	1.6	1.6	3.9
Other services	7.9	8.0	13.0
Professions	4.5	3.6	5.8
Unallocated	18.4	16.6	14.6
Total self-employment income	73.5	60.1	78.2
Wages and salaries	20.9	12.8	20.9
Company profits	5.7	27.1	0.9
	As percentage of recorded sectoral income		
Self-employment income	7.9	12.1	23.5
Wages and salaries	0.3	0.4	0.8
Company profits	0.4	4.1	0.2

sistent figures were produced, however, they would almost certainly be underestimates since the method makes the implausible assumption that the expenditure measure of national income is accurate. Insofar as expenditures are in fact underestimated, the amount of unrecorded income is greater than the discrepancy method reveals. At best, discrepancy measures are only indicators of the trend in the growth of the unobserved economy.

The Inland Revenue's not implausible broad judgment

The most frequently quoted estimate of the unobserved economy in the United Kingdom is the 7.5% of the GNP figure suggested as "not implausible" (House of Commons, 1979) by Sir William Pile, the former Chairman of the United Kingdom's Board of Inland Revenue. His successor, Sir Lawrence Airey (House of Commons, 1980, Q4637 and QQ4658–60, 1981, 1982) has successively accepted this figure, put forward a range of 6–8%, and most recently suggested the lower part of the 6–8% range as an estimate of the magnitude of the U.K. unobserved economy. This series of estimates reflects judgments made in the IR about the level and frequency of non-reporting by the self-employed and the employed, judgments that presumably reflect IR experience in administering the tax system.

The basis of the IR assessment was to calculate for various suggested magnitudes of the hidden economy the implied level of unreported income for each member of the working population. On this basis, a hidden economy of 15% implied an average annual level of under-reporting of £720 per member of the working population in March 1979. This figure was judged to be implausibly high by Sir William Pile (House of Commons, 1979). It was, however, thought to be not implausible to assume that each self-employed person underreported £1,000 each year and that perhaps one in four or one in five of employees had undeclared second incomes of an annual average of £1,000. These two assumptions produced aggregated underreporting of about £2 billion and £6 billion, respectively, and if some allowance is made for evasion by companies, underreporting of interest payments, and so on, a total of £9 billion or 7.5% of national income is within the bounds of possibility.

If the IR method and assumptions are applied to current data on the U.K. economy, it suggests an underground economy of £15 billion, or average annual underreporting of around £1,750 by each self-employed person and one-quarter of employees.

If these assumptions are compared to the CSO estimates based on discrepancy measures of the hidden economy, it becomes clear that the major difference between the estimates is due to the assumption made about moonlighting. Both the CSO and the IR assume that under-reporting by the self-employed generates a hidden economy of about 2% of national income each year. The CSO then assumes that hidden income from employment, such as undeclared tips, adds a further 0.5% but treats moonlighting – working for an undeclared second income – as income from self-employment. So whereas the IR estimate implies that moonlighting by employed persons generates a hidden economy of 5%, the CSO estimate makes no specific provision for this category of un-observed activity. Although Sir Lawrence Airey has sought to lessen the impression of a large difference of views between the CSO and the IR by arguing that much of the difference is because different phenomena are being measured (House of Commons, 1981, Q2004), this major divergence on the amount of moonlighting is in fact the main explana-tion for the difference, and it is presumably susceptible to more accurate measurement.

Existing data suggest that less than 10% of the working population have second jobs (Alden, 1978), which is difficult to reconcile with the much higher IR assumptions since at least some of this income is re-

181

ported. What is, of course, difficult to assess is how accurate these data are: If those who do not report secondary employment income also respond negatively to survey questions on whether they have second jobs – or refuse to respond to surveys – the formal data are of little use. This point is discussed further when we examine the microdata analysis of income–expenditure divergences.

Compliance measures of tax evasion

The SSRC Working Group took the view that the Taxpayers Compliance Measurement Program (TCMP) carried out by the U.S. Internal Revenue Service "provides by far the most firmly-based figures of hidden economic activity at present available" (SSRC, 1981, paragraph 2.1). Under current British law a full TCMP cannot be carried out since the IR does not have powers of random audit. Tax inspectors may only question a taxpayer's return of income if they have cause to be dissatisfied. A further obstacle to using a TCMP in the United Kingdom is that there is no equivalent to the American Exact Match File to aid in assessing the extent of hidden economic activity.

The TCMP estimates of unreported income, however, provide an interesting contrast to the U.K. estimates reported in Table 7.2. Table 7.3 sets out the TCMP estimates and calculates the amount of underreporting that would be implied if the estimates were valid for the United Kingdom. The TCMP estimated underreporting of self-employment income at 36–40% in the United States in 1976, compared to the CSO estimate of 23.5% for the United Kingdom in 1977. With respect to employment income, the TCMP estimated underreporting to be between 2 and 3%, which is appreciably higher than the 0.8% in the CSO estimate but much lower than the figure of about 8% implied in the IR procedure.

The TCMP showed an overall reporting rate for individual income of 92–94% in the United States; sectorial differences in the U.K. reported economy cause the overall reporting rate aggregated over the TCMP sectorial estimates to be rather lower, at 88.6–91.2%. The level of non-reported individual income then turns out to be between £13 billion and £17 billion, or between 7.5 and 10% of national income in 1979.

Obviously this application to the U.K. data of U.S. data proves nothing about the magnitude of the underground economy in the United Kingdom. None of the reporting rates are intuitively implausible, however, so the figures emphasize the importance of obtaining more accurate estimates of the frequency and level of underreporting of the various types of income.

Table 7.3. *An application of TCMP estimates of unreported individual income to the United Kingdom, 1979 (billion pounds)*

Type of income	Reported income, 1979	TCMP estimate of reporting rate (%)	TCMP, implied reportable income	TCMP, implied non-reporting income
Self-employment	15.3	60–64	23.9–25.5	8.6–10.2
Wages and salaries,	96.6	97–98	98.6–99.6	2.0–3.0
Rents, dividends, and interest	10.4	84–92	11.3–12.4	0.9–2.0
Pensions	8.1	84–88	9.2–9.6	1.1–1.5
Capital gains	0.6	78–83	0.7–9.8	0.1–0.2
Total	131.0	88.6–91.2	143.7–147.9	12.7–16.9

Source: U.K. income data from *National Income and Expenditure,* 1980 edition (HMSO, 1980); TCMP reporting rate estimates from *Estimates of Income Unreported on Individual Income Tax Returns* (U.S. Internal Revenue Service, 1979), Table 2.

Although a full TCMP is not possible in the United Kingdom, the IR has recently begun a more formal attempt at compliance measurement in the case of self-employment income (House of Commons, 1982). A random sample of 5,500 Schedule D (self-employment income) cases, representing about 1 in 300 of all such cases, was drawn at the end of 1981. Each district inspector of taxes was asked to examine the files relating to those cases from his district and to suggest

a the likelihood that an investigation of the return would show an understatement of liable income and
b the extent of the justification for starting an investigation.

Table 7.4 sets out the results of this investigation, which, it must be emphasized, were based solely on the judgment of the tax inspectors. It shows that it was thought that investigation had a probable yield in one in five cases, with a possible yield in a further two in five cases. In three out of ten cases there were plenty of grounds on which a formal investigation could legally begin, whereas a further four in ten provided some grounds. Overall, then, six in ten cases had a possible or probable yield, whereas seven in ten gave some or plenty of grounds for investigation. At present, only 3% of self-employment income returns are investigated each year.

It is now intended to test the validity and accuracy of these judgments by actual investigation of a selection of those cases where the predicted

Table 7.4. *Preliminary results of U.K. Inland Revenue self-employment income compliance measurement study (N = 5,500)*

Predicted result of investigation	Assessed degree of justification for investigation
Probable yield, 22%	Plenty, 31%
Possible yield, 42%	Some, 39%
Nothing of consequence, 37%	None, 29%

Source: House of Commons, 1982.

result is a possible or probable yield and there is thought to be some or plenty of justification for an investigation. The results of this validation exercise will provide the best "hard" data so far on the actual levels of tax evasion by the self-employed.

It will be remembered that the IR guesstimate of a hidden economy of 7.5% of national income implied underreporting of £1,750 by each self-employed person in 1981. If this new assessment that two in five of the self-employed have no understatement of any consequence is correct, the remaining 60% needed to have average underreporting of about £3,000 each in order to maintain the overall self-employed contribution to that IR guesstimate. For what it is worth, my judgment is that £3,000 is at the top end of the plausible range of average understatement.

Household survey evidence on income–expenditure discrepancies

While expressing considerable skepticism about hidden economy estimates based on discrepancies in the national accounts, the SSRC Working Group considered that the matching of income and expenditure information at the level of individual households could be a useful way to measure participation in the hidden economy and to quantify the value of such participation (SSRC, 1981, paragraph 2.1). More generally, discrepancies between the reported income and the expenditure or living standards of particular households at the very least suggest the possibility of hidden economic activity generating unreported income.

Such a discrepancy has most often been noticed in the case of the self-employed. The Royal Commission on the Distribution of Income and Wealth (1979), for example, contrasted the living standards of the employed and self-employed in the United Kingdom in 1975. Their findings show that the self-employed appear to have a significantly higher standard of living than the employed – and the gap increases if the comparison is performed for data standardized by income and age. It is possible that the discrepancy could be explained suggesting that the self-employed tend to have more wealth that they use to purchase durable goods, but there is no evidence to support this contention.

This divergence in living standards led me in previous papers to compare the expenditure of self-employed households with that of employed households with similar levels of income (Dilnot and Morris, 1981, pp. 64–72). The results of that analysis may be summarized briefly.

The database for the comparison was the Family Expenditure Survey (FES) for each of the years 1971–77. The FES is a continuous, multi-purpose income and expenditure survey with an annual effective sample of about 7,000 households (about a 70% response rate). Expenditure details are collected by means of detailed diaries of spending kept over a fourteen-day period. Income data reflects a mixture of weekly or monthly and annual data.

Media comment had suggested that the self-employed appeared to be able to spend higher proportions of income than other households, and the initial analysis of the data bore this out. In each of the seven years for which data were examined, self-employed households had higher expenditure–income ratios, both in general and at particular income levels, than employee-headed households in a variety of occupational groups. In particular, it appeared that the discrepancy was greatest for self-employed households reporting relatively low levels of income.

Closer examinations of the data revealed, however, that although the measure of employment income was essentially current income, self-employment income was measured using the most recent twelve-month period for which figures were available. The consequential lag in the data was enough to explain most of the discrepancy: Once the data were "corrected" by a rather approximate adjustment for this bias, the self-employed no longer appeared to be out of line in their expenditure–income ratio.

This analysis left four important questions unanswered. Do the self-employed (and other households) simply exclude any expenditure financed by unreported income from their reported expenditure? Does participation for a two-week period in the FES have a tendency to cause a temporary regularization of spending (and perhaps earning) patterns in households? Is participation in the hidden economy a factor behind the 30% non-response rate in the FES – and the 40% non-response rate of the self-employed? And, lastly, regardless of whether the reported expenditure–income ratio of the self-employed is any different from that for other households, do the divergences between expenditure and income among households in general indicate the presence of unreported

185

income? Unfortunately, only this final question has received any empirical analysis.

Dilnot and Morris (1981, p. 58) screened an FES microdata file for 1977 to isolate those households whose incomes and expenditures were discrepant. (They had previously adjusted self-employment income for the lag mentioned previously.) They sought to "trap" out of the analysis those households where income–expenditure discrepancies might have had explanations other than hidden economic activity. For example, they excluded from their lower bound estimate households headed by pensioners or by somebody temporarily away from work since they argued that excesses of expenditure over income were plausibly explained either by the running down of assets or the temporary incurring of debt. These households were included in their upper bound estimate of the size of the hidden economy.

After these and other traps they then assumed that any household whose expenditure exceeded its income by more than 20% (subject to a minimum of £3 weekly) had unreported income. The lower bound estimate then suggested 9.6% of respondent households had an average weekly discrepancy of £31, leading to an estimate of £3,200 million, or 2.3% of GNP, in 1977 for unreported income. The higher bound estimate suggested figures of 14.8% of households with an average weekly discrepancy of £30; this implied unreported income of £4,200, or 3.0%, of 1977 GNP.

Dilnot and Morris (1981, p. 58) state explicitly that their purpose is to cast a skeptical light on high estimates of the hidden economy. Three features of their analysis induce a counter-skepticism about their relatively low estimates: The nature of the traps used, the choice of a 20% discrepancy as the cutoff point, and what they admit to be the implausible assumption that non-respondents to the FES participate in the unobserved economy to no greater an extent than survey respondents.

Dilnot and Morris (1981, p. 65) discuss a number of non-hidden economy explanations for expenditure income divergences and then state that "where any of these reasons appeared a significant course of entry to the black economy population, we developed systematic traps to exclude such households, but when the trap might be too strong we included it in our lower-bound estimates but not in the upper bound." They do not, however, give any precise listing of the range of traps used, nor of the impact of the empirical data of the operation of each trap. One particular trap they mention is especially problematic: the exclusion of households with high expenditures because of an unusual major purchase. It might equally be suggested that such major purchases (e.g., consumer durables or holidays) are particularly likely to be

Table 7.5. *Size of underground economy (%) on alternative assumptions about FES non-respondents, 1977*

Percentage of non-respondents assumed to have unreported income	Average weekly amount assumed to be unreported by FES non-respondents			

A. *Dilnot and Morris lower-bound estimate*

	£31	£41	£51	£62
9.6	2.3[a]	2.5	2.7	3.0
14.4	2.6	2.9	3.1	3.4
19.2	3.0	3.3	3.6	3.8
25.0	3.4	3.7	4.1	4.4
50.0	5.2	5.7	6.2	6.7

B. *Dilnot and Morris upper-bound estimate*

	£30	£40	£50	£60
14.8	3.0[a]	3.3	3.6	3.9
22.2	3.5	3.9	4.4	4.8
33.3	4.1	4.8	5.5	6.2
50.0	5.1	6.2	7.2	8.2

[a] Dilnot and Morris's (1981) estimates.
Notes: Dilnot and Morris assumed that the 30% of FES non-respondents had the same likelihood to participate in the hidden economy (9.6% on their lower estimate) and the same average under reporting (e.g., £31) as the 70% who responded. The table shows the result of assuming various different likelihoods and amounts for the non-respondents.
Source: Adapted from Dilnot and Morris, 1981, Table 2.

financed by unreported income, being in the nature of windfall spending from windfall income.

The decision to view only discrepancies of over 20% of income as indicative of hidden economic activity was "pragmatic": "At higher levels we seemed to be excluding households which seemed on the basis of all other information potential black economy candidates while 10 to 15 per cent brought in groups which obviously were not" (Dilnot and Morris, 1981, p. 66). Although it is clear that a lower cutoff would have had less effect on the estimated level of underground activity than on the numbers assumed to be involved, one is given no information on the sensitivity of the results to a lower cutoff nor on the factors that make some households "obviously" not "black economy candidates."

The third objection is quantitatively probably the most serious. Dilnot and Morris assumed that the 30% of households who do not respond to the FES had similar average levels and frequencies of unobserved activity as the 70% who did, despite the fact, for example, that the response rate is lower among the self-employed than among employees. This assumption led the chairman of the IR to say (House of Commons, 1981, Q2205) with respect to their resulting estimate, "I personally would not put a lot of weight on that because it is derived from the Family Expenditure Survey and the response to that survey is about 70 percent, and the 30 percent who do not respond are atypical of the 70 percent who do respond, and you have room for the black economy hidden away there."

Table 7.5 sets out the results Dilnot and Morris would have obtained on a variety of alternative assumptions about the hidden economic activity of FES non-respondents. For example, their lower bound estimate of 2.3% is increased to 3.0% if it is assumed that non-respondents are twice as likely to have unreported income, and it goes up to 3.8% if it is further assumed that they have twice as much of such income. If it is assumed that half of the non-respondents have hidden income of twice the value of that of respondents; the lower end upper bound estimates become 6.7 and 8.2%, respectively.

It is clear, therefore, that the treatment of non-respondents affects the results significantly, even if reservations concerning the analysis carried out on respondents are left aside. Even relatively cautious assumptions about non-respondents would raise the Dilnot and Morris lower bound estimate to around 4% of GNP.

Monetary aggregates and the hidden economy

Three categories of approaches based on the analysis of monetary aggregates have been used in attempts to examine the U.K. unobserved economy. They are the relative demand for large- and small-denomination notes method, the currency–deposit ratio method, and Feige's transactions method. The general skepticism in the United Kingdom about the value of this class of methods is expressed by the SSRC Working Group: "The problems of identifying stable demand for money functions are well known and have already been the subject of a considerable amount of research. It seemed extremely unlikely that the pattern of residual errors in such relationships could be reliably ascribed to the Hidden Economy" (SSRC, 1981, paragraph 2.1). The results of using the three methods in the United Kingdom are reviewed briefly next.

United Kingdom

The big-bill method

The hypothesis underlying the "big-bill" method appears to be that hidden economic transactions require payment in cash and that a growth in the demand for large-denomination notes is particularly indicative of hidden activity, since formal economy transactions involving large payments would be conducted by check or credit card. One suspects that the hypothesis has its origin in anecdotes about self-employed tradesmen with wads of large-denomination notes in their back pockets.

In a previous paper I suggested that inflation had "substitution" as well as "nominal income" effects on currency holding; that is, that people do not simply increase the number of notes they carry to counteract inflation but that they substitute larger for smaller denomination notes in order to carry an approximately constant number of notes over time. This hypothesis was investigated using U.K. data for the period 1972–8. The analysis indicated that the number of large-denomination notes had increased by less than the substitution effect hypothesis would explain and consequently concluded that the large-denomination note hypothesis was not an especially useful approach to measure the hidden economy (O'Higgins, 1980, pp. 17–21). Subsequent researchers have reached similar conclusions (Macafee, 1980, p. 85; Feige, 1981, p. 207).

Currency–deposit ratios

It can be argued that much of the current interest in measuring the unobserved economy in developed economies stemmed from Gutmann's (1977) controversial 1977 estimate that subterranean transactions were worth 10% of measured GNP. Gutmann assumed that over time the increased used of checks and credit cards would cause a relative decline in the demand for currency. Yet, he argued, the ratio of currency to narrow money supply, M1, had consistently grown in the United States since 1961. By assuming the 1939–41 level of the ratio to be normal and arguing that "the difference between this and recent values of the ratio may be taken as a measure of the amount of currency held for illegal purposes" (p. 27), he estimated the amount of currency fueling the unobserved economy, and on the assumption that the amount of economic activity generated by one dollar was similar in both the legal and subterranean economies, he concluded that the subterranean economy was at least 10.4% of recorded GNP.

The U.S. debate on Gutmann's methodology was reviewed and his method applied to U.K. data (O'Higgins, 1980, pp. 11–16). Table 7.6

189

Table 7.6. *Currency in circulation and the money supply, 1963–81*

Year	Currency,[a] £m	Currency as percentage of MI[b]	Currency as percentage of M*[c]
1963	2,254	32.5	21.5
1964	2,353	32.1	21.0
1965	2,512	33.2	21.0
1966	2,685	34.5	21.1
1967	2,780	34.4	20.6
1968	2,856	33.8	19.3
1969	2,922	34.7	19.3
1970	3,149	35.0	19.5
1971	3,435	33.7	19.0
1972	3,900	32.8	17.4
1973	4,299	33.3	15.3
1974	4,800	35.5	14.7
1975	5,511	35.5/33.9	15.6
1976	6,328	33.8	16.5
1977	7,217	33.7	17.4
1978	8,422	32.8	17.6
1979	9,416	32.9	17.4
1980	9,935	33.1	15.9
1981	10,473	31.7	14.4

[a] Notes and coins in circulation with the public; the annual figures (in all columns) are based on simple averages of the unadjusted figures for March, June, September, and December of each year.
[b] MI is currency plus U.K. private sector sterling sight deposits. From 1963 to 1968 they include 40% of transit items to make them comparable to later data. A large break occurs in the MI series in 1975; the two figures given in the table indicate the approximate magnitude of the break.
[c] M* is MI plus U.K. private sector sterling time deposits.
Source: Bank of England Quarterly Bulletin, September 1970 to March 1982.

updates the data in that analysis and provides figures for the ratio of currency both to M1 and to M*, a wider money supply concept that includes M1 plus U.K. private sector sterling time deposits. Gutmann was criticized for not using this latter ratio in his analysis.[2]

The currency–M1 ratio provides no support, on Gutmann's assumptions, for the hypothesis of hidden economy growth in the United Kingdom. The data in Table 7.6 show slight upward trends during the 1946–70 Labour government, a gentle S-shaped curve during the

[2] Gorman, as quoted in Ross (1978).

following years of Conservative rule, and a light drop again from 1977 onward.

The wider ratio of currency to M* shows a fairly steady decline during the 1960's and early 1970's; by 1974 it was only about two-thirds as great as in 1963, which is consistent with the hypothesis of a declining relative demand for currency. From 1974 the ratio rose to a peak in 1978 but has since resumed its decline.

To seek to replicate Gutmann and reach conclusions about the size or trend of the hidden economy on the basis of data such as these and without setting out clear assumptions about the reasons people hold currency would not even merit the description. As presented, the data tell us nothing about the hidden economy.

A more elaborate attempt to relate the demand for currency to the hidden economy in the United Kingdom was recently made by Matthews (1981, pp. 7–20). It was assumed that an individual's preferred currency–deposit ratio was governed by "certain qualitative uses and functions which are themselves responsive to economic variables" (p. 7). It was also rather more implausibly assumed that decisions about currency and deposit holdings were independent of other portfolio decisions.

The choice of currency or deposit then depend upon the quality factors that affected each form of holding. The quality of deposits is increased by the rate of inflation and the rate of interest payable and is also assumed to increase over time due to increases in the efficiency with which they can be used for payments. Consequently, it is hypothesized that the current–deposit ratio will be negatively related to these variables.

Currency, however, has "anonymity," a valuable quality for hidden economy transactions. It was assumed that this quality would be more highly valued as average income taxes on households and average sales taxes increased. It was also, however, assumed that some people, rather than having a combination of recorded and moonlighting income, might choose to specialize in the hidden economy while being unemployed. Therefore, the currency–deposit ratio was predicted to be positively related to unemployment and to average household income and sales tax rates.

The analysis took the logarithmic form of an ordinary least squares regression of the currency–deposit ratio on these six variables and recorded national income [as measured by GDP (E)] for each quarter from 1973 quarter 3, to 1979, quarter 2.

Interpretations of the results will differ. Matthews argued that "given the crudeness of our black economy variables it is heartening that two out of three variables appear correctly signed and significant" (p. 13).

The results indicated that the interest rate and inflation variables were insignificant; the time trend variable is consistently significant but positive when it was hypothesized to be negative. The sales tax variable was usually insignificant (and perversely signed when significant). However, both the unemployment and the income tax variables were correctly signed and significant.

Since the dependent variable was a ratio of two variables, each of which had certain qualities hypothesized, the failure of part of the model casts doubt about whether the model-based interpretation of the "successful" results is correct. For example, the failure of the rate of interest to have a significant impact on the currency–deposit ratio may indicate that the assumption that currency–deposit ratio and holding decisions are independent of wider portfolio decisions is incorrect. In this case, changes in deposit holdings (and thus in the currency–deposit ratios) might have nothing to do with the hidden economy qualities of currency.

Matthews calculates hidden economy magnitudes from the parameters of the unemployment and income tax variables in the modeled equations. These produce an average lower bound estimate (excluding the unemployment rate variable) of 3% of recorded GNP and an average upper estimate of 10.9%. The model therefore suggests that unemployment generates considerably more hidden economic activity than does taxation.

Matthews's lower and higher bound estimates of the magnitude of unobserved economic activity as a percentage of reported GDP assuming a zero hidden economy in 1973 are displayed in Table 7.7.

As indicated in the preceding, I would argue that their validity is weakened by the questions concerning the interpretation of the results of the model from which they are derived.

Table 7.7. *Matthews's estimates of unobserved activity, percentage of GDP*

	Lower (%)	Higher (%)
1974	0.5	0.8
1975	2.7	6.5
1976	3.4	10.8
1977	3.1	11.5
1978	2.3	10.6
1979	3.3	11.0

Source: Matthews (1981).

Transactions analysis of the unobserved economy

The transactions approach pioneered by Feige (1979, 1981) for the United States and since applied to a number of countries is too well known to need any description. As with Gutmann's approach, one's reaction depends upon one's view about the interpretation of the relationship between monetary aggregates and real economic activity.

Feige's results for the United Kingdom show the unobserved sector growing from 0% of the observed sector in 1960 to around 15% in 1979. Within these two decades seven main periods can be identified, three of which show sharp growth, two sharp declines, and two relative stability. The periods are displayed in Table 7.8.

In the latter half of the 1970's, when the British economy (and society) was particularly troubled, the unobserved sector was relatively static according to Feige's (1981, Table 3) results.

There are two aspects of Feige's results I would like to discuss to lead to the conclusion of this chapter: first, the relationship of these results to other evidence examined here and, second, the interpretation of Feige's results in the context of other data about the British economy during these periods.

The evidence is varied: Dilnot and Morris and the CSO present the lowest estimates at around 3%; my reworking of Dilnot and Morris's results would suggest that their analysis makes anything less than 4% implausible; the IR is now suggesting 6–7%; the Matthews upper bound estimates are of the order of 11% for 1979, whereas Feige suggests 15%.

Only three estimates, those by the CSO, Matthews, and Feige, present figures that allow examination of trends in the hidden economy, and the CSO evidence has two versions: that by Macafee and that summarized in the more recent data presented in Table 7.1 of this chapter. The Macafee results for the initial residual difference show trends not

Table 7.8. *Feige's estimates of the growth of unobserved sector, United Kingdom*

1960–1,	growth, from	0 to 6%
1963–6,	growth, from	6 to 12%
1969–71,	decline, from	12 to 8%
1971–4,	growth, from	8 to 22%
1974–5,	decline, from	22 to 15%

Source: Feige (1981).

unlike those presented by Feige, though of very different orders of magnitude. Both show a minor peak in the latter part of the 1960's, relatively rapid growth during the first part of the 1970's, a major peak in 1974, and comparative constancy in the second half of that decade. The more recent CSO estimates shift the peak of the national income discrepancy measure to 1976, with rapid growth from 1973 to 1976 and decline since. The Matthews data show rapid growth from 1974 to 1976 and constancy since.

Two points therefore emerge: First, each measure shows relatively rapid hidden economy growth in the early 1970's although they disagree on whether the growth period was 1971–4 or 1973–6; second, each measure shows no relative growth in the hidden economy during the latter part of the 1970's (although this was the period in which public criticism of high tax rates was most voluble).

The divergence between the measures concerning the timing of hidden economy growth in the early 1970's may be simply the result of lagged effects some measures do not capture. But the differences make it difficult to comment confidently on the causes of such hidden economy growth as there may be. The point is best illustrated by reference to Feige's model and results.

Feige contends that "even in a fundamentally healthy economy, shifts from the observed to the unobserved sector can induce the perception of declining real income, rising unemployment, reduced productivity and higher prices" (p. 206). When discussing his results, he observes that "they suggest that the massive recession and soaring inflation recorded in the mid 1970's might be partly explicable in terms of a statistical illusion induced by the growth of the unobserved sector" (p. 211).

However, the periods his results identify with a growing unobserved sector are in fact those when official statistics show the economy to be performing relatively well.

The three periods of fastest economic growth in the United Kingdom since the 1950's were 1959–61, 1963–5, and 1970–3. Since 1975 unemployment has been measured at 2% or less only in 1960–1 and 1964–6. In the 1970's the unemployment rate was as its lowest in 1973 and 1974. Each of these periods is identified in Feige's results as a period of rapid growth in the unobserved sector.

One further point about the period from 1975 to 1979 is worth making. The economy was, formally at least, subject to considerable government regulation during this period. A "social contract" restricted earnings increases, and various forms of price regulation and control were toughened up. If the hidden economy is indeed a safety valve from regulation, one would have expected it to grow during this period. Yet none of the measures indicate that it did so.

These comments are obviously not intended to "prove" anything conclusively. Lagged effects may be distorting the relationship between the "real" hidden economy and our measures of it. We are still at an early stage in attempting to measure the unobserved sector and in due course may establish measures that indicate that the standard theory (that the size of the hidden economy is positively related to high taxes, low "official" growth, high unemployment, and inflation) is correct.

The fact that the data are, as discussed here, more compatible with the hypothesis that the hidden economy grows during periods when the formal economy is tight should, however, suggest caution in presenting the standard theory, which focuses on the supply conditions that might act as incentives to hidden economic activity. Viewed from the demand side, a positive relationship between the formal and the hidden economies is less surprising. When the formal economy is doing well, people have more disposable income with which to pay others to do some of the classic hidden economy activities, such as home improvements and extensions. They may also have less time for household activities such as do-it-yourself work and, thus, be more likely to employ someone to do it for them. Demand side explanations such as these require further attention if the causes of changing levels of hidden economic activity are to be properly understood.

Conclusions

The research of the past two years does little to disprove the old equation that number of opinions equals number of economists plus 1. The size of the hidden economy has been variously estimated as between 2.5 and 15%; I remain content with a 5% guess. Two points of agreement appear to emerge with respect to trends in the size of the hidden economy: that it grew during the early 1970's and that it was static during the later 1970's. These trends appear, however, to conflict with a number of the most commonly advanced hypotheses concerning the causes of growth in the unobserved economy. Skepticism is therefore still justified about the origins of the "footprints in the sands" of the formal economy.

CHAPTER 8

The underground economy in the Federal Republic of Germany: a preliminary assessment

ENNO LANGFELDT

In recent years, increased interest has been expressed in the underground economy of the Federal Republic of Germany. This unobserved sector of economic activity has been featured in numerous newspaper articles and has become a concern to institutions engaged in economic policy. In its 1977 annual report, the Deutsche Bundesbank stated (p. 23) that "cash payment is unequestionably gaining ground in some fields, notably in the 'grey areas' of business activity where services are rendered without taxes and contributions to the social security system and are settled in cash." Similarly, the German Council of Economic Advisers (Sachverstanndigenrat) (1980, paragraph 296; 1981, paragraph 373) stated that the growth of the "Schattenwirtschaft" indicates resistance against increasing tax burdens and excessive regulations.

To shed some more light on this neglected part of the German economy, this chapter attempts to estimate the size and the growth of the unobserved sector in Germany. After defining the phenomenon under study, we review the existing evidence on the German unobserved sector and present some new empirical evidence based on different methodologies that have been applied in other countries, especially in the United States.

Definitions

As a first step, one must make an effort to clarify the confusion in the literature resulting from different definitions. Terms like "subterranean" or "underground" may be misleading because they create the impression of illegal and immoral activities. Most authors (Feige, 1980; Frey, 1981; Tanzi, 1980) define the unobserved sector as a complement of the observed sector. It includes therefore all those economic activities that are not measured by the current official measurement system. The rather general definition naturally leaves room for different concepts. It seems therefore necessary to agree on some conventions, especially with respect to the measurement of the unobserved economy. They concern the use of a turnover or a value-added concept, the inclusion or exclusion of economic activities that are beyond the traditional national accounts framework, and the taxonomic classification of different aspects of unobserved activity.

Although it is sometimes more difficult to estimate the value added than the total transactions volume, it is useful to define unobserved activity in terms of the net use of resources or incomes generated. This concept is equivalent to the national accounts convention and the way in which economic policy targets are formulated. Questions concerning the evasion of sales taxes will however require a gross concept.

In the traditional national accounts framework, with the main exception of owner-occupied and rent-free accommodation, all private transactions involving goods and services that are not exchanged for money are excluded. This omission is due to valuation problems. There is widespread agreement among economists that the concept of production underlying the national accounts is too restrictive.[1] Limiting the concept of unobserved economic activity to one consistent with the national accounts framework neglects a very important and increasing sector of unobserved activity, the household economy. In spite of all existing valuation problems, this sector should be part of the analysis of the unobserved sector since otherwise an important possibility of substitution is neglected.

Most of the estimation methods employed to measure unobserved economic activity have relied on a single characteristic of the activity. The monetary approaches concentrate on the estimation of the *monetary* unobserved activities by subtracting observed monetary transactions from total monetary transactions. Other methods focus exclusively on the estimation of the *undeclared* income or the calculation of irregular *employment*. It is therefore not surprising that the estimates differ considerably since they concentrate on different aspects of the unobserved economy.

Review of the existing evidence on unobserved activities in Germany

The existing evidence on the German unobserved sector consists of the following:

1 Anecdotal evidence indicating in how many different forms the unobserved sector has developed in Germany.

[1] See I. A. Eisner (1978), Juster (1966), Kendrick (1979), and Nordhaus and Tobin (1972)

2 Estimates by the Craftsmen Association that the turnover of illicit work in the handicraft sector amounted to some DM 30 billion in 1978. This was roughly 10% of the total turnover in the handicraft sector. Hamer (1978) suspects that clandestine work in this branch is more likely to be of the order of 20%.

3 The observation that the amount of fines for illicit work has markedly increased from DM 1.4 million in 1976 to DM 3.7 million in 1980.

4 The conjecture that the vigorous increase of currency holdings in the late 1970's – as compared to gross national product (GNP) – can be partly attributed to the existence of the unobserved economy (Bundesbank, 1977, p. 23).

5 Estimates by the Ministry of Labor and the construction industry that illegal temporary employment in the construction sector includes some 200,000 persons.

6 Measures of the discrepancy between income reported to the tax authorities and income recorded in the national accounts.

The estimate by the Craftsmen Association is in gross terms. However, the interpretation of the figures creates problems since the price per unit of output in the unobserved sector is only 30% of the official price in the handicraft sector. It would therefore be necessary to establish whether the turnover estimates of illicit work are valued at official or actual prices.

According to Hamer (1979, p. 114), it would be appropriate to assume actual prices. This implies that since non-labor input is negligible, the unobserved value added in the handicraft sector is about 3% of GNP. Comparing this figure to the amount of fines for illicit work, it appears that only a small part of clandestine work is actually penalized. The increase in fines may be the result of both more intensive prosecution and a growing amount of illicit work.

Evidence concerning the increase in currency holdings in the late 1970's can largely be explained in terms of the low opportunity costs of holding currency (Langfeldt and Lehment, 1980). The average denomination value of notes in Germany has grown roughly in proportion to the price index. The proportion of large-denomination notes is relatively high as compared to the United States. However, the Netherlands and Switzerland exhibit a significantly higher proportion of large-denomination notes.[2]

The estimates of illegal employment in the construction sector are on the order of 20% of total official employment in this sector. However,

---

[2] The composition of bank note series in these countries in 1975 is shown by Fase and Nieuwkerk (1977, p. 84).

these figures are rather dubious as indicators of unobserved activity as it is not known whether these illegal workers were employed during the whole year. The value added created by illegal employment is recorded on the expenditure side of the national accounts; only their incomes are not reported to the tax and social security administration. Thus, the available evidence does not give a comprehensive estimate of the size and development of the German unobserved sector. Before presenting our own preliminary estimates of the unobserved sector, we show the results of the calculated discrepancy between income reported to the tax authorities and income in the national accounts because they might provide information about the development of tax evasion in Germany.

The discrepancy approach

This approach examines the discrepancy between the income reported to the tax authorities – adjusted for differences in the concepts of taxable income and national accounts income – and the independently estimated income from the national accounts statistics. A reconciliation of the two concepts in West Germany has been calculated by Petersen (1981) for the years 1961, 1965, 1968, 1971, and 1974 and is shown in Table 8.1. The results show that the discrepancy measure, which is the complement of total income reported to the fiscal authorities in relation to national income, shows a declining trend. The illegal underreporting of income decreased from 16.7% in 1961 to 4.8% in 1974. Looking at the separate results for the income of employees and other income, it

Table 8.1. *Discrepancy between income reported to tax authorities (adjusted for conceptual differences) and the national income (billions of DM)*

	1961	1965	1968	1971	1974
Adjusted income of employees reported to fiscal authorities	148.8 (91.9)	216.7 (92.1)	249.6 (91.8)	393.4 (96.4)	549.1 (97.9)
Adjusted other income reported to fiscal authorities	68.4 (70.3)	89.8 (72.8)	117.2 (79.2)	159.1 (87.0)	186.6 (88.1)
Adjusted total income reported to fiscal authorities	217.2 (83.3)	306.5 (85.5)	366.8 (87.4)	552.5 (93.5)	735.7 (95.2)

Note: Numbers in parentheses are percentage of national income.
Source: Petersen (1981, p. 30).

appears that taxation of employees covered by the pay-as-you-earn system leaves less room for underreporting than other incomes covered by the assessment procedure. This discrepancy of some 5% of national income in 1974 comes rather close to the results calculated for the United States (see Feige, 1980, p. 18).

This estimate should however be viewed with caution. The declining trend in non-compliance may be the result of changes in the measurement procedures for collecting both tax statistics and national income statistics. By definition, the discrepancy method measures only those incomes that are included in the national accounts but are not reported to the tax authorities. The discrepancy method does not provide a measure of the size of the unobserved sector; it can only give a hint as to the efficiency of the fiscal administration.

Some more comprehensive estimates of the monetary unobserved activity in Germany

To arrive at more comprehensive estimates of the size and growth of the German monetary unobserved sector, three different methods discussed in the international literature were applied to the German case:

1 simple currency–demand deposit ratio (Gutmann, 1977),
2 estimation of tax-induced currency holdings from a demand-for-money function (Tanzi, 1980), and
3 transactions method (Feige, 1979).

These methods, based on monetary information, only yield estimates of the monetary unobserved sector. They do not take account of barter activities. The results of the investigations by Kendrick (1979) and Eisner (1978) for the United States suggest that the non-monetary unobserved sector may be large and shows a dramatic growth relative to the official economy. Comparable estimates of the non-monetary unobserved sector in Germany are not available. We therefore concentrate exclusively on the monetary unobserved sector.

In addition to the methods based on monetary statistics, we also explore an estimation method based on labor market data that attempts to measure the labor force potential available for monetary as well as non-monetary unobserved activities.

The currency-ratio method

The currency–demand deposit ratio method when applied to the U.S. economy suggested an unobserved monetary economy of approximately

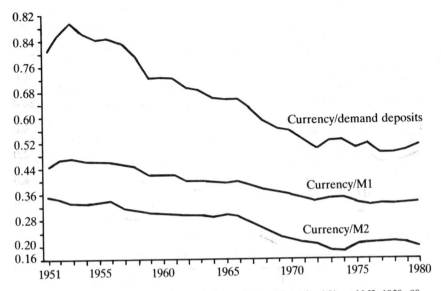

Figure 8.1. Development of currency relative to demand deposits, M1, and M2, 1950–80. (*Source:* Monthly report of the Deutsche Bundesbank, various issues, own calculations.)

10% of GNP. Moreover, the method suggested rapid growth of the monetary unobserved sector as the result of a rising ratio of currency to demand deposits (Gutmann, 1977).

Figure 8.1 shows that in Germany the ratio of currency to demand deposits actually *declined* sharply from 1951 to 1980. The ratios of currency to M1 and M2 show the same development. A change in the trend can only be observed during the last few years. There is, however, much evidence that the irregular sector has grown relative to the official economy during the last thirty years. Therefore, it seems necessary to have a closer look at Gutmann's assumptions, especially with respect to their validity in the German case.

The assumption that currency is the exclusive medium of exchange in the unobserved sector is too rigid. Because the risk of detection is rather low, it seems reasonable that irregular purchases are paid for by check as well. Surveys from Norway (Isachsen, Klovland, and Strom, 1981) and estimates of the Internal Revenue Service (Feige, 1980, p. 21) indicate that between one-fifth and one-third of unobserved transactions were paid by check rather than by currency. Gutmann's assumption of an equal income velocity of money in the unobserved and observed economies has also been questioned. Whereas Cagan (1958, p. 13) argues that the unreported income produces an abnormal demand for currency to hoard. Feige (1979, p. 7) suspects that the irregular sector – due to the importance of services – is more integrated than the official sector and therefore is likely to have a higher income velocity.

The most severe shortcoming of Gutmann's approach, however, is his assumption that the currency–demand deposit ratio is solely affected by the unobserved activity. Since Cagan's fundamental study on the demand for currency relative to total money supply in 1958, there is widespread agreement that besides irregular activities many other variables affect the currency ratio. In Germany, the development of a more sophisticated financial system has contributed to the decreasing currency ratio. Due to all these shortcomings the currency-ratio method has not been applied to calculate the monetary unobserved economy in Germany.

The estimation of tax-induced currency holding from a demand-for-money function

Tanzi (1980) used a modified version of Cagan's original model deriving the demand for currency as an explicit function of several exogenous variables including the level of taxes. He therefore avoided the critique that the ratio of currency to demand deposits is solely influenced by changes in taxes. After having specified a statistically significant relationship, Tanzi simulated the amount of currency attributable to the increase in taxes, which is taken as a proxy for tax evasion. Multiplying these extra-currency holdings by the normal income velocity of money, he obtained two different estimates of the monetary unobserved economy. The first is based on a base period where taxation was rather low, and the second is based on zero taxation.

There is no clear-cut answer as to which dependent variable will show the tax evasion motive properly. Tanzi used the ratio of currency to the money supply M2 to prevent shifts between demand and time deposits from influencing the results.[3] The currency–demand deposit ratio is often favored for long-term analysis, for it allows the elimination of the rate of interest from the list of explanatory variables. However, because currency and demand deposits show different elasticities of substitution with respect to other financial assets, we did not follow this suggestion. Klovland (1980, p. 23) estimated tax evasion directly from a demand-

---

[3] For the United States Garcia (1978) has argued that demand deposits have been strongly influenced by new financial techniques such as repurchase agreements, automatic transfer systems, or NOW accounts.

for-currency function because of the significantly positive relationship between demand deposits and tax rates.

In the German case we tried all three different dependent variables to determine the tax-induced currency holdings. Whereas Tanzi (1980) used three different tax rates – the ratio of personal income taxes to personal income net of transfers, the top-bracket statutory tax rate, and the weighted-average tax rate on interest income – we only used the ratio of total taxes to GNP.[4] It should be noted that although the average marginal tax rate would be a better indicator for tax evasion, such a time series is not available for Germany. The other exogenous variables incorporated in the analysis are an income variable, an opportunity cost variable, and the ratio of the cost-of-living index to the general price index as measured by the GNP deflator.[5] Let

C = currency held by public, excluding vault cash
D = demand deposits
M2 = money supply M2, currency plus demand deposits plus time deposits
Y = real GNP
Y_{cap} = real national income per capita
r = three-month money-market rate
P_1/P = ratio of cost-of-living index to implicit GNP deflator
T = total taxes, including social contributions, in relation to GNP
P = implicit GNP deflator

Assuming the adjustment of the actual variables to the long-term desired variables follows the conventional stock adjustment process, the following models were subjected to empirical tests:

$$\ln(X)_t = \beta \ln a_0 + a\beta \ln Y_t + a_2\beta r_t + a_3\beta(P_1/P)_t \\ + a_4\beta T_t + (1 - \beta)\ln(X)_{t-1} + u_1$$

where X alternatively is expressed as C/D [equations (1) and (2)], C/M2 [equations (3) and (4)], and C/P [equations (5) and (6)]. The income variable is alternatively measured by real GNP or real national income per capita. Additionally, all variables were expressed in natural logarithm form, thus assuming a constant elasticity instead of a constant semi-elasticity of the coefficients a_2, a_3, a_4. It is to be expected that the

---

[4] Total taxes include all taxes and contributions accruing to the public sector and the social security system. The extension of taxes by social security payment is due to the compulsory character of these payments in Germany, which are therefore giving additional incentives for non-reporting of incomes.

[5] According to Neldner (1977), this price ratio has a significantly positive influence on currency–deposit ratios in Germany.

P_1/P and T variables show positive signs, whereas the signs of the other coefficients depend on the relative size of the elasticities with respect to currency, demand deposits, and M2.

The regressions with the best fit for the preceding equation are shown in Table 8.2. Since it is the intent of the analysis to determine the size of tax-induced currency holdings, we concentrate on the sign and the significance of the T-variable. Given the significantly negative T-coefficient of the $C/M2$ equations, it may be the case that demand and time deposits have been created in connection with irregular activities. On the other hand, the low income elasticity might indicate that the T-variable has picked up some effects of trend growth. The C/D and the C/P equations show the correct sign for they indicate that an increase in tax rates brings about a greater relative use of currency. According to equation (5), at the end of the adjustment process the demand for real currency has increased by 4.9% if tax rates rise by one percentage point. Although it is evident that the explanation of C/D, $C/M2$, and C/P in Germany requires further empirical work, we shall use these equations to estimate the tax-induced monetary unobserved activity. Equations (1), (2), (5), and (6) were used to simulate the increase in currency holdings attributable to the rise in the tax burden. Using the real currency demand function yielded slightly higher estimates than using the currency–demand deposit ratios. Because these estimates would be biased downward if demand deposits are held for tax evasion purposes, only the results calculated with equation (5) are shown in Table 8.3.

We followed the approach of Tanzi (1980) and calculated two different measures. First, we estimated the unobserved activity induced by the increase in taxes between 1950 and the terminal period. Second, we estimated the total unobserved activity associated with the year-end level of taxation. The simulated extra-currency holdings were multiplied by the income velocity in the observed sector.[6] The results in Table 8.3 indicate that in 1980 DM 54 billion, or 3.7% of GNP, can be attributed to the increase in the tax burden since 1950.[7] The existence of taxes has generated unobserved income of some DM 187 billion in 1980. Given the differences in the specification, especially the different formulations

---

[6] In Germany empirical analysis has shown that changes in money supply M1 show the closest connection with changes in observed economic activity. We therefore took the money supply M1 adjusted for the extra-currency holdings to calculate the income velocity of money.

[7] Klovland (1980) simulated currency holdings in the unobserved sector on the basis of long-term desired values. However, it seems to be inconsistent to link desired currency holdings with the actual income velocity of money. Because of the extraordinary low speed of adjustment [0.14 in equation (5)], a simulation on the basis of the desired extra-currency holdings would lead to a significantly higher monetary unobserved sector.

Table 8.2. Determinants of C/D, C/M2, and C/P in Germany (1952–80)

Equation number	Dependent variable	Coefficient estimates								Lagged endogenous variable	$\bar{R}^2$	SEE	ϱ	Durbin H-statistic
		Constant	$\ln y$	r	$\ln r$	T	$\ln T$	P_1/P	$\ln P_1/P$					
(1)	$\ln(C/D)$	5.64 (3.20)^b	-0.488 (3.29)^b	0.011 (5.27)^b	—	0.0057 (1.03)	—	—	—	0.317 (1.51)	0.9904	0.021	0.67 (4.84)^b	—
(2)	$\ln(C/D)$	4.45 (2.56)^b	-0.485 (3.44)^b	—	0.081 (5.96)	—	0.296 (1.54)	—	—	0.378 (1.94)^a	0.9901	0.021	0.69 (5.04)^b	—
(3)	$\ln(C/M2)$	2.92 (1.84)	-0.096 (0.56)	-0.0040 (1.27)	—	-0.017 (2.16)^a	—	-0.0008 (0.08)	—	0.498 (3.04)	0.9772	0.030	0.75 (6.15)^b	—
(4)	$\ln(C/M2)$	0.960 (0.34)	0.0008 (0.00)	—	-0.0020 (0.09)	—	-0.771 (2.68)^b	—	0.870 (1.53)	0.465 (3.16)^b	0.9787	0.029	0.77 (6.39)^b	—
(5)	$\ln(C/P)$	0.29 (2.28)^a	-0.014 (0.22)	-0.0054 (3.03)^b	—	0.0099 (3.62)^b	—	0.0045 (0.97)	—	0.861 (12.89)^b	0.9960	0.017	—	1.22
(6)	$\ln(C/P)$	-2.80 (1.42)	0.102 (0.82)	—	-0.033 (2.81)^b	—	+0.340 (3.11)^b	—	0.408 (1.12)	0.790 (8.62)^b	0.9956	0.018	—	1.45

^{a} Significant at 10% level.
^{b} Significant at 5% level.

Note: Results are from ordinary least squares regression. Equations (1)–(4) have been adjusted for first-order serial autocorrelation by Cochrane–Orcutt method. Numbers in parentheses are t-values.

Table 8.3. *Estimates of the monetary unobserved activity by tax-induced currency holdings calculated with equation (5) (billions of DM)*

Year	Illegal money (1)	Legal money M1 (2)	Income velocity of legal money (3)	Unobserved economic activity	
				DM (4)	Percentage of GNP
With lowest taxes					
1976	5.86	170.82	6.58	38.55	3.4
1978	7.32	208.93	6.17	45.16	3.5
1980	8.38	229.64	6.50	54.47	3.7
With zero taxes					
1976	19.07	157.61	7.14	136.16	12.1
1978	22.77	193.48	6.67	151.88	11.8
1980	26.57	211.45	7.05	187.32	12.6

Note: Column 4 = column 1 × column 3.

of the tax variable, the similarity between the results for the United States calculated by Tanzi (1980, p. 450) and those for Germany is astonishing.

Even if the demand for currency with respect to increases in tax rates could be properly identified, there still remain some crucial assumptions underlying the simple currency-ratio method. Currency is still assumed to be the exclusive medium of exchange in the hidden sector, and the income velocity of money is assumed to be the same as that in the observed sector. These arguments have already been discussed. We therefore consider the additional assumptions underlying Tanzi's method.

In the theory of tax evasion it is widely accepted that in addition to the monetary rewards in terms of non-paid taxes, many other factors such as (a) the attitude toward government, (b) basic religious and cultural development, (c) the severity of penalties, and (d) the ease of evading taxes determine tax evasion. These factors are not measurable; however, their omission leaves out important factors influencing tax evasion. Besides the fact that tax rates might be a too simple proxy for tax evasion, other factors affect the development of the unobserved economy, such as the various regulations introduced by government. For these reasons, the estimates of tax-induced irregular activities tend to underestimate the size of the total monetary unobserved income.

The transactions method

Feige (1979) suggested an alternative macroeconomic approach of measuring the monetary unobserved activity. Whereas Gutmann and Tanzi especially relied on changes in the stock of currency, Feige believes that information on the development of the total volume of transactions supported by currency and demand deposits will lead to more accurate estimates of the size and growth of the irregular economy.

According to the quantity theory of money, total transactions reveal a relatively constant relation to total income. Since estimates of the transactions volume from the payment side are generally available and are not biased by the development of the underground economy, they can be used to estimate total income, comprising observed as well as unobserved income. Thus, if a proportional relationship between transactions and income exists, a significant increase in the volume of transactions relative to observed income (GNP) indicates a stronger growth of the monetary unobserved sector.

Total transactions incorporate not only purchases of newly produced goods and services but also purchases of intermediate goods and services, existing assets, and purely financial transactions. Given the increasing stock of capital and wealth and the structural changes in the German economy, it is necessary to carefully analyze whether changes in the monetary transactions volume are caused by factors other than those that can be attributed to unobserved activities.

In order to apply Feige's methodology in the German context, an estimate of the total value of transactions supported by currency and demand deposits is necessary. Assuming that there was no irregular activity in the chosen base year, we arrive at estimates of the total economic activity for the succeeding years by dividing the total value of transactions by the base-year ratio of transactions to income. Subtracting observed activity leaves as a residual the estimate of the unobserved income.

For Germany a consistent set of data is only available for the period 1950–80. Due to the division of the country, earlier figures are not comparable. It is rather difficult to determine a base year in which the unobserved activity can be assumed to be negligible. In the early 1950's, highly progressive tax rates,[8] many regulations, and the excess supply

---

[8] In its annual report for 1950 the central bank states (p. 23) that in the first two years after the currency reform of 1948 currency hoarding in connection with tax evasion has taken place.

Table 8.4. *Average lifetime of notes by denomination, 1948–81*

	Denomination							
	1000	500	100	50	20	10	5	All notes
Lifetime, years	6.1	4.7	3.1	1.7	1.3	1.3	2.5	1.8

Source: Deutsche Bundesbank, internal reports.

of labor were factors that typically encouraged unobserved activities. It seems therefore more reasonable to take the mid-1950's as a base period. However, it should be kept in mind that even during this period some unobserved activities were no doubt present in the German economy.

In order to estimate the total value of monetary transactions, it is necessary to determine the turnover of demand deposit and currency. Demand deposit turnover can be estimated from data on debits to accounts of non-banks arising from transfers, direct debits, and check clearings, and these statistics are collected by the Deutsche Bundesbank.[9] Comparable figures for the turnover of currency, however, are not directly available. Since only figures on the stock of currency are published, Feige (1979) suggested a method for estimating the yearly turnover of currency by using information on the rate of destruction of soiled and unfit currency. In order to implement this method, we assumed that the average note outstanding could sustain 125 income-producing transactions before being withdrawn as unfit for further circulation.[10] According to the Deutsche Bundesbank, the average lifetime of notes over the period 1948–81 was 1.8 years. The lifetime of notes increases substantially with the denomination value due to a lower velocity and a more careful handling (Table 8.4).

As compared to other countries, the lifetime of German notes appears to be rather short. We therefore investigated the destruction of worn-out notes more closely. Dividing the average annual stock of currency by the yearly redemptions yields a measure of the lifetime of notes over time. The ratio shows strong fluctuations before 1968 and a rather stable movement afterward. The strong changes in redemptions are mostly the result of institutional effects on the note issue. After the

[9] Deutsche Bundesbank, monthly report, III, Table 23.
[10] This figure was estimated by Laurent (1970) for the United States during the 1890–1965 period. Feige (1980) reported that an engineering study of the wearing characteristics of new currency issues revealed total lifetime transactions on the order of 200–60.

currency reform in 1948 notes of the Deutsche Reichsbank were replaced by notes of the Bank Deutscher Lander. After the constitution of the Deutsche Bundesbank in 1957, the circulating notes were again substituted step by step. This means that the lifetime of notes as calculated by the Deutsche Bundesbank is likely to be biased downward by the substitution of notes. It is therefore more plausible to assume an average lifetime of notes of approximately three years. Due to the uncertainty about the impacts of note issue, changes in the quality standard of notes, and the central bank's behavior on the destruction of soiled notes, we assumed a constant lifetime of notes for the whole period. To take account of the uncertainty with respect to number of total transactions per note and the average lifetime of notes, we experimented with four different values (35, 43, 57, and 62) for the velocity of currency. Before carrying out the final calculations, it was necessary to investigate whether intermediate transactions, purely financial transactions, or transfers of existing assets behaved differently than transactions with respect to final goods production. In this case the transactions value has to be corrected to arrive at an estimate of the unobserved monetary activity.

The examination of the time path of intermediate goods transactions yielded no clear-cut answer as to whether the total monetary transactions value had been influenced by changes in the degree of intra-industry trade. Comparable official input–output tables for Germany exist only since 1965. The volume of intermediate transactions as a fraction of total final transactions increased slightly from 0.90 in 1965 to 0.94 in 1975. However, it is doubtful whether this indicates that the degree of integration has declined, for the input–output tables classify industries according to the type of production rather than their market involvement.

It is to be expected that with an increasing stock of real assets, transfers of existing assets will increase more strongly than sales of newly produced goods and services. In order to model the ratio of existing asset transfers to sales of new assets, we examined the ratio of automobile title transfers to new car registrations. The time path of this ratio is displayed in Figure 8.2.[11] Between 1956 and 1980 the volume of title transfers increased two times faster than new registrations. It is likely that the relation between transfers of existing and newly produced goods followed a similar trend for other assets. We therefore assumed that the volume of the transfers of existing assets matches the volume of private consumption and investment multiplied by the ratio shown in Figure

---

[11] Property transcriptions are only available from 1956 onward.

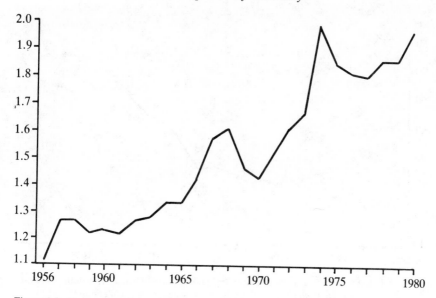

Figure 8.2. Ratio of numbers of property transcriptions of cars to new car registrations, 1956–80. (*Source:* Statistical Office, Statistical yearbook, current issues.)

8.2. This measure is admittedly arbitrary; however, no more precise information was available.

In order to arrive at an estimate of transactions net of financial transactions, it is necessary to subtract out those debits arising from various types of other financial transactions. However, the requisite debit figures are not available. Stock data are available for many monetary assets, but the desired flow data are not recorded. In spite of these problems, we tried to estimate purely financial transactions within the debit figures by adding up the following items:

market value of all stock and bond sales,
amounts paid into savings accounts and into accounts of building and
  loan associations,
interest paid on loans and yearly changes in stocks of loans of non-banks
  as a proxy for repayments, and
average yearly stock of short-term time deposits (up to one year maturity) as a proxy for debits arising from shifts to time deposits.

The resulting estimates of financial transactions per unit of GNP are shown in Figure 8.3. It is evident that especially in the late 1960's the financial system expanded rapidly, thus contributing to the increase in

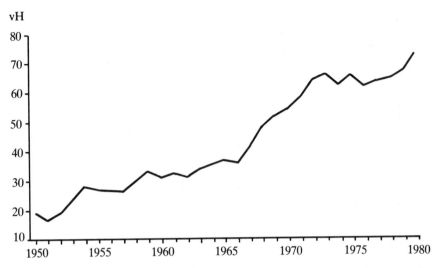

Figure 8.3. Financial transactions per unit of GNP, 1950–80. (*Source:* Monthly report of the Deutsche Bundesbank, various issues, own calculations.)

monetary transactions. It is likely that the financial flows are underestimated; therefore, the estimate of the financial transactions seems to be conservative.

After correcting monetary transactions for transfers of existing assets and purely financial transactions, the unobserved activity was calculated as follows. The year 1956 was chosen as benchmark period. For the following years the corrected transactions volume was divided by the base-year ratio, and then official GNP was subtracted. The remaining amount yields a measure of the income generated in the monetary unobserved sector.

Taking 1956 as the base period and assuming that currency turns over an average of 62 times per year, the transactions approach leads to the conclusion that in 1980 the monetary unobserved sector in Germany amounted to some DM 400 billion, or 27% of GNP.[12] This is a shockingly high result but is very well in line with the estimates obtained by Feige (1979) for the United States. Figure 8.4 presents the estimates of the monetary unobserved economy as a percentage of official GNP along with the average tax rate. It shows that especially in the 1970's the unobserved sector has grown more rapidly than the regular economy.

---

[12] Contrary to expectations, assuming less than 62 annual transactions per unit of currency leads to slightly higher estimates of the monetary unobserved sector.

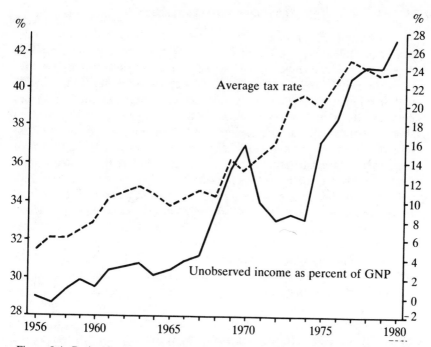

Figure 8.4. Ratio of monetary unobserved income to GNP in Germany estimated with transactions approach, 1956–80. (*Source:* Statistical Office, Statistical yearbook, own calculations.)

Since assumptions are necessary to arrive at the obtained estimates of the monetary unobserved sector, they must be viewed as presumptive. There still exist different possible sources of under- and overestimation. It is doubtful that in the chosen base year 1956, all economic activity was confined to the official sector. By assuming no unobserved income in the base period, we have therefore underestimated the magnitude and growth of the monetary unobserved sector. A higher estimate of the irregular economy would also result if because of greater integration, the income velocity in the unobserved sector was higher than in the observed sector. On the other hand, in the German case it is evident that total monetary transactions have been strongly enlarged by financial transfers as well as by transfers of existing assets. The estimates for these factors can be on the low side since the flows are conservatively estimated, thus leading to an overestimation of the monetary unobserved sector.

The labor market approach

To get an impression of the development of the unobserved sector, it can be useful to have a closer look at official labor market statistics. Anecdotal evidence reveals that unobserved activity in Germany is rather labor intensive. An increasing irregular sector should therefore coincide with a relative decrease in officially recorded employment.[13] This can manifest itself in lower participation rates, higher unemployment, a shorter work week, an increasing number of holidays, or a more extensive absenteeism from work. Figure 8.5 shows the development of the participation rate, weekly hours worked, and unemployment rate in Germany. The evidence seems to confirm the hypothesis that the mid-1950's can be taken as an appropriate benchmark period for an estimation of the irregular activity in Germany. The participation rate reached its maximum in 1957 at a level of 48.7%, whereas weekly hours of production peaked with 48.72 hours in 1955, and unemployment was declining rapidly. This period can be interpreted as the golden age of the official economy. The introduction of a market system in 1949 and the existence of a motivated, mobile, and skilled labor force led to large productivity increases. At the same time the economy was deregulated, and the marginal burden of taxes and social security contributions declined. It is likely that during this period resources were shifted to the official, monetized, market sector.

During the 1960's this development reversed only slightly. However, the decrease in the participation rate can be explained more by demographic developments (relative increase of children and aged people) than by a change in the labor market behavior. The special participation rates in the age group from 25 to 60 remained high (male workers) or even increased (female workers). Only the development of the weekly hours of production may indicate a reduced attractiveness of the official sector. However, the vigorous inflow of foreign workers still offered a chance for promotion of skilled workers in the official sector, as is indicated by a positive wage drift.

The 1970's can be roughly characterized as a period with a growing public sector acquiring resources for the provision of public goods as well as for redistribution. This development can be mainly attributed to the announcement of the public "employment guarantee." The government tried to solve the rising unemployment problems by granting subsidies for further education as well as for earlier retirement. These

---

[13] Employment figures in Germany are calculated not on a survey basis but by a census covering all enterprises.

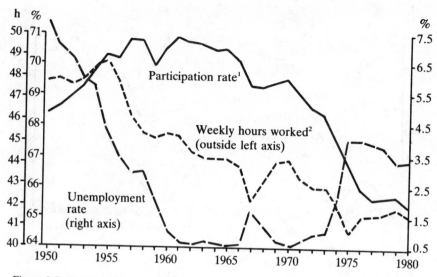

Figure 8.5. Development of participation rate, hours worked per week, and unemployment rate in West Germany, 1950–80: (1) labor force participation (including foreign workers, age group 15–65 years): (2) average paid weekly hours of work of blue-collar workers in industry.

measures could only be financed by additional taxes and social security contributions. Increasing regulations were necessary to prevent a misuse of subsidies. Thus, the incentives to work in the unobserved sector increased strongly. Do-it-yourself activities as well as working in the monetary unobserved sector are likely to have expanded rapidly during this decade.

The actual demand of German trade unions for a shortening of life-time work as well as for a shorter work week seem to indicate that a considerable potential for do-it-yourself work and for illicit work still exists. The fact that the dramatic rise in unemployment up to now is not accompanied by social disturbances but by relative acquiescence (Shankland, 1980) may be attributed to the provision of generous unemployment benefits while there are opportunities to obtain an additional tax-free income in the irregular sector. The strong increase in transfer payments in general is likely to lead to the practice that people claim transfer payments and work off the books at the same time because otherwise they would often loose their claims.

Adding up the working hours resulting from a decline of the participation rate and the average weekly hours of production below their top level and the total volume of unemployment yields a measure for the

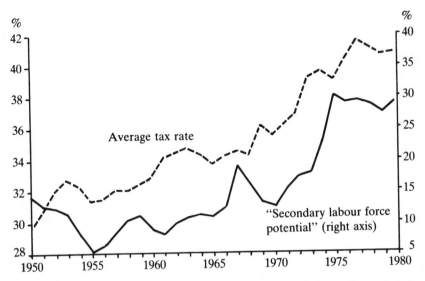

Figure 8.6. Development of labor market potential available for unobserved sector relative to hours worked in official sector and average tax rate in Germany, 1950–80. (*Source:* Statistical Office, Statistical yearbook, own calculations.)

potential labor force available for total unobserved activities. However, it should be kept in mind that this reflects a notional supply curve of labor for irregular activities. It can be expected that higher incomes coincide with an increasing demand for "leisure."[14] Figure 8.6 shows the development of the potential labor supply for unobserved activities as a fraction of hours worked in the official sector. The rate significantly decreased in the early 1950's. After reaching a bottom in the mid-1950's it continually increased until 1980. The peaks in 1967 and 1975 reflect the strong increase in unemployment during a recession. In general, the declining participation rate and the shortening of the work week contributed to the growing labor potential not used in the official economy.

It is likely that the relative decline in official hours worked to a large degree can be taken as an indicator for the relative growth of the unobserved sector. However, the estimates cannot directly be compared to those obtained from the money demand approach and the transactions method since they incorporate monetary as well as non-monetary unobserved activities. Additionally, they can give only information on

[14] There has been a long debate on the labor–leisure relationship in economic literature. However, a widely accepted definition of "leisure" is not yet available.

the relative growth of the unobserved sector. To arrive at an estimate of the size of the unobserved sector, it would be necessary to make an assumption about the productivity in this sector. In spite of these shortcomings, further research based on labor market statistics should be carried out, especially incorporating the effects of increasing holidays and absenteeism as well as demographic developments.

Conclusions

This chapter attempted to estimate the size of the monetary unobserved sector in West Germany. The estimates should be regarded as preliminary, since crucial assumptions had to be made to arrive at quantitative estimates. The estimate based on the calculation of tax-induced currency holding suggests a monetary unobserved economy approaching some DM 50 billion in 1980; this comes rather close to the estimates of the Craftsmen Association. Due to the same rather restrictive assumptions, these estimates should be regarded as being on the low side. The results obtained with the transactions approach lead to the conclusion that in 1980 about DM 400 billion, or 27% of GNP, were not accounted for by the official statistical measurement system. Due to the difficulties arising from calculating those parts of total monetary transactions that can be referred to as purely financial transactions, the transactions approach would seem to yield estimates on the high side. However, none of these estimates takes account of barter activities. Up to now, estimates of the non-monetary unobserved sector in Germany are not available.

To sum up, all results reveal that the unobserved economy in Germany is already a cause for concern: All methods used indicate a dramatic growth especially during the last decade.

CHAPTER 9

The underground economy in Sweden

INGEMAR HANSSON

Sweden's tax rates are among the highest in Europe, especially on marginal earnings. Accounting for the effect of direct and indirect taxes as well as income-dependent transfers, the marginal tax rate amounts to 75% for the average income earner.[1] Dividing the economy into a taxed and an untaxed sector, this means that the value of the gross marginal product of labor in the taxed sector must be four times as high as the value of the (gross and net) marginal product of labor in the untaxed sector in order to give the same net remuneration for marginal labor time.

The high marginal taxes thus give a strong incentive for time allocation to untaxed activities such as home production and leisure. Moreover, there are strong incentives for tax avoidance that can be accomplished through payments in the form of fringe benefits and through excessive borrowing in order to obtain deductible interest expenditures. Finally, tax evasion carries a high premium due to the high tax rates.

For all these reasons, high marginal tax rates tend to produce a relatively small tax base and distortions in the allocation of resources. Some, but not all, of these factors tend to give a small observed economy as measured by national account statistics.

After many years of experience, most economists, politicians, and the mass media recognize these effects of high marginal taxes; yet their quantitative importance remains a matter of much debate. The four largest parties in Sweden, covering 95% of the seats in the parliament, consider the effects to be sufficiently severe to call for a reduction in the marginal tax rates. Three of these parties, covering 75% of the seats, have agreed on a tax reform that decreases the marginal tax rate from 75% to roughly 70% for the average income earner.[2]

This tax reform dampens the incentives for untaxed activities, but the wedge between gross and net returns from taxed activities is still very substantial.

This chapter mainly focuses on the unobserved economy in the form of tax evasion in Sweden. Tax evasion is defined as the underestimate of

[1] See Hansson (1980).
[2] Proportional taxes would require a tax rate somewhat above 50%.

reported income that arises due to unreported income or false deductions in the tax returns for the income tax. Available studies of the magnitude of tax evasion are surveyed and evaluated, leading to a best guess for the size and the development of tax evasion over time in Sweden.

Survey studies

In several studies, the occurrence of tax evasion is examined by direct questions in surveys. In 1966, the Swedish Institute for Public Opinion Research (SIFO) asked: "Have you ever tried and managed to avoid to pay tax for an amount that you should have paid tax for?" An affirmative answer was given by 12%. For two similar questions tax evasion was confirmed by 28% in the governmental report SOU (1970, p. 25) by 7% through "too low reported income ever" and by 10% through "too high deductions ever" in SIFO (1979) and by 19% through "too high deductions ever" in Warneryd and Walerud (1981). The latter study was confined to males, and other studies (SIFO, 1980a, 1981) show higher tax evasion for men.

In some studies, the time period was restricted to one year, giving affirmative answers for "received black money for a job or service during 1980" from 14% in SIFO (1980a) and 12% in Warneryd and Walerud (1981).

According to these surveys, 10–30% of the population is involved in this type of tax evasion. The results reveal no clear tendency of increasing or decreasing tax evasion over time. This comparison is, however, disturbed by differences in the questions between different surveys.

SIFO (1966) also included questions on the amounts for unreported income. Among the 12% that admitted underreporting, 71% claimed that the amount did not exceed 500 Kr ($85), 10% checked the interval 500–999 Kr ($85–170), 8% the interval 1,000–3,999 Kr ($170–680), and 4% above 4,000 Kr. The remaining 7% did not check any interval. To get a rough picture of the indicated magnitude as percentage of gross domestic product (GDP), note that the interval midpoints and 8,000 Kr for the upper interval with a proportional distribution of people who did not answer gives an underreported income corresponding to 0.5% of GDP for 1966.

Distribution of unreported income

Several studies also examined the frequency of unreported income for different subgroups. A higher frequency was found for men (SIFO,

1980a, 1981), for younger people (SIFO, 1966, 1980), respectively for middle aged (SIFO, 1979, 1981), for entrepreneurs as compared to wage earners (SIFO, 1979, 1981), for workers as compared to middle and upper class (SIFO, 1980), and for high income for a given age group (SIFO, 1979). Elsewhere (SIFO, 1966) the share was higher in urban areas, whereas SIFO (1980) gave the same share for urban and rural areas.

Warneryd and Walerud (1981) found that the frequency for received black money was significantly higher among higher income groups, those with greater opportunities for tax evasion, and lower perceptions that their evasion would be detected. Examining the frequency in different occupational groups, SIFO (1981a) found the highest frequency among students (35%) followed by construction (26%), housewives (22%), manufacturing (13%), trade (13%), and finally health and social care (11%).

Payments of black money

Surveys typically show higher frequency for admitted payments of black money. In SIFO (1979) and Warneryd and Walerud (1981), 28 and 42%, respectively, admitted having made payments of black money. Again, the difference is partly explained by the fact that the later study includes males only.

When the time period was confined to one year, the share decreased to 19% (SIFO, 1980a). Among people admitting black payments in the later study, 81% claimed that the amount did not exceed 1,000 Kr ($170), 17% checked the interval 1,000–10,000 Kr ($170–1,700) with a remaining 2% above 10,000 Kr. Calculated on the interval means and 20,000 Kr, these figures indicate black payments amounting to 0.4% of GDP for 1979.

The frequency of admitted black payments is highest for entrepreneurs and lowest for workers. The share increases with income for a given age group (SIFO, 1979) and is highest for the upper and upper middle class (SIFO, 1980a). Finally, the share decreases with age, is higher for men, and is similar for urban and rural areas (SIFO, 1980a).

Warneryd and Walerud (1981) conclude that payments of black money increase significantly with house ownership, education, opportunity for tax evasion, household size, a more lenient attitude to tax crime and tax evasion, and the frequency of tax planning. Payments of black money decrease significantly with age, the perceived risk that tax evasion will be detected, and income (contrary to the result in SIFO, 1980a).

221

Attitude to tax crime

In both 1958 and 1978, SIFO conducted comparable surveys in order to examine changing attitudes toward tax crime. The 1958 survey revealed that 77% of respondents regarded the underreporting of taxable income a serious or fairly serious offense. The 1978 survey found that 75% of the respondents shared this view. Of the 1958 respondents 16% regarded under reporting as a non-serious crime, whereas 22% of the 1978 respondents held this view. These results thus indicate a development toward a slightly more lenient attitude toward tax crimes.

Summary and evaluation of the surveys

To summarize, tax evasion is confined to less than a third of the population according to these surveys, whereas the indicated magnitude for tax evasion does not exceed 1% of GDP. Survey studies are likely to underestimate tax evasion for several reasons. Respondents probably tend to understate their own involvement in the black sector, particularly when responding to an unknown interviewer. The importance of the nature of the interview procedure is reflected in the results for Norway reported in Isachsen and Strom (1981). The share admitting participation in the black market was 26% in a survey with personal interviews as compared to 40% in a more anonymous survey where answers were sent by mail.

Moreover, surveys probably involve a systematic error due to a higher tendency for overall non-response and question-specific non-response particularly among those most likely to be engaged in unobserved sector activities. Finally, the questions are often limited to a specific type of tax evasion such as "received black money for a job or a service." The nature of the question may therefore tend to exclude other forms of underreporting such as the income for sale of goods, tax evasion through barter, incorrect deductions, and so on. These surveys may possibly indicate a lower bound for tax evasion. They may, however, involve a substantial underestimate.

The method may be more reliable for an evelution of the development of tax evasion over time, but the results may be disturbed by trend changes in the tendency to admit tax evasion among evaders.

Discrepancy in national account statistics

Sweden has a long tradition of extensive and fairly carefully administered statistics on economic activities. Official GDP is calculated mainly on the basis of expenditure data. Data sources are avoided where tax considerations tend to produce underestimates. Income statistics are, on the other hand, mainly based on income reported for tax purposes. The national account statistics therefore provide a fairly promising basis for an estimate of tax evasion applying the discrepancy method. Hansson (1981) applied this method to estimate tax evasion in different years as the discrepancy between households' total expenditures on consumption, savings, taxes, and so on, and total income estimated from income reported on tax returns.

An examination of different items on the expenditure and income sides revealed different sources of error for estimated tax evasion. These sources of error required both upward and downward revisions depending upon the reporting unit. Upward adjustments were made to take account of tax evasion for farmers, for interest income and dividends, and for exaggerated deductions from salary and wage income. Moreover, the low estimate of tax evasion involves a small upward adjustment for some type of consumption where there is a likely underestimate from "The Family Expenditure Survey 1978," whereas the high estimate of tax evasion involves a somewhat larger upward adjustment. The estimated range for tax evasion was widened in both directions to take account of possible errors in the measurement, especially for expenditures on housing and house investment, dining outside the home, compensation for work expenditures, and interest income.

Through these adjustments, the initial discrepancy of 15.0 billion Kr is changed to the range 16.5–27.3 billion Kr as an estimate of the amount of tax evasion for 1978. This range corresponds to 4.0–6.7% of GDP for 1978. Analogous results for 1970–9 are reported in Figure 9.1.

The low estimate for tax evasion as share of GDP is 3.8% on average, whereas the high estimate averages 6.4%. The short-run variations shown in Figure 9.1 are probably mainly due to errors. Except for these variations, the results show a roughly constant tax evasion as share of GDP for this period. This unexpected result is further discussed in what follows.

The preceding estimate covers tax evasion in the household sector including personal firms but excludes tax evasion in other sectors such as corporate firms and the public sector. Taxable income in these other sectors is, however, very small as compared to taxable income in the household sector.

Moreover, some, but not all, types of barter in the household sector are excluded from measured consumption and investment, implying that estimated tax evasion excludes taxable income from such barter. Finally, the estimate excludes tax evasion due to unreported income from illegal activities as sale of narcotics, theft, bribes, and so on, since

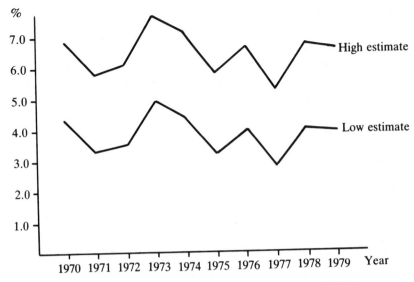

Figure 9.1. Underestimated taxable income as share of GDP.

the expenditure side in national account statistics does not include this type of expenditures.

More generally, the discrepancy method may involve an underestimate of tax evasion due to underreporting of expenditures on goods and services purchased from the black sector. The Swedish statistics are, however, partly designed to avoid this problem, and the reported estimate involves additional adjustments to take account of this type of error. The estimated range, 3.8–6.4% of GDP, may therefore be interpreted as a best guess for the size of tax evasion except for the aforementioned additional types of tax evasion.

The degree of uncertainty using this method is substantial since tax evasion is calculated as the difference between two large sums. Even a modest error in one of the sums may produce a large error in estimated tax evasion.

Discrepancy between reported and actual hours of work

Competition from the black economy in Sweden is considered to be especially severe for construction and maintenance activities. On behalf of associations of entrepreneurs in these sectors, Myrsten (1980) estimated the amount of black work for these types of activity. The number

224

of hours worked in the black sector was calculated as the difference between estimated total hours of work including some overtime and reported hours of work in the official sector.

For employed painters, full-time work involved 1,800 hours in 1974. Allowing for a 5% unemployment rate, a 10% sick leave rate, and a 2% rate for lost time due to job changes results in an average expected hours of work of 1,500 hours. Official work hours were reported to be 1,250, suggesting an estimated 250 hours of unrecorded work. In addition, Myrsten assumed overtime work of 100 hours, giving a total of 350 hours of work per employee.

For self-employed painters, reported income for tax purposes was calculated to correspond to 1,000 hours of work. Under the assumption that total hours of work was 2,000 hours, this suggests 1,000 hours of unrecorded work for a typical self-employed painter. These calculations lead to the conclusion that the number of hours worked in the black sector amounted to 30% of reported hours. Corresponding calculations for other subsectors of construction and maintenance gave an estimated share for hours of work in the black sector of 10% for lumber and cement, 16% for plumbing, and 25% for electric installations. Taken together, the hours of work in the black sector amounted to 15% of reported hours of work for the occupational groups examined by Myrsten.

Kjell Olsson, at the Associated General Contractors for Home Builders of Sweden, applied the same method to three major construction firms, concluding that the number of hours worked in the black sector was 10% of reported hours. These calculations involve several sources of error. Information on total hours of work including overtime is very scarce and the estimated amounts are essentially educated guesses. The measurement of reported hours of work is also subject to error, especially for the self-employed. Work in the black sector is conducted not only by registered employees but also by retired persons and those registered in other sectors. Finally, reported hours of work may be lower than estimated total hours of work as a result of work in other sectors and leisure, education, and training activities.

The severity of these deficiencies is somewhat dampened by the fact that the investigators have a good working knowledge of the institutional arrangements in the sectors studied.

Relation to other results

In order to compare these results with earlier studies, it is necessary to convert unrecorded working hours to a measure of the share of value added in the black sector. Under the assumption that the price per hour of work in the black sector is 60% of the price per hour in the recorded sector, the estimated range for hours worked, 10–15%, corresponds to the range 6–9% for value added.

Anecdotal information suggests that the share of unrecorded income in construction and maintenance exceeds the share of such income in the entire economy. This hypothesis is supported by SIFO (1980a), which reveals that 26% of the respondents working in the construction sector acknowledged work in the black sector, whereas the comparable share for the entire sample was only 14%. The estimate of 6–9% can thus be interpreted as an upper bound for the total share of unrecorded income. Applying the SIFO figures yields a share of 3–5% for overall unrecorded income.

Estimates based on currency–deposit ratio

The business magazine *Veckans Affarer* applied the simple currency ratio method to estimate the size of the unobserved monetary economy in Sweden. The result was that this sector amounted to 10% of GDP statistics. This estimate has been cited extensively in domestic and international literature.[3]

A close examination of this study reveals, however, very serious deficiencies in the estimate. It is highly unlikely that the restrictive assumptions required by this estimation method are valid for Sweden during the period 1920–75. During this period there has been a secular shift away from cash wage payments to payments by account transfers, thus violating the assumption of a fixed currency-to-demand-deposit ratio. Moreover, cash payments for goods and services have been replaced by checks, giro, and credit card payments. More generally, check payments to and from private individuals were quite rare in the beginning of the period, whereas this form of payment has now become commonplace. Feige (1979) has also challenged this method on the grounds that it incorrectly assumes that cash is the sole medium of exchange in the unobserved sector. This critique is also germane for Sweden. Finally, the method requires the assumption that the unobserved sector was negligible for the period 1922–33. Yet the method implies that the unobserved economy was then as high as 20% of the observed sector during the five-year periods preceding and following this base period. *Veckans Affarer*'s application for Sweden was based on

---

[3] See Delorozoy (1980), Isachsen and Strom (1980, 1981), Klovland (1980), Magnusson (1980), and Persson (1979).

the quotient between currency and total time and demand deposits. No rationale is offered for the inclusion of time deposits in the denominator of the ratio; however, it is well known that changes in inflation, interest rates, and tax rules are likely to influence time deposits versus currency to an even greater extent than the influence between demand deposits and currency. Neglecting the other variables that affect the overall ratio therefore casts serious doubt on the manner in which the method was applied. Finally, the inclusion of time deposits is conceptually inappropriate since time deposits do not serve as a final medium of exchange.

The time series for the currency-to-total-deposits ratio is displayed in Figure 9.2. The right scale in Figure 9.2 shows the implied estimate for the unobserved monetary economy as a share of the observed monetary economy. This method thus gives the implausible result that the share for the unobserved monetary economy increased from 0% in the 1930's to over 100% for 1957–65 and thereafter decreased dramatically reaching a low point in the mid-1970's. Moreover, this recalculation reveals a different result from the one reported in the original paper.[4]

My conclusion is that the often cited result from *Veckans Affärer* should be dismissed from the set of useful results concerning the size of tax evasion in Sweden.

Other applications of the currency ratio method

The direct application of the simple currency ratio method as employed by Cagan (1958) and Gutmann (1977) for Sweden yields implausible results. The share for the unobserved monetary economy is estimated to increase from 0% for the base year 1939 to above 100% for 1957–61 and thereafter decreases to 5% in the middle of the 1970's.

If the method is adjusted to the Swedish method of payment by a replacement of demand deposits by demand deposits plus deposits on postal giro, any base year with data available before World War II (1926–38) implies a negative unobserved monetary economy for most years after the war. My conclusion is that the simple currency ratio method is unlikely to give reliable results for Sweden, probably as a result of the aforementioned changes in the method of payment during the relevant time period.

Klovland (1980) applied the method developed by Tanzi (1980), involving an econometric estimate of the relation between different types of currency ratios and tax rates to calculate the size and the develop-

---

[4] The author of the original paper has not been able to explain how his results were calculated or why the results differ.

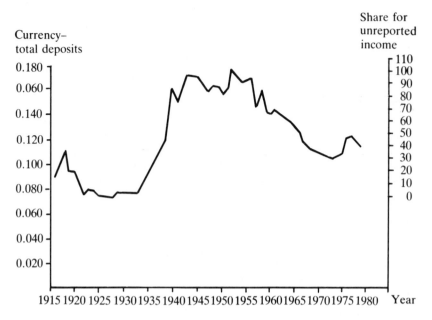

Figure 9.2. Ratio of currency to total deposits and estimated share for unobserved monetary sector.

ment of the unobserved monetary economy. The method is applied for Sweden and Norway. The results are, however, highly sensitive to the specification of the model and the selected measure for velocity. In some cases the estimated coefficients for the tax parameters were negative, implying a negative share of unobserved monetary income for the economy.

These results thus reveal such large variations that they are unlikely to provide a reliable base for an estimate of the size of the unobserved monetary sector.

Revealed underreporting

The tax administration authority, Riksskatteverket, makes occasional data revisions for different subsectors of the economy. The revisions are focused on sectors and taxpayers with a high expected degree of under-reporting. This limits the value of the results as a base for an estimate of total tax evasion.

Calculated in 1978 prices, these revisions revealed underreported income per examined case amounting to an average 35,100 Kr ($5,900)

228

for mink farmers, 18,000 Kr ($3,100) for firms in advertising and public relations, 14,300 Kr ($2,400) for architects, 68,300 Kr ($11,600) for lumber, 21,900 Kr ($3,700) for a selection of various types of taxpayers, and 29,300 Kr ($5,000) for a selection of taxpayers with complicated tax returns. The first four revisions covered less than five years, the fifth revision involved two years, and the last involved one year. If the reported income for the corresponding one- to five-year period amounted to 100,000–400,000 Kr ($33,900–67,800) on average for the examined taxpayers, the revealed underreported income amounted to 8–16% of reported income. The lack of more exact information on the size of reported income for examined individuals and firms gives a considerable source of error in these calculations. Additional serious errors arise through the focus of revisions on sectors and taxpayers with high expected underreporting and the fact that audits discover only a part of the unreported income for the examined taxpayers.

Central Bureau of Police

As a final piece of evidence on the size of tax evasion in Sweden, a committee at the Central Bureau of Police, Rikspolisstyrelsen (1977), estimated that tax evasion detected by the tax authorities through "tax crimes of more systematic type" amounted to 500–1,000 million Kr: "If the probability of detection is set as high as 5–10%, this estimate gives a minimum value of five billions of Kr per year and a maximum value of twenty billions of Kr per year." This estimate corresponds to 1.4–5.4% of GDP for 1977. However, the estimate does not include minor tax evasion for wage earners due to the expressed limitation "tax crimes of a more systematic type." Moreover, the largely unsupported estimate of the detection probability involves a large source of error.

Estimated range for tax evasion based on these studies

This section makes a best guess for the size of tax evasion based on the presented available estimates for Sweden.

Compared to other available estimates, the discrepancy estimate based on national accounts appears to be relatively reliable. The estimated range 3.8–6.4% of GDP may therefore be taken as a starting point for this summary. This estimate excludes

1 tax evasion through illegal activities such as the sale of narcotics,
2 some tax evasion through barter, and
3 tax evasion outside the household sector.

These exclusions require an upward adjustment of the estimates of tax evasion.

Most of the other estimates do, however, suggest a smaller magnitude for tax evasion. SIFO results in the range 0.4–0.5% of GDP and the 1.4–5.4% estimate from the Central Bureau of Police indicate a lower range in spite of the more narrow definition of tax evasion in these cases. These low results, combined with the 3–5% range based on Myrsten–Olsson's calculations, suggest a downward adjustment of the range for tax evasion. The range 8–16% for detected underreported income in revisions should probably be substantially reduced to compensate for the systematic selection of sectors and individuals with high expected underreporting.

These studies suggest a downward adjustment of the upper estimate, 6.4%, from the national accounts estimate, whereas the results are consistent with the lower estimate, 3.8%. This suggests the range 3.8–5.5% as a best guess for the size of tax evasion in Sweden as a share of GDP in the end of the 1970's. For 1980 this corresponds to 3,300–4,800 Kr ($560–810) per adult Swede.

This final estimate is based on five different studies of tax evasion applying different methods. As discussed previously, the source of error for each separate study is quite large. The presence of several studies contributes to the reliability of the final estimate, but the margin of error is still relatively large.

Development of tax evasion over time

Mass media often transmit anecdotal information that indicates that tax evasion is growing over time in Sweden, and politicians devote an increasing interest to this field. The perception of growing tax evasion is also expressed by economists, for example, Myrdal (1978), Du Rietz (1980), and Myrsten (1980). The author shared this view at the start of the current research.

A close look at available studies of tax evasion in Sweden does, however, reveal the lack of systematic evidence supporting the common perception of growing tax evasion. The survey studies indicate a slight change toward a more lenient view of tax crimes but offer mixed evidence for the development of tax evasion over time. The most relevant study of the question based on national account statistics suggests constant tax evasion as a share of GDP during the 1970's.

The conclusion is that the results from the few available studies of the development of tax evasion over time raises serious doubts about

230

the correctness of the common perception of growing tax evasion in Sweden.

Possible explanations for hypothetically constant tax evasion

Sweden has experienced a long period with increasing taxes. The marginal tax rate, including direct taxes, indirect taxes, and income-dependent transfers, has increased from 59% in 1965 to 75% in 1980 for the average income earner. Such a tax increase is likely to increase tax evasion. Indeed, the view that tax evasion increases over time may partly be interpreted as a prediction of the effects of tax increases.

The resources devoted to audits of tax returns have, however, increased during the 1970's, and firms are obliged to keep books on their income and expenditure to an increasing extent. These factors may provide a tendency to lower tax evasion.

Moreover, the share of value added in the public sector and in large firms increases, which may tend to lower tax evasion. In these cases, internal control often requires fairly rigorous reporting of income and expenditure. The possibilities of distorting reports to tax authorities are hampered if people without close ties to the employer are involved in this reporting.

The likely tendency to increasing tax evasion as a result of increasing taxes may thus have been counteracted and neutralized by these two factors involving tendencies to decrease tax evasion. This provides a possible explanation for the indicated constancy for tax evasion as a share of GDP in Sweden.

Observed and unobserved economy

This section examines the size of the unobserved economy in Sweden on the basis of the preceding estimates of tax evasion. The unobserved economy, defined as economic activities that are not included in national account statistics, may be divided into economic activities that generate income that should be taxed according to the tax law and other economic activities. The latter group includes cooking your own food, repairing your own car or house, care and education of your own children, and so on. This division of the unobserved economy into a taxable and non-taxable unobserved economy is similar but not identical to Feige's (1979) division of the unobserved economy into a monetary and non-monetary unobserved economy. Since GDP is calculated from the expenditure side, the discrepancy between the expenditure side and the

231

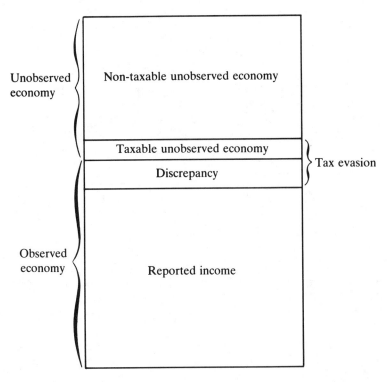

Figure 9.3. Disaggregation of observed and unobserved economy.

income side is included in the observed economy. The relation between the different groups of economic activities is shown in Figure 9.3. The figure reveals that the taxable unobserved economy may be calculated as tax evasion minus the discrepancy in national account statistics.

One of the preceding methods estimates tax evasion as the discrepancy between expenditure and reported income after adjustment for minor likely underestimations on the expenditure side. This method is therefore not suitable for estimation of the taxable unobserved economy. However, the other four methods for estimating tax evasion are independent of national account statistics. These estimates of tax evasion may therefore be compared to the discrepancy in national account statistics in order to evaluate the size of the taxable unobserved economy.

All four estimation methods indicate tax evasion that indeed is lower than the discrepancy in national accounts statistics. This in turn indicates a relatively small taxable unobserved economy in Sweden. Since each of these four methods involves large sources of error, the reliability of this conclusion is also subject to question. As a reasonable cautious conclusion, these results show that it is unlikely that the taxable unobserved economy exceeds, say, 10% of GDP. Since the monetary unobserved economy probably is smaller than the taxable unobserved economy due to exclusions of barter, these results also indicate a quite small monetary unobserved economy in Sweden.

Evaluation of unobserved and untaxed sectors: measurement errors in official statistics

This section examines the importance of the measurement errors in official statistics that arise due to the existence of an unobserved economy.

If the analysis is confined to those economic activities that are intended to be measured by national account statistics, measurement errors in GDP arise mainly as a result of the taxable unobserved economy. The preceding estimate of a quite small taxable unobserved economy indicates that such measurement errors are likely to be small.

Table 9.1 shows the magnitude of the measurement errors for the growth rate when the taxable unobserved economy amounts to 10% of the observed economy and this share grows with one percentage point per year. Given these upper bound assumptions for the size and growth of the unobserved taxable economy, the error in the growth rate in Table 9.1, 0.9%, is small as compared to the decrease in the growth rate for the observed economy in Sweden from 4.8% in 1960–70 to 1.4% in 1970–8.

If the price level in the unobserved taxable economy is 50% of the price level in the observed economy for year 1 and 49% in year 2, an observed rate of inflation of 10% corresponds to a rate of inflation of 9.4% for the entire taxable economy. Again, the measurement error is small as compared to the increase in the recorded rate of inflation, from 4.0% in 1960–70 to 9.0% in 1970–8.

The measurement errors for growth and inflation are thus small given our estimates for the size and growth of the unobserved taxable economy. In order to explain a major part of the stagflation in Sweden during the 1970's, the unobserved taxable economy must be considerably higher and grow considerably faster than is indicated in the estimates given here.

If the analysis is expanded to also include the non-taxable unobserved economy, the unobserved economy is likely to be quite large as compared to the observed economy. The measurement of the observed

233

Table 9.1. *Measurement error in growth rate*

Year	Observed taxable economy	Unobserved taxable economy	Total taxable economy
1	100	10	110
2	102	11.22	113.22
Growth rate, %	2	—	2.9

economy may then, of course, provide poor information of the development of the total economy.

In a general equilibrium model of the Swedish economy with a taxed and an untaxed sector, Hansson and Stuart (1982) simulate a model for which tax increases have decreased the yearly growth rate of the taxed sector by 1.1–1.6 percentage points for the period 1965–79. The tax increases are, however, also simulated to have increased the growth rate of the untaxed sector by 0.4–0.5 percentage points. Since these sectors are of equal magnitude, the simulated effect on the total economy is a decrease in the growth rate of 0.4–0.6 percentage points. The difference between the growth rates for the total economy and the taxed sector thus amounts to 0.7–1.0 percentage points in these simulations.

Efficiency effects

This section analyzes the efficiency effects of economic activities in the untaxed sector including the subsector of tax evasion. The 75% marginal tax rate in the taxed sector means that gross returns from taxed production must be four times as high as gross returns from the untaxed sector in order to give the same net return. An equilibrium with equalized net returns from the taxed and the untaxed sectors thus involves considerable efficiency losses due to a too small taxed sector. As an example, production in the untaxed sector may be more costly due to higher transaction costs and restrictions to small-scale technology in order to keep the activity within the untaxed sector. For the subsector that evades taxes, small-scale technology may be selected to escape detection. In addition, costs arise for non-monetary punishments, risk of punishments, and "moral" costs.

Production in the untaxed sector may be competitive as compared to production in the taxed sector due to the large wedge between gross and net returns in this sector.

The untaxed sector, including the subsector that evades taxes, not only draws resources from the taxed sector but also exchanges resources within the sector and draws time and effort from untaxed uses such as leisure. In this case the untaxed economy gives mutual gains from exchange of services that arise due to this exchange or that otherwise would have been produced within the household. As an example, a car mechanic and a painter may gain by exchange of services without losses for other taxpayers if the alternative is to repair their own cars and paint their own houses. If, as in the earlier case, the alternative is to buy these services from the taxed sector, the production in the untaxed sector may involve efficiency losses due to less efficient methods of production and losses for other taxpayers.

To summarize, the untaxed sector involves efficiency losses for resources that are drawn from the taxed sector and efficiency gains for resources that are exchanged within the sector or drawn from other untaxed users.

An evaluation of the efficiency effects of the unobserved economy must thus consider the extent to which resources are drawn from these alternative uses. Since gains from exchange are small and close to an equilibrium, this suggests that a proportional decrease of all types of activities in the untaxed sector involves net gains over some range. Further contractions of the untaxed sector may involve elimination of exchanges within the untaxed sector with considerable mutual benefits and shifts of resources from the untaxed sector to the taxed sector where the latter is almost as efficient as the former.

This admittedly loose discussion and illustration indicate that there may exist some intermediate efficient level for untaxed activities that is sufficiently large to allow for the most beneficial exchanges within the untaxed sector and sufficiently small to avoid an excessive reallocation of resources from the taxed into the untaxed sector.

A similar analysis can be applied in order to determine the optimal level of tax evasion. The optimal level of tax evasion is sufficiently large to allow for the most beneficial exchanges and sufficiently small to avoid an excessive drain of resources from the taxed sector.

The indicated, somewhat trivial policy conclusion is to select an intermediate level for tax revisions and punishments in order to get this level of tax evasion.

In addition, efficiency gains may arise from a discriminating policy that focuses tax revisions and punishments on activities that are likely to draw resources from the taxed sector, with a more lenient policy for tax evasion that mainly draws resources from other untaxed uses of time and effort. As an example, tax revisions might focus on underreporting in manufacturing firms rather than on barter income of babysitting and minor repair services among neighbors.

Distribution effects

The untaxed sector, including the subsector of tax evasion, also affects the distribution of real income among different groups. The existence of tax evasion redistributes real income in favor of producers and consumers of goods and services that evade taxes at the expense of other taxpayers.

At the margin, benefits are balanced by costs in the form of expected punishment, risk, and moral costs, while intramarginal benefits may involve considerable redistribution effects. In competitive subsectors with a perfectly elastic supply of production factors and constant returns to scale, the entire benefit of tax evasion is pushed forward to consumers through lower prices. More generally, the absence of taxes in the untaxed sector favors people with comparative advantages in this sector. People with skills and interest in repair and care services thus gain as compared to people with skills that mainly can be used in the taxed sector. The existence of tax evasion and, more generally, untaxed economy activities also hamper government efforts to redistribute income on the basis of recorded income.

Concluding comments

To summarize, tax evasion and, more generally, untaxed economic activities involve both positive and negative efficiency effects. Redistribution effects arise that are, to a large extent, beyond the control of official redistribution policies.

For tax evasion, these conclusions, together with the findings of a rather limited amount of tax evasion, suggest that efficiency and redistribution effects are rather small as compared to the large interest in tax evasion shown by public and mass media. This concern may perhaps instead be explained in terms of prospects of large individual gains from tax evasion, the involved gamble or risk element, the conflict with the principle of equal treatment of persons with equal actual income, and the potential challenge to social coherence.

When the perspective is broadened to include the entire unobserved economy, the much larger size of this economy is likely to involve more important efficiency and redistribution issues that to a large extent are unobserved in statistics and in traditional economic analysis.

CHAPTER 10

The irregular economy of Italy:
a survey of contributions

BRUNO CONTINI

Some preliminary history

The Italian debate on the unobserved economy dates back to the early 1970's when several authors of labor market studies pointed out the rapid decline in the labor force participation rate. During the late 1950's, the official overall participation rate (defined here as the ratio of labor force to total population) was nearly 45%, comparable to that of most industrialized countries. During the late 1960's, it declined to 39%, and by the mid-1970's it had dropped to less than 35%, far below the trend of all of Italy's neighbors, let alone of countries such as France and the United States, where female participation rates were already rising and have indeed risen remarkably during the last decade. The idea developed that the massive outflow from agriculture – far from being completed – might explain a fraction of the decline at the most; the rest reflect increasingly wider segments of the population of working age holding unrecorded jobs of various kinds and yet claiming not to belong to the active population for fear of losing these jobs.

With the passage of time, there was growing confirmation that the participation rates estimated by ISTAT (Italian National Income and Product Accounts Authority) via the Quarterly Survey on the Labor Force (QSLF) had widely underestimated the extent of individual participation in the active population. It was observed that participation rates were falling for some categories of workers (women of all ages and the young and the aged of both sexes) but not for male workers in their "prime" years. Thus, as aggregate demand had ceased to grow at the pace of the early 1960's, it appeared that business firms were selecting their work force according to each worker's productivity, with the "stronger" workers retained and the "weaker" being expelled from the labor force much in the same way as in a Ricardian model of land exploitation. The next step in the direction of arousing scholars' interest was Frey's discovery (1975a) of a remarkable increase of work-at-home activity related to the garment industry of Lombardy, which took place simultaneously with a vast reduction of recorded female blue-collar employment.

237

Numerous field studies and community surveys soon followed up these leads, yielding growing evidence of the importance of semi-hidden labor in all branches of productive activities.[1,2]

A brief historical survey of the irregular economy in Italy

The peak of the Italian postwar export-led growth was reached in 1962. At this time, it was commonly believed that Italy was near full employment. Industrial wages had increased more slowly than average productivity, investment was high, and the productive system had expanded rapidly in the exporting sectors (although considerably less so in sectors aimed at supplying domestic demand). In 1962, wages began to increase more rapidly as a natural consequence of the progressive opening of the European Economic Community (EEC) labor market. The ensuing decline in profits forced Italian manufacturing industries to search for new cost containment strategies. The period from 1963 to 1972 was consequently characterized by a massive labor-saving effort on the part of industry. This was carried out in two ways. The first was that of increasing labor productivity by concentrating male workers of "prime age" in the industrial labor force. This was achieved by a substantial reduction of women's participation, by a progressive lowering of the retirement age, and by hiring practices that excluded the younger members of the labor force. The second was that of decentralizing the production of labor-intensive items that were not amenable to assembly line production. The institution of craft shops, the setting up of small-scale manufacturing units, and the more extensive utilization of work-at-home were all aimed at recovering full labor flexibility. Throughout the years of the boom, wide and stable wage differentials between major classes of the labor force (male vs. female and skilled vs. unskilled) were a distinguishing feature of Italy's labor market. During the mid-1960's these differentials began to decrease under union pressure for equalization, although there were no corresponding gains in average productivity. On the contrary, during those years productivity differentials were moving further and further apart. The 1963–4 slowdown in eco-

---

[1] It goes beyond the historical note to emphasize that the interest in discovering more about the patterns of utilization of irregular workers was a direct outgrowth of a political involvement on the part of many young scholars of the Left who were anxious to know if and how the system was responding to the harm inflicted by the labor movement during the late 1960's and early 1970's.

[2] See Bergonzini (1973); Boltacchiari, Crespi, and Segatori (1976); Brusco (1975); Canullo and Montanari (1978); Comune di Modena (1978); Deaglio (1974); and Frey (1975b).

238

nomic activity struck a mortal blow to the construction industry at a time
when demand for low-cost housing, services, and social infrastructures
was rapidly expanding in urban and industrialized areas. The construction boom of the earlier decade had attracted a substantial labor mi-
gration from the southern regions of Italy. Widespread discontent and
grievances among the more disadvantaged workers began to come to
a head. Absenteeism and dissatisfaction increased rapidly, especially
among women workers who found it increasingly difficult to divide their
time between market work and domestic activities. Occasionally, absenteeism was tentatively accepted by the unions on the grounds that it
was a kind of indirect compensation for poor living conditions and for
a lack of adequate social services. All in all, unit labor costs of the
"secondary" components of the labor force (i.e., women and the young
and the aged of both sexes) increased and started to move ahead of the
costs of "primary" workers, thus harming employment opportunities for
the weakest fringes of the labor force.

Towards the end of the 1960's, the situation was ripe for the "re-
venge" of the market. Money wages in the official labor market could
not be held down (real wages were still lower than in all of the other
neighboring countries), and therefore, a parallel market for "irregular"
labor services began to develop. The supply of irregular labor grew
rapidly, as did the demand for its services. Many workers seemed to
prefer precarious forms of employment – which yielded money wages
below the official market rates but allowed a high degree of flexibility in
the allocation of their time – to forced inactivity. Firms that had the
option of utilizing irregular labor, either directly or by subcontracting
to small-scale manufacturers, were eager to take full advantage of this
prevailing attitude.

On the demand side, payroll tax avoidance provided an incentive to
hire irregular workers. Other cost-saving incentives included the avoidance of union contracts, piece rate payment, and retention of unlimited
flexibility of labor utilization in terms of working hours and layoffs. On
the supply side, too, incentives to conceal the employment status are
powerful. Income tax evasion is the most obvious one, but the flexibility
of working time – especially for women but also for the young and
the aged of both sexes – is equally important for understanding the
seemingly everlasing supply of irregular labor.

A framework for the labor market approach

The framework that has become common to all Italian studies on the
"irregular" labor market can be represented as follows:

I   Non-active population (ISTAT definition)
    (1) Unavailable for work
    (2) Available for irregular activities
II Unemployed (drawing unemployment benefits)
    (1) Not working
    (2) Holding temporary jobs while waiting for permanent positions
III "Officially" employed (with social security coverage)
    (1) Holding only one job
    (2) Multiple job holders
IV Clandestine aliens (in working age)

In this schema, irregular activities include items I.2, II.2, III.2, and IV. The term "irregular activities" covers any job performed or service rendered outside the social security system. Irregular activities include overtime work paid under the table by otherwise regular employers and/or performed against negotiated agreements as well as many part-time and temporary jobs (which firms often keep off the books in order to avoid conflict with the unions, which have been openly hostile against them), personal services, illegal building activities, and unregulated apprentice work. Thus, the vast majority of the so-called irregular jobs are by their very nature unprotected, often precarious, and beyond any form of organized social control.

There is no doubt that the size of the irregular economy is closely related to the flexibility of labor utilization, which may be defined as the possibility of firms to adjust the size of the labor force according to their needs. This possibility depends on the institutional characteristics of the labor market in a particular country and on the fiscal system. In Italy, payroll taxes and indirect charges add 50–70% to the basic pay (substantially more than in any of the other EEC countries). This is, taken by itself, a powerful incentive for tax evasion on the side of the employers.[3] Moreover, labor legislation applying to all firms with more than fifteen employees requires that jobs cannot be terminated unless the firm can prove the existence of "a just cause." Various forms of just causes aimed at protecting job security exist in most European countries, although they are nowhere as strict as in Italy.

Multiple job holding

Rigorous sample studies aimed at measuring the extent of multiple job

---

[3] Payroll taxes are the major financial sources for the social security system. Revenue from direct taxation is lower in Italy than in most Western countries in spite of the marked progressiveness of income taxation due to income tax evasion in the middle- and high-income brackets.

holding in the Italian economy were undertaken in the ISFOL-Doxa surveys (1977, 1981). It estimated that, in 1974, 1,068,000 officially employed people held two or more jobs (i.e., 5.5% of the official labor force). Gallino (1975) provided indirect estimates of the same order of magnitude.

It is well known that many multiple job holders in the urban areas are employed in the public sector where the working schedule has traditionally been very light. A normal schedule often runs from 8 am to 2 pm for less than 30 effective hours a week. This is a peculiar compensation for pay levels that have often been lower than for comparable jobs in the private sector. Multiple job holding is also very common among factory workers in the large industrial areas.

The aim of later contributions was that of identifying some qualitative characteristics of multiple jobs and multiple job holders rather than that of improving the overall estimate. Sample surveys conducted in the Turin metropolitan area indicated that 90% of the multiple job holders were men, their average age higher than that of women holding more than one job and their education significantly lower. Multiple job holding appeared to be a steady activity (80% of the workers had held more than one job over the last four years). Business firms offered mainly white-collar jobs (bookkeeping, sales jobs, computer programming, tax consulting) whereas households requested personal services, maintenance, and repair jobs. Hourly pay offered for second jobs normally exceeded the official take-home pay.

Another example of significant research in a very different social context is that of Canullo and Montanari (1978). Their survey included 1,984 workers, all residents of four rural villages in Central Italy. Of those interrogated, 14% held more than one job, and sometimes neither would be regular. Of the multiple job holders, 41% were part-time farmers; 20% of the second jobs were in the manufacturing sector, and 39% were in the services.

Work-at-home in the manufacturing sector

The basic study on this aspect of the irregular economy in Italy is by Frey, Livraghi, and De Santis (1975), which gives a detailed picture of the emerging organization of the hosiery, garment, and textile sectors in the early 1970's. According to their estimates, workers-at-home in these sectors of manufacturing exceeded 500,000. All were women, often in their teens or early twenties and over fifty. Most lived in relatively wealthy rural areas and could therefore easily engage in some form of part-time farming.

Table 10.1. *Work-at-home in manufacturing, 1972–3*

Workers-at-home	Product	Regions
480,000	Hosiery	Emilia, Veneto, Tuscany, Marche, Puglia
150,000	Textiles	Piedmont, Tuscany
150,000	Shoes	Veneto, Tuscany
155,000	Toys	Liguria, Tuscany
100,000	Auto accessories	Piedmont, Lombardy
90,000	Garments	Tuscany, Emilia, Lombardy, Puglia, Laxi
80,000	Leather products	Veneto, Tuscany, Lazio, Lombardy
68,000	Gloves	Campania
30,000	Cosmetic products	Sicily, Calabria
40,000	Plastic products	Piedmont, Lombardy, Tuscany
25,000	Tiles	Veneto, Umbria, Abruzzi, Sicily
20,000	Electrical motors	Lombardy
15,000	Bicycles	Lombardy, Marche
15,000	Glass	Tuscany
12,000	Furniture	Tuscany
170,000	Miscellaneous	Veneto, Lombardy, Lazio
1,600,000	Total	(manufacturing only)

Sources: S. Brusco, "Prime Note per un Studio del Lavoro a Domicilio," *Inchiesta*, April–June 1973.

Another early study of the mechanical sector is that of Brusco (1975), who discovered that work-at-home was also widely utilized for the assembly of bicycles, motorcycles, and cars, with a vast majority of unskilled women workers paid by piece rate.

During the middle and late 1970's, there was an increase of field studies, all aimed at discovering the emerging organization of this apparently new mode of production. Table 10.1 provides a summary of estimates of the presence of workers-at-home in the manufacturing sector at about 1972–3.

Irregular working activities

Various estimates of irregular activities at large have been constructed on the basis of findings from the QSLF. In the CERES (Centro Ricerche Economiche e Sociali, Milano) study (1978) the population is classified by sex, age, and professional status (Table 10.2). Fragments of information from various sources were pooled together with appropriate weights, yielding a ratio estimate of irregular activity in the population control totals given by the QSLF.

Table 10.2. *CERES estimates of the irregular labor force in 1977 (in thousands)*

Age bracket	Men	Women	Total
14–29	520	890	1410
30–49	0	600	600
50 and over	450	810	1260
Total	970	2300	3270

Table 10.3. *Estimates of non-agricultural irregular working activities in the mid-1970's*

Manufacturing	1.6 million
Construction	0.6 million
Retail and wholesale trade	1.4 million
Services (other)	1.0 million
Total	4.6 million

Source: B. Contini, *Lo Sviluppo di un'Economia Parallela*, Banca Commerciale Italiana, Milano (1979).

The CERES estimate of 3,270,000 irregular workers implies a real participation rate of 44.7% (against 36.1% ISTAT old series and 38.9% ISTAT new series). No key to judge the statistical significance of these figures is provided by CERES. It should be pointed out that CERES counts workers, not jobs. Thus, the fact that there are no "irregulars" among male workers between 30 and 49 years of age means simply that none were found who only had irregular jobs. However, many of the officially unemployed were also active in the irregular sector while searching for a job and drawing unemployment compensation. Hence, the number of irregular positions in 1977 was certainly higher than 3,270,000. One estimate [reported in Contini (1979) and reproduced in Table 10.3] puts this number at around 4.6 million, not counting the irregular jobs of the agricultural sector. This, too, is likely to under-estimate the extent of irregular activities. For instance, the number of clandestine working aliens – both seasonal and permanent – appears to have grown rapidly in Italy throughout the 1970's. In default of ad hoc surveys, estimating their number is at best an educated guess.[4] CENSIS

---

[4] The Ministry of Internal Affairs occasionally releases data on temporary residence permits granted to aliens.

(Centro Studi Investimenti Sociali, Rome) puts it at around 1 million for 1978, their presence being concentrated in the agricultural sector and domestic services. Fishing and the retail trade appear to be dominated by workers of North African origin and in domestic services for the Somali (almost all women) and for the Latin and Central Americans.

The skills required for most irregular activities are usually very modest. One important exception is found among the multiple job holders (Gallino, 1980; Brusco, 1975). These often have special skills that are in great demand, both in the white- and blue-collar sectors. This finding is in line with available information about other countries.

Micro-approaches to the estimation of the irregular labor supply

Colombino (1978) was the first to produce a testable model of family-generated labor supply estimated by means of micro-observations. Del Boca and Turvani (1979) discussed the different roles of the family in rural and urban contexts and its connection with the supply of irregular labor. In the rural areas, the "extended" family, with all its members engaged in various market and non-market activities within a seasonal framework, is ideally suited to meet the demands of a highly flexible industrial structure based on small business firms. In metropolitan areas the range of consumer choices and expectations becomes larger, but at the same time the often disorderly development of urbanization and industrialization produce environmental externalities that increase the costs of transaction in goods and labor markets. Thus, people must increasingly rely on the family organization as a unit for producing goods and services. Likewise, the need for a high degree of flexibility of one's own time induces many to search for job opportunities on the irregular labor market where flexibility is the rule of the game.

Growth and determinants of the irregular economy

The aim of the Italian studies mentioned so far is that of establishing the magnitude of the irregular sector as a whole or of some important subsectors and of eventually specifying its qualitative characteristics. The development of the irregular economy in the course of time and its macro-determinants have been studied by Contini (1979 and 1981). As a basis for his estimation of the relevant variables, he adopted the following equation:

$$FLT = OT + OA + U_1 + U_2 \tag{10.1}$$

FLT = potential labor force
OT = permanent employment in industry
OA = permanent employment in agriculture and services[5]
U_1 = official unemployment
U_2 = irregular labor force

The potential labor force was estimated on the basis of two surveys of the non-working population conducted by ISTAT in 1971 and 1975.[6] Here U_2 is a residual indicator that comprises most of the irregular labor force, that is, marginal and irregular workers of all sectors, including underemployed, seasonal workers, part-timers, as well as the "discouraged" fraction of the population in working age that is excluded from the official count of the labor force. To a large extent, the discouraged fraction overlaps with the former categories.

These calculations suggest that U_2 reached a minimum of 1.6. million in 1962 (at the peak of the boom), more than doubled to 3.8 million in 1972, and widely fluctuated from then onward around a trend that is still moving upward, although at a slower pace than before. This corresponds to the ratio of irregular employment to the total labor force of about 16–18% at the end of the 1970's:

$$\frac{U_2}{\text{FLT}} = f(a, c, e) \quad \text{where } c = \frac{W}{\pi} \tag{10.2}$$

Equation (10.2) is a crude, reduced form that indicates the determinants of the rate of irregular employment in a small open economy. There is one structural determinant from the supply side, namely, the flight from agriculture a, which was still a massive phenomenon in the early 1970's despite the uncertainties in the non-farm sectors. The main cyclical determinant from the demand side is unit labor cost c in the "regular" economy, defined as the ratio of money wages W to average productivity π in real terms (exogenous in the short run). Any increase of c will cause the economy to shift supply from the official sectors to the irregular mode of production. The third variable is the exchange rate e between the Italian lira and the Eurodollar, the implication being that the labor cost indicator relevant for the determination of the degree of competitiveness of Italian goods on the world market should be ex-

---

[5] Official data on "permanent employment" have been available through 1974. "Permanent" means work for more than 32 hours a week. The 1975–7 data have been estimated.

[6] These surveys aimed to improve the definition of the non-active population and develop means to detect it. The survey was replicated in 1977 and served as a basis for the reformulation of the questionnaire currently used by ISTAT.

pressed in the currency in which contracts are usually denominated. This model would require explicit measurement of unit cost differentials, but no reliable data could be found. The assumption was therefore made that official wages have been substantially higher and have moved at a more rapid pace than those paid on the irregular market. Estimation was performed on the basis of quarterly data for the 1965–77 period and yielded the following equation (*t*-ratios in parentheses):

$$\frac{U_2}{\text{FLT}} = \underset{(8.11)}{35.04} - \underset{(2.81)}{0.0035a} + \underset{(3.67)}{0.022c} - 0.016e_{-1}$$
$$(R^2 = 0.89, \text{DW} = 2.36) \tag{10.3}$$

The flight from agriculture, *a*, explains approximately 55% of the variance of U_2/FLT. The rest is well explained by unit labor cost and by the exchange rate, confirming that the devaluation implicit in flexible changes has kept the relevant unit labor cost lower than that expressed in national currency. The elasticity of substitution between unit labor cost and the exchange rate is approximately −2. Thus, with *a* constant, the growth rate of the irregular economy would have been stable around its 1978 level (16.8%) if an annual increase of 10% in the labor cost per unit of output were countered by a 5% depreciation of the lira against the Eurodollar.

Small-scale industry and recourse to irregular work

Much of the literature on the unobsereved economy of the Western world indicates that hidden activities take place mainly in the services and in house maintenance and repair. In Italy the unobserved economy has also taken hold in the manufacturing sector. Does the Italian case therefore run counter to experience? The branches of manufacturing known to include the bulk of irregular activities cover a wide range of consumption good production. All are highly labor intensive, economies of scale do not play a major role, and the technology easily lends itself to piece rate pay. Moreover, the size of firms that operate in these sectors is typically small compared to the rest of manufacturing, which makes concealment easy and union control less tight.

There is also another explanation. Large-scale production can often be broken down into self-contained processes that may widely differ from a technological point of view or in terms of the labor intensity required to perform them. The highly labor-intensive processes can be profitably subcontracted to firms that have access to cheap labor. Until now, there are a considerable number of such firms in Italy's irregular economy that have adopted the role of substitutes (subsidiaries) for (to) the better known international subcontracting firms. Decentralization of production and subcontracting to small-scale businesses appear, therefore, to be the distinguishing features of the Italian manufacturing sector in the 1970's. Direct utilization of irregular labor is confined to small and very small businesses, whereas indirect recourse to the irregular labor market touches almost everybody. Large firms subcontract to small ones, and these in turn subcontract to even smaller ones, right down to the work-at-home level. One would therefore expect to find differences in behavior – and a substantially better performance – of small businesses vis-à-vis the larger ones since the former have almost free access to the irregular job market. Several indicators of small- and medium-size businesses indeed point in this direction (Contini, 1981). Small firms, more so than larger ones, have added to their stock of fixed capital during the 1968–73 period across all branches of manufacturing. In addition, small businesses have decreased the number of workers, whereas larger firms have increased employment. Indeed, employment figures refer to official employment, providing a hint at the extensive substitution of officially employed workers for irregular workers by smaller entrepreneurs. Unions have prevented the same from happening in larger establishments. Finally, gross (before-tax) profit shares on value added have been much higher among the small firms during the mid-1970's than among the large ones. Other studies have pointed in the same direction. Brusco (1975, 1979) estimated cost curves for different stages of the production process in several industries (garments, hosiery, and tile manufacturing) and in areas where work-at-home activities were traditionally very extensive. He discovered that whereas economies of scale were present in firms with antiquated machinery and shop layout, their impact was not nearly as important as that of firms that had invested in new technology and modified their organizational structure accordingly. Thus, decentralization of production may take place without the loss of economies of scale. In addition, there are the cost savings allowed by recourse to highly flexible labor. Where these developments have taken place, the expansion of small manufacturing units has been very high, but recourse to work-at-home appears to be on the decline.

The irregular economy Italian style versus other definitions

As we have seen in this survey, Italian authors apply the term "irregular economy" in a sense that is somewhat more narrow than other definitions that have occasionally been suggested. The following classification by type of activity provides a useful framework (Barthelemy, 1981):

a Household production and non-market activities
b Irregular working activities
c Work performed by clandestine workers and minors
d Criminal activities

The first three categories represent legal activities performed in an illegal fashion. The final category represents illegal activity. This classification distinguishes between criminal activities (i.e., drug trade, narcotics, gambling, prostitution, bribing, and laundering of stolen money and goods) and all other activities that are legal but may be performed against fiscal and/or labor legislation. Studies of the Italian labor markets refer to activities b and c, and these are the categories most likely to be affected by labor legislation and fiscal incentives. The underground (hidden) economy in its broadest sense includes all four activities.

Estimates of the size of the irregular GNP

The emphasis of most Italian research has been on the interpretation of the development of the irregular labor force rather than on efforts to estimate the fraction of total income produced in the irregular sector. For many of those who used the labor market as the main indirect indicator of irregular activities, there was a natural method to quantify the share of irregular income in total economic activity. Given the number of irregular workers and the average productivity of these workers, it is possible to derive irregular income estimates once estimates on the number of workers are transformed into estimates of the number of irregular jobs. A very conservative estimate of this kind (Contini, 1979) calculates the share of GNP accounted for by irregular labor to be approximately 7.5% of the official GNP in 1977. In the same year ISTAT undertook a major revision of GDP estimates in order to take better account of the unrecorded activities. The criteria for revising the existing indicators were twofold:

a increasing the employment data to account for irregular, unrecorded positions in each sector and
b updating the estimates of per capita value added generated by firms with less than 20 employees, still linked to a sample survey of small industrial businesses conducted in 1967.

Table 10.4 reveals the sizable revisions in the GDP that were necessitated by these improvements in estimation methods. The GDP figures

Table 10.4. *Differences between old and new estimates of gross domestic product (after ISTAT revisions 1977)*

Sectors	In current liras (billions)		1977	Percentage variations		
	1975	1976	1977	1975	1976	1977
Agriculture	—	18	305	—	+0.2	+2.3
Industry	5,324	6,760	9,069	+11.1	+11.0	+12.4
Energy	5	−21	119	+0.1	−0.3	+1.3
Manufacturing	4,650	5,987	7,808	+14.3	+13.7	+15.3
Building	699	794	1,142	+7.2	+7.2	+8.6
Private services	2,530	3,132	3,878	+5.3	+5.4	+5.6
Trade and hotel services	2,321	3,092	4,084	+14.0	+15.1	+16.6
Transportation	750	559	851	+12.1	+7.1	+8.7
Others: banks and insurance	−541	−519	−1,057	−2.2	−1.8	−3.0
Public services	2,452	2,899	3,552	+19.3	+18.7	+18.4
Total GDP	10,306	12,808	16,990	+9.0	+8.9	+9.8

were increased by 8.9% for 1976 and by 9.8% for 1977. Thereafter, the GDP year-to-year variations were linked to the revised 1977 figures.

There is wide consensus that ISTAT has moved in the right direction with the 1977 revision. According to Blades (1982), Italy's national accounts now cover a higher proportion of undeclared activities than most of the other industrialized countries of the Western world. The current understatement of GDP due to undeclared legal activities has been estimated to be on the order of 6% (Frey 1979).

Other indirect estimates have been provided by Alvaro (1979), who suggested that the share of unrecorded GNP was 14%, and by Forte (1979), whose estimate was 15% for 1979 plus another 7% due to under-estimation of income generated by residential housing. These estimates also include unreported incomes of professionals, independent workers, and shopkeepers, which the labor market studies fail to cover.

The only estimate based on a somewhat naive version of the *C/D* method is reported in Saba (1980). Not surprisingly, Saba's figures are higher than those reported in other studies. Whereas the normal GNP grew at an average annual rate of 16.7% during the years 1968–78, the average growth rate of the irregular GNP is calculated at 30.8%. Thus, by the end of 1978, the share of the irregular GNP was estimated to exceed 30% of the officially reported figure, whereas it was below 10% in 1968.

A synthesis of contemporary Italian research

Summarizing the state of current and past research on the irregular economy in Italy, the following may be observed. There have been several large surveys on specific sectors of industrial activity, and of those conducted only a few were based on rigorous statistical sampling. However, we have witnessed an upsurge of field research and community studies. These provide many important insights into local situations but leave much to be desired from a statistical point of view in that few generalizations are possible and no inferences about underlying population parameters may be drawn. Several authors have decided to check the findings of field research and community studies against existing statistical indicators of the labor force and of activity rates. Their aim was to search for systematic discrepancies between the official data and the alternative findings. Some succeeded in improving existing estimates; others managed to provide a more satisfactory macro-interpretation of recent developments. Finally, there are two ISTAT special surveys on the non-active population (1971, 1975), both confirming that the real participation rate was substantially higher than that revealed by the QSLF. These special surveys provide the basis for the new format of the Quarterly Survey as initiated in January 1977. It is specifically aimed at uncovering activities that previously escaped the ISTAT findings. According to this newly designed survey, the average participation rate in 1977 was 38% rather than the 35.9% estimated by the old survey. This appears to be a step in the right direction, although there is a widely shared belief that the amount of underestimation of the activity rates in the new ISTAT series is still considerable.

CHAPTER 11

The hidden economy in Norway with special emphasis on the hidden labor market

ARNE JON ISACHSEN and STEINER STROM

Studying the hidden economy requires an operational definition of it. Feige's (1979) definition is "those economic activities that go unreported or are unmeasured by the society's current techniques for monitoring economic activity" (p. 6). Tanzi's (1982) definition of the hidden economy is "gross national product that because of unreporting and/or underreporting is not measured by official statistics" (p. 70). Macafee (1980) offers yet a third definition.

In light of these various definitions, it is not surprising that the various methods that have been employed to estimate the hidden economy often measure different things. Estimations based on the development of the composition of the money stock will not include barter transactions. Analysis performed by the Internal Revenue Service focuses on unreported income that implies tax evasion, whereas the GNP concept of income is broader than taxable income. Nevertheless, the lack of a general and operational definition of the hidden economy should not keep researchers from trying to measure parts of it, bearing in mind that different methods most likely capture different unregistered activities.

We have attempted to measure the hidden economy of Norway in terms of a micro- and a macro-approach. The micro-approach, based on a survey study conducted in September 1980, is rather novel. The macro-study is more traditional as it focuses on the development of the stock of currency.

The micro-approach was solely related to unreported income from work. The main purpose of the survey was to collect data in order to test hypotheses concerning the effects of marginal taxes, penalty charges, probabilities of detection, and demographic factors on the supply of labor in the hidden economy.

Allingham and Sandmo (1972) modeled the tax declaration decision as a decision problem under uncertainty. Ignoring the labor supply decision, they could concentrate on the portfolio aspects. In such a framework a change in the (average) tax rate will have the traditional income and substitution effects working in opposite directions when the

251

tax-reporting individual is risk averse. Changes in the probability of detection and in the penalty rate generate substitution effects with unambiguous signs.

When the Allingham–Sandmo approach is extended to allow for a variable labor supply, all the partial derivatives become ambiguous (Weiss, 1976; Baldry, 1979; and Pencavel, 1979). Isachsen and Strom (1980) demonstrate that unambiguous results can be obtained by assuming a specific utility function yielding an inelastic *total* supply of hours of work.

Despite the increasing number of theoretical contributions, few, if any, have tried to test empirically how various factors influence the behavior of the agents in the hidden economy, or to quote Pencavel (1979, p. 124): "In view of this, what this literature requires is a healthy infusion of empirical work to confront these hypotheses with actual behavior and to resolve the ambiguities derived here."

Lack of relevant data is obviously a problem. Based on completion of 877 questionnaires, each containing 45 questions, we have been able to generate data that makes it possible to start confronting theory with observed behavior.

At the outset it is pertinent to warn against placing too much confidence in the results. Measuring what is supposed to be hidden is likely to give results that abound with uncertainties.

The macro-approach

We shall very briefly go through the estimation of the size of the hidden economy based on the macro-approach. With some few, but important, changes, the estimates given are based on Klovland (1980) and Isachsen, Klovland, and Strom in Tanzi (1982). The method of estimating the size of the hidden economy is based on the demand for currency assuming that higher tax rates will promote tax evasion, which in turn will increase the demand for currency. This last assumption is supported by the results of the survey study discussed in the third section.

The following variables are needed:

C = currency held by public
P = price index
Y = real GDP
i = rate of return on time deposits
π = rate of inflation
CON/Y = private consumption as share of GDP
t = gross marginal tax rate
θ = stock adjustment parameter, $0 \leq \theta \leq 1$

252

The model can be specified as

$$\ln C - \ln C_{-1} = \theta(\ln C^* - \ln C_{-1}) \tag{11.1}$$

where C^* is the long-run demand for currency, and

$$\ln\frac{C^*}{P} = a_0 + a_1\ln Y + a_2 i + a_3\pi + a_4\frac{CON}{Y} + a_5 t \tag{11.2}$$

The coefficients are expected to be signed as follows: $a_1 > 0$, $a_2 < 0$, $a_3 < 0$, $a_4 > 0$, and $a_5 > 0$. These coefficients were estimated by a single-equation approach ignoring the obvious simultaneity involved. A fourth-degree Almon lag of the tax variable was employed since the effects of higher tax rates on tax evasion are likely to be spread out in time. The coefficient attached to the tax variable a_5 is the sum of the lagged coefficients. Annual data were used, covering the period 1952–79.

The estimation gave the following result (t-values are in parentheses):

$$\ln\frac{C}{P} = \underset{(3.65)}{-1.250} + \underset{(3.41)}{0.309\ln Y} - \underset{(2.54)}{0.024i} + \underset{(0.03)}{0.003\pi} + \underset{(1.44)}{0.001\frac{CON}{Y}}$$
$$+ 0.007t + 0.534\ln\frac{C_{-1}}{P} \tag{11.3}$$

All the estimated coefficients, except for the coefficient attached to the inflation rate, have the expected sign.

To proceed with estimation of the size of the hidden economy, we rewrite (11.3) as

$$\ln C = \ln P + \hat{a}Z + \hat{a}_5 t \tag{11.4}$$

where the term aZ includes the a's and the other variables except for the tax rate. Here $\hat{a}$ and $\hat{a}_5$ are estimated values.

Predicting currency holdings at time τ is then

$$\hat{C}_\tau = \exp(\ln P_\tau + \hat{a}Z_\tau + \hat{a}_\tau t_\tau) \tag{11.5}$$

To obtain in estimate of the size of the hidden economy, we selected 1952 as a base year. Thus, if the tax rate had remained at the 1952 level, the predicted value of currency holdings would have been

$$\hat{C}_{52,\tau} = \exp(\ln P_\tau + \hat{a}\hat{Z}_\tau + \hat{a}_5 t_{52}) \tag{11.6}$$

The difference $\Delta C_\tau = \hat{C}_\tau - \hat{C}_{52,\tau}$ would then give the increase in the amount of currency needed to fuel the tax evasion part of the economy compared to the normal currency needs in this part of the economy in 1952. We next assume that no tax evasion took place in 1952 or in

253

preceding years. The difference $\Delta\hat{C}_\tau$ would then yield an estimate of all currency circulating in the hidden economy at time τ. Inserting observations for the assumed exogenous variables, we obtain the following estimate for $\tau = 1978$:

$$\Delta C_{1978} = 2.9 \text{ billion Kr} \qquad (11.7)$$

To complete the story, we need an estimate of the income velocity of currency. Due to the Norwegian bank giro system, transaction balances have been enlarged to include a fraction of time deposits. Thus, the transaction balances employed, M1, include total currency, ordinary checking accounts, wage accounts, postal giro deposits, and 10% (a qualified guess) of total time deposits. In accordance with Tanzi (1982) and others, we assume that the income velocity of currency in the hidden economy equals the velocity of M1 money in the official parts of the economy. Hence, for 1978 we obtained

$$V_{1,78} = \frac{Y_{78}}{M1_{78} - \Delta C_{78}} = 5.0 \qquad (11.8)$$

where $V_{1,78}$ is the velocity rate, Y_{78} is the official GDP in 1978, $M1_{78}$ is M1 money in 1978 (with parts of time deposits included as explained previously), and ΔC_{78} is estimated in (11.7).

If Y_{78}^b denotes the GDP contribution from the black economy in 1978, then

$$Y_{78}^b = V\Delta C = 5.0 \times 2.9 = 14.5 \text{ billion Kr} \qquad (11.9)$$

and

$$\frac{Y_{78}^b}{Y_{78}} = 0.063 \qquad (11.10)$$

or the black economy is 6.3% of the GDP in the registered parts of the Norwegian economy in 1978.

It is important to notice that this estimate includes all kinds of tax-evading activities. In the next section we will estimate income connected with non-reporting of labor income.

The main results of the survey study

The survey was conducted by a professional private Gallup institute (Markeds-og Mediainstituttet) in September 1980. In concluding the regular interview, the interviewer asked the respondent to receive a questionnaire on the hidden labor market to be filled in and mailed within a week. Of 1198 persons being interviewed, 958 accepted (80%) of which 877 complied by mailing the questionnaire within the next two weeks. This means that of the total sample, 73% complied with the request. Among those who did not want to receive the questionnaire (240 persons), there was an overrepresentation of people aged 65 years and over. For some of the results reported we have corrected for this bias in our sample by proper weighting. Data from the regular interview provided us with some basic socioeconomic information such as sex, age, marital status, place and type of residence, and income. We have no information on the 81 persons that initially agreed to take part in the survey but did not return the questionnaire.

Compared to the population of the country, in our final sample of 877 persons there was an overrepresentation of men aged 25–39 years.

Before reporting the main results of the survey, one further comment on the method is in order. A few months prior to our investigation, the newspaper *Verdens Gang* (VG) reported the results of an interview survey performed by another Gallup institute (Scan-Fact) on the hidden economy. This survey covered 1,002 persons, and respondents were directly interviewed. The results of the two surveys[1] on the question of whether the respondent, over the last 12 months, had participated in the hidden labor market are compared in Table 11.1. Table 11.1 indicates that in a direct-interview survey, people are less willing to acknowledge participation in the unregistered labor market than in a combined interview–postal survey. The reason for this may be that to acknowledge openly one's unregistered economic transactions is more difficult than filling in a questionnaire. Provided one is reasonably certain of preserving anonymity, one may feel less uneasy about putting a few check marks in the proper boxes of a questionnaire.

At any rate, it seems safe to assume that both methods will underestimate the size of the hidden labor market. One way to get a grasp of the degree of underreporting would be to have the correct data on hidden economic activities on a subset of the sample and compare that a priori knowledge with what emerges from the questionnaire. Needless to say, such an approach is quite demanding and was deemed infeasible at the present stage of the project.

The disparities revealed in Table 11.1 remind us of the uncertainties involved in interpreting the results of the survey method when applied to such a sensitive topic as the hidden economy. The main conclusions of our survey approach can be summarized as follows (notice that the

---

[1] Although the questions in the two surveys were not identically worded, the difference was so moderate as to be ignored.

Table 11.1. *Participation rates in the hidden labor market, last 12 months, percentage of sample*

1. Worked in hidden market	20	16
2. Paid for work in hidden market	29	16
3. Worked and paid	9	6
4. Participated in hidden labor market (line 1 + line 2 − line 3)	40	26

Note: In the VG survey the data are not weighted according to sex and age. For proper comparison, our results are given in unweighted form. Results shown are of two surveys both conducted in 1980.

estimates given are adjusted in order to correct for the unrepresentative nature of the sample):

Over the last 12 months (1979–80) 18% of the population above the age of 15 years acknowledged *income* from unreported work, whereas 26% stated that they had *paid* for unregistered services. Taken together, 37.5% of the population had been active in the unregistered labor market over the previous 12 months as buyers and/or sellers. The estimate of 37.5% is adjusted, whereas the estimate of 40.0% in Table 11.1 is unadjusted, derived directly from the answers of the questionnaire.

Forty percent of the respondents answered that at least once in the past they had worked in the hidden economy.

Sixty-five percent answered that they would work in the hidden economy if they had the opportunity.

Hours worked by males and females decline with age. On the demand side the pattern differs among sexes. The demand for irregular labor services reaches a maximum for males between 25–54 years of age. For females there are two maxima: 25–39 years of age and 55 years and over.

Demand for hidden labor services increases with years of schooling. *Supply* of hidden labor services first increases and then decreases with years of schooling.

Based on market wages and on answers on the number of hours worked in the hidden economy, the size of the hidden labor market is estimated to be 5.5 billion Kr. Compared to the GDP of 1979 this amounts to 2.3%. If we base the estimate on what the respondents answered on what they thought were their "neighbors'" participation in the black markets, the estimate is increased to 3.5%.

Buyers of unregistered labor services are generally quite pleased both

256

Table 11.2. *Survey regressions, male propensities I–III*

	"Would if possible" (I)		"Once in the past" (II)		"Last year" (III)	
	Estimated coefficients	Significance level	Estimated coefficients	Significance level	Estimated coefficients	Significance level
A						
Constant term	0.788	0	0.206	0.24	−0.019	0.90
Regular wage rate after marginal tax	−0.003	0.20	−0.002	0.45	−0.003	0.35
Irregular wage rate	0.001	0.43	0.003	0.01	0.001	0.15
Irregular wage rate after penalty charge	−0.001	0.49	−0.002	0.36	0.001	0.47
Probability of detection	−0.579	0	−0.624	0	−0.406	0
Index of gambling	0.027	0.22	0.062	0.02	0.028	0.24
B						
Under 40, unmarried	0.226	0.01	0.257	0.01	0.282	0
Under 40, married, without children	0.228	0.02	0.147	0.20	0.257	0.01
Under 40, married, with children	0.144	0.03	0.112	0.15	0.105	0.14
Above 40, unmarried	0.180	0.19	0.219	0.18	0.146	0.33
Above 40, married children	0.147	0.03	0.073	0.36	−0.006	0.94
C						
Cities	0.077	0.13	0.020	0.74	0.140	0.01
Rural districts	0.010	0.88	0.138	0.08	0.117	0.10
D						
Farm houses	0.192	0.16	0.108	0.51	0.119	0.43
Semi-detached houses	−0.018	0.82	0.061	0.50	0.131	0.12
Apartments	−0.044	0.55	−0.004	0.96	0.016	0.84
Lodgings	0.056	0.72	0.127	0.49	0.082	0.62
Other residences	−0.374	0.04	−0.188	0.38	0.036	0.85

Table 11.2. (Cont.)

	"Would if possible" (I)		"Once in the past" (II)		"Last year" (III)	
	Estimated coefficients	Significance level	Estimated coefficients	Significance level	Estimated coefficients	Significance level
E						
7–9 years of schooling	0.003	0.97	0.048	0.51	0.083	0.20
10–12 years of schooling	0.051	0.45	0.119	0.15	0.104	0.16
University	−0.129	0.12	−0.089	0.36	−0.138	0.12
F						
Teaching	0.103	0.32	0.279	0.04	0.122	0.23
Functionary, secretaries	0.230	0.10	Reference group	Reference group	0.078	0.59
Administrators, salesmen, accountants	0.065	0.41	0.224	0.06	Reference group	Reference group
Sales staff	0.101	0.37	—	—	−0.088	0.47
Housing, children day care	0.198	0.48	−0.024	0.94	0.213	0.49
Manufacturing industries, constructions	0.037	0.62	0.233	0.03	0.108	0.15
Agriculture	0.087	0.55	0.272	0.14	0.344	0.03
Public relations, etc.	−0.318	0.03	−0.125	0.48	−0.154	0.29
Craftsmen	Reference group	Reference group	0.285	0.01	0.300	0
Drivers	−0.020	0.86	0.088	0.55	0.199	0.10
Engineers, mechanics	0.233	0.06	0.299	0.05	0.276	0.03
Lawyers, doctors	−0.129	0.46	0.133	0.29	0.133	0.47
Other occupations	0.006	0.95	0.193	0.10	0.147	0.09
Students, pupils	−0.196	0.22	0.172	0.39	0.049	0.78
Without regular work	0.044	0.61	0.291	0.20	0.022	0.91

with the quality of work and the ease with which such work is supplied.

There is a general feeling that the hidden labor market will increase over time and become more acceptable in society.

There is a tendency that the participation rate for younger people has increased relative to other age groups over the last decade.

A final finding in the survey study is that about 80% of the hidden labor services is paid in cash. This gives some justification to the underlying assumption of the macro-approach, namely, that transactions in the unregistered sector of the economy are settled in currency.

The behavior of the tax evaders: some empirical tests

In the survey the respondents were asked to estimate their marginal tax rate, the penalty rate, and the probability of detection. Since they also answered what their gross and net incomes were the preceding year, we could compare the "true" marginal tax rate with what they considered it to be. Their answers on the penalty rate question could be compared with the actual rules, and the estimate of the probability of detection could be compared with qualified guesses made by ourselves. The result of these comparisons was that the marginal tax rates were overestimated, but the gap between the estimated and the true marginal tax rates decreased with higher income. On the other hand, people in lower income brackets overestimated the probability of detection and the penalty rate as well. The *net* result of these three misunderstandings could just as well be that the low-income people chose the optimal tax evasion level.

The answers given in the survey were used as observations of the variables. For several reasons the answers may not yield the intended information. First, our interpretation of the answers could be wrong. Second, the respondents might suppress the true answers. Finally, as already indicated, their estimates might not be in accordance with true values. However, what matters for individual behavior is perception, not reality.

The survey contained several demographic and socioeconomic questions. In what follows we give the main conclusions obtained from several regressions. In all regressions the same set of independent variables are used. The independent variables are grouped in the following six categories:

A. Economic variables. The economic variables included are those suggested by the economic theory of tax evasion extended to allow for a variable labor supply. Thus, marginal wage income [i.e., the gross wage rate per hour multiplied by 1 minus the marginal tax rate] is used as one variable rather than introducing wage rates and tax rates separately. The wage rate in the unregistered labor market enters the relations separately as well as with the penalty charges deducted. The probability of detection is included separately.[2] Finally, we have included a gambling index constructed on the basis of the respondent's participation in the state lottery, the state football pools, bingo, and trotting races. The hypothesis is that tax evasion is rooted in the agent's inclination to take risks and gamble. There are, of course, other explanations of a possible relationship between tax evasion and gambling. Through participation in gambling, unregistered income can be whitewashed. That is, unregistered income used in state football pools may yield a tax-free and legal prize. Further, people without a regular job may choose to fill their spare time with gambling as well as with temporary employment in the unregistered labor markets.

B. Demographic factors. The following categories are specified:

Less than 40 years old, unmarried with and without children
Less than 40 years old and married with and without children
Above 40 years old.

C. Place of residence. Three categories are specified: sparsely populated areas, cities, and rural districts.

D. Type of residences. Farmhouses, single-unit houses, semi-detached houses, apartments, lodgings, and others.

E. Education. Seven to nine years of schooling, 10–12 years of schooling, universities.

F. Occupation. Eighteen different occupations are specified. The exact specification is given in Tables 11.2 and 11.3.

In the survey the following three questions are asked:

I If you had the opportunity, would you evade taxes? ("Would if possible.")
II Have you at least once evaded taxes? ("Once in the past.")
III Have you received unregistered labor income the last 12 months? ("Last year.")

If the answer was yes, the value 1 was attached to the answer. If no, the value was 0. Thus, the dependent variable is dichotomous, and the independent variables are continuous or polytomous. The presence of dichotomous and polytomous variables indicates the logit method as

---

[2] For a theoretical exposition, see Isachsen and Strom (1980).

the appropriate method of estimation. However, this was not done. Instead, the more cruder and simpler method of linear regression was applied with dummy variables representing the categorical variables B–F. The estimated values of the dependent variables I–III will vary between 0 and 1 and can be interpreted as estimates of the frequencies of the different kinds of participation in the hidden economy. To illustrate how Tables 11.2 and 11.3 should be interpreted, an example is offered. If the subjective probability of detection is increased from 0.1 to 0.2, the value of variable I will decrease from 0.5 to 0.46. Thus, the frequency of evading taxes "if one had the opportunity" is estimated to decrease by four percentage points, from 0.5 to 0.46.

The results of the regressions are displayed in Tables 11.2 and 11.3. We distinguish between males (Table 11.2) and females (Table 11.3) because their opportunities in the labor markets are significantly different.

In category B above 40, married without children is used as a reference group.

In category C the reference group is sparsely populated areas.

In category D the reference group is single-unit houses.

In category E the reference group is 7–9 years of schooling, and in category F the reference group varies over the different cases.

A notable result is that the probability of detection has a highly significant impact upon all three frequencies for males and upon frequencies I and II for all females. Thus, increased surveillance of economic activity giving the impression of a higher probability of detection should be an effective way of combatting the growth of the unregistered labor market.

For males, wage rates, marginal tax rates, and penalty charges have the intuitively expected signs, and some of them are even significantly different from zero at acceptable levels of significance (0.05–0.10). It should be emphasized that the few coefficients significantly different from zero accords with theory that allows for labor supply to vary. As stated in the preceding, theory gives no definite answer as to the sign of the partial derivatives.

The demographic factor under 40, especially if unmarried, seems to have a decisive influence on the male's propensity to engage in unregistered work. When it comes to frequencies based on experiences (II and III), the expectations of an overrepresentation of male craftsmen and mechanics is confirmed. For females the gambler index has a significant influence on both wishes to take part in the unregistered labor market (I) and on past participation (II). The expectation of an

Table 11.3. *Survey regressions, female propensities I–III*

	"Would if possible" (I)		"Once in the past" (II)		"Last year" (III)	
	Estimated coefficients	Significance level	Estimated coefficients	Significance level	Estimated coefficients	Significance level
A						
Constant term	0.481	0.02	−0.064	0.78	−0.354	0.02
Regular wage rate after marginal tax	0.007	0.08	0.002	0.69	0.006	0.04
Irregular wage rate	−0.001	0.56	0.001	0.66	0.002	0.07
Irregular wage rate after penalty charge	−0.003	0.31	0.001	0.77	0.001	0.85
Probability of detection	−0.767	0	−0.286	0.04	−0.110	0.23
Index of gambling	0.090	0.01	0.081	0.02	0.042	0.07
B						
Under 40, unmarried, without children	0.146	0.40	0.261	0.15	0.311	0.01
Under 40, unmarried, with children	0.141	0.46	0.355	0.06	0.358	0
Under 40, married, without children	0.079	0.60	0.153	0.34	0.109	0.28
Under 40, married, 1 child	0.222	0.12	0.183	0.23	0.019	0.85
Under 40, married, children	0.097	0.45	0.209	0.11	0.133	0.12
Above 40, unmarried	−0.010	0.60	0.561	0.05	0.055	0.65
Above 40, married children	0.025	0.80	0.041	0.80	0.120	0.23
C						
Cities	−0.053	0.50	−0.026	0.75	0.018	0.73
Rural districts	0.057	0.56	0.008	0.93	0.126	0.06

D						
Farmhouses	-0.523	0.01	-0.330	0.09	-0.146	0.27
Semi-detached houses	-0.011	0.93	-0.042	0.72	0.044	0.56
Apartments	0.111	0.36	-0.033	0.79	0.074	0.37
Lodgings	0.033	0.90	-0.279	0.31	-0.143	0.44
Other residences	0.217	0.57	0.048	0.90	0.116	0.65
E						
7–9 years of schooling	0.056	-0.54	0.037	0.69	0.020	0.74
10–12 years of schooling	0.001	0.99	-0.025	0.81	-0.011	0.87
University	-0.055	0.69	-0.050	0.72	-0.086	0.35
F						
Teaching	-0.076	0.63	0.152	0.33	-0.019	0.87
Functionary, secretaries	0.118	0.31	Reference group	Reference group	-0.020	0.80
Administrators, salesmen, accountants	0.343	0.02	0.153	0.46	0.127	0.37
Sales staff	0.068	0.55	0.125	0.30	Reference group	Reference group
Housing, children day care	0.248	0.05	0.241	0.05	0.158	0.06
Manufacturing industries	0.014	0.94	0.208	0.26	-0.030	0.79
Cleaning	0.222	0.18	-0.010	0.95	0.014	0.86
Nurses	Reference group	Reference group	0.014	0.90		
Other occupations	0.144	0.33	0.262	0.08	0.053	0.59
Students, pupils	0.391	0.42	0.650	0.19	0.659	0.05

overrepresentation of females in the child day care business is also confirmed. For women, the demographic factor under 40, especially if unmarried with children, seems to have a decisive influence on past participation in the unregistered labor markets.

The labor supply function

In addition to questions I–III, the respondents also reported on how many hours they worked unregistered during the last 12 months. These answers are taken as observations of the fourth dependent variable:

IV Number of hours worked unregistered last year.

The following function for the supply of unregistered labor supply was assumed:

$$\ln(N_B + 1) = \alpha_0 + \alpha_1 W_R(1 - t) + \alpha_2 W_B + \alpha_3 W_B(1 - \tau)$$
$$+ \alpha_4 p + \alpha_5 z + u$$

where

N_B = number of hours worked per year in unregistered market
W_R = hourly wage rate in regular market
t = marginal tax rate, $t \geqslant 0$
W_B = hourly wage rate in unregistered market
τ = penalty rate, $\tau \geqslant 0$
p = probability of detection measured in percentages
z = vector of socioeconomic variables whose content is suppressed here
u = normally distributed error term

The results are given in what follows. The figures in parentheses are significance levels:

Males:

$$\ln(N_B + 1) = 2.060 - 0.016 W_R(1 - t) - 0.001 W_B$$
$$(0.0) \quad (0.14) \qquad\qquad (0.82)$$
$$+ 0.100 W_B(1 - \tau) - 0.020p + \alpha Z$$
$$(0.13) \qquad\qquad (0.0)$$

Females:

$$\ln(N_B + 1) = -0.170 + 0.150 W_R(1 - t) + 0.005 W_B$$
$$(0.63) \quad (0.19) \qquad\qquad (0.26)$$
$$+ 0.003 W_B(1 - \tau) - 0.004p + \alpha_5 Z$$
$$(0.73) \qquad\qquad (0.20)$$

264

Except for the coefficients associated with W_B, all coefficients in the regression equation for males have a plausible sign, although we again remind the reader that the general theory of tax evasion implies no expected signs. If the behavior is guided by economically based decisions under uncertainty, however, some of the economic variables should be expected to have a significant influence on the behavior. The coefficients associated with wage rates and tax rates are not significant at the 5% level. At that level only the coefficient associated with the (subjective) probability of detection is significant. The results indicate that if the probability of detection increases by one percentage point, say, from 0.10 to 0.11 (from 10 to 11%), the number of hours worked in the unregistered economy will, on average, decrease by 2%, say, from 100 hours per year to 98 hours per year.

In the case of females no coefficients associated with the economic factors are different from zero at acceptable levels of significance. It thus seems that the reason females work unregistered is not a result of a calculated decision under uncertainty, as could be the case for males. A more reasonable explanation in accordance with our findings in Tables 11.2 and 11.3, as well as with common observations, is that females work unregistered due to the lack of regular job opportunities.

Another way of putting it is that *schwartsarbeit* for men are side jobs. Males are in a position to say yes or no to side jobs to complement or to replace some hours otherwise worked in the regular market. This decision might be explained by the more elaborate theory of tax evasion. Females, on the other hand, are not in this position. Their decision of taking jobs in the unregistered market therefore might not be a result of a calculated decision under uncertainty but the only way of getting a job at all.

CHAPTER 12

Canada's underground economy

ROLF MIRUS and ROGER S. SMITH

Measurement of unobserved economic activity in Canada has proven to be an elusive task. In this chapter, we define the two broad concepts of the unobserved economy, summarize the findings of studies that have dealt with this topic in the Canadian context, and present new estimates of unmeasured gross national product (GNP).

Defining the phenomenon

Although it is agreed that unobserved economic activity is the result of a complex interaction of legal, economic, political, cultural, and other institutional factors that vary from country to country, it is also apparent that there is no uniformly accepted definition of unobserved economic activity. It is therefore important to clarify possible concepts of unobserved economic activity at the outset.

It is useful to decompose total economic activity into money-based and non-monetary transactions (Feige, 1980). Non-monetary activities comprise both market activities (i.e., exchange) and non-market ones whether legal or illegal in nature. Included in this group are in-kind consumption and cooperatively organized exchange of professional services. The fact that this component of economic activity is so difficult to measure has resulted in the convention to exclude most non-monetary transactions from GNP. To the extent that shifts occur from the monetary observed to the non-monetary unobserved sector, the National Income and Product Accounts will present a biased picture of economic growth. Despite the obvious importance and far-reaching implications of non-monetary economic activity (Kendrick, 1979; Eisner, 1978), this essay will concentrate on the monetary portion of unobserved economic activity.

Two concepts of the unobserved monetary economy can be distinguished. First, there is the sum of all unreported taxable money income, which forms the base for tax evasion. Second, there is the monetary value of economic activity that should conventionally be included in GNP but is nevertheless unrecorded. These two broad definitions, in turn, subsume aspects of the unobserved economy that have been the subject of investigation by some researchers. For example, grey labor markets are part of both tax evasion and unobserved GNP. The difference lies in the extent to which such unreported labor income is taxable. The tax evasion notion of the unobserved economy also includes all unreported but taxable capital gains from wealth transfers, whereas unobserved GNP only includes the unrecorded expenditures that result from such income.

Previous Canadian studies

The earliest work on Canada's unobserved economy was carried out at the Bank of Canada. Both the studies by Haas (1978) and Wong and Rose (1980) are unpublished internal research memoranda and have therefore not been widely circulated. They are based on the role of currency as a medium of exchange in the unobserved economy. Haas studied real per capita currency holdings with the expectation that such holdings should decline as a result of the introduction of credit cards and other financial innovations. Observing an increase during the 1960's and 1970's, he concluded that this must be attributable to growing unobserved economic activity. On the basis of 1953–5 as a benchmark period and using M1 velocity, Haas estimated that by the end of 1977 an extra 11.1% of GNP went unreported.

Although this methodology is open to the objections that demographic changes have been ignored, that the velocity has not been adjusted to reflect unobserved activity, and that the income elasticity of real per capita currency holdings is assumed zero,[1] the approach is promising in that it avoids the difficulties besetting the methods used by Gutmann (1977) and Tanzi (1982), namely, drawing inferences about additional currency holdings by studying the movement of currency relative to demand deposits or a broader monetary aggregate.

Wong and Rose (1980) showed that the Gutmann approach encounters difficulties in the Canadian setting. Dividing total demand deposits into their two components, they found that currency declined relative to personal checking account balances throughout the 1970's, so that the observed increase in the currency–demand deposit ratio had to be due to rapid growth in current-account balances. In addition, when bank note quality and the share of currency transfers in total transactions are assumed constant, they show that currency transfers relative to demand deposit transfers declined from the 1950's to the late 1970's. This decline implies that the stock of currency grew at a rate insufficient

---

[1] These criticisms are made by Wong and Rose (1980).

to support much growth in unobserved transactions. As a result, Wong and Rose rejected the Gutmann methodology for Canada. They instead favored Feige's transactions method as the theoretically strongest among the monetary approaches but did not pursue it beyond the currency component.

Mirus and Smith (1981) attempted to apply the transactions methods to Canadian data but encountered difficulties with the adjustment for purely financial transactions. Without such an adjustment, implausible results were obtained. After omitting check-clearing transactions in major financial centers and assuming 125 lifetime transactions per bank note, they arrived at an unobserved economy of 28.1% of GNP by 1976 using 1939 as their benchmark. They also provided estimates of income evading taxes by means of Tanzi's method, expressing the currency–demand deposit ratio as a function of, among others, the average personal tax burden. On the basis of their regression analysis, they calculated that extra currency holdings attributable to an increasing tax burden might imply income equivalent to 5.3–7.8% of GNP evading taxes in 1976.

In her study of tax evasion, Ethier (1982) provided some evidence on the discrepancy between national accounts income and individual and corporate incomes reported to the tax authorities. During the decade of the 1970's, this discrepancy declined from nearly 30 to 14%. It is difficult to interpret this trend as well as the remaining gap. Is the decline due to a drift from monetary income to income in kind or is it due to the increase in the coverage of taxable income resulting from the inclusion of social insurance pensions (1972) and family allowances (1974) in the tax base? The measured increase in compliance may also have been the result of increased enforcement activities.

Ethier also applied Tanzi's approach and found that currency holdings were significantly affected by the tax burden, measured as the average marginal tax rate on filers. Ethier's estimates suggest that tax evasion in 1980 amounted to 8.8% of the actual tax revenues collected from individuals and unincorporated business.

Methodological observations

Depending on which of the two concepts of unobserved monetary activity is employed – and the previous Canadian studies have not always made that distinction clear – different methodologies are appropriate. For this reason the review of the Canadian measurement attempts affords an opportunity to evaluate the strengths and weaknesses of the various methodologies used.

Currency ratio methods as advocated by Gutmann and Tanzi have proved problematic. They fail to take account of changes in financial innovations and changes in interest rates. Reliance on the currency ratio to isolate the effect of increases in the tax burden ignores consideration of other contributing factors such as audit probabilities and changes in social attitudes. Moreover, the implicit assumption that tax evasion applies only to cash income leads the method to produce underestimates of evasion since underreported capital gains income is unlikely to be related to currency usage.[2]

These methodological difficulties are largely avoided by Feige's transactions method. From a theoretical perspective, this method is better suited to accomplish its objective. Its objective is, of course, to measure the second concept of unobserved monetary economic activity: unrecorded GNP. By including check-based transactions, it overcomes the overly narrow focus on currency. By adjusting for purely financial transactions, it remains true to its goal to measure unrecorded production activity.

If there are questions to be raised about Feige's approach, they pertain largely to the availability of the empirical data required for its implementation. Since confirmation of the existence and the growth of the unobserved economy depends on an increase in the ratio of total to final transactions and since such an increase can be observed, one has to show that it is not due to an increase in the prices of intermediate relative to final goods or to a decrease in vertical integration that necessitates more intermediate transactions per dollar of final output. While the methodology clearly takes account of these considerations (Feige, 1979), it is often empirically difficult to adduce clear evidence with respect to these questions. An increasing total–final transactions ratio can also be the result of more purely financial transactions, such as transfers between checking and savings accounts, asset transfers, and the like. Once again, it is difficult to obtain accurate data on purely financial flows, and thus the results of the method must be judged by the availability and accuracy of the empirical data required to make the necessary conceptual adjustments. In the absence of a thorough tax compliance study by the Canadian authorities, Feige's approach remains the only comprehensive macro-approach that passes the initial requirement of theoretical acceptability.

Other approaches such as labor market studies based on survey data are likely to be marred by problems of non-response or untruthful response. Nonetheless, they can provide important corroborative or

---

[2] Langfeldt (1982) points out these limitations.

non-supportive evidence. Indirect evidence yielded by other simple economic indicators may also prove helpful in any initial assessment of the preconditions for the existence of an unobserved sector.

Simple indicators

In casual discussions one encounters references to the increase in large-denomination bank notes, the availability of time for second jobs, and the increasing tax burden as indicators of the existence of an unobserved economy. Whereas the theoretical links between these indicators and the size of the phenomenon are tenuous, impressionistic evidence of this nature may prove beneficial if only to provide some description of the Canadian institutional setting.

Large-denomination bank notes

If currency is the prevalent medium of exchange in unobserved economic activity and if wealth from such activity, especially the illegal kind, is held in this form so as to prevent it from being traced, one might expect a growing unobserved sector to be reflected in a growing proportion of large-denomination bills. Indeed, between 1969 and 1979, when GNP grew by 226%, $100 and $1,000 notes grew by 288 and 641%. However, as pointed by O'Higgins (1981), this increase cannot be viewed as un-ambiguous evidence of growing unobserved economic activity. It may simply reflect the public's attempt to replace lower with higher denomination notes in the face of inflation. The fact that between 1960 and 1980, the average note denomination grew by 241.7% while the con-sumer price index (CPI) grew by 283.8% is consistent with this view.

The Canadian consumer tax index

To answer the question of how the average Canadian family's tax burden has been changing over time, the Fraser Institute publishes the Canadian consumer tax index at two-year intervals.[3] This index shows the propor-tion of total income the average family would have paid in taxes of all kinds: personal federal and provincial income tax, sales taxes, property taxes, profits taxes, social security, liquor taxes, and many others. Table 12.1 shows the increase in this index in nominal and real terms as well as the ratio of personal income taxes to personal income net of transfers.

Since this index only reflects the revenue going to government and not

---

[3] See Pipes and Walker (1982).

Table 12.1. *The tax burden of the average Canadian family*

Year	Total income, average family	Taxes paid	Nominal increase over 1961 (%)	Real increase over 1961 (%)	Personal income tax relative to personal income
1961	$ 7,582	$ 1,675	—	—	0.078
1969	11,323	3,117	86.1	48.3	0.134
1972	14,154	4,203	150.9	79.6	0.154
1976	21,872	5,979	257.9	79.8	0.155
1980	33,685	10,306	515.3	119.1	0.155

Source: Pipes and Walker (1982, pp. 44 and 45). The average personal income tax burden is calculated from the Cansim series.

the resulting benefits to residents, it reflects a partial picture. Nevertheless, a tax bill that more than doubles in real terms over two decades can be viewed as a cause for a switch to the unobserved sector. As more and more Canadians made the discovery that a substantial portion of total income is going to the various forms of taxation, this awareness, combined with the widely shared perception of the complexity and unfairness of the system, may well explain decisions to supply and demand goods and services in markets where taxes can be avoided.

The potential supply of labor for unobserved activity

Ethier (1982) had dismissed the labor market approach on the grounds that in Canada, contrary to Italy or West Germany, the labor force participation rate had been rising rather than falling. Despite such an increase, it is possible that population growth, reductions in the average work week, and increased unemployment combine to swell the potential supply of labor for unobserved activities. Using 1970 as the base year, Table 12.2 presents evidence that in the Canadian case the potential supply of labor for unobserved activity has fairly steadily increased during the last 12 years. This potential supply of unobserved labor is comprised of those already employed but working fewer hours per week, those not reporting themselves as looking for work, or the unemployed.

Taken together, the readings of these simple indicators obviously do not permit strong conclusions. But they are suggestive: In Canada there was significant growth in incentives and available time for diverting economic activity to the unobserved sector. The fact that large-denomination notes have not grown disproportionately is not incom-

Table 12.2. *The potential supply of labor for unobserved activity*
(1970 = 100)

Year	Potential supply of hours per week increase over 1970 (%)
1971	5.6
1972	5.8
1973	6.1
1974	9.3
1975	14.3
1976	16.8
1977	20.1
1978	19.6
1979	18.3
1980	20.1
1981	20.4
1982	34.2

Notes: Calculated from Labor Force Status of the Population and Average Hours Worked per Week in Manufacturing as published by the *Bank of Canada Review*, April 1983, pp. S118/19, S126. The series is defined as [(1 − participation rate) × civilian population over 15 + unemployed] × 39.7 + (39.7 − average weekly hours in manufacturing) × labor force. Average weekly hours in manufacturing were 39.7 in 1970.

patible with the existence and growth of the unobserved sector. It may well be that increased use of checks, lack of ready acceptability of large bills in day-to-day transactions, as well as reliance on U.S. currency explain the changing denomination structure.

Currency demand

A review of Canadian attempts to gauge the unobserved economy reveals a belief that both its size and growth should be detectable from the behavior of monetary aggregates or their components. In light of the deficiencies of the currency ratio approaches, it appears useful to focus on currency demand separately. Currency is uniquely demand determined and does not bear an implicit interest rate, as do sight deposits. Its role as transactions medium is therefore captured by inventory models that show optimal cash holdings as the result of cost minimization.[4]

[4] In the context of inventory models the optimal cash holdings imply an elasticity of 0.05 of real currency demand with respect to real GNP (Baumol, 1966).

The existence of an unobserved money-based sector with payment practices similar to those in the observed sector would suggest that there are inexplicably large real-currency holdings. If this sector is growing in relative terms, one should observe an increase in the measured income elasticity of real-currency holdings when observed GNP declines as a fraction of total output. However, the 1968 introduction of credit cards to Canada and their subsequent acceptance by consumers undoubtedly also affected currency demand. Although their impact on demand deposits is somewhat ambiguous, because debit balances ultimately tend to get settled by demand deposits, it is reasonable to suggest that credit card use has lessened the need for cash transactions. The empirical researcher therefore confronts the unenviable situation where confirmation of a growing unobserved economy requires evidence of increasing income elasticity of currency demand when the biased GNP measure is used as an independent variable; yet at the same time financial sector innovations, coupled with increasing sophistication of the public in managing its cash balances, suggest that this income elasticity should have declined in recent years.

In order to investigate the structure of currency demand, the demand function for real per capita currency holdings is specified as follows:

$$c(t) = a_1 + a_2 D(t) + a_3 y(t) + a_4 D(t^*) y(t) + a_5 r(t) + a_6 T(t) + e(t)$$

$$(12.1)$$

where

$c(t)$ = natural logarithm of real per capita currency holdings (using the CPI) for year t

$y(t)$ = natural logarithm of real per capita GNP (using the CPI) for year t

$D(t^*)$ = dummy variable, 0 for $t > t^*$,
$\qquad\qquad\qquad\qquad$ 1 for $t \leqslant t^*$

$r(t)$ = interest rate .

$T(t)$ = natural logarithm of personal tax burden in year t

$e(t)$ = error term

In effect, we are searching for a significant coefficient a_4 of the dummy variable D indicating a change from time t^* onward of the per capita real income elasticity a_3. Utilizing annual average data for currency, the years 1968, 1970, and 1972 are of greatest interest. In 1968 credit cards were first introduced and the personal tax burden increased dramatically. In the course of the next five years the average tax burden increased

274

more than 25%, and credit card use became widespread. Regression results are shown in Table 12.3.

Equations (1)–(3) in Table 12.3 reveal no significant change in the dummy shift variable for the real income elasticity; hence, no net structural change can be ascertained for these three years. One can possibly interpret the absence of such a change in structure as indirect corroboration of the existence of unobserved economic activity in that the lower per capita currency holdings, induced by credit card use, were counteracted by additional holdings to support transactions not included in measured real GNP per capita. This, of course, amounts to forcing the hypothesis to fit the data. Still, equations (5) and (6), although based on very few observations, suggest an increase in the real income elasticity, and equation (4) reveals a positive, but insignificant, effect of the personal tax burden on currency holdings.

Finally, it is worth noting that the estimated values of the real income elasticity are compatible with growth in the unobserved economy since they exceed the theoretical optimum of 0.5.

Although no significant conclusions can be drawn, this approach may prove useful in future work as data availability permits further tests of structural change. There are hints in the results of equations (5) and (6) that currency demand is characterized by some instability, the causes of which are not well understood but may be related to the unobserved economy.

Estimates by means of the total transactions method

As the transactions method is well known,[5] it will not be discussed in detail other than to emphasize that it relies on the assumption that the ratio of total non-financial transactions to total final output is relatively constant. Since total final output is simply the sum of observed and unobserved output, knowledge of the transaction–income ratio, the total volume of non-financial transactions, and the observed level of output permits residual estimation of the unobserved component of total income.

Total check-based transactions

Data are available for all of Canada's check-clearing centers, but the

---

[5] See Feige (1979) for a detailed description of the approach and Feige (1980) for refinements.

Table 12.3. *Per capita real currency demand, 1960–82*

Equation number	Characteristic of c	a_1	a_2	a_3	a_4	a_5	a_6	ϱ	Adjusted R^2, DW
1	1960–82, $t^* = 196$	-4.86(4.97)	1.19(1.26)	0.55(1.69)	0.36(1.24)	-0.054(2.21)	—	0.95	0.47, 1.70
2	1960–82, $t^* = 1970$	-4.29(3.77)	0.52(0.50)	0.70(1.86)	0.16(0.50)	-0.051(1.94)	—	0.93	0.40, 1.32
3	1960–82, $t^* = 1972$	-4.34(5.05)	0.45(0.43)	0.70(2.32)	0.13(0.40)	-0.051(1.95)	—	0.94	0.47, 1.20
4	1960–82	-4.07(8.27)	—	0.72(4.64)	—	-0.600(2.24)	0.000(1.34)	0.82	0.50, 0.92
5	1960–72	-4.08(7.69)	—	0.72(4.34)	—	-0.037(1.19)	—	0.76	0.62, 1.06
6	1971–82	-2.34(2.08)	—	1.21(3.36)	—	-0.187(4.10)	—	0.49	0.61, 1.43
7	1960–82, $t^* = 1970$	-3.79(6.39)	—	0.857(4.27)	-0.0002(0.02)	0.054(2.12)	—	0.92	0.42, 1.24

Notes: Numbers in parentheses are t-values; ϱ = first-order serial correlation coefficient.

elimination of purely financial transactions requires ad hoc experimentation. Three alternative transaction measures were constructed in order to account for purely financial transactions.

a Total check-based transactions were estimated for all clearing centers other than Toronto, Montreal, Vancouver, and Calgary. The growth rate of transactions in these non-financial centers was then applied to the 1949 volume of transactions in the financial centers in order to arrive at the first estimate of total adjusted check-based transactions.

b Total adjusted check-based transactions were estimated as the sum of transactions in all clearing centers other than Toronto and Montreal.

c Total adjusted check-based transactions were estimated as the sum of transactions in all clearing centers other than Toronto minus the sum of the market value of stocks sold at the Montreal and Toronto Stock Exchanges and the value of gross new issues and retirements of Canadian dollar denominated bonds.

Again following Feige, total federal personal and corporate income taxes as well as employer and employee contributions to social insurance were subtracted from these total check transactions. Since transactions data exclude federal government transactions, observed output was measured net of government expenditures on goods and services.

Currency transactions

An experiment regarding the lifetime of Canadian bank notes[6] helped support the assumption of 200 lifetime transactions. Coupling this assumption with estimated average life spans of the various bank notes, it was possible to construct a series for currency turnover.[7] The resulting estimated sums of currency and check transactions relative to GNP (net of federal government expenditures for goods and services) is given in Table 12.4 for each of the aforementioned cases. Inspection of these ratios reveals a slight, but steady, decline in the ratios during the 1960's, with subsequent sporadic increases since then. This observation might

---

[6] Thanks are due to Drew Mackenzie for designing this test on 30 fresh notes, and simulating more than 14,000 folding transactions. The notes were considered "worn" when a tear, hole, or perforation arose. Assuming two folds per transaction, the average note supported 240 transactions. We use the somewhat more conservative number of 200 lifetime transactions.

[7] For 1978–2 we used the average life of bills published by the *Bank of Canada Review* (January 1982), p. 18. For 1964–77 we used our calculations, which are based on the age of worn-out bills in 1968. There were only minor differences between these two sets of note lives.

Table 12.4. *Ratios of total to final transactions*

Year	(a)	(b)	(c)
1949	13.32	10.41	11.78
1950	12.61	9.74	11.23
1951	12.03	9.17	10.63
1952	11.77	8.94	10.36
1953	11.89	9.04	10.22
1954	11.70	8.99	10.15
1955	11.12	8.57	9.91
1956	10.94	8.39	9.85
1957	10.72	8.23	9.67
1958	10.94	8.26	9.38
1959	10.91	8.11	9.67
1960	10.93	8.04	9.83
1961	11.38	8.34	10.12
1962	11.25	8.18	10.06
1963	11.40	8.13	10.12
1964	11.14	7.89	10.04
1965	11.13	7.81	10.06
1966	10.99	7.67	9.94
1967	11.26	7.80	10.06
1968	11.10	7.76	9.81
1969	10.97	7.65	9.65
1970	10.83	7.50	9.59
1971	10.95	7.54	9.60
1972	10.99	7.69	9.86
1973	11.25	7.79	10.03
1974	11.66	7.93	10.40
1975	12.56	8.38	11.13
1976	12.25	8.16	11.04
1977	12.01	8.07	10.98
1978	11.73	7.86	10.31
1979	11.80	7.90	10.15
1980	12.44	8.35	10.72
1981	11.98	8.76	11.20
1982	12.36	8.73	10.96

reflect a slow process of increasing vertical integration that then either subsides or is swamped by the effects of the emerging unobserved sector.

To give the results a conservative flavor, the ratio for the year 1972, rather than 1970, was chosen as the benchmark for calculating the implied unobserved economy as a fraction of officially measured GNP. Table 12.5 shows that regardless of the method of adjusting for financial

Table 12.5. *The implied unobserved economy (percentage of GNP)*

Year	Adjustment procedure			Real GNP growth (%)
	(a)	(b)	(c)	
1973	2.25	1.26	1.62	7.54
1974	5.80	3.10	5.17	3.59
1975	13.50	8.53	12.26	1.19
1976	10.81	5.82	11.31	5.52
1977	8.75	4.62	10.75	2.10
1978	6.33	2.12	4.35	3.71
1979	6.98	2.53	2.76	3.03
1980	12.53	8.13	8.26	0.03
1981	8.52	13.20	12.93	2.02
1982	11.81	12.84	10.53	−5.00

fluff, very similar patterns result for the evolution of the unobserved sector. There appears to be rapid growth up to the mid-1970's, a decline to 1978–9, and resumed growth since then except for the deep recession in 1982. The decline during the second half of the 1970's coincides with a decline in the average tax burden due to the indexing of the federal income tax against inflation effective in 1974. The existence of a wage–price controls program for 1975–8 may also have had an impact on the size of this sector by affecting the relative price of observed and unobserved output. However, it is less clear that this should have led to a net decline.

Although the results appear plausible in terms of order of magnitude, several caveats are necessary. To the extent that unobserved activity existed before 1972, the estimates represent a conservative figure. The fluctuations in the estimated unobserved sector remain somewhat puzzling. Large supply elasticities and fluctuations in demand are implied for this sector. Whereas these are perhaps not implausible, given the nature of the unobserved economy, it is difficult to discern a consistent pro-cyclical or countercyclical movement in the estimates. The real GNP growth rates in Table 12.5 show the recession years 1974–5 accompanied by dramatic growth in the estimates of unobserved economy activity, yet during the 1982 recession, the unobserved sector contracts in two of the three estimates. The recession of the mid-1970's was accompanied by accelerating inflation whereas the deep recession of 1982 was accompanied by decelerating inflation, but it is unclear how this difference should affect the growth of the unobserved sector. Finally, it can be seen that the results are quite sensitive to the type of adjustments made to incorporate the effects of purely financial transactions. No adjustments were included to account for debits due to cash withdrawals and shifts between demand deposits and time deposits. To the extent that these flows have increased over time in non-financial centers, the possibility remains that some financial fluff may still be included in the estimated check transactions series.

To summarize, the results suggest that the unobserved sector has shown considerable fluctuations over the 1972–82 period and that it currently may amount to 10% of observed GNP. These estimates are far from precise, and little is known about their confidence intervals.

To date, no systematic research has been undertaken to examine the causes of the growth of the unobserved economy in Canada. The prevailing hypothesis is that the sector's apparent growth has been encouraged by increases in the marginal rates of taxation, the growing complexity of the tax structure, and a decline in taxpayers' perceptions of the fairness of the system. Although public discussion of tax evasion has substantially increased, Revenue Canada's number of special investigators of tax evasion has remained stationary at 530 in the last few years, and prosecutions as well as investigations completed show a downward trend.[8] The growth of the unobserved economy does suggest that informal markets may play an important role in limiting governmental interference with free-market activities through the imposition of taxes and regulations.

[8] Department of National Revenue, *Inside Taxation*, 1980–2.

CHAPTER 13

The underground economy in France

PHILIPPE BARTHELEMY

This chapter examines four aspects of the research on the underground economy in France. After a brief review of the historical interest in the subject and a discussion of the most frequently employed terminology, I report on the results of several regional surveys that have been conducted in order to gain an insight into the nature of the problem of "clandestine labor." This will be followed by a survey of the empirical estimates of tax evasion in France and by a macro-economic estimate of the size and growth of the underground economy in France employing Tanzi's (1980) estimating method.

Terminology

French legislation concerning clandestine labor dates back to 1936. Immediately following the Matignon accord, which established paid holidays, a law was passed in June 1936 forbidding paid work during paid holidays. In October 1940, a multiple-job-holding law was adopted: "No one may undertake an industrial, commercial or professional job on his own account unless he is registered either in the commercial register or the trade register and unless he pays the social and taxation charges levied on that profession." The adequacy of these laws was severely questioned by Mr. Antoni who, in his report on the fight against clandestine labor prepared on behalf of the Economic Council (March 1950), drew special attention to "the disquieting extension of the clandestine labor market." The current legislation concerning clandestine labor was adopted in July 1972, largely as a result of pressure exerted by professional organizations that frequently put forward the argument of unfair competition. The law states that labor shall be considered clandestine if it concerns the non-occasional "remunerated exercise of an activity dealing with production, transformation, repairs, or the supply of services necessitating inscription on the commercial register and/or the list of trades, or consisting of commercial activities effected by an individual not figuring on the list of trades or the commercial register and not meeting the social and fiscal obligations inherent to that activity."[1]

---

[1] A detailed analysis of the law and its application can be found in C. Choain (1982).

Since the passage of this law, employer organizations and trade associations have increased their demands for more severe measures against clandestine workers. The Metton report on means to fight clandestine labor proposed an increase in the penalties for clandestine labor and an extension of the meaning of the term to include occasional activities as well.[2] This extended concept of illegal activities is referred to as "black labor."

Two aspects of the French legal conception of clandestine labor that have been more or less copied by various other countries[3] are worth noting. First, there are the proposals to step up the fight against hidden labor that nevertheless exclude a category of acceptable domestic activities. Second, distinctions are made between various types of black labor depending on the motivation behind it. Thus one can distinguish between black labor performed for the sake of survival (hunger justifies the means), parasitic black labor (the unacceptable type), and convivial labor in the sense defined by Ivan Illich as an alternative to labor in the public and private market sectors. Convivial labor is performed in what has become known as the third sector.

Whether seen from the point of view of supply or demand, black labor is motivated by conventional economic considerations of financial gain. However, autonomous forms of production such as communities or associations are guided by different incentives. They are motivated not by the search for profit but by the desire to produce something important without delay. The third sector is characterized by its emphasis on creativity rather than remuneration.

The theoretical basis for the third sector also has its origins in a new concept of time use that discards the traditional dichotomy of work time and leisure time. Instead, the third sector employs the three-way partition – market labor–non-market labor–non-labor – under the conviction that "it is necessary both to have a better mastery of time, and to be able to use the time thus freed to improve upon non-market goods from non-market labor."[4] Delors and Gaudin (1979) provide a detailed description of the third economy, focusing on its place in the economy at large, its method of organization, and its financial aspects. The third sector coexists with the market economy and with the administrative sector. It is based on small, mainly decentralized economic units, and its finances are initially secured through public subsidies and

---

[2] *Rapport sur les moyes à mettre en oeuvre pour lutter contre le travail clandestin*, National Building Federation, Paris, February 1979.
[3] Belgium, July 6, 1976, and Luxemburg, August 3, 1977.
[4] Greffe and Gaudin, 1980, p. 92.

subsequently by membership fees and the sale goods and services on special markets. The third sector has received growing attention in the French literature on the informal economy. Two French authors, Barthelemy and Rosanvallon, have each developed a definition of the underground economy. Although their definitions are not fundamentally opposed, their points of view are markedly different.

Rosanvallon (1980) includes the underground economy as one component of what he terms global activities:

$$\begin{matrix} \text{Global} \\ \text{social} \\ \text{activity} \end{matrix} = \begin{matrix} \text{official} \\ \text{private} \\ \text{economy} \end{matrix} + \begin{matrix} \text{official} \\ \text{public} \\ \text{economy} \end{matrix} + \begin{matrix} \text{underground} \\ \text{economy} \end{matrix}$$

The author quite correctly points out that the underground economy seems, to many people, to be an official pseudo-economy, based on the fact that certain underground activities (e.g., domestic activities) have, in a sense, been re-integrated into the traditional economy. However, it is equally important to see the underground economy as a phenomenon in its own right and to study it in the larger traditional economic context. As characteristic criteria of the underground economy, Rosanvallon successively rejects

1 size (both small-scale and large-scale activities are included),
2 legality (help provided within a family is not clandestine labor), and
3 market characteristics (some goods are sold, others are not).

The criterion he accepts is that of the connection between the underground economy and the state. Underground exchanges are carried out on the borderline of state control, and there are two ways in which this may be done: (a) concealed (the occult economy) and (b) autonomously (the autonomous economy). His definition for the underground economy is therefore as follows:

Underground economy = occult economy + autonomous economy

The occult economy is defined as illegal with regard to state regulations. There is an organic relationship between the occult economy and the market economy, and its existence is seen as the product of the social rigidity of an official economy. The autonomous economy does not infringe upon state regulations: "It is based on forms of social organization which have no tax consequences (neighbors, family in the broad sense of the word) or on the activities which give rise to taxation because they are free or reciprocal (domestic labor)."[5]

---

[5] Rosanvanlon, 1980, p. 19.

283

Barthelemy's (1981) classification of hidden activities is composed of four components: clandestine labor, black labor, the underground economy in the strict sense, and the underground economy in a broad sense. Clandestine labor involves regular work done outside the current social and taxation norms as defined by French law. Black labor (which includes clandestine labor) comprises concealed activities of an occasional nature including the activities of students, retired people, multiple job holders, and unemployed in a small-scale and occasional way. It is the lower intensity of fraudulent salaried activities that distinguishes black labor from clandestine labor. The underground economy in the strict sense of the term includes undeclared labor as well as legal activities not reported to tax authorities and illegal prohibited activities. It therefore includes fiscal evasion, barter, theft, corruption, bribery, smuggling, embezzlement, prostitution, and drug traffic. The underground economy in the broad sense of the term includes all of the preceding activities as well as a series of domestic activities and communal, charitable, and group activities.

Reports and survey evidence

The available documentation on the underground economy in France is fairly abundant, though frequently it is too subjective to be used without reservations. The main body of sources can be divided up into two categories: reports from social partners and administrative reports. Both have the issue of black labor as their main subject. Characteristic of the reports belonging to the first category is the overall condemnation of illegal workers. The arguments provided for such an attitude vary according to the nature of the organization publishing the paper in question. Unanimity is also characteristic of the official reports in the second category. Fabre (1979), Sequin (1979), Delorozoy (1980), Fau (1980), Dupeyroux (1983), and Ragot (1983) all agree that black labor is extensive, though unmeasurable. All believe that one ought to distinguish between large-scale defrauders and occasional clandestine workers, and all deem it necessary to strengthen the methods of control.

Both approaches are inadequate for an analysis of the phenomenon of black labor. Any condemnation of black labor requires a detailed examination of the motives of all participants in illegal activities. Such an examination is absent from the preceding studies. In addition, the distinction between black labor and the underground economy is not always clearly drawn, with the result that many French studies produce empirical estimates of its size without a clear-cut operational definition of the phenomenon being measured. However, black labor has also been the subject of several direct surveys that have yielded interesting results. Tahar's monograph (1980) on the leather industry in the Tarn region traces the economic chain of undeclared labor from the tanning of hides to the sale of leather products by street vendors.

Le Bars (1980) has studied black labor in the building industry of the Paris region, and Foudi (1981) has investigated black labor activity among the unemployed workers in the region of Lille.

In the le Bars (1980) study, the sample was composed of young men between the ages of 24 and 43. The average age was 32. All individuals had lived in a given area for a long time and were thus well integrated. All had professional training. Half of the black workers questioned were salaried employees, 20% laborers, 10% middle managerial staff, and 10% unemployed. The average of the net declared monthly salaries (excluding those of the unemployed) was twice the legal minimum wage (SMIC). In only 20% of all cases was black labor a vital financial necessity. For 60% of those interviewed, the motivation was financial, although black labor was not a dire necessity. Twenty percent of the men had no financial motivation. They either attempted to obtain professional qualifications or wished to be integrated into society. The income from black labor varied with each individual and ranged from 2,500 FF to 36,000 FF per annum. The average income was 17,000 FF per year. The average time devoted to black labor – 12 hours a week – is of little significance. One group worked between 1 and 3 hours per week, another between 6 and 15 hours a week. All participants questioned knew that black labor was illegal. However, aware of the risks and the penalties, they were not dissuaded. On the contrary, it pushed them toward black labor all the more.

On the demand side, the positions are less easily classified. They belong to all socio-professional categories, their incomes vary from 3,000 FF to 11,000 FF per month, and their ages vary from 27 to 82. The only thing they have in common is the fact that 90% of them turned to undeclared labor for the first time out of financial necessity; the remaining 10% got involved in illegal activities when helping someone out.

This study of black labor in the Paris region is interesting for two reasons. From a methodological point of view, it provides an apt illustration of the kind of surveys that should now be applied to other professions and in other regions. In this way, the overall picture of French black labor could be brought more into focus. From an analytical point of view, the study enables one to examine the basis of supply and demand for black labor. In this context, Giran (1981) has recently published a paper establishing the theoretical connection between the official and the unofficial labor market.

Foudi's (1981) study concerned the behavior of the unemployed when confronted with the option of black labor. The study is based on interviews of prime aged unemployed males from the region of Lille. All were searching for employment and had been registered at the National Employment Agency (ANPE) for more than three months. The greatest achievement of this study was to disprove the popular idea that the "professional" undeclared work force is composed of those who are unemployed and on the dole. In a sample of ninety-four individuals, only forty cases of black labor were discovered. Moreover, in twenty-five cases the contribution of income earned to the family resources was small and insignificant; in only three cases did the income from black labor amount to more than half the legal minimum wage (SMIC). In addition, it was found that out of thirty-one individuals who had done undeclared work before becoming unemployed, only eleven had increased their practices in this sector once officially unemployed. However, the study is not limited to the quantitative aspect of black labor among the unemployed but provides an insight into the broader social life of those interviewed.[6] Those men whose income from black labor was large can be divided into three categories:

1 undeclared workers in real misery (poverty forced them to black labor),
2 contractors (the professional undeclared in the building sector), and
3 unemployed men undergoing retraining (involved in jobs that could soon become their official occupation).

For individuals with very little income from undeclared work, a series of socioeconomic factors provided an explanation. One of these was the reduction of the demand for labor due to a drop in the purchasing power of those offering employment and the increase of domestic do-it-yourself activities. Other factors varied with each individual questioned (deterioration of health, inability to borrow the necessary equipment from employers, and the fear of being caught). From a sociological point of view, the studies done in Paris and Lille are complementary. They both shed light on the motivations and difficulties of multiple job holders and the officially unemployed confronted with the option of "every-day undeclared work." Their contribution is that they reveal both sociological and economic descriptions of underground activity, but given their limited regional scope, it is difficult to use these studies to obtain national estimates of the size of underground activities.

---

[6] The study also extends to the domestic activities of the unemployed questioned. However, these activities do not increase noticeably with the advent of unemployment.

Estimating tax evasion in France

Estimates of tax evasion in France have been made by the General Income Board for the Tax Council.[7] Its first study appeared in 1972, and since 1978 regular publications have appeared with the aim of evaluating the reliability of income declarations. The first study contains a survey of 40,000 taxpayers, the sample determined by two criteria: (1) level of taxable declared income and (2) category of prevailing income.

On the basis of these criteria, 86.3% (i.e., 34,500) of the taxpayers initially examined were excluded since their prevailing income consisted of salaries, wages, pensions, and life annuities. Consequently, the sample survey subjected 4,165 units to a careful audit in order to determine an aggregate estimate of French tax evasion. The main results of this survey are summarized in Tables 13.1 and 13.2.

Before studying the results, one should not fail to take into account the following:

a The sample study concerned only those taxpayers who admitted to a tax liability. Thus, the estimate excludes non-filers as well as filers who claimed no tax liability.
b The registered evasion is that which has been disclosed by the tax inspectors. Consequently, it is impossible to form an estimate of the amount of undisclosed tax evasion.

From Table 13.1 it appears that those taxpayers whose prevailing income was composed of salaries, wages, pensions, and life annuities represented 86.3% of all taxpayers and that the proportion of those who would have been corrected had systematic verification applied to all taxpayers would only have amounted to 18.2%. Conversely, it was the smaller category, comprising the recipients of profits from non-commercial activities (and taxed according to the checked declaration system), that would have been subjected to the higher degree of correction, namely, 85.2%. One can also observe that the average amount of unpaid tax was low for the larger category and high for the smaller category. The average increased rate for corrected taxpayers also shows great disparities according to the prevailing incomes. The taxpayers whose main income was composed of industrial and commercial profits (taxed according to the lump-sum system) were corrected at a rate of 43.8%, whereas those who earned salaries, wages, pensions, and life annuities were corrected at a rate of 10.3%. Notably, the average increased rate of taxpayers whose prevailing income was composed of

[7] Conseil des Impôts, 1979.

287

Table 13.1. *Estimates of tax evasion by type of income*

Type of prevailing income	Percentage of taxpayers	Percentage of corrected taxpayers	Average increased rate for corrected taxpayers	Average value of unpaid tax (in FF of 1971)
Salaries, wages, pensions, and life annuities	86.3	18.2	10.3	790
Industrial and commercial profits, taxes and according to lump-sum system	7.2	43.1	43.8	3,875
Industrial and commercial profits, taxed according to real profit system	1.3	78.5	21.9	6,510
Profits from non-commercial activities, taxed according to administrative evaluation system	1.1	45.2	21.9	4,415
Profits from non-commercial activities, taxed according to checked declaration system	0.3	85.2	16.1	10,160
Land and real estate incomes	1.1	50.6	32.1	4,630
Stocks and share incomes	0.7	32.5	14.6	5,830
Other incomes	2.0	34.8	12.3	1,270
Total or average	100	22.0	17.4	1,848

Source: Conseil des Impôts, "Le rapport au Président de la Republique relatif à l'impôt sur le revenu," *Journal Officiel*, 1979, p. 161.

non-commercial profits taxed according to the checked declaration system was only 16.1% (i.e., below the average of 17.4%). When tax evasion is studied according to the net total income before corrections (Table 13.2), one observes (with the exception of one case) that the higher the proportion of corrected taxpayers, the larger the average value of the unpaid tax. However, the average increased rate of corrected taxpayers declines as the declared incomes rises, with one exception, for the income bracket 30,100–50,000 FF. Thus, the big taxpayers appear to evade more tax than the small ones, although their evasion is proportionally less. On the basis of these figures, income tax evasion in France was estimated to amount to 4.4 billion FF, which was approximately 14% of the declared income tax.

Evasion of the value-added tax (VAT) has recently been studied by the General Tax Board (GTB) and by the General Customs Board

Table 13.2. *Estimated size of tax evasion*

Net total income before corrections	Percentage of taxpayers	Percentage of corrected taxpayers	Average increased rate for corrected taxpayers	Average value of unpaid tax (in FF of 1971)
Less than 15,000	43.9	16.4	29.0	638
15,100–20,000	19.1	14.8	17.2	847
20,100–30,000	19.9	27.7	16.5	1,125
30,100–50,000	11.9	35.8	20.3	3,054
50,100–100,000	4.1	38.3	13.0	4,045
More than 100,000	1.1	61.7	10.6	9,262
Average	100	22.0	17.4	1,848

Source: Conseil des Impôts, "Le rapport au Président de la Republique relatif à impôt sur le revenue," *Journal Officiel*, 1979, pp. 162–4, 167 (extracts).

(GCB)[8]. These results have been published in the sixth report of the tax council (1983). In its policy of tax control, the GTB focuses on the areas where inaccuracies in the declarations are most likely to occur. As a simple extrapolation of results for all people subject to VAT would most probably lead to an overestimation of the size of evasion, an index of overestimation has been defined as the ratio of the examination results of those obtained if the choice of subjects and areas were to be purely random. With the aid of the indexes arrived at and the results provided by the tax controls, it becomes possible to estimate VAT evasion. On the basis of these studies, the amount of evasion of VAT was estimated to be 6,434 billion FF in 1979. However, it is most likely that the amount of evasion is underestimated since:

1 The estimate concerns only the disclosed evasion; one must add all evasion uncovered by the inspectors.
2 The study excludes all industrial and commercial firms with a turnover lower than 150,000 FF for firms supplying services and lower than 500,000 FF for all other firms. This exclusion seems all the more unfortunate since evasion tends to increase when turnover figures are lower. Indeed, it is easier to evade VAT when one is directly in contact with the ultimate consumer than when one sells by way of intermediate consumption to firms that have the right to deduct VAT paid

[8] In France, VAT is collected by the General Tax Board (~71%) and by the General Customs Board (~29%).

for their purchases. It is the smallest firms that are frequently situated at the end of the production process.

3 Several activities subject to VAT have been excluded from the estimate (i.e., farming, non-commercial activities, civil building societies).

In order to evaluate the total amount of VAT evasion, it is necessary to include the estimate derived by the GCB. This estimate was derived by means of a sample survey relating to three fields within the jurisdiction of the GCB: (1) clearance of commercial transactions, (2) transits, and (3) travelers. As in the case of the estimate published by the GTB, the results of the GCB underestimate the true situation because of the following:

1 The most serious attempts at evasion escape all attempts of evaluation insofar as the smugglers do not clear the goods. Smuggling automatically falls beyond the scope of the investigations.

2 The sample survey only concerns one of the three checking processes of the GCB. The three processes are direct checking (in the customs office or in transit), deferred checking (during the following month), and a posteriori checking (with confidential information about individuals who are suspected of evasion). The survey is only concerned with the direct-check procedure and thus tends to understate the true degree of VAT evasion.

3 The sample represents a small fraction of the annual traffic (1.32% for customs declarations, 0.02% for transit permits, and 0.018% for travelers).

If we extrapolate these findings to all taxpayers who are subject to VAT, evasion would amount to 1.4 billion FF for 1979, or 1.8% of all VAT collected. Total VAT evasion as estimated by the tax council, however, amounts to 7,834 billion FF (6.434 billion FF for the GTB and 1.4 billion FF for the GCB). In conjunction with these surveys, the tax council has also attempted to find an estimate of the amount of VAT that theoretically should be collected if no underestimates existed. This was done in the following manner. First, VAT returns that had been *effectively* levied by the government were computed by means of figures to be found in the national accounts. Then, VAT returns that *theoretically* should have been levied were computed, taking into account all economic activity as measured by the different items of the national accounts input–output tables. The difference between theoretical VAT and effective VAT is termed the VAT gap. In order to deduce an estimate of VAT evasion, one only had to correct this gap by taking into

Table 13.3. *Estimated VAT evasion*

Years	VAT gap (in billions of FF)	Proportion attributable to exemptions, deductions, and legal delays	Residual gap (VAT evasion) (in billions of FF)	Percentages of VAT returns	Percentages of GDP
1970	9.1	1.8	7.3	10.3	0.9
1971	10.3	2.2	8.1	10.2	0.9
1972	10.2	2.2	8.0	8.9	0.8
1973	10.5	2.0	8.5	8.8	0.8
1974	12.2	2.8	9.4	8.2	0.7
1975[a]	13.2	3.0	10.2	7.5	0.7
1976[a]	—	—	—	—	—
1977	19.5	5.7	13.8	8.9	0.7
1978	17.3	4.4	12.9	7.1	0.7
1979	14.5	2.5	12.0	5.6	0.6
1980	20.3	5.2	15.1	6.2	0.6
1981	24.0	5.9	18.1	6.6	0.7

[a] Average of both years (1975 and 1976).

Source: Conseil des Impôts, "Sixième rapport au Président de la Republique relatif à la ' TVA," *Journal Officiel*, 1983, p. 181.

account legal exemptions, deductions, and delays that come from legal rules concerning VAT payments and abatements. The results of this investigation are provided in Table 13.3. They suggest that VAT evasion is approximately 1% of GNP.

A currency-ratio-based estimate of unreported income in France

At present, there are no macroeconomic estimates of France's unrecorded income since several of the estimating methods that have been applied to other countries have been difficult to implement in the French context. As the French national accounts do not provide pre-correction figures of the revenue and expenditure aspects of the GDP, an application of the IRD method [the initial residual difference method used by Macaffee (1980) for the United Kingdom] proved impossible.

Several monetary methods, however, may be modified to apply to France. Contrary, however, to Gutmann's (1977) findings for the United States, the trend of C/D (currency–demand deposit ratio) for France has shown a marked decline since World War II. This suggests that the

simple currency ratio method used by Gutmann (1977) could not usefully be applied. Feige's (1979) transactions method, based on Fisher's
equation of exchange, cannot be used either since no data on the transactions velocity of money are available. The only available data are
those on income velocity. However, a future investigation into the determinants of transactions velocity [as employed by Feige (1979, 1981)
for the United States and the United Kingdom] should yield interesting
results.

For these reasons we have employed the monetary method Tanzi
(1982) used for the United States. In France, it is possible to apply this
method to data for the period 1959–79. The French national accounting
system was changed in 1976 to fit in with the accounts of other European
countries. However, conceptually consistent data have only been made
available as far back as 1959. Consequently, 1959 is the base year for our
study. This constraint should not present a handicap as 1959 marked a
turning point in the French economy from a period of reconstruction,
instability, and protectionism to a period of liberalization, political
stability, and the opening up of a new area of trade with the formation
of the Common Market.

As to the dependent variables, we had to make a choice of three
possible ratios: C/D; $C/M1$; or $C/M2$. Although Tanzi makes use of the
ratio $C/M2$, we have not adhered to this choice for several reasons.
First, the broader definition of deposits does not correspond to transaction balances but includes savings deposits that must first be converted
to currency or demand deposits before being used as a means of payment. Any use of this broader definition requires information on the
costs of holding money, and such an appropriate interest rate series is
not available for France. Moreover, there have been no interest payments
on current accounts in France since 1967. It would have been possible to
work with $C/M1$, but the resulting econometric relationships are not
satisfactory. We have therefore chosen to examine the ratio of currency
to demand deposits, although this ratio also has several drawbacks as an
indicator of underground activity. Currency is not the sole medium of
exchange in clandestine activities, and it is also likely that variations in
C/D have occurred due to shifts between term deposits and current
accounts rather than as a result of shifts between the official and the unreported sector. Thus, C/D is affected by perfectly legal factors as well
as by factors relevant to clandestine activities. Each of these factors
influences the ratio through long-term and short-term effects. As we
have used annual data, the short-term effects can be disregarded. However, long-term effects require close examination. As Table 13.4 shows,
C/D has dropped sharply since World War II. Two main groups of

292

Table 13.4. *Monetary ratios (%)*

	1945	1950	1955	1960	1965	1970	1975	1980
C/M1	57	51.1	48.8	41.7	36.9	32.2	24.8	20.8
D/M1	43	48.9	51.2	58.3	63.1	67.8	75.2	79.2
C/D	133	104	95	71	58	47	33	26

factors may explain this tendency. To the first belong the rise in the level of real income, the introduction and increasing use of credit cards, the fact that checks are free of charge, the efforts made by the banks to multiply the number of accounts, and the considerable degree of urbanization. In order to take these factors into account, we have used the level of real GDP per capita as a proxy variable. To the second group of factors belong the increasing tendency to pay wages and salaries by check or transfer, the growing use of monthly payments, and the increase in the number of wage earners in the labor force. The variable chosen to represent the latter group of factors is the proportion of wages and salaries in the gross disposable income of the households. We are not able to define a proxy variable to represent activities as varied as drug traffic, smuggling, or prostitution.[9] Consequently, we focus more particularly on the effects of tax evasion on *C/D*.

Although it is impossible to deal directly with the size of illegal activities, we may assume that they are nevertheless partially represented, considering that a proportion of the funds necessary for these activities probably comes from tax evasion. In order to estimate the incentives for tax evasion, it is necessary to construct an appropriate tax rate variable for the French situation. In light of the fact that VAT accounts for almost 45% of tax revenue, we have chosen to represent the average rate of taxation as the ratio of personal income tax revenue plus VAT to pre-tax household income. The decision to underreport income depends not only on direct taxation but also on indirect taxation.[10] With our variables defined in this way, we empirically estimated the following equation:

$$\ln \frac{C}{D} = a_0 + a_1 \ln W + a_2 \ln T + a_3 \ln Y \qquad (13.1)$$

where

[9] No study similar to that of Simon and Witte (1981) has been attempted for France.
[10] Other tax variables have been tested, but the results obtained were not as good as with this tax variable.

C/D = currency–demand deposit ratio

W = ratio of wages and salaries to gross disposable household income

T = ratio of personal income tax plus VAT to household income before tax

Y = index of real GDP per capita

For the years 1959–79, we arrived at the following results:

$$\ln \frac{C}{D} = 9.82031 - 0.086 \ln W + 0.917 \ln T - 1.636 \ln Y$$
$$\phantom{\ln \frac{C}{D} =} (6.09) \quad (-0.17) \quad\quad (2.99) \quad\quad (-12.92)$$
$$R^2 = 0.976 \quad F = 236.436 \quad DW = 1.282$$

In order to arrive at an estimate of unreported income in France for 1979, we follow Tanzi's (1980) method to first derive the amount of currency induced by changes in the tax rate between its initial level in 1959 and its 1979 value. These calculations suggest that some 36,900 million FF of currency can be attributed to the change in the tax variable between its original level and that of 1979. The method then requires a second assumption, namely, that the amount of income generated by these estimated tax-induced currency holdings can be derived by simply multiplying the estimated tax-induced currency by the observed income velocity in the official economy. The National Council for Credit estimates that the ratio of GDP to M1 (income velocity) is 4.188. Using this velocity figure in conjunction with the estimated tax-induced currency yields an estimate of unreported income of 154.5 billion FF, or some 6.3% of GDP. Alternatively, since our estimates suggest that 36.9 billion FF of currency actually were used to produce unreported income, we must first subtract this amount from M1 in order to estimate the corrected income velocity in the official economy. Using this second and preferred method, we find that income velocity in the official sector was 4.472, and applying this figure to tax-induced currency yields an estimate of unreported income of 165 billion FF, or 6.7% of GDP.

Our estimate of the size of unreported income in France has several drawbacks. One of these is the limited nature of the available data, which prevents us from adopting other estimating methods and from comparing the results. These initial results for the French economy rely completely on the implicit assumptions embedded in Tanzi's method and thus neglect all other factors affecting unreported activity other than changes in tax rates. As such, they should probably be regarded as lower bound estimates.

PART III

The underground economy under central planning

CHAPTER 14

The Soviet second economy in a political and legal perspective

F. J. M. FELDBRUGGE

Official Soviet sources project an image of an economy that is totally centrally controlled: Central planning is comprehensive, and the means of production are in the hands of the state. (The legal distinction between state ownership, cooperative ownership, and social ownership, which is of minor importance in political and economic terms, is disregarded here.) This image is not significantly altered by the official toleration of a modest private sector. It was well known to Western observers that the official economy did not always function as it was supposed to. The criminal code contains several provisions dealing with violations of the established economic system, and the Soviet press regularly reports on prosecutions for such violations and on other abuses of the system. Nonetheless, such incidents did not detract seriously from the overall picture. This began to change only after the opening up of two new channels of information during the last fifteen years: the emergence of a vast reservoir of unofficial (*samizdat*) sources from the Soviet Union and the arrival of large numbers of Soviet emigrants in the West, many of whom brought with them extensive and intimate knowledge of the functioning of the Soviet economic system. As a result of these developments, the traditional view of the Soviet economy as a system that was planned, owned, and controlled from the center had to be revised. It became customary in this respect to speak of the "second economy" of the Soviet Union, a system that presumably would coexist with and be supplementary to the official, first economy. It is the purpose of this chapter to investigate the relationships between this second economy and the politico-legal system of the USSR.

Definition and nomenclature

Further reflection on the topic reveals two interrelated questions: What is it precisely that we are looking at and what are we going to call it? In other words, the questions of definition and nomenclature. The first obstacle we encounter is the familiar conundrum of defining a complex phenomenon that we suspect to hide behind specific manifestations visible to us. Such definitions inevitably contain an element of arbitrariness; they may result in the undesired exclusion or inclusion of certain elements. The definition, however, is a tool; if it does not work well, it can be thrown away. The minimum requirement is that it embraces the core elements, which we assume to be connected. In the case of the second economy of the USSR (I use this term provisionally at this moment) it is not difficult to identify a number of such core elements, as they have been described in recent sources: the existence of a flourishing private market in certain goods and commodities, extensive productive activities of private individuals and groups, the institutionalization of corruption and bribery, and utilization of the front of the official economy for private entrepreneurial activities, to mention a few of the most conspicuous.

The first attempt to tie together these various elements within a general definition was made by Grossman in his pioneering essay on the second economy of the USSR.[1] He suggested that the second economy comprised all production and exchange activities that fulfilled at least one of the two following tests: (a) being directly for private gain and (b) being in some significant respect in knowing contravention of existing law.[2] Although the definition has undoubtedly proved usable, there is something inherently unsatisfactory in its combination of two quite disparate elements: private gain and illegality. What does an act that is lawful and for private gain have in common with an act that is unlawful and not for private gain?

Ginsburgs and Pomorski suggest two definitions, a wider and a narrower one, and, upon reflection, opt for the former. The wider definition describes the second economy as "any private, spontaneous economic activity beyond direct control by the central planner"; the narrower definition reduces the concept to "spontaneous, private activity officially denounced as harmful and, hence, prohibited by law."[3] Although the authors prefer the wider definition in principle, the narrow one is in fact operational because, as they point out, their "interest focuses primarily on the responses of the second economy, [and therefore] it seems natural to structure the discussion following the major types of criminal conduct recognized in the penal legislation." This, incidentally, illus-

---

[1] G. Grossman, "The 'Second Economy' of the USSR," *Problems of Communism*, 1977, No. 5, pp. 25–40.

[2] Ibid, p.25; the same definition is retained by Grossman in "La seconde économie et la planification économique soviétique," *Revue d'études comparatives Est-Ouest*, 1981, No. 2, pp. 5–24, at p. 6.

[3] In an as yet unpublished paper (see note 18) G. Ginsburgs and S. Pomorski, "Enforcement of the Law and the Second Economy."

trates my point about the instrumental character of the definition to be given. A certain malaise concerning both definitions of Ginsburgs and Pomorski may be felt on account of the use of the term "spontaneous"; at least to the present author this term seems unusually ambiguous.

Much attention to the matter of definitions is devoted by Wiles in the German version of his study on the parallel economy.[4] The central concept is anti-systemic conduct (*systemwidriges Verhalten*), "which concerns anything which does not conform to the actual economic system of the country in question" (my translation, F. F.). Its complement is *systemkonformes Verhalten*, which is also called official conduct. I cannot consider this terminology entirely satisfactory because it begs the question whether the actual economy system (*tatsächliches Wirtschaftssystem*) should not, in any normal meaning of the word, embrace the parallel (or second) economy. Anti-systemic behavior is also designated as *unrechtmässig*, while at the same time the latter qualification is contrasted with *illegal*. This would imply that in Wiles's view anti-systemic behavior is not to be branded as ipso facto unlawful (against the law) but as unjust, contrary to natural justice, or perhaps simply contrary to the prevailing system. After some additional considerations Wiles forwards an enumerative definition that equates anti-systemic behavior with unlawful distribution or production plus tax evasion plus evasion of price controls plus theft plus corruption. The last four elements concern illegal transfers; the first two involve illegal added value.

The legal criterion is again made decisive by Katsenelinboigen, who has attempted to describe the different kinds of markets in the Soviet Union. In his study on "coloured markets" he uses two sets of characteristics: their legality (legal, semi-legal, and illegal markets) and their relationship to the centralized planning system (immanent, socialist, and rudimentary markets).[5] The latter aspect comes into consideration in forecasting the future of the various subdivisions of the second economy, which is otherwise analyzed according to its relationship with the criminal law.

The advantage of using a legal criterion for determining what constitutes the second economy is the relative sharpness of the distinction (relative, in view of the haziness of many of the pertinent definitions of

---

[4] P. Wiles, *Die Parallelwirtschaft; eine Einschätzung des systemwidrigen Verhaltens (SWV) im Bereich der Wirtschaft unter besonderer Berücksichtigung der UdSSR*, Bundesinstitut für Ostwissenschaftliche und Internationale Studien Köln, 1981, pp. 8–10.
[5] A. Katsenelinboigen, "Coloured Markets in the Soviet Union," *Soviet Studies*, 1977, No. 1, pp. 62–85.

second-economy activities in Soviet criminal law). On the other hand, defining the second economy principally by reference to the illegality of its constituent activities begs the question of why the legislator proscribed precisely those activities. This leads us to the following consideration: The most appropriate definition of the second economy depends very much on the standpoint of the observer. He may be primarily interested in specific economic or legal ramifications of the phenomenon. If one attempts to view second-economy activities within the context of the political and socioeconomic system prevailing in the Soviet Union, a definition should take account of the essential characteristics of this system. It proclaims and tends to be, as stated in the first sentence of this chapter, a totally centrally controlled economic system. There can be no doubt that the political and social system are in close harmony with the economy in the sense that they are also determined by rigid and comprehensive central control.

In the economy central control is expressed chiefly through two institutions: central planning and state ownership of the means of production. It is clear that these two institutions are intimately connected; already long ago they have been described as the dynamic and the static aspects of the Soviet economic system.[6] Comprehensive planning of the Soviet variety can only be realized where central authority is in unchallenged control of the means of production. There are various legal instrumentalities for achieving such control; the Soviet regime has opted for a system wherein the bulk of the means of production are in immediate and undivided state ownership, with the remainder assigned to a plurality of cooperative owners (mainly kolkhozes). The legal and economic independence of the individual cooperative is hardly less minute than that of the individual state enterprise, so that, apart from its formal legal nature, cooperative ownership can be regarded as a form of indirect state ownership. For the sake of completeness it should be added that there still exists a legally recognized but otherwise extremely limited and totally insignificant possibility of individual ownership of means of production.

Conversely, state ownership (whether direct or indirect) of the means of production, as demanded by Marxist–Leninist political ideology, naturally entails comprehensive central planning; it would be utterly irrational first to concentrate all means of production in the hands of a single owner and then to allow their uncoordinated utilization.

Once these essential characteristics of the Soviet economic system

---

[6] R. Maurach in his comments on article 4 of the 1936 constitution of the USSR, in his *Handbuch der Sowjetverfassung*, Isar, München, 1955, p. 55.

have been grasped, it is not difficult to perceive the vital role of the legal system in the functioning of the economy and to understand why definitions of the second economy so easily refer to legal standards. An economic system of the Soviet type is in many respects a highly artificial and therefore vulnerable construction. If its weaker sections are not propped up by a number of legal commands and prohibitions, collapse is imminent and widespread. The greater the comprehensiveness and integration of the system, the more serious the effect of a single malfunctioning. It is no exaggeration to assert that the entire Soviet economic system would be fatally affected if only one of a small number of vital prohibitions were lifted. The most important among these are the provisions of the criminal code against speculation (article 154), the exercise of forbidden professions (article 162), commercial middlemen (article 153), and foreign trade transactions and foreign currency speculation (article 88). The term "speculation" in this context may be misleading because the criminal code defines speculation as the buying and selling with the purpose of making a profit. There are a great many other provisions in the criminal code directed against specific economic activities, but the common element of the aforementioned offenses (and a few others as well) is that they cover activities that are universal in all countries and all times and in which people will engage more or less spontaneously as long as they are not specifically prevented from doing so. What this amounts to is that if the expectation turns out to be correct, private citizens will enter the sphere of lawful and reported economic activity on a large scale. A very significant sector of the economy will thereby become desocialized and decontrolled. This would destroy the ideological claim of having an economy where the means of production are in the hands of society. It is this claim that largely determines the organizational structure and legal arrangement of the Soviet state and its economy. These cannot remain as they are without legal prohibitions and safeguards.

Keeping this in mind, we may proceed to a definition of the second economy. Such a definition could take as its starting point the consideration that the Soviet economy pretends to be, and is to a considerable extent, totally centrally controlled, that is, based on comprehensive central planning and central (state) ownership of the means of production. If this is regarded as the first (official) economy, then the second economy can be defined as its complement. Together they would make up the whole of the economic life of the USSR. The second economy then would cover those economic activities that escape central control on account of their not being determined by central planning and/or not being embraced by state ownership of the means of production.

301

The definition just given has important points of similarity with the wide definition of Ginsburgs and Pomorski, who speak of "economic activity beyond direct control by the central planner." It is equally close to the views developed by Birman in his study on "second and first economies and economic reforms." The latter author argues that the most apt terminology would be to designate the "inherently socialist forms of the economy" (*posledovatel'no-sotsialisticheskie formy khoziaistva*) as the first economy and all the rest as the second economy.[7] But after stating his preference in this respect, he declares that he will follow Grossman's usage, albeit with some modifications. As a result, Birman's definition of the second economy consists of an enumeration of various activities, arranged according to two criteria, both of them legal: What is the legal character of the activity (legal, semi-legal, illegal) and what are the property relations involved? We shall return to Birman's classification in the following section of this study.

Perhaps the most important consequence of the definition of the second economy advanced here is that its comprehensive nature leads to the inclusion of activities that are perfectly legal, particularly the important private sector in Soviet agriculture. It is my contention that in the perspective adopted here such a consequence is desirable and advantageous. It highlights what Pomorski (and other authors) have elsewhere designed as the machine model of the Soviet economy[8]:

The Soviet economy, indeed the Soviet society as a whole, is organized according to a machine model: one centre of political and economic disposition, supplied with maximum relevant data and equipped with infallible tools for their interpretation, makes all the important decisions. The decisions, conveyed to various parts of the system, are faithfully carried out, and their implementation is quickly and exactly reported back to the center. Underlying the machine model is a fundamental assumption, that is, the assumption of ideal cooperation.

In this view, any economic activity that takes place outside or detracts from the centrally controlled economic machine is part of the second economy. In this way the definition allows the collection under a single formula of a great variety of activities, the connection between which may not be immediately obvious.

The definition is also affected by the common disease of the unclarity of some of its constituent parts. We have attempted to explain the con-

---

[7] I. Birman, *Second and First Economies and Economic Reforms*, Occasional Paper No. 108 of the Kennan Institute for Advanced Russian Studies, in Russian, p. 7.

[8] S. Pomorski, "Crimes against the Central Planner: 'Ochkovtiratel'-stvo,'" in D. Barry, G. Ginsburgs, P. Maggs, Eds., *Soviet Law After Stalin, Part II: Social Engineering Through Law*, Sijthoff, Alphen aan den Rijn, 1978, pp. 291–317, at pp. 306–7.

cept of central control of the economy by reference to the twin concepts of central planning and central (state) ownership of the means of production. The latter concept is sufficiently precise, even if, as in this chapter, it is not taken in its strictly legal meaning. State ownership is defined in article 11 of the Soviet constitution and more extensively in the Russian civil code. In this chapter state ownership is assumed to embrace also the legal categories of collective and social ownership, as defined in the USSR constitution and the Russian civil code; that is, I use state ownership in the meaning that Soviet law attributes to socialist ownership (as opposed to personal ownership). It is much less clear, however, what central planning embraces. One cannot say, for instance, that private agricultural production is wholly outside the world of central planning in the Soviet Union. In drawing up its plans for agricultural production, the state certainly takes private production into account. In present times the state even takes positive measures to improve certain aspects of private agriculture.[9] Without getting into details, I propose to limit the concept of central planning to those economic activities that are formally included in the plan.

A final observation with regard to the definition proposed concerns the term "economic activities." This obviously also displays some inherent vagueness. Without attempting to resolve them, an example may be of some help. Regular and routine theft of liquid fuel by professional drivers, who resell it on the black market to private car owners, is a well-known and well-documented phenomenon in the Soviet Union.[10] It should be regarded as an economic activity, which forms part of the second economy. The occasional theft of a can of fuel by a bystander is not an economic activity, although the totality of all such thefts will have a forecastable and measurable effect on the economy.

This finally leaves us with the matter of nomenclature. What name should be given to the phenomenon that has provisionally been designated as the second economy? Once again, the point may be made that there is a certain amount of legitimate variety flowing from the different perspectives selected by various authors. Where the focus of a study is on unlawful economic practices, there it is entirely in order to speak about the illegal market and economy. In the framework of this chapter, where the concept of a centrally controlled economy is the pivotal idea, it would not be helpful to use a terminology that refers

---

[9] Cf. B. Rumer, "The 'Second' Agriculture in the USSR," *Soviet Studies*, 1981, No. 4, pp. 560–72.

[10] D. O'Hearn, "The Consumer Second Economy: Size and Effects," *Soviet Studies*, 1980, No. 2, pp. 218–34, at p. 221.

primarily to the legal character of the activities concerned. In other words, "black market," "illegal economic activities," and similar designations are unsuitable. "Private economy" has to be rejected because, as we shall see, the centrally controlled economy is interwoven with and penetrated by the economy we want to describe, so the second economy is not only a private economy. It would also be paradoxical to refer to our subject as "unobserved economy," when the whole point of the present exercise is to observe, analyze, and explain the very same. The most practical way out of the terminological quandary is to go for a neutral term that has little precise meaning by itself. The most ready candidates presenting themselves are "parallel," "second," and "unofficial" economy. "Parallel" and "second" economy have been used by several authors, and as "second economy" seems to be the most frequently employed expression when referring to the Soviet economy, I propose to conform to the latter usage.

Sources

Collecting information on the second economy of the USSR presents a few special problems. Most of the basic information-gathering techniques cannot be utilized in situ by Western students. Moreover, the perusal of Soviet economic statistics often requires special skills, whereas the equally important criminal statistics are treated as state secrets. All this raises high barriers for a satisfactory quantitative analysis of the phenomenon, a question to which we shall return in the next section.

When it comes to the question of a more general insight into the morphology of the Soviet second economy, its social significance, its relationship to the political system, and so on, the picture becomes rosier. Surprisingly, perhaps, the most detailed description of the rich variety of second-economy activities is supplied by the Soviet press itself. Soviet newspapers and magazines report frequently on the manifold economic irregularities brought to light. Within the confined space of an annual volume of the *Current Digest of the Soviet Press* (which covers the entire spectrum of the Soviet press), there were more than 50 items concerning the second economy in 1981.[11] This means that there must be at least tens of thousands of such reports in the entire Soviet

---

[11] In order to illustrate the point of the richness of the Soviet press as a source of information on the various types of second-economy activities, the examples given in this chapter have all been taken from the most recent available volume of the *Current Digest of the Soviet Press* (CDSP).

Soviet second economy in political and legal perspective

press during the last two or three decades. Occasionally Soviet newspapers and magazines carry more general articles in which the phenomenon of the second economy or some of its aspects are discussed. Such contributions often limit themselves to castigating the activities concerned and to calling for increased vigilance and repression. In some instances, however, authors have put forward more imaginative and innovative suggestions.[12] Knowledge gleaned from the official press may, as usual, be supplemented through the reading of *samizdat* literature.[13] *Samizdat* sources have from their inception in the 1960's devoted considerable attention to economic problems, and in that context there has been quite a lot of reporting on and analysis of second-economy activities.

Samizdat writing finds a natural extension in the works of Soviet emigrés published in the West. Of particular interest among them for our present topic are the books by Valerii Chalidze on crime in Russia,[14] Vladimir Bukovskii's autobiography,[15] Voslenskii's study on the *nomenklatura*,[16] Zemtsov's "Party or Mafia?"[17], and a host of shorter studies by these and other authors.

Many Western visitors to the USSR have included discussions of the second-economy phenomenon and related anecdotal evidence in more general works of the Soviet Union.[18]

All such works provide in one way or another first-hand information on the second economy. This reservoir of primary knowledge has fed a by-now impressive collection of secondary Western studies. Among

---

[12] In an article exposing "underground millionaires," A. Rubinov suggests the introduction of income tax forms for people who make expensive purchases; *Literaturnaia Gazeta*, July 1, 1981, CDSP, 1981, No. 40, p. 17. A similar suggestion is made by F. Kuznetsov in *Pravda*, November 9, 1981, CDSP, 1981, no. 45, p. 19. In a more widely ranging and candid survey of various manifestations of the second economy the economist V. Rutgaizer (in *Pravda*, November 16, 1981, CDSP 1981, No. 46, pp. 18–19) recognizes the inevitability, for the time being, of many such activities and even advocates a certain liberalization in the wake of the Hungarian and East German experience; this should be accompanied in his opinion by the simultaneous introduction of income tax for the entire population.

[13] Some of the principal older *samizdat* treatises on the Soviet economy are briefly discussed in my book *Samizdat and Political Dissent in the Soviet Union*, Sijthoff Leyden, 1975, pp. 213–214. More up to date is C. Allen, "A Survey of Economic Samizdat," *Radio Liberty Research*, September 12, 1979, RL 268/79.

[14] V. Chalidze, *Criminal Russia*, Random House, New York, 1977.

[15] V. Bukovskii, *To Build a Castle*, Viking, London, 1978.

[16] M. Voslensky, *Nomenklatura – Die herrschende Klasse der Sowjet-union*, Fritz Molden, Wien, 1980.

[17] I. Zemtsov, *Partiia ili Mafiia? Razvorovannaia respublika*, Editeurs Réunis, Paris, 1976.

[18] H. Smith, *The Russians*, Ballantine, New York, 1976, especially the chapter "Corruption: Living *na levo*," pp. 81–101.

these, Gregory Grossman's pioneering essay of 1977, published in *Problems of Communism*, has already been mentioned.[19] Other important contributions may be found in *Soviet Studies* and *Survey*.

The size of the Soviet second economy

Estimating the size of the second economy in the USSR is surrounded by the same obstacles that similar operations entail in Western countries plus quite a few additional ones caused by the scarcity and inaccessibility of the relevant Soviet data. A preliminary difficulty is produced by the question of definition, referred to in the beginning of this chapter. It is hardly necessary to point out that if one wants to talk about the Soviet second economy in quantitative terms, it makes an enormous difference whether, for instance, data concerning legal agricultural production from the private plots are included.

Once the researcher is clear in his own mind about the meaning to be given to "second economy," he has to select a method of finding and analyzing quantitative data. A number of Western authors have addressed this particular problem of methodology.[20]

At the initial level there are the educated guesses of former Soviet

---

[19] A research conference on the second economy of the USSR organized by Professor Grossman took place in Washington DC in January 1980; the following conference papers have been at my disposal, through the courtesy of their respective authors: S. Pomorski and G. Ginsburgs, "Enforcement of the Law and Second Economy"; G. Schroeder Greenslade, "Regional Dimensions of the 'Second Economy' in the USSR" (Occasional Paper No. 115 of the Kennan Institute for Advanced Russian Studies); J. Vanous, "Private Foreign Exchange Markets in Eastern Europe and the USSR" (Occasional Paper No. 114 of the Kennan Institute for Advanced Russian Studies); I. Birman, "'Vtoraia' i 'pervaia' ekonomiki i khoziaistvennye reformy" ["Second and First Economies and Economic Reforms"] (Occasional Paper No. 108 of the Kennan Institute for Advanced Russian Studies); D. O'Hearn, "The Second Economy in Consumer Goods and Services" (Occasional Paper No. 113 of the Kennan Institute for Advanced Russian Studies); G. Ofer and A. Vinokur, "Private Sources of Income of the Soviet Urban Household," Rand Corporation Report R-2359-NA, Santa Monica, 1980; K. Bush, "Books in the Soviet Second Economy," *Radio Liberty Research*, November 23, 1981, No. 468/81. An expanded version of Wiles's paper was published in German by the *Bundesinstitut für ostwissenschaftliche und internationale Studien*, P. Wiles, *Die Parallelwirtschaft; eine Einschätzung des systemwidrigen Verhaltens (SWV) im Bereich der Wirtschaft unter besonderer Berücksichtigung der UdSSR*, Köln, 1981.

[20] G. Schroeder and R. Greenslade, "On the Measurement of the Second Economy in the USSR," *Ass. for Comp. Econ. Studies Bull.*, Vol 21 (1979), No. 1, pp. 3–22; D. O'Hearn, op. cit., Consumer note 10, pp. 219–21; P. Wiles, *Die Parallelwirtschaft* (note 19), pp. 20–2; G. Grossman, "Notes on the Illegal Private Economy and Corruption," in *Soviet Economy in a Time of Change* (A Compendium of Papers Submitted to the Joint Economic Committee, Congress of the United States), Vol. 1, Washington DC, 1979, pp. 847–52.

citizens who have mentioned for the second economy percentages of from 10 to 50 of the official, first economy. The same source is utilized on a larger scale and in a more organized manner by Ofer and Vinokur, who base themselves on a family budget survey of about a thousand Russian emigré families now living in Israel.[21] Their basic conclusions are that the urban private sector accounts for 10–12% of total family income and that about 18% of all consumption expenditures are made to private people. In all, however, private activity in the urban consumer sector does not add more than 3–4% to Soviet GNP estimates.

On the basis of data from Ofer and Vinokur and similar sources, official Soviet statistics, and some amount of guesswork, Wiles offers an estimate of 12–13% of per capita personal income being derived from the second economy.[22]

The picture would change considerably when the legal sector of the second economy is also included. In this case more reliable data, albeit somewhat dated, are available. According to CIA estimates for 1968, 10% of Soviet GNP originated in the legal private sector, of this 76% was in agriculture, 22% in housing construction, and 2% in services. In Grossman's opinion, the share of the legal private sector has decreased since 1968.[23]

Speaking of the overall effect of the Soviet second economy in quantitative terms, the wisest course is surely to agree with most other authors who limit themselves to calling it considerable or significant. It is different when the attention is directed at specific sectors or at specific geographical areas. In such cases various methods sometimes allow more precise statements because Soviet sources themselves directly or indirectly supply the necessary data, and Soviet press reports occasionally quote precise figures concerning specific illegal practices in a particular city or province. These figures are often the results of spot checks; the performance of a given economic unit (a store, filling station, etc.) is closely monitored for a day or a week and then checked against "normal" performance. O'Hearn has collected a large number of such press report data and used them in quantifying important parts of the consumer sector of the Soviet second economy.[24] They indicate that in many areas the second economy has outstripped the official one, a fact that is abundantly confirmed by other Soviet press reports and by observer reports. For instance, the quoted market share of the second

---

[21] Ofer and Vinokur, op. cit., note 19, especially p. 70.
[22] Wiles, *Die Parallelwirtschaft*, note 19, p. 65.
[23] Grossman, op. cit, note 1, p. 35.
[24] O'Hearn, op. cit., note 10, pp. 219–29.

economy of petrol and lubricants in Kazakhstan is 80%, of house repairs and decoration in Moscow 70%, of house repairs in Georgia 98–99%. Press reports concerning the unlawful acquisition of fuel for private cars may provide a good example of the difficulties encountered in trying to form a more precise picture of a particular activity in the second economy. Other sources mention ten filling stations in Kursk taking in 273,000 rubles, against 88,000 rubles during an equal but unsupervised period the year before; 13.5% of petrol consumed in Omsk in 1971 being bought legally from the state; filling stations' receipts in Orel rising by 200–1000% during supervised periods.[25] All this accords with an *Izvestiia* report stating that by the most conservative estimates more than a third of private motor cars drove on illegally acquired fuel. However, this only permits us to say with reasonable confidence that the actual figure is probably between 40 and 90%.

No similar study has been made for the production sector, although similar fragmentary data crop up regularly in the Soviet press. For instance, according to newspaper reports, private construction activities by regular gangs of builders (*shabashniki*) had completed projects to a value of 70 million rubles in the province of Kurgan, whereas official state construction enterprises accounted for only two-thirds of this amount during the same period.[26]

Vanous has devoted a special study to private (illegal) foreign exchange markets in Eastern Europe and the USSR. On the basis of his calculations for other East European countries, a prudent estimate of the volume of hard currencies channelled into the black market of the USSR during 1977 would amount to the equivalent of $500 million.[27]

Treml's pioneering studies on alcohol consumption in the USSR have also covered the question of illegal distilling (*samogon*). During the entire period of 1957–72 the figures for production and consumption of *samogon* remain in the vicinity of at least 40% of total production and consumption of hard liquor.[28]

An important aspect of the study of the size of the second economy is its geographical differentiation. This aspect emerges in many general discussions of the subject and is the object of a special study by Ger-

[25] Ibid., p. 221.
[26] See three articles in *Komsomol'skaia Pravda*, April 14, 15, and 17, 1981 (CDSP, 1981, No. 17, pp. 6–8), reporting on the activities of moonlighting gangs of construction workers in West Siberia.
[27] Cf. Vanous, op. cit., note 19, pp. 42–43.
[28] V. Treml, "Alcohol in the USSR: a Fiscal Dilemma," *Soviet Studies*, Vol. 27, 1975, pp. 161–77.

trude Schroeder Greenslade.[29] Wiles, in his study on the "parallel economy" of the Soviet Union, has attempted a geographical and urban/rural breakdown of his estimates of the share of second-economy activities in the composition of personal incomes. A point invariably made in these studies concerns the special position of the Caucasian republics, particularly Georgia. The latter republic has earned the special attention of students of the Soviet second economy by its apparent leading position in this respect, a position probably rooted in its geographical position, its climatological characteristics, and the historically shaped national character of its inhabitants. In Wiles's estimate, rural Georgia tops the league with 32% of personal income derived from the illegal sector of the second economy.

By way of a general conclusion, the first thing to be said is that reasonably firm and precise figures concerning the overall effect of the second economy can as yet not be given for two reasons. First, it is impossible to provide a definition of the second economy that draws a clear and meaningful (i.e., non-arbitrary) dividing line between the second and first economies. Second, even if it were possible to design such a definition, there is no sufficient database available to produce the figures desired.

At more specific levels, that is, for specific economic sectors and/or specific geographical areas, reasonably reliable figures can occasionally be given. They confirm what already was known from differently oriented studies, that the second economy is of considerable and sometimes preponderant importance in the production of consumer goods and services. The interwovenness of the first and second economies in the production of capital goods is an issue that does not lend itself easily to quantification.

The forms of the second economy

In describing and classifying the forms in which the second economy manifests itself, it is again the perspective adopted by the observer and the definitions flowing from this that determine the approach to be selected. In a legally oriented view of the second economy the most natural procedure is to arrange various second-economy activities according to the various criminal offenses under which they may be subsumed: speculation, plan fraud, bribery, cheating customers, the exercise of forbidden trades, and so on. This is, understandably, the procedure

---

[29] Greenslade, op. cit., note 19.

followed by Ginsburgs and Pomorski in their study on enforcement of the law and the second economy.

A more detailed description is offered by Birman on the basis of his classification of the entire Soviet economy.[30] The latter is subdivided by him into nine main sectors, each of which consists of several subsections:

1 the state sector (institutions financed from the state budget and institutions that have to pay their own way – *khozraschet* organizations);
2 the cooperative sector (kolkhozes, fishing, trading, building, and other cooperatives);
3 the quasi-capitalist sector (state-controlled enterprises with certain specific legal characteristics, such as "Inturist" and Soviet banks for foreign trade);
4 the intermediate sector (various supportive activities in the socialist economy, of dubious legality themselves, such as the activities of private building teams – *shabashniki* – for kolkhozes, the utilization of private agents – *tolkachi* – by state enterprises, agricultural production by industrial enterprises for the benefit of their own personnel, etc.);
5 private and lawful commercial activities (trading on the kolkhoz market, letting of private apartments, certain permitted forms of private employment);
6 private and lawful productive activities (agriculture on private plots, hunting, fishing, building, and repair of private dwellings);
7 the semi-legal private sector (permitted private activities without payment of the prescribed taxes, acceptance of tips, industrial production by kolkhozes, etc.);
8 illegal private economic activities (theft of public property, unauthorized use of public property, forbidden productive activities, bribery); and
9 illegal private trade (selling illegally acquired goods, speculation, currency transactions).

Of these activities, Birman considers the last three entirely and 5 and 6 in part to make up the second economy.

A convenient beginning of a description of the various forms of the second economy, and in this I follow Grossman's example, may well be the admission that the Soviet economy does not even officially pretend to be totally centrally controlled. Complete socialization of production is certainly an officially acclaimed ideal and has indeed been realized to

---

[30] Birman, op. cit., note 7, pp. 3–4.

a very high degree, but there still remains a private sector that is not entirely insignificant and is accorded official recognition. The most authoritative recent expression of this recognition is in article 17 of the 1977 constitution of the USSR[31]:

Individual labor activity in the sphere of trades and crafts, agriculture, serving the everyday needs of the population, as well as other forms of activity based exclusively on the individual labor of citizens and the members of their families are permitted in the USSR in accordance with the law. The state regulates individual labor activity, ensuring its utilization in the interests of society.

This provision lends constitutional respectability to a plethora of activities, of which private agriculture is the most important and the best known.[32] Notwithstanding the nationalization of land and the virtually complete socialization of the agricultural work force, individual families of collectivized farmers will normally receive the use of a small plot (up to 0.5 hectare, but usually smaller) to provide for their own needs. The surplus production of this private plot (*priusadebnyi uchastok*) may be sold on the so-called kolkhoz market. But what in theory was meant as a modest concession to the realities of life in the country has turned out to be a major and irreplaceable source of food production. According to the official data for 1979, the private plots were responsible for the following percentages of nationwide production: potatoes, 59%; vegetables, 31%; meat, 30%; milk, 29%; and eggs, 33%.[33]

Another important area of private economic activity is in the construction of houses. In rural areas owner occupancy is the rule, and taking the entire Soviet Union, about half the population lives in privately owned houses and apartments.[34]

In other sectors of private production and service the picture is complicated. Certain professions and trades cannot be exercised legally because they are affected by general prohibitions proclaimed by the criminal code. For instance, the law forbids speculation, which is defined as the buying and selling of goods with the purpose of making a profit. This provision obviously prevents the legal exercise of a great number of professions and trades, which are not themselves forbidden outright. In other cases specific activities are expressly proscribed, and the most important source in this respect is the Statute on Crafts and

---

[31] Quoted from F. Feldbrugge (Ed.), *The Constitutions of the USSR and the Union Republics*, Sijhoff and Noordhoff, Alphen aan den Rijn, 1979, p. 85.

[32] Cf. K. Wädekin, *The Private Sector in Soviet Agriculture*, University of California Press, Berkeley, 1973.

[33] *Narodnoe Khoziaistvo 1979*, Moscow, 1981, p. 222.

[34] Grossman, op. cit., note 1, p. 26.

Trades of May 3, 1976.[35] It lists a number of forbidden activities, of which the most important are the preparation of food products (except for one's own use or from self-produced materials), the production of chemicals and leather goods, and the transportation of passengers or goods. Activities not covered by any of the general or specific prohibitions are in principle permitted but subject to a fairly restrictive system of registration and permission. Such permitted activities may only be exercised within the district of residence of the permission holder, at a fixed address, and for the period of one year, to mention the most important restrictions. The scale of all legal private economic activities is further circumscribed by the constitutional prohibition of all forms of privately hired labor. (There is an exception for house personnel.) This means that the size of legitimate private enterprise is limited to the size of the family.

Summing up the significance of the legal private sector of the Soviet economy, one could say that it is restricted to specifically defined activities and that, operating in small production units, it is of very considerable importance within its permitted sphere of operation.

Another observation concerning the legal private sector in the USSR may usefully be inserted at this point, namely with regard to consumptive freedom. The Soviet society of today is far removed from the strict military model, where even food, clothing, and shelter are centrally distributed and where almost no consumers' options remain open. Of course, in a negative way, the Soviet regime controls consumer behavior by not making certain goods available. This will often force Soviet citizens to buy certain other goods (or services) that are on sale. Otherwise, where there is a choice of goods, or where supply is more than just adequate, or where for some other reason a good is not regarded as essential by the consumer, the population is actually free not to make use of the offer made by the state. This is a very significant factor in connection with the second economy because a great many goods and services officially produced are in fact rejected by the consumer in the Soviet Union, usually on account of their perceived poor quality.

A survey of the legal side of the private sector of the economy provides a convenient introduction to a description of the entire second economy, precisely because legal, semi-legal, and illegal activities constitute a single intricately interwoven network. The transition from legal to illegal can easily be illustrated by the example of private agriculture. This, by itself, is legal, provided it is carried out outside normal work-

---

[35] Official publication of the Statute in *Sobranie Postanovlenii Pravitel'stva SSSR*, 1976, No. 7, item 39; see also E. de Jong, "Statute on Handicraft-Artisan Trade," *Rev. of Socialist Law*, 1976, No. 4, pp. 266–7.

ing hours and on the piece of land assigned for the purpose. But, as the peasant will usually derive a higher income from his private plot, the arrangement tends to favor an undisciplined approach to work in the collective or state farm. More seriously, in view of the permanent and universal shortages in supplying the individual farmer with everything required for work on the private plot, the only realistic alternative is to carry off the necessary implements, fertilizer, building materials, and so on, from the kolkhoz or sovkhoz. The surplus product of the private plot may be sold, legally, on the so-called kolkhoz market, usually located in the nearby town. The most readily available means of transportation will often be a truck "borrowed" from the kolkhoz. With regard to the selling of the agricultural produce, it will often be more attractive to the producer to sell, illegally, to a middleman, who can offer a more reliable and regular outlet. Moreover, most illegal phases of the transactions will inevitably require the at least tacit permission or active cooperation of third persons, who will expect something in return (farm managers and overseers, truck drivers, etc.).[36] This pattern returns in most cases of legal private activities of an economic character; legal and illegal practices are inseparably bound up.

At this point a few words should be said about the paradoxical term "semi-legal" (cf. Birman's "intermediate economy," Katsenelinboigen's "grey market," etc.). Generally speaking, this term may be applied to activities and transactions that contain an element of illegality but for one reason or another do not attract serious governmental repression. The sources of the illegality and the motives for official inaction are varied. The transaction may have been on behalf and in the interest of a state enterprise; it may have been private and legal but unrecorded and thereby in avoidance of taxation; or it may have been officially encouraged but lacking a firm basis in law, to mention only a few possibilities. A well-known example of the first category is the time-honored practice of *tolkachi*, unofficial agents of state enterprises who ensure through informal negotiations (not excluding bribery) that the enterprise receives necessary supplies, permits, specialist labor, and generally, anything required to make the enterprise fulfill its plan.[37] The second category embraces the letting of apartments and holiday houses (dachas), private tuition, paid services by doctors, dentists, nurses, lawyers, (although such services are in principle available free of charge), and numerous other privately produced services.[38] An important example of

---

[36] Cf. Grossman, op. cit., note 1, p. 26; K. Simis, "The Machinery of Corruption in the Soviet Union," *Survey*, 1977, No. 4, pp. 35–55 at p. 36.
[37] Cf. J. Berliner, *Factory and Manager in the USSR*, Cambridge, MA, 1957.
[38] D. Simes, "The Soviet Parallel Market," *Survey*, 1975, No. 3, pp. 42–52 at pp. 46–8.

Table 14.1. *Second economy activities in the Russian criminal code*

Article of Russian criminal code	Description of offenses	Maximum penalty for most serious form of offense	Normal position in Western legal systems
78	Smuggling	10	Lower penalties
88	Violations of rules for currency transactions	15 or death	Lower penalties
87	Making or passing counterfeit money or securities	15 or death	Lower penalties
89–97	Theft and other appropriation of socialist property	15 or death	Lower penalties
152	Issuing low-quality, nonstandard, or incomplete products	3	No direct parallel
152–1	Distortion of plan fulfillment accounts	3	No direct parallel
153	Private enterprise and commercial middle-men activities	5	No direct parallel
154	Speculation	7	No direct parallel
154–1	Buying up grain products for cattle feed	1	No direct parallel
155	Illegal use of trademarks	6 months	Similar penalties
156	Cheating public in stores, restaurants, etc.	7	No direct parallel
156–1	Violations of rules for liquor trade	1	No direct parallel
156–2	Receiving unlawful rewards from customers	3	No direct parallel
156–3	Violation of trade regulations by shop personnel	3	No direct parallel
157	Issuing low-quality, nonstandard, or incomplete merchandise	2	No direct parallel
158	Illicit production, storage and sale of alcoholic beverages	5	Similar penalties
159	Forgery of postal values or transportation tickets	3	Similar penalties
162	Engaging in forbidden trade	4	No direct parallel
163	Illegal fishing	4	Similar penalties
164	Illegal hunting of seals or beavers	1	Similar penalties
166	Poaching	1	Similar penalties

Article	Crime	Maximum term (years)	Comparison
166–1	Trading in unstamped furs	1	No direct parallel
167	Private mining or prospecting	5	No direct parallel
169	Illegal woodcutting	3	Similar penalties
170	Abuse of authority or of official position	8	No direct parallel
171	Exceeding official power or authority	10	No direct parallel
172	Negligent performance of official duty	3	No direct parallel
173	Accepting bribes	15 or death	Lower penalties
174	Giving bribes	5	Lower penalties
174–1	Acting as intermediary in bribery	15	Lower penalties
175	Documentary fraud by an official	2	Similar penalties
196	Making, selling, or using forged documents, seals, etc.	5	Similar penalties
199	Unauthorized taking of land or construction	1	Similar penalties
208	Acquiring or transferring property illegally acquired	7	Similar penalties
212–1	Unauthorized use of motor vehicles	3	Similar penalties
224	Production and possession of narcotics	15	Similar penalties
224–1	Theft of narcotics	15	Similar penalties
224–2	Incitement to use narcotics	10	Similar penalties
225	Cultivation of plants containing narcotic substances	8	Similar penalties
226	Keeping dens of debauchery or of gambling; pandering	5	Similar penalties
226–1	Keeping dens for use of narcotics	10	Similar penalties
228	Production of or trading in pornographic materials	3	Similar penalties

an officially promoted activity that lacks a firm legal basis is the recent campaign to encourage industrial and commercial enterprises, other state institutions, and army units to engage in agriculture to serve the needs of their members.[39] A reasonably firm construction of the relevant laws on the subject would regard such activities as *ultra vires* and therefore impermissible, but this point has become completely academic since the existing practice received the most positive accolade from the regime in a combined resolution of the Central Committee of the Party and the federal Council of Ministers in 1978.[40]

Western literature on the Soviet second economy has painted a rich and detailed picture of the latter, and there is no need here to repeat what has been done elsewhere. Instead I propose to pay some more attention to the question of classification. This is not unduly complicated when a strongly legal focus is selected. The enormous variety of second-economy activities may then be subsumed under a limited number of offenses, as defined in the criminal code. Table 14.1 prompts a number of observations that are of direct relevance to the subject of this chapter.

The comparison with Western legal systems

The first difficulty in comparing is that there is a great lack of uniformity in the West. Many economic offenses in Western countries are encountered only in a few legal systems. Even where an offense is fairly commonly included in Western criminal law, penalties may still vary enormously in the allowed range as well as in the actual practice of courts and enforcement agencies. More insidiously, many offenses that superficially look quite similar may in fact turn out to be strongly different phenomena in the USSR as compared with the West. Trading in foreign currency (or currency speculation as it is called in Soviet law), for instance, may be a more or less serious offense in certain Western countries that maintain currency restrictions; in the Soviet Union, however, it is regarded as an "anti-state" crime, almost on a par with treason, espionage, and the like.

The different nature of the Soviet economy

An attempt to make fruitful comparisons with Western legal systems is seriously hampered by the fundamentally different character of the

---

[39] See Rumer, op. cit., note 9.
[40] "On auxiliary agricultural households of enterprises, organizations and institutions," resolution of December 4, 1978, *Resheniia partii i pravitel'stva po khoziaistvennym voprosam*, Vol. 12, 1977–9, Moscow, 1979, pp. 594–7.

Soviet economy, as discussed before and as reflected in the legal system. The universally known crime of theft, for instance, is broken up in Soviet law into theft of socialist and personal property, with their own ranges of penalties. The various offenses known as "official crimes" (articles 170–175 of the criminal code) receive their peculiar Soviet coloring from the fact that there is no private sector in the Soviet economy, in education, services, and so on. Therefore, almost anybody in any position of authority in Soviet society is an official.

The absence of tax evasion as an offense

In particular, the absence of tax evasion as a specific offense appears almost incredible to a Western observer. The explanation is of great significance for the entire question of the second economy of the USSR. The Soviet state owns and controls almost the entire economy. It is in a position to derive the bulk of its income directly from the state economy. The overwhelming majority of the population is directly or indirectly employed by the state and has no alternative source of income. A very low rate of income tax is withheld from better paid employees. Apart from this, a small number of citizens is either self-employed (the constitution forbids privately hired labor) or allowed to earn extra money privately. The first category consists mainly of small craftsmen, the second of teachers and various types of medical personnel. The former are assessed for their annual income according to certain standard guidelines; the latter are obliged to account for their extra income according to a precisely prescribed system of bookkeeping. In theory this system eliminates the need to recruit the assistance of earners of private income to contribute to the collection of data for fiscal assessment. Any irregularities introduced by them may be covered by specific provisions of the criminal code, such as article 175 (documentary fraud by an official) or article 196 (forging documents) and others. The main point, however, remains that by virtue of the nature of the Soviet system of collecting state income, income tax and similar taxes paid by individual citizens are unimportant, and consequently tax evasion by individuals is of almost negligible significance.

The manifold activities reflected in the list of offenses provided by Table 14.1 may or may not be part of the second economy, as defined in this study. Some of them (e.g., article 153, private enterprise) inevitably are; theft of socialist property, however, will quite often not be connected with the second economy. Moreover, the relative importance of various offenses in connection with the second economy is different; the illegal use of trademarks, for instance, is hardly to be compared with

317

such a key offense as bribery. These considerations make the criminal code an unsuitable starting point, from our perspective, for a more extensive description of the second economy. The most important consideration, however, in this respect is that most second-economy activities encompass several distinct offenses and that to some extent it is a matter of chance how certain activities should be qualified according to criminal law. In this way a classification of second-economy activities based on the criminal code may separate what should remain united.

The aforementioned example of privately conducted agriculture might entail theft of socialist property (e.g., fertilizer), unauthorized appropriation of land, services of commercial middlemen, speculation, abuse of power, and at several stages, bribery.

It is more promising in this respect to apply a typology based on economic functionality. This approach is taken, among others, by Birman and Katsenelinboigen, who look at such items as the place of the agent within the economic system (state enterprise or institution, kolkhoz, individual employee, or entrepreneur), the type of goods or services involved (producer or consumer goods, producer and recipient of service), the location of the activity concerned within the economic system (industry, agriculture, trade, etc). Instead of reproducing their systematic analyses and without a pretense at comprehensiveness, I shall attempt to present a reasonably balanced picture of the second economy by grouping the most frequently encountered and/or most significant activities into clusters of similar behavior.

Vynos (siphoning off, carrying out, diversion of state property)

Given a state-controlled economy of the Soviet type, state property is omnipresent, and every working citizen is in direct contact with it at his place of work. Most reliable sources agree that theft of socialist (state) property is almost as widespread as state property itself. A comparatively innocent and universal form of it is the taking home of small quantities of goods, or goods of little value, such as tools or materials.[41]

---

[41] In 1981 several hundred pilferers of meat from meat-packing plants in the southern Ukraine were apprehended, according to *Pravda*, December 15, 1981 (CDSP, 1981, No. 50, p. 20); in *Pravda* of November 11, 1981 (CDSP, 1981, No. 45, p. 18), the police chief of Odessa province complained that "pilfering and petty theft by employees have been widespread at enterprises in Odessa province"; *Sovetskaia Rossiia* of June 20, 1981 (CDSP, 1981, No. 31, p. 15), contains a report from a number of correspondents about the universality of the "I-brought-it-from-work" practice in many cities of the Russian republic; the most successful practitioner (until his arrest) was a bulldozer

One author relates how nobody in a company of Moscow intellectuals knows where to buy stationery because it was never bought.[42] This phenomenon of course is well known in the West too.

At a more serious level there is the more substantial theft of building materials by persons who have access to them, especially store attendants and transportation workers. Such thefts are the principal source of supply for the illegal building trade but also for semi-legal construction works for state enterprises and kolkhozes.[43]

Official sources have admitted that at least one-third of the fuel needs of private car owners are met by illegal diversion of state-owned fuel.[44] Other sources indicate that the actual figure is much higher, in the region of 80%.[45] This example illustrates the institutionalized character of the activity: It is not a question of an individual prospective consumer snatching a can of petrol at a station, but a regular and general practice by which truck drivers will systematically falsify their fuel consumption sheets and dispose of the surplus through routine channels.[46]

A related area is the theft of goods in transit by warehousemen and transportation personnel.[47] Such goods are normally disposed of on the black market. Store personnel, particularly in shops selling clothing and foodstuffs, are traditionally underpaid. They will supplement their incomes by putting aside part of the store supplies to be sold from under the counter.[48] The permanent shortages and scarcity of many such goods strongly promote such practices. Not only are they hard to detect, but not infrequently they are tied to a wide network of protection,

operator from Magadan who had accumulated 30,000 rubles' worth of gold dust at his place of work: *Izvestiia*, June 14, 1981 (CDSP, 1981, No. 24, p. 19).

[42] Birman, op. cit., note 7, p. 16.

[43] Cf. Chalidze, *Criminal Russia* (note 14), p. 166; *Pravda*, October 28, 1981 (CDSP, 1981, No. 43, p. 19), reported on a building materials scandal to the value of 400,000 rubles in which an Armenian operator had bribed a number of officials from the State Supply Committee for Timber Products to deliver thousands of cubic meters of round timber to Samarkand Province, where it was sold to private builders.

[44] See note 9. *Izvestiia*, November 24, 1981 (CDSP, 1981, No. 47, p. 26), contains an article that explains how pump attendants can accumulate an unaccounted-for surplus.

[45] O'Hearn, op. cit., note 10, p. 226.

[46] O'Hearn, op. cit., note 10, p. 221.

[47] *Vecherniaia Moskvase*, July 20, 1981 (CDSP, 1981, No. 36, p. 15): a gang of 24 railroad workers and accomplices convicted of 28 thefts from railroad cars; a report in *Sel'skaia Zhizn'*, January 6, 1981 (CDSP, 1981, No. 35, pp. 11–12), complains about the colossal losses sustained by fruit and vegetable growers in Georgia through the incessant pillage during transportation.

[48] Four persons employed at a Moscow fruit and vegetable warehouse had accumulated the sum of 100,000 rubles by diverting goods in various ways to the black market; *Trud*, July 17, 1981 (CDSP, 1981, No. 38, p. 20).

bribery, and kick-backs, involving local police, government, and party officials.[49]

A somewhat different version of the siphoning off of state property is the practice, engaged in by some enterprise managers, of diverting part of the enterprise production away from the official channels and outlets and into illegal trade.[50] In another variety of this practice supplies may be diverted to engage in pseudo-official but in fact private production. The latter practice has even its own criminal provision, article 153, paragraph 1: "Private enterprise activities with the use of state, co-operative or other public firms.[51] In all these cases the proceeds may be pocketed privately by the persons involved or received by the enterprise but in some way kept out of the books. This practice again makes clear that a single second economy activity may embrace a number of different offenses.

In these various manifestations of *vynos* theft is usually, but not always, the central offense. The most characteristic element of *vynos* is that goods belonging to the state are diverted from their official destination by persons who have some amount of control over these goods and who reroute these goods according to regular patterns to other sectors of the economy. Of course, common theft is also well known in the USSR, but it is not very illuminating to regard the incidental activities of ordinary thieves as a species of the second economy.

Using state property for private purposes

The use of state property for private aims is obviously related to the activities described in the previous paragraphs. A closer look at the practices concerned will explain the differences. It is quite common for officials of a certain rank to take advantage of facilities that are under

---

[49] Simis, op. cit., note 36; also see S. Staats, "Corruption in the Soviet System," *Problems of Communism*, 1972, No. 1, pp. 40–6.

[50] A report from *Literaturnaia Gazeta*, March 25, 1981 (CDSP, 1981, No. 15, p. 13), illustrates the practice: A reporter from the paper had gone to the provincial capital of Krasnodar in the Northern Caucasus; he was unable to buy soap, toothpaste, or other toiletries in the state shops but found an abundant supply on the black market at strongly inflated prices; the officials from the Ministry of Trade in Moscow assured him that sufficient supplies had been sent to Krasnodar. See also the case cited in note 44.

[51] A small ring of operators in cahoots with the minister of local industry of the Chechen-Ingush autonomous republic and the deputy minister of local industry of the Russian federation had a number of enterprises in the Chechen-Ingush republic producing unaccounted-for goods, which then were sold illegally all over the Russian republic: *Trud*, April 9, 1981 (CDSP, 1981, No. 19, p. 14). An article in *Pravda*, October 22, 1981 (CDSP, 1981, No. 42, p. 21), reports on the activities of illegal subsidiary enterprises of kolkhozes from all over the USSR.

their control. Managers and other high-ranking staff of an enterprise may have houses or dachas built by enterprise personnel and from materials belonging to the enterprise.[52] Or such work may be carried out by friendly business partners. Another example would be the execution of home repairs at the expense of the enterprise. The motor car is also of considerable importance in this respect. The official car can be used privately or put at the disposal of relatives. Chauffeurs of important officials are regularly permitted to "moonlight" as cabdrivers, as even foreign visitors have often noticed.

Although such activities may involve theft of state property, the emphasis is rather on the improper *use* of state property. Also, the activities of the principal beneficiaries (with the exception of the moonlighting driver) are directed at the immediate satisfaction of their consumer requirements and do not feed further stages of the second economy.

Administrative power as a source of income

In a society of the Soviet type, where state control, state ownership, and state interference are extremely pervasive, permission and cooperation of state officials is required at almost every step. This holds true for the individual citizen as well as for any activity within the state-run economy. Cooperative behavior of officials, or the denial of it, which goes beyond the strict call of duty, may be motivated by a number of considerations: personal feelings toward the petitioner, the desire to improve one's standing with higher ranking officials, and so on. Where such behavior is wholly or partly directed toward economic consequences, it enters the area of the second economy. The most useful distinction to make with regard to the latter type of behavior is based on its purpose: Is cooperation extended or refused for private gain or in the interest of a section of the state economy? Parenthetically, let it be stressed once more that, as in most distinctions made in the description of the second economy, there are no sharp borderlines. Often enough the activities envisaged in this paragraph will serve both personal interest and the interest of the organization in which the agent is employed. Moreover, the smaller the section of the state machinery being favored, the more indistinguishable corporate and private interest become.

The most quoted examples of the use (or rather abuse) of administrative power as a source of private income are naturally from the area of close contact between the individual citizen and the administration,

---

[52] *Izvestiia*, November 4, 1981 (CDSP, 1981, No. 44, p. 17): The paper's correspondent reports from Barnaul that several officials had luxurious country homes built and fitted out at the expense of the enterprises they were heading.

where the former addresses the latter in order to acquire some kind of concession of permission. Acceptance of bribes in the form of money or goods is widely reported in connection with the granting of driving licenses, the allocation of permits to buy a car, the allocation of living space and the granting of residential permits, admittance to educational institutions, and so on.[53] Official inaction, for a consideration, is common in cases of traffic offenses, but also on a larger and more institutionalized level, in administrative collusion with second-economy networks.[54] Indeed, many second-economy activities can only take place because a number of officials who should counteract them prefer to look the other way, not without profit to themselves.

The use of administrative power or an official position in order to further the interests of a section of the state economy is possibly even more widespread than the same use for the purpose of private gain. Not every link of the network of the official economy is in contact with individual citizens, but there are always contacts with other parts of the state organization. The latter traffic is predominantly of an economic nature, since the entire economy is in principle run by the state. At managerial as well as at lower levels of the state economy there are copious opportunities to utilize administrative discretion for furthering the interests of one's own economic or administrative unit. In fact, it would hardly be an exaggeration to say that this is the way the official economy functions. Enterprise management has a legitimate area of discretion and a much larger zone of actual freedom. Within these limits enterprises will engage in deals concerning supplies, spare parts, use of materials, buildings, labor reserves, credit and finance, and so on. Some of these deals may be completely legal, but many of them will be considered semi-legal; that is, they are tolerated or disregarded by the immediately concerned supervisory agencies (whose inaction, when bought for certain economic advantages, itself becomes a second-economy activity). In other transactions illegality becomes preponderant, for instance, where one side of the transaction consists of the unauthorized payment of money, which in fact constitutes the crime of bribery.

---

[53] *Izvestiia*, May 22, 1981 (CDSP, 1981, No. 21, p. 18): A group of instructors at a Frunze technical college were convicted of bribery; they charged 25 rubles for a passing grade in correcting examination papers. *Literaturnaia Gazeta*, July 1, 1981 (CDSP, 1981, No. 40, p. 17): The head of a welfare agency in Baku, in charge of allocating cars to disabled drivers, sold permits to other drivers; when he was arrested, he owned two apartments, a dacha with a swimming pool, old paintings, antiques, and 34 kilograms of gold. *Izvestiia*, December 1, 1981 (CDSP, 1981, No. 48, p. 21): A doctor in Magadan issued medical certificates to people who wanted to stay away from work, charging 10 rubles per workday.

[54] Simis, op. cit., note 36, pp. 52–55.

Speculation

Speculation is the name Soviet law gives to what in other societies is the basic commercial transaction: buying and selling with the aim to make profit. The law does not draw a distinction between private citizens and entities of the socialist economy. Presumably the latter, who alone are allowed to engage in legitimate trade, do not do so with the aim of making a profit (although they are normally required to make a profit: the *khozraschet* principle) but rather for the purpose of serving the common good or some similar aim. To be quite clear, the law does not forbid citizens outright to participate in contracts of sale. What is objectionable in the Soviet view is to engage in buying and selling as a regular source of income. The line between what is legal and what is forbidden is again hazy, a pervasive feature of Soviet criminal law, which enables the authorities to intervene whenever they consider this to be desirable and keeps the citizen in a permanent position of legal uncertainty.

Speculation will often appear as the ultimate link in a chain of second-economy activities (such as the earlier quoted example of private agricultural production), but it occurs also as a more or less independent activity. It takes place against the general background of an officially induced or tolerated scarcity in a number of consumer goods. The unsatisfied demand for such goods may be met from production within the second economy or through importation from abroad. The most important categories of goods produced by the domestic second economy (produced directly or siphoned off from the official economy) are farm produce and other foodstuffs, wine, liquor and beer, cars, spare parts for cars and domestic appliances, clothing, books,[55] and records.[56] Foreign-made goods enter the country through foreign tourists and through Soviet citizens who have the opportunity to travel abroad. The most important item is clothing, and anybody who has walked around in a major Soviet city will have observed the popularity of Western-made clothes. It is probably safe to say that none of these have ever seen the inside of a Soviet shop. The opportunity to bring in Western textiles, ostensibly for one's own use, but in fact in order to sell them privately at hugely inflated prices, is one of the most materially valuable privileges

---

[55] K. Bush, "Books in the Soviet Second Economy," *Radio Liberty Research*, November 23, 1981, RL 468/81. Also see O'Hearn, op. cit., note 10, pp. 223–4.

[56] A minor but still quite significant item on this market is tickets for the theatre or the opera. Several correspondents write that it is impossible to obtain tickets for popular performances at the box office, although they can be bought easily from speculators; *Sovetskaia Rossiia*, October 13, 1981 (CDSP, 1981, No. 50, p. 21).

a Soviet citizen may seek. Other imported objects are watches, books, household appliances, and similar objects of not too large a size.

An adjunct of the flourishing market in imported Western goods is the foreign currency trade.[57] This is not only fueled by the demand of prospective Soviet travelers and the unrealistic exchange rate offered by the Soviet government, but also by the ease with which foreign money can be utilized in various second-economy transactions. Currency transactions are almost at the nadir of illegality in the official scale of values; they are dealt with in the chapter on crimes against the state in the criminal code, and professional currency speculation regularly entails capital punishment. There appears to be an oddly ideological twist to this matter in the USSR, as other East European regimes display a much more relaxed attitude in this respect and have learned to live with and even profit from illegal currency deals by their citizenry.[58]

Forbidden trades and activities

Generally speaking, the official economy performs poorly in supplying goods and services to private consumers. Food and textile production and housing are the most glaring examples. The second economy has moved into this gap and supplies an important section of the market. Best known is the contribution of private agriculture, but in fact the share of the second economy is even larger in other sectors. There are indications, for instance, that in the area of household repairs the officially appointed agencies take care of only an insignificant portion of the work to be done.[59] Other jobs frequently carried out outside the officially provided networks are car repairs, house moving, other forms of transportation, and building. A crucial role in this respect is fulfilled by *shabashniki* (literally sabbath workers), teams of craftsmen who are available for specific jobs, especially in the construction business, and who move from place to place.

Many activities connected with the unofficial supply of the private consumer are illegal, either because they constitute the exercise of a forbidden profession or because they fall foul of another provision of the criminal code. In this respect, and in contrast to the situation pre-

[57] See J. Vanous, "Private Foreign Exchange Markets in Eastern Europe and the USSR" (unpublished discussion paper, see note 19). See also O'Hearn, op. cit., note 10, pp. 227–9, and Wiles, op. cit., note 19, pp. 74–6.

[58] Ibid.

[59] O'Hearn, op. cit., note 10, 225.

vailing in the Western world, the fact that such activities possibly imply a contravention of fiscal laws is hardly a consideration for either the authorities or for the persons engaging in such activities.

Of the numerous and variegated activities covered by the general label of forbidden trades,[60] two deserve a special mention. One, the provision of transportation for payment by persons who own or control means of transportation, has been referred to previously. The other one is the illegal distilling of liquor. The alcoholism problem in imperial Russia was already of exceptional proportions, and the situation seems to have worsened since. Moreover, the consumption of alcohol is the most common and the easiest way to spend money that can be spent on very little else by large sections of the population. Under these circumstances alcohol assumes the function of an alternative currency, a phenomenon of great importance in the second economy, where payments are often made in alcohol. The attitude of the Soviet government is ambivalent, on account of the enormous income derived from high duties on a vast turnover. The result is a situation one observer has described as an economy afloat in alcohol. All these conditions together create a most favorable climate for illegal distilling. *Samogon* (home-distilled alcohol) reportedly accounts for a quarter of the total production of distilled liquor (2,000 million liters of pure alcohol).[61]

The exercise of forbidden trades and crafts not only is directed at the satisfaction of the demands of individual consumers, but also supplies the socialist sector of the economy. Particularly the construction business routinely makes use of the activities of *shabashniki* to meet the needs of kolkhozes and state enterprises.[62]

As many other second-economy activities, the successful operation of forbidden trades and crafts has a spiral-like effect: the second economy supplements the unsatisfactory performance of the official economy – as the level of dissatisfaction declines, there is less incentive for the authorities to improve the performance of the official economy – the demands of the second economy increase – the potential of the official economy gradually atrophies.

---

[60] Among the more bizarre activities one might mention are the melting down of gold acquired by buying up gilded articles from the public by a gang of Baku entrepreneurs who sold the gold thus obtained to dentists and to black market speculators [*Izvestiia*, November 26, 1981 (CDSP, 1981, No. 47, pp. 23–4)] and the trade in lids for jam jars apparently flourishing in many cities [*Nedelia*, September 7/13, 1981 (CDSP, 1981, No. 36, p. 18)].

[61] V. Treml, "Alcohol in the USSR: A Fiscal Dilemma," *Soviet Studies*, 1975, No. 2, pp. 161–77, at p. 163; see also Wiles, op. cit., (note 19), pp. 73, 97–8.

[62] See note 26.

Private enterprises

A number of reports from official and unofficial sources indicate that second-economy activities are sometimes of such complexity and so firmly organized and institutionalized that there is every reason to speak of private enterprises existing outside the official system of exclusively state-owned or controlled enterprises. What we have in mind especially are enterprises in the production sector. There are indeed complex and permanent second-economy operations in the trading sector, but these do not normally require a large material basis. They consist essentially of a network of personal relationships. A different situation arises in production, where normally materials, machinery, and a workplace are required. The chief manifestations of private production enterprises are the fully underground private factory and the private factory working behind the facade of a state enterprise. The latter form is the most common and has been mentioned before in connection with other second-economy activities.[63] The scale of the operations may be quite considerable: one source mentions a private factory of television sets.[64]

Bribery

Bribery occupies a peculiar position among the numerous and variegated second-economy activities in that it is usually present in any more complex transaction. Bribery, or more precisely the value transferred as the object of bribery, thereby serves as the universal lubricant for the entire second economy. It would be pointless to attempt to describe the endless varieties in which bribery may occur.[65] As a possible object of bribery, according to Soviet law, is regarded not only money but also any other material object that has a money value and any factors, services, actions, or omissions to which a material value can be put.[66] Grossman has drawn attention to the useful distinction between ordinary, or ad hoc, bribery and the traditional custom of *prinoshenie* (literally bringing to), "a general and regular way of ingratiating oneself with authority."[67] The

---

[63] An interesting example is mentioned in *Pravda*, March 22, 1981 (CDSP, 1981, No. 12, pp. 20–1): an illegal poster-printing enterprise using the presses of Moscow print shops to print posters and other work on stolen paper for provincial organizations.

[64] O'Hearn, op. cit., note 10, p. 220.

[65] Staats, op. cit., note 49, and Simis, op. cit., note 36.

[66] Cf. Kommentarii k Ugolovnomu Kodeksu RSFSR, Moscow, 1971, p. 374; a curious consequence of this view is that the granting of sexual favors in return of some kind of dereliction of official duties does not constitute bribery because such favors are regarded by Soviet law as not having a material value.

[67] Cf. Grossman, op. cit., note 1, p. 32.

latter practice reemerges in various shapes in the second economy, for example, in the regular payment of protection money or in the availability of free meals and drinks to officials in exchange for their benevolent disregard of certain activities.[68] In such cases *prinoshenie* would undoubtedly be covered by the criminal code's definition of bribery.

Bribery, looked at from the perspective adopted in the previous paragraph, again reinforces the point that a classification of second-economy activities according to merely legal criteria may hinder a more general understanding: It occurs at almost any point of the economy and embraces a great variety of socioeconomic and political situations, from the conductor who accepts a packet of cigarettes and allows the passengers to smoke in their compartment to the virtual sale of a ministry of a union republic.[69] A legal typology concerns the form rather than the content of second-economy activities.

The symbiosis of the first and second economies

One of the insights yielded by the foregoing survey of clusters of second-economy activities is that many of the latter are located and occur within the official economy. It would be misleading to present the second economy primarily as the dealings of individual entrepreneurs who, far removed from the ostensibly centrally controlled official economy, would constitute a parallel network operating side by side with the official one. This image, to be sure, is largely correct with respect to those activities that supplement and replace a defective performance of the official apparatus. In the survey provided in the foregoing section such activities are found especially within the bracket of "forbidden trades and professions." As reported, the poor performance of the official sector and its adequate replacement by the services of the second economy mutually reinforce each other.

In many other areas, however, it is not so much a matter of parallel and separate operations in the official and the second economy but

---

[68] Cf. Simis, op. cit., note 36, pp. 50–2. In the trade scandal in the Chechen-Ingush republic, mentioned in note 51, the local minister of local industry received a monthly bribe of 1,500 rubles, while his colleague in Moscow received a monthly sum of 400 rubles.

[69] Simis, ibid., p. 42, mentions that the bribes for securing appointment as minister in one of the Transcaucasian republics range from 100,000 rubles (Minister of Social Security) to 250,000 rubles (Minister of Trade). Simis's data from Azerbaidzhan are based on information from I. Zemtsov. The latter adds the interesting information that one of the ground rules in the purchasing of party or government posts is that the price should not exceed the annual income yielded by the post in question; I. Zemtsov, "The Ruling Class in the USSR," *Crossroads*, 1979, No. 2, pp. 5–60, at p. 35.

rather of close relationships and widespread interpenetration. Numerous ordinary economic activities are located partly in the official and partly in the unofficial sector. This holds true for small-scale transactions of individual consumers as well as for much larger operations taking place between units of the state economic system. With regard to the former, it should be sufficient to point out that there is a very considerable second-economy input in the production of food, and that the food trade is riddled with second-economy activities. As to the impact of second-economy activities within the state economic system, the situation is no longer that there are wide and important connections between the two spheres but that the second-economy activities have become an essential element in the functioning of the state economic system. It is probable, from the picture emerging from official and *samizdat* reports, that at least a number of sectors of the economy would collapse without the operation of personal networks to secure supplies, materials, labor, and so on, without the activities of the *tolkachi*, without the additional income state enterprises derive from unplanned and unaccounted for production, and so forth.[70] In this respect, the term "parallel" economy may even produce the wrong impression, insofar as the activities referred to do not take place inside an independent circuit but are by now inseparable from the normal operation of the official economy. Soviet sources, of course, tend to deny the institutional and structural connections between the two economies and project by the same token the image of a parallel economy as a separate and insignificant sphere of action of individual criminal operators.

If one accepts this view regarding the far-reaching integration of the official and the second economy, then the next consideration that comes in sight is this: Quantitative assessments of the relative strengths of aspects of the official and second economies become questionable. Even where it would be possible, for instance, to estimate the amount of *samogon* (home-distilled liquor) produced within a specific period and in a specific area, who could still guarantee that there would be no second-economy input in the amount of officially produced liquor within the same period and area?[71] In fact, it has often been reported that official and illicit distilling constitute a system of communicating channels (and this is even more so for the liquor trade).

---

[70] Cf. Grossman, op. cit., note 2, pp. 6–7. See also Wiles's section on "Benign planning violations," op. cit., note 19, pp. 31–2, 88–9.

[71] A section in *Izvestiia*, October 28, 1981 (CDSP, 1981, No. 43, p. 19), explains how legally produced vodka can be diverted into illegal retail networks by making use of a 2.1% allowance for spillage and breakage at the bottling plant. Two employees of a vodka plant in Omsk had diverted 365 cases of vodka in this way.

Another consequence of the widespread integration of official and second economies is that it seriously affects the officially projected view of total economic control from the top. If it is true that the official economy functions in part through its recourse to second-economy operations, then the central planners lack the full information needed to exercise such control as well as the will or the power to do so.

Second economy and political organization

A realistic assessment of the economic significance of the second economy on the USSR inevitably leads to wider ranging questions, such as: Why has it been allowed to assume its present proportions? What is its function within the political system of the the USSR? And so on.

The official Soviet line on the significance of the second economy is to belittle it: The socialist economy is by and large working well and is ultimately superior to the capitalist system; there may be occasional difficulties in certain sectors, which may provoke unstable or criminal elements to attempt to exploit such situations; however, such conduct is quantitatively and qualitatively of very limited effect on the overall rosy picture of the socialist economy. Due to insufficient information on the Soviet second economy, this line is still implicitly accepted by large sections of the Western public.

Even where more detailed knowledge of the Soviet economic scene is available, there remains the problem of reconciling such knowledge with the traditional Western view of the Soviet Union as a rigidly centrally controlled, almost totalitarian political system. If the party and the government are indeed all-powerful, why do they not put an end to economic practices that seem to run counter to the basic ideological tenets of the system and are usually illegal to boot? The answer can only be that there must be a more complex connection between the second economy and the prevailing political system.

Grossman had indeed, in his original study on the Soviet second economy, already referred to this connection in passing when he noted "that very probably there is a close organic connection between political-administrative authority, on the one hand, and a highly developed world of illegal economy activity, on the other."[72] On a more specific point, planning frauds (*ochkovtiratel'sto*), Pomorski had argued compellingly that such frauds were symptomatic of the inherent bureaucratic conflicts between the central executive and subordinate operational entities.[73]

[72] Grossman, op. cit., note 1, pp. 32–33.
[73] Pomorski, op. cit., note 8, p. 306.

In the meantime studies and reports by recent Soviet emigrés have considerably enriched our understanding of the connection. Many of them have spent their lives in the Soviet Union working in the higher spheres of the bureaucracy; they brought with them an intimate and detailed knowledge of the actual operation of the Soviet economic system. This information, added to the available reservoir of knowledge, allowed the construction of a general picture offering a satisfactory answer to the questions posed at the beginning of this section.

It is essential to recognize that the relationship between the political system, the official economy, and the second economy is fundamentally different from the situation prevailing in Western countries. The maintenance of central power overrides all other considerations; once this is realized, many incomprehensible aspects of the Soviet system of economic management become clear. The Soviet economy is not run with a view toward making the country richer, satisfying consumer demands, or even catering to the desires of the elite but in order to maintain and enlarge the power of those in possession of it. This point is made forcefully and authoritatively by the most eminent Soviet lawyer, the chief draftsman of the Soviet civil code, Ioffe, after his arrival in the West[74]:

Once this point is grasped, the usual questions asked by Western observers of the Soviet system seem naive: Why cannot the leadership make the economy work? Why does one economic failure follow another? Why is every economic measure more stupid than the last? In fact, the leadership has made the economy work splendidly as the source of its dictatorship. In this regard, Soviet economic policy has never suffered a single real failure, and each new economic measure has appeared as effective as any previous one. The Soviet economy is inefficient only as a source of material wellbeing. This criterion, however, has nothing to do with real Soviet economic efficiency. The measure of material welfare is simply incompatible with the aims of the Soviet system.

The most fundamental characteristic of the Soviet economy is that it finds itself almost completely in the hands of the state; it is owned by the state, albeit not in a strictly legal sense. The state in its turn is owned by the party, "the leading and guiding force of Soviet society and the nucleus of its political system and of state and social organizations" (article 6 of the USSR constitution). The party, finally, is controlled from the top through the mechanism of democratic centralism and represents a pyramidical structure organized along strictly hierarchical

[74] O. S. Ioffe, "Law and Economy in the USSR," *Harvard Law Review*, 1982, pp. 1591–1625, at p. 1625.

lines. The higher a person's position in the party, the greater his say in the affairs of the state and, consequently, of the economy. The entire arrangement is justified and legitimized by the officially propounded ideology of Marxism–Leninism: The state is said to be the state of the working people, whose interests are represented by the party. The same constitutional provision (article 6) adds: "The CPSU exists for the people and serves the people." The will of the party (i.e., the will of the entire Soviet people) is enunciated by its leaders. As the leaders control almost all media of expression through the party and the state, they can pride themselves on the unanimous support of the entire population, and this again strengthens their claim on a position at the political summit of the country.

One of the principal instruments through which the party machine maintains a firm grip on the country's political and socioeconomic system is its monopoly of personnel selection. This operates chiefly through the device of the *nomenklatura*, a list of positions that may only be filled after prior vetting and approval by the competent party agency. There are nomenclatures at all hierarchical and territorial levels, with the *nomenklatura* utilized at the level of the Central Committee at the top, and in this way a totally integrated system of personnel selection and control has been put into operation.

Appointment to a *nomenklatura* position implies incorporation into the power elite. Nomenclatures of various levels embrace all leading positions in the party, the state apparatus, the economy, and in public life in general. But apart from the official powers that such positions confer upon their incumbents, *nomenklatura* posts also plug into an elaborate network of other advantages and privileges.[75] The most important of these, as related by Matthews in his well-known study of this subject, are not of an immediately monetary nature (with the exception of a "13th month" payment, also known as "hospital allowance," *lech-posobie, bol'nichnaia zarplata*).[76] For several decades higher party functionaries used to receive a secret additional pay packet (*kremlevskii paek*), the Kremlin ration, which was paid in special "certificate rubles" usable only in special stores with low prices and scarce goods and thereby worth several times their nominal value. The emission of certificate rubles seems to have been discontinued, and it is uncertain whether the Kremlin ration is still being paid out.

[75] See especially Zemtsov, op. cit., note 69; Voslensky, op. cit., note 16, pp. 304–308 ("Das Nomenklatura-Bakschisch").

[76] M. Matthews, *Privilege in the Soviet Union – A Study of Elite Life-Style Under Communism*, Allan and Unwin, London, 1978, especially Chapter 2, pp. 36–58, "Special Elite Benefits."

In accordance with one of the dominant characteristics of the Soviet economy, the scarcity and/or low quality of many consumer goods and services, the emphasis within the system of privileges is not on monetary values but on goods and services in short supply. Members of the elite have access to special facilities in food supply, medical care, housing, and leisure. This is usually done by making available special stores, clinics, hospitals, housing units, holiday homes, and so on, to specific categories of personnel. Other elements of the system of privileges are the opportunity to travel abroad, the use of an official car, membership of elected bodies (such as soviets), which itself is an additional source of privilege and prestige, and so forth. The least tangible but most pervasive advantage to be derived from a position within the *nomenklatura* apparatus is the network of personal relations and the accompanying security of "having arrived" in Soviet society.[77]

A very important aspect of the privilege system is that it reflects itself in the hierarchical structure of the ruling class. The special facilities and privileges for this class are themselves graded and distributed according to the beneficiary's position within the hierarchy. In this way the privilege system does not only identify and reward membership of the elite but also maintains discipline and structure within the elite itself.

Powerful imagination is not required to grasp that the twin networks of the second economy and of a privileged elite do not lead a wholly separate existence. Some of the privileges accorded to members of the elite do in fact owe much of their attractiveness to their second-economy value. Trips abroad allow the lucky traveler to purchase goods not available on the domestic market; access to special shops has a similar effect. At a more general plane, membership of the *nomenklatura* class offers its incumbents the opportunity to utilize an official position and its powers as a source of further advancement, favor, and indeed financial reward through the second economy in the shape of direct bribery, presents, protection, the possibility to engage in advantageous deals, and so forth.

The interaction of the two networks of the second economy and the privileged elite results in a political system that several observers have even characterized as a kleptocracy[78]: Recruitment into the party establishment is akin to joining a band of robbers – the individual contributes loyalty and obedience to the organization and in return receives his share of the proceeds. It may be worthwhile to have a closer look at this

---

[77] Cf. Wiles, op. cit., note 19, p. 19.
[78] Grossman, op. cit., note 1, p. 33; Simis, op. cit., note 36, p. 55; Wiles, op. cit., note 19, pp. 5–6.

thesis that the major factor of cohesion of the political establishment of the USSR is not its ideological commitment but the material interests of its members in exploiting their positions in the second-economy market.

If this thesis is true, it would be irrational for the top leadership to clamp down decisively on the second economy (as the officially proclaimed ideology would seem to demand) because this would undermine the very foundation of their own power. The fall of Khrushchev retains its value as a warning signal that the leaders' possibility of antagonizing the higher and middle echelons of the party with impunity is strictly circumscribed.

A superficial examination of Soviet sources may yield the impression that the regime is indeed strongly committed to stamping out second-economy activities. A closer look, however, tells us that official campaigns are full of nuances, both in the types of activities and the categories of persons they are aimed at. The most energetic measures, up to capital punishment, are usually reserved for private entrepreneurs who operate outside the sphere of the governmental officials. The most obvious examples are professional dealers in foreign currency and other purely black market operators. Punishment for second-economy activities decreases, according to the rough rule of thumb and, other things being equal, with the closeness of a person's connections to the party establishment and with the elevation of his position therein. Especially in the peripheral republics of the Caucasus and Central Asia there have been a number of far-flung economic scandals involving numerous participants, where at one end of the spectrum the individual black marketeer got shot, whereas at the other end the minister of the union republic involved was merely assigned to another well-paid *nomenklatura* position.[79]

Another point deserves to be made with regard to the personal involvement of high-ranking party and government officials. If the thesis of the kleptocracy, as outlined in the preceding, is accepted, one could expect involvement of all strata of the establishment in second-economy profiteering, although it would still be unlikely that the top leadership should allow exposure of its own members in such practices. Public admission that members of the highest leading circles themselves were involved in officially condemned second-economy operations might undermine their collective legitimacy via-à-vis other ranks within the party and thereby weaken their hold on supreme power. The pattern of exposure as displayed in the Soviet press is in accordance with the kleptocratic thesis. With only very occasional exceptions, exposures stop

---

[79] Several examples are in Simis, op. cit., note 36.

just before the highest level, that is, the Politburo, but affect the next highest level of top officials of the federal establishment and of the supreme leaders in the smaller union republics. They involve federal ministers, such as Ishkov (USSR Minister of Fisheries) in 1980 or Furtseva (USSR Minister of Culture) in 1974, republican party first secretaries, such as Akhundov (Azerbaidzhan, 1969) and Mzhavanadze (Georgia, 1972), and other top leaders in union republics, such as the prime minister and the Supreme Soviet Presidium chairman of Uzbekistan, Kurbanov, and Nasriddinova in 1974. The subsequent fate of such officials conforms to the pattern indicated before: There is usually no prosecution, but the offending leader is quietly removed to a less visible and prestigious position. At lower levels the exposure of official involvement in second-economy activities is more frequent, and the penalties tend to increase.[80]

This naturally leads to the question as to why certain activities are prosecuted and punished and others, presumably, are not. An answer, in the kleptocratic model, can be given without great difficulty. Access to the advantages supplied by the second economy is one of the basic attractions and rewards of membership of the establishment. The individual black market operator, who is outside the establishment, has no claim to these advantages and may therefore be prosecuted without reservations if the interests of the members of the establishment are not at stake. A member of the party elite, even the very highest, may similarly be prosecuted if it has been decided to eject him from the establishment. Otherwise, a decision to punish a member of the elite for participation in second-economy activities will be weighed carefully. Against the tacit admission that such participation is itself a normal aspect of elite membership may stand the wish to punish a specific individual. This wish may be motivated by the initiation of new policies directed against certain economic activities or evoked by the conduct of the individual himself. Highly institutionalized systems of corruption, second-economy networks, and so on always have their own informal rules, and individuals who overstep the bounds imposed by such rules must be disciplined. The typical cases of prominent officials exposed in second-economy scandals, as reported to the Soviet press, concern instances of excessive greed, too blatant corruption, ostentatious display of wealth, and similar situations where the offending officials upset the smoothness and discretion of the privilege system itself. Of course, an

---

[80] This seems to me to be a more plausible explanation than Wiles's thesis that the party promotes the most honest and most competent to the highest posts; Wiles, op. cit., note 19, pp. 36, 5.

official may also be caught by bad luck: For example, a specific activity may be exposed by accident or he may become the victim of a feud between higher party members.

In all these cases the vagueness of the criminal law definitions of various second-economy activities remains a crucial factor; it allows a highly flexible use of the criminal law as an instrument of discipline. Since almost every member of the party elite, and indeed virtually every citizen, is involved in the operation of the second economy, everybody is at the mercy of the authorities, who hold *lettres de cachet* against anybody.

The Soviet regime continues to adhere to the ideal of a communist society, which would call for dynamic domestic policies and would certainly demand the most energetic measures against the second economy. The evidence, however, suggests that this adherence is purely verbal and that the operative domestic policies are more modest and more conservative: maintenance of the prevailing system of distribution of power and privilege, of which the second economy is an integral part.

The second economy of the USSR in a comparative perspective

The second economy of the Soviet Union coexists, as we have seen, in a curious symbiosis with the official economy. This relationship is affected by numerous domestic factors located in the political and socioeconomic system of the USSR. Among the external factors bearing on it, the various experiences of other East European countries exercise a noticeable pressure. In some of these countries state control of the economy has been less comprehensive, either by allowing a larger private sector or by relaxing central control of individual state enterprises. There have always been indications that such experiments have been closely watched by Soviet leaders, for whom the optimal balance between economic performance and political control is a permanent dilemma. Given the increasing, although still modest, economic pluralism within the Soviet bloc, the experience of countries such as Hungary and Poland may provide the Soviet leaders with important pointers for future policy shifts. These may in turn alter the present relationship between the official and the second economy in the USSR. In this regard the currently favorable treatment accorded to private agriculture is worth mentioning.[81] Not for many decades have Soviet leaders displayed such a warm and positive attitude toward the labor of the individual kolkhoz or sovkhoz farmer.

[81] See Rumer, op. cit., note 9.

This may indeed be a sign of an incipient willingness to relax somewhat the rigidity of totally central control.

If the Soviet second economy is compared with analogous phenomena in the Western world, the first difference that catches the eye is in their respective legal backgrounds. Second-economy activities in the Soviet Union typically run afoul of the criminal law, whereas analogous activities in the West are usually motivated by fiscal considerations. This point is highly significant and reflects the fundamentally different character of the societies concerned. A Soviet-type economy, with its almost exclusive control of production and trade by the state, can only be kept in operation if it is backed up by criminal sanctions forbidding all activities that would encroach upon the state's monopoly position. Western governments, on the other hand, do not own the economy in the manner in which the Soviet government does and have to look elsewhere for the financial and other material means to realize their intentions. Some governments, depending on the dominant political ideas, are prepared to appropriate significant sectors of the economy in order to secure adequate income for the state. But whatever approach is preferred, collection of taxes from the population and from private enterprise remains a principal and in most cases the chief source of government income.

Viewed in this manner, the common element of the second economies in the East and West appears to be a popular, grass-roots reaction against the state-imposed system of collecting the government's income. Of course, as long as state-like institutions have existed, there have been schemes for inducing the population to pay for them, and people have resisted such schemes. In this sense a second economy is a perennial fixture of public life. What has increased its worldwide significance is the growth of its scope and ramifications. This no doubt is simply a reflection of the growth of the dominant role of the modern state. It is more than a curious coincidence that there are remarkable parallels in the reactions of officialdom in the East and West to the increasing weight of the second economy. The emphasis is always on repression – more inspectors, higher penalties, closer supervision – while the argument that less government intervention would almost automatically result in lower popular resistance is seldom given prominence. This is perhaps only to be expected, as it will not appear as rational to an organization to allow its own power and influence to decrease.

Until about the beginning of the Industrial Revolution governments were by and large content with maintaining peace and security, both externally and internally. They did not believe, as a rule, that they possessed the potential to embark on a wholesale restructuring of society, and they did not entertain corresponding ambitions. The picture changed when the Industrial Revolution gave birth to the industrial proletariat and to social conditions widely regarded as unacceptable. Simultaneously, the spectacular growth of scientific knowledge and technological ability seemed to provide the tools for remaking society along lines that were considered more appropriate. The reply of the Western world was the welfare state. In Eastern Europe a Marxist-inspired system was adopted or imposed, of which the Soviet state is the prototype. Both are characterized, although in very different degrees, by an enhanced role of the state in the economy, and in both cases this has engendered the emergence of a lively second economy.

Modern states, in the East as well as the West, have usually adopted an ambiguous stance vis-à-vis the second economy. Although it is officially condemned and measures are taken against certain aspects of it, other aspects are allowed to carry on with impunity, on the understanding that their overall effect is beneficial to official policies or at least that their effective repression would demand an inordinately high price.

There are, however, serious drawbacks to this seemingly pragmatic approach. One of the fundamental concepts underlying the more active intervention of the modern state in economic life is the idea of the public good, of the commonality of interests, of social solidarity. It may be argued that it is ultimately on the vitality of such ideas that the consistency of our society hinges. A lively second economy indicates increased resistance on the part of the population against government interference in the economy, and consequently an at least partial rejection of the societal ideals that legitimize such interference and, by the same token, a withdrawal into a pursuit of private interests. A government that overreaches itself, in the perception of many of its citizens, in its attempt to control the economy undermines the operation of the very social ideals in the name of which it purports to act and, consequently, the cohesiveness of society as a whole.[82]

Modern governmental management of the economy, whether of the welfare state form or of a Soviet type, has its roots in traditional rationalism. The availability of scientific knowledge and technological ability promotes an awareness that society can be structured along rational and utilitarian lines. The rise of the second economy and then its grudgingly tolerated existence have turned this awareness into a fallacy because the more realistically the state attempts to implement

---

[82] The space available in a study of this format does not allow any serious discussion of other attempts to view the second economy from a more elevated position. In this respect Wiles's excursions on the religious and national dimensions of the problem are of great interest; op. cit., (note 19, pp. 47–55.

its blueprints for the economy of the future, the more patent the gap between plan and reality becomes. The apparent rationality of the plan begets the apparent irrationality of the second economy. Could it be that the problem is not so much with the second economy but rather with the role the modern state has assumed? Is modesty only a virtue in individuals?

CHAPTER 15

Second economy and socialism:
the Hungarian experience

ISTVAN R. GÁBOR

This chapter examines the extensive presence of the second economy in Hungary as an important cause and consequence of the structural limits and dilemmas of state regulation in a socialist economy[1]. In addition, the second economy is studied as an essential reason why the population considers the system to be a relative success.

We define the second economy as the field of all those economic activities through which the population – legally or illegally – acquires incomes not as employees in the socialist sector.[2] The self-supplying activities of the households belong to the second economy insofar as they are income-producing activities.[3] Fundamentally, therefore, our definition of the second economy is the same as that of Grossman (1977),

---

[1] The author wishes to thank the Social Sciences Institute of the Central Committee of the Hungarian Socialist Workers' Party for its generous material assistance while writing this chapter.

[2] The economic activities of the population are defined as activities conducted by individuals or households (a) voluntarily and (b) without physical or moral coercion of others on the condition that the inputs (money, time, effort, etc.) (c) are experienced by the performers as a sacrifice and (d) are used in quantities of significance to them (e) with the anticipation of a satisfactory yield (at least of the return of the inputs, either as the sole goal of their activity or as a restricting condition in pursuing a goal of a different nature (f) in money or that can be exacted in money or rent or in kind of use to the performer that could be purchased for money (g) within a foreseeable period of time and (h) within reasonable risk limits. Accordingly, non-economic activities are defined as those activities to which any of the criteria listed in the preceding definition does not apply. As implied by this definition, not all economic activities of individuals and households are at the same time income-producing activities (changing "capital" for rent income; entrepreneurial activity; small-scale production; wage labor). Economic activities also include those activities aimed at the rational, economical use and spending of incomes. The distinctive feature of such economizing activities is that, contrary to the income-producing activities, the performers do not regard the labor input, only the actual expenditure, as a cost.

[3] In accordance with the definition in footnote 2, a self-supplying activity can fall into the category of economic activities – and thus belong to either income-producing or economizing activities – depending on (1) whether the given needs of the performers are met through purchases on the one hand and (2) whether there exists any alternative use of their manpower in the form of income-producing activity. If option 1 is unattainable, the activity must be regarded as non-economic in character, whereas the absence of option 2 only precludes the activity to be classified as income producing (however large an amount of income it may generate for the performer).

who regards all those activities aimed directly at private gain or being in some significant respect in knowing contravention of the law as belonging to the second economy.

We have, however, made three minor modifications:

1 The economizing activities of the population in an attempt to rationally and economically use and spend their incomes are not counted as part of the second economy.[4]
2 All acts performed by employees in the first economy to increase their official earnings by using their bargaining power with their employers – although such acts are directed at private gain – are not part of the second economy but of the first.
3 Also excluded from the second economy are all irregularities committed by employees (mainly in management positions) in the first economy directed at obtaining advantages for their organization in the first economy. This is regardless of the fact that they generally wish to improve their own positions as well. Such infringement of the rules, based on an "acceptance of the common lot," can be regarded as a characteristic form of operation in the first economy.

Economic background

The coexistence of a socialized and a second economy in Hungary explains the schizophrenic duality of economic behavior in the country as a whole. Both economies operate according to different principles and are regulated in different ways. They are separated from one another with regard to the flow of capital and the movement of economic organizations.[5] They are linked to each other by the flow of consumer goods and of manpower. Although the first economy is made up of large-scale production units subordinated to the organs of economic guidance, the second economy is one of small-scale production, of an entrepreneurial nature, and operating on a private basis. In the final analysis, the great difference between the role of the market (money and prices) in either accounts for their conflicting relationship.[6]

Although the earnings of their working members impose strict budget

---

[4] We do not consider these activities as belonging to the first economy either since both economies are regarded by definition as alternative fields of income acquisition for the population. We regard them as indispensable for the operation of the (first) economy in which the dual function attributed by the economy to households (as a basic institution of labor supply and consumption) is linked and thereby achieved.

[5] For an extensive analysis of this "separation" see Galasi (1982).

[6] For the following discussion of the distinction between the two economies and its consequences for the first economy, I am indebted to Kornai (1980).

constraints on the consumption possibilities of the households, the mere accounting function of money and prices dominates in the first economy. The enterprises in this sector must carry out economic activities, adjusting to market forces conditioned by the central authority. The fulfillment of their expansionary aspirations (generally characteristic of the organizations) depends on the resource allocation decisions taken by the organs of economic guidance. In the case of state ownership of the means of production, there can not be private appropriation on which the interrelated system of price-regulating markets for goods and services could be based. In contrast to the households, which can acquire goods to the limits of the purchasing power of the incomes they earn and must therefore strive for a balance between the two, the behavior of units operating in the first economy is characterized by low market sensitivity, low cost sensitivity, and an insatiable appetite for resources. Besides the futility of the profit incentive, their quasi-unlimited appetite for manpower as a resource is reflected by the fact that they constantly strive to pay more.and higher wages.

The central economic authority ought, therefore, to limit the outflow of enterprise earning and judge enterprises' demands for supplementary resources. However, as the artificial production cost price system is an inherent component of the economy, the profitability of operation cannot be evaluated on the microlevel. Consequently, the economic planning authority is unable to cope with this task adequately.

In contrast, therefore, with the demand-constrained capitalist economy, the socialist economy functions as a resource-constrained system that perpetuates shortages and is accompanied by relatively low efficiency in exploitation of the production factors operated by the enterprises.

There is a chronic shortage not only on the market for production factors but also on the consumer goods market. This is so because the enterprises draw away not only part of the supply of consumer goods from the private consumers (i.e., households) but also capital and manpower from the enterprises producing consumer goods and from the development of the infrastructure for the population. The central economic authority cannot exert effective control in this respect either because the development possibility for the consumer goods industry and the infrastructure as well as the formation of resources to be used for this purpose depend on meeting the investment and manpower demands of the producing enterprises and, in particular, of those producing capital goods.

The shortage makes production in the first economy more costly than it need be, given the level of technology and the available equipment.

Production factors are frequently condemned to forced idleness. There are disruptions in the continuity of production, and the execution of investment projects meets with long delays. However, the shortage also leads enterprises to create reserves in order to avoid possible problems caused by late deliveries or failures to deliver and in order to anticipate the need for resources and manpower required for future expansion. This makes the shortage even more poignant.

In this situation of chronic shortage, the sellers or suppliers are at a definite advantage over the buyers or clients. Sellers can easily pass on their costs to buyers. The households as ultimate consumers can therefore only acquire the goods they desire at a price that is far too high compared to their incomes and to the technical level of the first economy.

The unlimited appetite of the first economy for factors of production (especially manpower) and the chronic shortage on the consumer goods market corrupt the relationship between consumers and state enterprise and give rise to public opinion that sanctions the misappropriation of workplace materials. In the end, it leads to the emergence of so-called parallel markets within the first economy. Curiously, though, in the case of this shortage economy, all self-supplying productive activities performed by the population as additional work are deemed desirable since they ease the burden on the resources of the first economy. Also, due to the nature of the shortage economy, the population's labor in the second economy proves more profitable than work performed for wages and salaries in the first economy. Consequently, the second economy as the field of income-producing activities exerts an attraction on manpower, and spontaneous processes are set going toward the strengthening, specializing, and differentiating of the goods-producing organizations operating there. As a result of their strengthened position, these units in the second economy become increasingly dependent on the first economy to ensure the objective conditions for their operation (i.e., materials, tools, machines, services). The state is therefore called upon, to a certain extent anyway, to legalize the necessary exchange between the two economies. However, the appropriation of materials not available through legal channels nevertheless becomes an unmistakable practice in first-economy workplaces. The resulting additional costs for the first economy, which are expressed in the price of its products, in turn improve the profitability of activities in the second economy. The shortage economy practically excludes the possibility that the output of the second economy will saturate the market. In fact, the first economy even withdraws from those areas of activity where it operates at a loss, leaving the field to second-economy entrepreneurs. It

342

is also continually creating new markets for second-economy activities, for example, by creating a demand for services for the increasing number of appliances it produces. Finally, it is increasingly obliged to be a consumer of the products and services of the second economy. Clearly, to an extent, the spontaneous increase of work performed in the second economy as well as improving the productivity there coincide with state aspirations directed at easing the burden on the first economy, raising the standard of living, and improving the supply of goods. At the same time, however, such an attitude runs counter to the declared guiding principles of state control over the distribution of the population's income. This leads to a weakening of the incentives for employees in the first-economy enterprises that are struggling with a shortage of manpower. It accelerates the decline in the relatively low productivity in the first economy and makes the profitability of activities in the second economy even more favorable.

Consequently, the state is constantly faced with a dilemma. Either it accepts the negative consequences outlined above or it attempts to redistribute incomes through the imposition of high and progressive taxes. However, in the best of cases, the consistent application of such tax rates would only lead to an increase in the volume of illegal activities and to a corruption of the relationship between taxpayers and the taxation authorities. In the worst case, it would lead to the shrinking of second-economy activities and thus to price rises, the deterioration of the supply of goods, and the creation of exceptionally high incomes in the second economy. This would place an additional burden on the first economy, already faced with a shortage of resources. However, if the state were to renounce the proportionalization of net incomes altogether, it would provide another incentive for people to enter the second economy and cause an expansion of its size. Consequently, the state can only apply this practice on a temporary basis.

The rise of second-economy incomes and the increasing divergence of income levels are becoming a source of social and economic conflict. They force the state to take decisions since sooner or later some of the units in the second economy reach the limits of expansion imposed by the state to guarantee the dominance of the first economy and to prevent citizens from becoming capitalists. Some entrepreneurs who have reached the limits of expansion refrain from further expansion by consuming those earnings that are in excess of the costs required to maintain their business at a steady level. Others purchase precious metals or invest in works of art and other valuable property. Others again exceed the limits of expansion in secret by taking recourse to illegal practices.

The state could try to control all of these consequences by widening the limits of expansion of the units operating in the second economy. However, this would only delay the appearance of the conflicts inherent in the relationship between the first and second economy, as the schizophrenic duality of the economy as a whole precludes the peaceful move of the relevant units into the first economy. Thus, due to the nature of the relationship between the two economies, the state is obliged to change from time to time the formal regulation of the second economy and the strictness with which regulations are applied. However, this changing treatment by itself gives rise to anomalies. First, it contributes to the erosion of business morality because instead of a long-term business policy, entrepreneurs in the second economy strive for quick enrichment at all costs. Second, it leads to the spread of corruption as bribed connections and the financed goodwill of officials can protect firms against the unpredictable changes in the behavior of the state. Thus, despite the theoretical possibility to conduct activities legally in the second economy, varying state regulations and the resulting self-defensive tactics of entrepreneurs in the second economy make it more and more difficult for outsiders to enter the most profitable sectors of the second economy. The monopolizing activities of a small group of entrepreneurs contributes to making full-time participation in the second economy by small-scale goods-producing families marginal and leads to an increase of small units that are poor in capital, less productive, and particularly sensitive to state regulation. Since the entrepreneurs with the exceptionally high incomes are also best able to weather the state restrictions, the restrictions make smaller units even more vulnerable. It can therefore be said that the second economy is becoming segmented and is taking on a hierarchical structure.

The negative consequences of the changing regulations lead the state to seek more viable ways to consolidate the development of the second economy, by means of compromises with those involved. However, the fact that the schizophrenic duality of the economy produces the same duality in the attitude and aspirations of the citizens makes this extremely difficult to achieve. Individuals and households as earners in the first economy and as consumers of its products have an interest in its improving productivity. However, as the majority of them are simultaneously active in the second economy, they have an equally immediate interest in the opposite. In their minds, the fact that higher incomes may be earned under primitive conditions in the second economy is rationalized as a direct consequence of inefficient handling of assets and manpower by managers in the first economy and of their refusal to allow people to earn more. They question the principles of wage policy, and a general attitude emerges that is tolerant of workplace lapses and slackness.

In the minds of the enterprise managers, however, the disparity of income in the two economies is rationalized as the consequence of varying regulatory conditions and of the limited operating autonomy of state enterprises. They consider the shortcomings of their operation to be largely attributable to the disparity in incomes in the two economies and do not consider that, conversely, their poor management might be the cause of these income disparities. In part, they call for restrictions on second-economy and other non-state organizations and in cases even for restrictions on small enterprises in the first economy. In part, they strive to become monopoly suppliers and/or buyers for the small producers and small entrepreneurs in a given sector. In this way, they would be able to influence the operation of the latter to suit the interests of their own organization. However, such asymmetry of the power positions inevitably leads to illegal bargaining between small producers and entrepreneurs on the one hand and representations of first-economy organizations on the other. Finally, the resulting isolation of the small producers and small entrepreneurs from the market due to their integration into larger organizations also forces into the background those qualities that are so important for the national economy in socialism: the flexible, market-sensitive, self-reliant nature of their operation, which provides a wide scope for individual inventiveness.

The paradoxical relationship between legality and regulation in the second economy

The intention of the foregoing analysis was to shed light on the state's varying treatment of the second economy and on the consequences this has in terms of its legality. In view of these consequences, it would be wrong to draw a distinction between the so-called legal private sector and other second-economy activities, considering that income-producing activities belonging to the latter can be related to the failures of state regulation. However, both in Hungary and in part of the Western literature dealing with the socialist economy, this distinction is nevertheless made.

In Hungary, for example, the latest measures allowing broader scope than ever before for income-producing activities in the second economy have given rise to the term "auxiliary supplementary economy." This term is used in political documents to refer to income-producing activities carried out by the population instead of or in addition to employ-

345

ment in the socialist sector, activities carried out within a legal framework, guided by economic self-interest but at the same time serving the common good. The purpose of this term is to distinguish these income-producing activities from illegal activities and to force out of general use the term "second economy," which is said to blur this distinction.[7]

Even before the appearance of this latest terminology, it was not considered appropriate to define small-scale agricultural production carried out on a part-time basis by village households as second-economy activities.[8] In fact, official statistics record the production value produced here within the socialist sector. The remarkable success of Hungarian agricultural policy as compared to that of other Eastern European countries (largely due precisely to the recognition of the importance of small-scale production) is also the argument most frequently put forward to disprove claims about the failure of state regulation. The present author's interpretation of the second economy has also been challenged by Marrese (1980), an American expert on the Hungarian economy. In his view, the legal private sector fits harmoniously into the institutional system of the socialist economy, promoting as it does the attainment of the economic policy goals. He does not deny that there are irregular and illegal aspects involved. However, according to Marrese, these are characteristic of all economic systems so that there is no reason for classifying the legal private sector in the second economy.

Holzman (1981) reaches the same conclusion by means of the elegant syllogism that if the state sector is not a second economy within the capitalist economy, then it is equally unjustified to regard legal private activities as a second economy in socialism. Although the views of Hungarian authors may be influenced by the fear that my emphasis on the illegal aspects of the legal private sector could lead to the imposition of restrictions, it is not likely that this consideration would be the main cause for their mistake. The more profound cause is their misidentification of the legal private sector in socialism with its counterpart in the capitalist economy. They are trapped in a kind of legal nominating that regards the economic phenomena of the world as being largely identical with the ideals of the legal system.[9] As a result, the most important characteristic of the private economy under socialism is not taken into account, namely, the paradoxical relationship between the legality and

---

[7] For a growing recognition of the propagandist aims behind the term "auxiliary supplementary economy," compare Héthy (1980) and Héthy (1983).

[8] Conflicting ideas about this issue may be found by comparing Gábor (1979a), Gábor (1979b), Radneoti (1979), and Varga (1980).

[9] On the pitfalls of such a procedure, see Weber (1964a, pp. 233–5).

the efficiency of the regulation of the second economy. The private economy under socialism does *not* in itself reveal a great deal about the extent to which its operation is actually controlled by the state.

In order to resolve this apparent contradiction, we must refer back to the consequences of the schizophrenic duality of the economy, which makes restriction of the participants' activities in this economy the only viable option for the state to control the operation of the second economy. This is done by what I shall term *control based on infringement of the rules* (CIR). It may best be understood by comparing this seemingly incongruous form of regulation to the so-called *control based on the application of rules* (CAR), which plays a significant role in the regulation of the private economy in the capitalist system.

The CAR assumes a system of rules, prescribed by the state, for sovereign participants in the economy. The success of its application depends on the effectiveness of the coercive institutions available to the state. It also largely depends on the extent to which the state is able to bring the subjects of the regulation to recognize the prescribed system of rules as legitimate. To achieve such a consensus requires the broad and public participation of the subjects of the regulation in defining the state's aspirations to be attained through the system of rules.

The CIR, however, assumes the permanent general possibility of exposure and punishment by the state as an external power. It is a system of rules that in theory excludes simultaneous legal activity in all respects by the subjects of the regulation who are sovereign participants in the economy. The attainment of the state's aspirations through this selective enforcement of necessarily systematically violated rules depends on the effectiveness of the coercive institutions available to it and on the coordination between the application of the rules and the aspirations at a given time. However, state control cannot compete with the inventiveness of the subjects of regulation in finding and exploiting gaps and contradictions in the rules for their benefit. The successful application of this type of regulation depends to a large extent on "informers." Thus, although the main threat to CAR is the undermining of the legitimacy of the aspirations to be asserted, the principal enemy of CIR is the silent complicity of the subjects of regulation. An equally important distinction is that the success of CIR cannot, by definition, be measured simply by the extent of infringements of the rules.

Although state regulation of the second economy is necessarily CIR, COD (*control based on orders and directives*) dominates the regulation of the first economy, which, as we have seen, closely interacts with the second economy. In its theoretically pure form, this means of control assumes theoretically applicable orders issued by the state to the participants in the economy in order to control their activity. The implementation of these orders depends on the strength of dependence, that is, the effectiveness of the means of reward and punishment that can be applied. However, since (1) the applicability of orders, (2) the efforts made by the subjects of the regulation to apply them, and (3) the results can never be perfectly supervised from above, the success of this type of regulation depends to a large extent on the state's ability to ensure the loyalty of the subjects of the control.[10] This loyalty can be attained by means of a system of informal bargains between the state and the subjects, in which the latter strive to have their own interests recognized as state interests and to exert an influence on decisions that affect them. The success of this form of regulation can be undermined by corruption, which takes the form of separate illegal bargains. Considering the schizophrenic duality of the Hungarian economy, the question arises as to how successful CIR – as the only suitable means of controlling the second economy – can be in the hands of the state. As already indicated, the success of CIR applied to the second economy largely depends on whether the behavior of the participants in this economy is characterized by informing on each other rather than by silent complicity. It is obvious that the fiercer the competition between the participants and the firmer their belief in the unconditional loyalty of those in positions of trust in the first economy, the smaller the risk that state aspirations to limit their self-interests will fail. However, as we have seen, the situation of the second economy is characterized by the fact that it operates in a situation of global excess demand for its products and its services. Consequently, there are no real grounds for informing among the participants. At the same time, the shortage economy perpetuates a state of affairs in which the second-economy units – forced into dependence on products and services of the first economy – cannot in general prosper without taking recourse to illegal means. This leads to the establishment of an extensive system of corruption sanctioned by custom, which undermines the faith of the participants of the second economy in the moral impeccability of state organizations and officials. This weakened faith and the serious business consequences of exclusion from the system of corruption would tend to make silent complicity the general rule of behavior. Thus, the syndrome of silent complicity and corruption, each assuming the support of the other and providing mutual cover, limits the restricting aspirations of the state in the second economy. However, it must be added that the "liberalism" of the state's treatment of the second economy cannot be unlimited either. The proclamation

---

[10] The ideas in this discussion of COD were inspired by Crozier (1963).

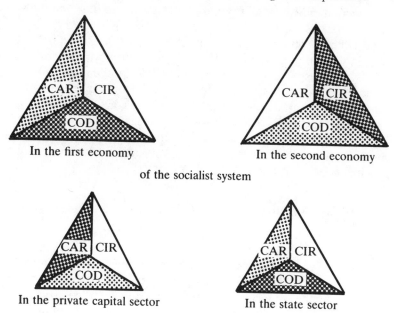

In the first economy   In the second economy

of the socialist system

In the private capital sector   In the state sector

of the capitalist system

Figure 15.1. Extent of direct economic role of state and way in which it is exercised.

and application of such a policy would undermine the loyalty of those in positions of trust in the first economy, loyalty that is indispensable for the state in asserting its aspirations because of the dominance of COD in this economy.[11] Returning to the principle of symmetry put forward by Holzman (the essence of which is the relatively analogous treatment of the relationship between the private and the state sectors in the capitalist economy and the socialist economy), Figure 15.1 sheds light on the pitfall of this procedure, as seen from the angle of regulation.

The triangles in Figure 15.1 illustrate the situation of the different economic sectors in terms of the amount of restriction imposed on the pursuit of self-interest and the extent of COD methods of regulation. This is indicated by the size of the triangles. In addition, the triangles show how these forms of regulation are combined. The dark third of each triangle indicates the dominant form of regulation, the medium-

---

[11] None of the reforms in economic management made in any of the CMEA countries during the past three decades has succeeded in shifting the emphasis to CAR. For Hungary see Antal (1979).

toned section indicates the form used to supplement this, and the white section indicates the form of regulation that is not used.

The triangles show that the private capitalist sector and the state sector in the capitalist system differ only in the proportional application of the two forms of regulation CAR and COD. In the state and private sectors of the socialist system – due to the schizophrenic duality of the economy – the state is obliged to use the contradictory forms of regulation CAR and CIR. At the same time, the two economic systems differ even more widely with regard to the extent of the state's direct economic role asserted through these forms of behavior control of the participants in the economy.

The competitive symbiosis of the two fields for acquiring income

In the previous section, we concentrated on the structural limits and dilemmas of state regulation of the second economy. We regarded the state as the active initiator. We pointed to the dual resistance to state aspirations by the subjects of the regulation, namely, the participants in the second economy and the enterprise management stratum that is largely excluded from the sources of income of this economy. However, the enterprise management stratum does not only have a hierarchical relationship to the state. It also personifies the role of employers to the participants in the second economy who – either personally or through members of their households – are simultaneously employees in the organizations of the first economy. This relationship between the enterprise management stratum as employer and the working masses as employees striving for the most advantageous combination of the possibilities offered by the two fields of income-producing activities provides another interesting insight into the contradictory relationship between the first and the second economy. As people freely entering into employment must manage their labor in order to raise the level of consumption for themselves and their families and keep pace with the general standard of living, wage differences play a decisive role in socialism in influencing the behavior of employees. Under these circumstances, the operation of the labor market will naturally be more effective if the relative wage differences can spread over a broad scale and if the influence of these differences on the level of consumption of the households can be more clearly marked.

Let us imagine a socialist economy without a second economy, in which the households are able to acquire earnings solely through employment in the first economy. The labor market in the socialist economy is characterized by a state of permanent global excess demand. This is particularly true for lower skilled workers. The chronic shortage of manpower means that workplace performance standards tend to be very low, and the labor market tends to overvalue unskilled jobs as compared to skilled jobs, thus narrowing earnings differentials. Rather than pursuing a professional career, the main path for material advancement is promotion within the hierarchy of classification, which makes it possible to acquire material advantages in the nature of privileges. This is, however, essentially independent of the operation of the labor market and can be regulated directly by the state.

In addition, under the conditions of the shortage economy, the poor contractual discipline in inter-enterprise relations and the frequent delays this causes in production make it difficult for employers to apply consistent and large-scale incentives based on the differentiation of earnings, as this can only be done in the case of a high level of organization and standard work requirements. As the shortage economy is accompanied by the practice of forming manpower reserves, labor capacity is not used efficiently. As a result, performance incentives inherent in the differentiation of earnings hardly come into play. For employers, earnings are primarily means of attracting additional manpower and of retaining their labor force. Only incidentally are they used for encouraging the workers to greater efficiency. With a high level of employment, the relative differentiation in earning to be achieved by the employers is more limited than at lower levels of employment. The lowest wages at any given time must be sufficient to provide for a modest life at the given consumption level, but at a given average wage level, the higher the level of employment, the higher the average level of consumption and with it the minimum wage level. In addition, at a higher employment level, the same income differences have less incentive power. Thus, as the level of employment rises, the attainable earnings differentials have a weaker and weaker role in influencing the workers' behavior.[12]

Significantly, the inadequate differentiation in incomes according to performance exists side by side with very large earning differentials due to the bargaining position of various groups of workers. This differentiation depends on the role these workers play in coping with chronic disorders in production and in resolving bottleneck situations.

---

[12] Further details on questions relating to the differentiation of earnings may be found in Gábor (1979c).

To what extent does the second economy relate to the preceding characteristics of the labor market in the "pure" socialist economy? Since they are largely the same households that acquire income from the second economy as those whose members are wage earners in the first economy, the second-economy incomes further deteriorate the ability of the first-economy earnings to ensure a livelihood, as they widen the gap between average earnings and the average consumption level. This makes it even more difficult to influence the workers' behavior by a differentiation of earnings. In addition, these second-economy incomes are distributed far more unevenly among households than earnings from the first economy. Consequently, in order to ensure the relative smoothness of production and to maintain or increase the enterprise's attractiveness on the labor market, employers are obliged to take into account the workers' unequal opportunities for earning second-economy income when determining earnings and performance requirements.

Those workers who are least dispensable because of their qualifications and experience must be ensured conditions for earning additional income and promotions within the enterprise so as to counteract the temptation of earning additional income in the second economy. Generally, this can only be achieved at the price of concessions in performance and work discipline requirements for other groups of workers. In this way, their parallel participation in the second economy is acknowledged or even facilitated. The situation is different again for those workers who have the opportunity to acquire second-income earnings through their actual jobs, a condition employers use as a trump card in their bargains over wages and performance requirements.

If we consider that, in addition to all this, the workers have widely differing attitudes toward the given workplace performance requirements and earning possibilities (depending on their status within the family or their income-earning strategy), it becomes clear that the partly competitive and partly symbiotic relationship between the two fields of income-producing activities perpetuates extremely unstable and highly complex labor market relations in the first economy, which is suffering from a shortage of manpower. The employers are obliged to adopt improvisations and defensive employment strategies, whereas the workers strive to occupy favorable positions on the labor market and to participate in the second economy. The fact that in Hungary the trade unions do not restrict the bargaining between employers and employees in determining the ratio between performance and wages undoubtedly contributes to perpetuating the present situation. In the final analysis, it is correct to regard this situation as the consequence of the labor market in the socialist economy rather than as a cause.

The size of the second economy in Hungary: 1970 – 1983

No reliable data are available concerning the size of the second economy in Hungary. The validity of those data that occasionally appear cannot be established due to the fact that no basic definitions are provided, nor is the method explained that was used to arrive at the relevant estimates. Even the widely quoted estimate that 16–18% of GNP is created in the second economy draws its credence solely from the prestige of the person who made the estimate.[13] However, if we accept this as a starting point and add the activity of the "semi-private" organizations that this estimate classifies in the first economy, at least one-fifth of the annual GNP can be attributed to activities performed outside the first economy.

Examining all second-economy activities on which quantitative data of any worth are available, certain conclusions can be drawn. The manpower input in small-scale agricultural production is equivalent to the full annual working time of approximately 800,000 people. This is 10% more than the work time basis for agricultural production units in the first economy.[14] The corresponding figures for private construction[15] and for legal private-trade activities are around 150,000 each.[16] Non-legalized trade activity is estimated at 100,000.[17] Private retail trade and

---

[13] Rezso Nyers's estimate is quoted in Juhász and Prugberger (1980).

[14] The data for small-scale agricultural production given here have been derived from several representative national surveys. The figure for the time input is based on a full census. The data for production value and income are estimates made on the basis of natural production data obtained from representative surveys conducted twice every year and with the aid of the regular observation of market prices and plant management cost norms.

[15] The manpower time requirement for a self-built house is considered to be equivalent to the legal annual work time basis of three persons.

[16] The official figures for the numbers involved in legal private trade activities do not include the number of auxiliary family members or occasional, seasonal, and part-time employees. For this reason and also because the working hours in private trade plants are generally longer than the legal working hours, we have taken into account approximately one and a half times the official figure for the numbers involved. The very high proportion of able-bodied women recorded formally as dependents in the families of self-employed persons is an indication of the important role of the help of family members. This proportion (28%) is almost as high as that in the households of the cooperative peasantry (30%), in contrast with the 14% for households of blue-collar workers and the 4% for white-collar households. According to a member of the ministry responsible for the state guidance of private trades, the figure increased approximately 1.5-fold between 1975 and 1980 (Kovacs, 1981).

[17] Estimate based on the parallel use of various methods. The so-called spare-parts rate method is based on the figures for retail trade spare-parts turnover. The estimated quantity used in private trade is deducted from this. Subsequently, the performance values for the remaining portion of spare-parts turnover are calculated on the basis of technically estimated norms. In contrast the so-called repair requirements method is

private intellectual activities together amount to approximately 50,000.[18] Finally, the various semi-private activities together amount to roughly the same figure. The total time input in the second economy corresponds to around one-quarter of that used in the first economy.

Small-scale agricultural production is carried out by 1.7 million households, which is 50% of all Hungarian households. Out of this total, the number of independent peasant farms is only 30,000 and declining. They produce one-third of the country's gross agricultural output and more than half of the net output. They consume approximately half of their produce and sell the other half. Out of the 86% of income from small-scale agricultural production that goes to the active households, 30% goes to the working class households, 23% to the households of the cooperative peasantry, and 18% to "mixed" households comprising both peasants and wage earners. The remaining 15% is divided equally between white-collar households and households carrying out full-time small-scale production.

The number of earners in the legal private trades is approximately 5,000 of whom 15,000 are officially registered as employees. Of the 100,000 independent tradesmen, only 60% carry out this activity as a full-time occupation (this figure was more than 80% in 1970); 10% are pensioners and 30% carry out their trade activity in conjunction with earning activities in the first economy. The number of households living solely from private trade activity does not amount to even half of the number of independent private tradesmen. Legal private trade activity produces 2–2.5% of GNP.[19] With a total of around 15,000 persons, legal private retail trade handles about 5% of the total retail trade turnover. Around half of the houses built each year (i.e., 40,000–50,000), including more than four-fifths of those in the villages, are built in the

---

based on an estimate of the average annual repair requirements for the stock of various consumer durables owned by the population (apartment, household appliances) using technically estimated breakdown norms. The performance of the legal service organizations is then deduced from the total repair requirement obtained in this way. The labor input figure given here is based on the assumption that the non-legalized tradesmen produce approximately two-thirds greater performance over the same amount of time as workers in the legalized service organizations. For further details on the methods of estimation see Razus (1975), Drexler (1977), Belyo (1981), and Drexler et al. (1981).

[18] Legalized and non-legalized together, assuming a ratio of $\frac{2}{3}:\frac{1}{3}$.

[19] The figures for the production value of legal private trade are determined with the aid of the county councils by first estimating the average performance value for a trade unit in each branch and then multiplying this by the average number of units for the given year. The figure obtained in this way is considerably underestimated since the councils are also the taxation authorities for the private sector in the given areas, and they are only able to counterbalance the effect of the unrealistically high tax rates (the shrinkage of the private sector) by approving or setting a much lower tax basis.

second economy, a proportion that has increased during recent years and may be expected to rise even further (up to about 85%). The share of legal private trades in housing construction carried out in the second economy is less than one-third. The share of legalized and non-legalized activities in the household repair sector is similar, but here the role of the second economy as a whole is more than five times greater than that of first-economy organizations. In other repair services, the gross performance value of non-legalized activities by the population can be estimated at around five times that of legal private trade and approaches that of the services provided by organizations in the first economy.[20] More than one-fifth of non-agricultural skilled workers regularly perform such activities.

Intellectual private activity can only be carried out on a full-time basis in exceptional cases. It can be carried out legally either in addition to full-time employment or pension (e.g., with a permit to conduct a private medical, veterinary, or architectural practice, which is presently the case for around 10,000 persons) or in different semi-private organizations (such as associations of solicitors, language teachers, or music teachers), in which the personal incomes earned are subject to taxation rules similar to those for private activities in the new collective entrepreneurial forms to be discussed later. The extent of non-legalized private professional activities is most probably not less than that of non-legalized activities in industrial and construction jobs. To conclude the discussion of the productive activities by the population, mention should also be made of renting apartments and rooms as a source of second-economy income. There are 110,000 officially reported sub-tenants, and 30,000 families officially rent rooms, apartments, and holiday homes for tourism. In addition, there is also the far greater extent of non-legalized accommodation for tourists, since four-fifths of the nights spent by tourists from abroad (as recorded in the number of border crossings) are spent in places of accommodation not officially recorded.

Net population incomes equivalent to at least one-third of wage-type incomes in the first economy are generated by the total of private activities listed in the preceding.

The other group of incomes derived from the second economy comprises such forms of income as tips received for services, "gratitude money" received by doctors, income from bribery in commerce and from official administrative bodies, the value of means of production misappropriated from the first economy and the income derived by

---

[20] The figure is derived from a survey conducted by means of a questionnaire (Drexler, 1977).

355

using those means for private benefit, and income from private work performed for personal benefit during working hours. This category does not include income from speculation in land and property or income derived from usury loans to private individuals, bootlegging, or prostitution. Thus, when considering only transactions related directly to employment in the first economy, the sum of these second-economy incomes is similar in volume to the total income from production and service activities performed in the second economy. Of this total, approximately 30% concerns the redistribution of income among the population, whereas 70% is at the expense of social ownership.[21] The incomes in the second economy that have been considered so far together amount to two-thirds of the wage-type incomes paid in the first economy. In view of the fact that the estimates are moderate and many sources of income in the second economy for which no quantitative information of any kind is available have not been taken into account, the real figure must even be higher than this. It also means that for the 75% of the population that, as empirical studies have shown, receive second-economy incomes, the second economy must be a source of income of similar importance as the first economy.

Among the many signs pointing at the growing importance of the second economy as a source of income, mention should be made of (1) the slow decline during the last few years in the statistically measured economic activity of the able-bodied population, (2) the shift from a decline to a slow increase in the number of first-economy agricultural earners at the end of the 1970's, and (3) the rapid rejuvenation of the labor force in legal private trades. They are all facts that can hardly be explained other than by the expansion and growing attraction of non-legalized and legalized activities in the second economy. The differentiation of participation in the second economy can be demonstrated concretely by the data series for small-scale agricultural production and legal private trades. They bear witness to the increasing degree of specialization and to the growing proportion of employment in branches that provide greater scope for entrepreneurial activity.[22]

---

[21] The source of the estimates (Lukacs, 1980) does not indicate the method used. We were only able to establish that the figures quoted are based on checks conducted by the Ministry for Domestic Trade and on the author's estimates.

[22] To give an indication of the extent of these trends, the following data are useful. Between 1970 and 1980 the proportion of private tradesmen under the age of 40 rose from 35 to 54%. According to a representative survey (Juhasz, 1978), the number of goods-producing units within the household plots of members of agricultural cooperatives rose from 30 to 57% between 1972 and 1977, and of this number, the proportion of those specializing rose from 10 to 30%. Within private trades, the numbers of self-employed in the engineering and construction industries, where the entrepreneurial

Second economy and socialism: the Hungarian experience

In 1981–82 a number of new small-scale entrepreneurial enterprises were legalized. Contrary to the expectation of the economic policy-makers, only those enterprises became popular in which participation could be combined with employment in the first economy or at least did not require any substantial material investment.[23] This means that the most rapid increase is in the so-called intra-enterprise – business work partnership – in which workers in the first economy perform work for their own employer after working hours for an entrepreneurial fee. In mid-1982 these partnerships had 6,000 members, and by the end of that year this figure had already risen to 20,000. In March 1983 it amounted to 30,000. Individual association members add an average of one-third to their working hours for an entrepreneurial fee that is 10–15% lower than the usual rates. The other entrepreneurial form that spread rapidly is that of renting or of operating first-economy commercial and catering units after paying a contract price. By the end of 1982, 20,000 people were already working within such a framework, and an additional 5,000 had taken over the operation of service units from their employers, also for a contract price. Finally, 15,000 people had formed independent economic communities, largely for services that were mainly professional services and for other activities requiring a very low level of operating capital. The so-called small cooperative form, which requires a more substantial material contribution, is not proving attractive, and only few such cooperatives have been formed.

The emergence of private and semi-private undertakings has added new color but has not changed the face of the second economy. At the same time it is highly probable that it has further expanded its scope. For it is only within a very limited circle that the new types of undertakings are proving to be realistic alternatives to the other ways of satisfying the population's needs within the second economy. They not only fail to present a competitive threat to the "traditional" private trades and small-scale private commerce but are also not bringing about any decrease in non-legalized activities. The majority are organized either to take over activities for the population previously performed by organizations in the first economy or to meet orders from first-economy organizations. In the latter case, they offer the possibility for a new and broader circle of workers to earn supplementary income in the first economy instead of or in addition to overtime, part-time, or occasional

---

nature is stronger, rose by 21 and 44%, respectively, between 1970 and 1978, in contrast with the increase of 3% for personal services largely covering traditional activities and the 20% decline in the light-industry sectors of a handicraft nature.

[23] See Laki (1983).

jobs and provide the enterprises with a means of stabilizing and encouraging their workers in more important posts by means of sources outside their wage budgets.

Thus, the new entrepreneurial forms may also use part of the surplus manpower capacity previously used for second-economy activities. However, assuming that the population's demand for such work (goods and services) will not decline, the consequence to be expected is a rise in the "free market" price of these services. This will in turn attract part of the manpower capacity used in the new entrepreneurial forms and induce people excluded from the new entrepreneurial forms to take advantage of the new opportunities offered for earning income. In Hungary the time spent on earning activities in the second economy is determined not by the population's willingness to undertake additional work but by the demand for such work and the possibility of acquiring additional income.

Thus, instead of (1) causing a spread of small undertakings operated on a full-time basis, (2) activating substantial financial resources of the population, and (3) placing a growing proportion of second-economy activities within a legal framework, the only change produced by the measures of 1981–2 has been that the second economy, as the alternative field of income-producing activities, has expanded by legally penetrating organizations in the first economy. This could easily create the illusion that by progressing in this direction, the competitive symbiosis of the two fields of income earning by the population could lead to a peaceful symbiosis and end the schizophrenic duality of the economy.

General conclusions

The socialist economy, as it exists in reality, is characterized by the simultaneous presence of two "productions forms." The first is the large-scale production-type first economy guided by the state, in whose organizations the workers act as wage laborers freely entering employment in exchange for wages. The second production form is that of the second economy. It is regulated by a market, operates on a private economic basis, and comprises individual and small-scale production and entrepreneurial units. These two economies are inevitably intertwined both in the national economic and in the sociological sense. They are mutually interdependent although due to their fundamentally different operating principles, the relationship between the two is of a conflicting nature. Accordingly, the second economy within the socialist economy cannot be equated either with the unobserved economy or

Second economy and socialism: the Hungarian experience

with the small-scale goods-producing and entrepreneurial sectors of the advanced capitalist economies. Because of the schizophrenic duality of the economy, state regulation of private economic activities in a socialist society follows a radically different pattern from that of the capitalist economy in which the degree of infringements (tax fraud and illegal employment) is uncertain and the effectiveness of state regulation not clear.

Finally, led by theoretical considerations, we reach the conclusion that in terms of scope and the effectiveness of state regulation, the presence of the entire second economy in a socialist system can be regarded as essentially of similar significance as the unobserved economy in the capitalist system. As in the case of the unobserved economy of the capitalist system, its spontaneous expansion can cause an increasingly serious disruption of the state's policy with regard to the economy.

Since the population's capacity for work in a socialist economy is not a production factor that can be taken into state ownership, the market distribution of consumer goods and the condition of the labor market – as in the capitalist economy – exert a decisive influence on consumer and employee behavior and on the performance of labor within family frameworks. If differences in the economic behavior of workers and households in the socialist economy may still be perceived, this must be due to the varying degree in which they are enabled to assert their consuming, producing, and employment aspirations.

The shortage economy nature of the first economy and the absence of the possibility for anyone to become a capitalist perpetuate goods market and labor market conditions that diminish the proportion of the population living from full-time small-scale production, as well as the proportion living solely from first-economy earnings, to a marginal level. The twofold economic status of individuals and households is a natural consequence. The population's livelihood strategy – including people's behavior as employees in the first economy – is greatly influenced by the global excess demand for manpower in the first economy and by the fact that productive activities that can be carried out in the households make it possible to earn a substantially higher income than could be received for the same amount of work in the first economy.

Hungarian research on the second economy has shown that the only way to resolve the increasing social and economic conflicts arising from the presence of the second economy and to resolve the dilemmas inherent in state regulation of private economic activity is a radical reform of the first economy. Reform is aimed at accepting the profit-oriented (or self-managing) socialist enterprise – operating as a market-sensitive and cost-sensitive undertaking – as the basic unit of the economy.[24] The closer alignment of the operating principles of the two economies, which can only be achieved in this manner, would open the way for the uniform incorporation of small-scale production and small-scale entrepreneurial private activities into the institutional system of the national economy, operating through controls based on the application of the rules.

[24] On the main current conceptions, see Barsony (1981), Antal (1982), Bauer (1982), and Kornai (1982).

Bibliography

Acharya, S. 1984. "The Underground Economy in the United States: Comment on Tanzi," *Staff Papers*, Vol. 31. International Monetary Fund, Washington, DC, December, pp. 742–6.

Alden, J. 1978. "Nature and Extent of Moonlighting in Britain." Paper presented to the Social Science Research Council (SSRC) Labour Studies Group, London.

1980. "A Comparative Analysis of Second Jobs in the USA and Great Britain." UWSIT Papers in Planning Research 17, University of Wales Institute of Science and Technology, mimeo.

Alden, J. and S. Saha. 1978. "Analysis of Second Job Holding in the EEC." *Regional Studies* 12: 639–50.

Algera, S. B., P. A. H. M. Mantelaers, and H. K. Van Tuinen. 1982. "Problems in the Compilation of Input–Output Tables in the Netherlands." *Lecture Notes in Economics and Mathematical Systems*. Vol. 203. Springer-Verlag, Berlin.

Allen, C. 1979. "A Survey of Economic *Samizdat.*" *Radio Liberty Research* RL 268/79, September 12.

Allingham, M. G. and A. Sandmo. 1972. "Income Tax Evasion: A Theoretical Analysis." *Journal of Public Economics* 1: 323–38.

Alvaro, G. 1979. "L'Italia sommersa che non paga le tasse." *Mondo Operaio* 32: 62–5.

Antal, L. 1979. "Development with Some Digression: The Hungarian Economic Mechanism in the Seventies." *Acta Oeconomica* 3–4: 257–73.

1982. "Gondolatok a gazdasági mechanizmus továbbfejlesztéséről." *Gazdaság* 3: 36–58.

Arrow, K. J. 1951. *Social Choice and Individual Value.* Wiley, New York.

Avery, R. B., G. E. Elliehausen, A. B. Kennickell, and P. A. Spindt. 1986. "The Use of Cash and Transaction Accounts by American Families." *Federal Reserve Bulletin*, February.

Baldry, J. C. 1979. "Tax Evasion and Labor Supply." *Economic Letters* 3, No. 1, 53–6.

Bank Deutscher Lander. 1951. *Geschäftsbericht für das Jahr 1950*. Bank Deutscher Lander, Frankfurt.

Bank of Canada. 1982. *Bank of Canada Review*. January, pp. 17–18.

Barro, R. J. and C. Sahasakul. "Measuring the Average Marginal Tax Rate from the Individual Income Tax." *Journal of Business (Chicago)* 56: 419–52.

Barry, D., G. Ginsburgs, and P. Maggs (Eds.). 1978. *Soviet Law after Stalin: Social Engineering through Law*, Law in Eastern Europe 20 (II). Alphen aan den Rijn: Sijthoff and Noordhoff, Netherlands.

Bars, J. J. le, G. Gamus, A. Cosset, and Y. Nottola. 1980. *Essai d'Analyse des Causes Socio-économiques du Développement du Travail Noir dans les Métiers du Batiment*. Societé d'Etudes pour le Développement Economique et Social, Etude pour le CORDES. SEDES, Paris.

Bársony, J. 1981. "Liska Tibor koncepciéoja, a szocialista vállalkozás." *Valéoság* 12: 22–44.

Barthelemy, P. 1981. "L'économie souterraine: concepts et mesures." Centre d'Analyse Economique, FEA, Aix-en-Provence, December.

Bauer, T. 1982. "A második gazdasági reform és a tulajdonviszonyok: szempontok az éuj gazdasági mechanizmus továbbfejlesztéséhez." *Mozgéo Világ* 10: 57–82.

Baumol, W. J. 1952. "The Transactions Demand for Cash," *Quarterly Journal of Economics* 66: 545–56.

Becker, G. S. 1965. "A Theory of the Allocation of Time." *Economic Journal* 75: 493–517.

　1976. *The Economic Approach to Human Behavior*. University of Chicago Press, Chicago and London.

Bell, D. 1973. *The Coming of Post Industrial Society* Basic Books, New York.

Belyéo, P. 1981. "A lakosság szolgáltatási igényei és kielégitésük lehetséges méodjai." Mimeo.

Bergonzini, L. 1973. "Professionalità femminile e lavoro a domicilio. Questioni generali ed esti di un'indagine statistica in alcuni communi dell'Emilia Romagna." *Statistica* 33: 323–39.

Berliner, J. 1957. *Factory and Manager in the USSR*. University Press, Cambridge, MA. Harvard.

Birman, I. 1980. "Second and First Economies and Economic Reforms." Occasional Paper No. 108, Kennan Institute for Advanced Russian Studies, Washington, DC (in Russian).

Black, D. 1958. *The Theory of Committees and Elections*. Cambridge University Press, Cambridge, UK.

Bibliography

Blades, D 1982. "The Hidden Economy and the National Accounts." *OECD Economic Outlook*, Occasional Studies, June, pp. 28–45.

Blockland, J. 1982. "Het officieuze circuit, een nadere begripsbepaling." *Statistisch Magazine* 2, No. 2.

Board of Inland Revenue. 1981. *123rd Report – Year Ended 31 March 1980*. Her Majesty's Stationery Office, London.

Boulding, K. E. 1971. *Collected Papers* (F. Glahe, Ed.). Colorado Associated University Press, Boulder.

Bradford, D. and H. Rosen. 1976. "The Optimal Taxation of Commodities and Income." *American Economic Review, Papers and Proceedings* 66: 94–101.

Brayton, F. and E. Mauskopf. 1985. "The Federal Reserve Board HPS Quarterly Econometric Model of the U.S. Economy." *Economic Modelling* July: 170–292.

Brennan, G. and J. M. Buchanan. 1980. *The Power to Tax. Analytical Foundations of a Fiscal Constitution*. Press, Cambridge.

Brusco, S. 1979. *Agricolutre Ricca e Classi Sociali*. Feltrinelli, Milan.

Buchanan, J. M. 1975. "A Contractarian Paradigm for Applying Economic Theory." *American Economic Review, Papers and Proceedings* 65: 225–30.

1976. "Taxation in Fiscal Exchange." *Journal of Public Economics* 6; 17–29.

1977. *Freedom in Constitutional Contract Perspectives of a Political Economist*. Texas A&M University Press, College Station and London.

Buchanan, J. M. and D. R. Lee. 1982. "Politics, Time and the Laffer Curve." *Journal of Political Economy* 90: 816–19.

Bukovskii, V. 1978. *To Build a Castle*. Deutsch, London.

Bush, K. 1981. "Books in the Soviet Second Economy." *Radio Liberty Research* RL 468/81, November 23.

Cagan, P. 1958. "The Demand for Currency Relative to the Total Money Supply." *Journal of Political Economy* 66 (August): 303–28.

Cameron, D. R. 1978. "The Expansion of the Public Economy: A Comparative Analysis." *American Political Science Review* 72: 1243–61.

Campbell, D. T. 1974. "Assessing the Impact of Planned Social Change." Dartmouth/OECD Seminar on Social Research Public Policies, September.

Campbell, D. T., et al. 1965. *Unobtrusive Measures*. Rand McNally, Chicago.

Canullo, G. and M. G. Montanari. 1978. "Lavore regolare e lavoro nero in alcuni Comuni delle Marche." *Lavoro Regolare e Lavoro Nero* (P. Alessandrini, Ed.). Edigraf, Rome.

Carlson, J. 1982. "Methods of Cash Management." *Economic Commentary* (Federal Reserve Bank of Cleveland), April 5.

Carson, C. S. 1984. "The Underground Economy: An Introduction." *Survey of Currency Business*. United States Department of Commerce/Bureau of Economic Analysis, Vol. 64, Number 5 (May 1984), pp. 21–37.

CBS. 1974. *Standaard Bedrijfsindeling*. CBS, The Hague.

CBS. 1983. *De produktiestructuur van de Nederlanse volkshuishouding*, deel XL. CBS, The Hague.

CERES. 1978. "Il lavoro nero nel 1977 in Italia." *Tendenze della Occupazione* 3:

Chadeau, A. 1985. "Measuring Household Activities: Some International Comparisons." *The Review of Income and Wealth* 31(3) (1985): 237–53.

Chadeau, A. and A. Fourquet. 1981. "Peut-on mesurer le travail domestique?" *Economie et Statistiques* 136: 29–42.

Chalidze, V. 1977. *Criminal Russia*. Random House, New York.

Choain, C. 1982. "Application jurisprudentielle de la loi de 1972 sur le travail clandestin." (Ed.). F. Stankiewicz, *Travail Noir Productions Domestiques et Entraide*. CNRS et LAST, Lille.

Colombino, U. 1978. *Il Potenziale Aggiuntivo del Lavoro in Italia: un' Esplorazione Econometrica*. Giappichelli, Torino.

Commune di Modena. 1978. *Il Lavoro a Domicilio nel Quartiere Madonnina*. Modena.

Connolly, W. 1981. *Appearance and Reality in Politics*. Cambridge University Press, Cambridge.

Conseil des Impôts. 1979. *Le Rapport au Président de la République Relatif à l'Impôt sur le Revenu*. Journal Officiel de la République Francaise, Paris.

1983. *Le Rapport au Président de la République Relatif à la TVA*. Journal Officiel de la République Francaise, Paris.

Contini, B. 1979. *Lo Sviluppo di un'Economia Parallela*. Edizioni di Communità, Milan.

1981. "Labor Market Segmentation and the Development of the Parallel Economy: The Italian Experience." *Oxford Economic Papers* 2: 401–12.

Copeland, M. A. 1952. *A Study of Money Flows in the United States*. National Bureau of Economic Research, New York.

Cramer, J. 1983. "Currency by Denomination." *Economic Letters* 12: 299–303.

Bibliography

Crozier, M. 1963. *Le Phénomène Bureaucratique*. Editions du Seuil, Paris.

Deaglio, M. 1974. "L'ocupazione invisible: il caso di un comune piemontese." *Biblioteca della Libertà* 52–3: 69–108.

Del Boca, A. 1980. "Segmentazione e mercati del lavoro dualistici. *Rivista Internationale di Scienza Sociali* July–December: 384–401.

Delorozoy, R. 1980. *Le Travail Clandestin*. Rapport au Président de la République. Chambre de Commerce et d'Industrie de Paris, Paris.

Delors, J. and J. Gaudin. 1979. "Pour la création d'un troisième secteur." *Problèmes Economiques* 1616: 20–4.

Deutsch, K. W. 1966. *The Nerves of Government, Model of Political Communication and Control*. Free Press, New York.

Deutsche Bundesbank. 1977. *Geschäftsbericht für das Jahr 1977*. Deutsche Bundesbank Frankfurt.

Dilnot, A. and N. Morris. 1981. "What Do We Do About the Black Economy?" *Fiscal Studies* 2: 58–73.

Dixit, A. and A. Sandmo. 1977. "Some Simplified Formulae for Optimal Income Taxation." *Scandinavian Journal of Economics* 79: 417–23.

Drexler, B. 1977. *A másodlagos gazdaságban végzett szolgáltatások helyzete és perspektivája*. Institute for the Development of Services, Budapest.

Drexler, B., A. Halfár, T. Sebestyén, and Gy. Maliga. 1981. *Épitöipari lakossági javitéo-karbantartéo szolgaltatás fejlesztése*. Institute for the Development of Services, Budapest.

Du Rietz, C. 1980. "Marginalskatter, moms och arbestsgivaravgifter bakom växande svart sektor." *SAF-Tidningen* 32: 8–9.

Dupeyroux, J. 1983. "Note sur les Activitiés Professionnelles Occultes." Rapport Rémis à Jean Auroux, Ministre Delegue aux Affaires Sociales, Charge du Travail, Paris, Mimeo.

Ehrlich, I. 1973. "Participation in Illegitimate Activities: A Theoretical and Empirical Investigation." *Journal of Political Economy* 81: 521–65.

Eisner, R. 1978. "Total Incomes in the United States, 1959 and 1969." *Review of Income and Wealth*, Series 24, No. 1, March: 41–70.

Enzler, J, L. Johnson, and J. Paulus. 1976. "Some Problems of Money Demand." *Brookings Papers on Economic Activity*, 1: 261–80.

Ethier, M. 1982. "L'Economie Souterraine: Revue de la Littérature et Nouvelles Estimations pour le Canada." Department of Finance, unpublished manuscript.

Fabre, R. 1979. *Une Politique de l'Emploi au Service de l'Homme*. Rapport Présenté à Monsieur le Président de la République.

Mission pour l'Emploi, Paris.

Fase, M. M. G. and M. van Nieuwkert. 1977. "The Demand for Bank Notes in Four Countries." *De Nederlandsche Bank N. V., Quarterly Statistics* 1 (June): 84–98.

Fau, J. 1980. "*Le Travail illégal.*" Rapport Rémis à Lionel Stoleru, Secretaire d'Etat auprés de Jean Matteoli, Ministre du Travail et de la Participation, Paris, mimeo.

Fédération Nationale du Batiment. 1979. "Rapport sur les Moyens a Mettre en Oeuvre pour Lutter contre le Travail Clandestin." Paris, mimeo.

Feige, E. L. 1975. "The Consequences of Journal Editorial Policies and a Suggestion for Revision." *Journal of Political Economy.* (December): 1291–5.

1979. "How Big is the Irregular Economy?" *Challenge* 22 (November–December): 5–13.

1980. "A New Perspective on Macroeconomic Phenomena. The Theory and Measurement of the Unobserved Sector of the United States Economy: Causes, Consequences, and Implications." Paper presented at the 1980 meetings of the American Economic Association, pp. 1–63.

1981. "The U.K.'s Unobserved Economy: A Preliminary Assessment." *Journal of Economic Affairs* 1: 205–12.

1982a. "A New Perspective on Macroeconomic Phenomena. The Theory and Measurement of the Unobserved Economy: Causes, Consequences and Implications." *Taxation: An International Perspective* H. Walker, Ed., International Burden of Government, Fraser Institute, Vancouver.

1982b. *Observer–Subject Feedback: The Dynamics of the Unobserved Economy.* E. J. Brill, Leiden.

1985a. "The Meaning of the 'Underground Economy' and the Full Compliance Deficit." *The Economics of the Shadow Economy.* (W. Gaertner and A. Wenig Eds.) Springer-Verlag, Berlin.

1985b. "The Equation of Exchange and National Accounting Systems: Does MV = PT? A Pilot Study of the Swedish Economy." Presented at the International Conference on Income and Wealth, Nordwijk, The Netherlands, pp. 1–106.

1986a. "An Analysis of Internal Revenue Service Estimates of Unreported Income." University of Wisconsin, Madison.

1986b. "The Role of Cash Payments in the U.S. Economy: The Currency Enigma." University of Wisconsin, Madison.

1986c. "A Re-Examination of the 'Underground Economy' in the United States: A Comment on Tanzi" *Staff Papers, International*

Monetary Fund 33(4): 768–81.

Feige, E. L. and R. T. McGee 1982. "Tax Revenue Losses and the Unobserved Economy in the UK." *Journal of Economic Affairs* 2: 164–172.

1983. "Sweden's Laffer Curve: Taxation and the Unobserved Economy." *Scandinavian Journal of Economics* 85: 499–519.

Feldbrugge, F. 1975. *Samizdat and Political Dissent in the Soviet Union.* Sijthoff, Leiden.

Feldbrugge, F. (Ed). 1979. *The Constitutions of the USSR and the Union Republics.* Sijthoff and Noordhoff, Alphen aan den Rijn.

Fiorina. M. 1981. "Short- and Long-term Effects of Economic Conditions on Individual Voting Decision." *Contemporary Political Economy.* (D. A. Hibbs and H. Fassbinder, Eds.). North-Holland, Amsterdam.

Fisher, I. 1911. *The Purchasing Power of Money*, Macmillan, New York.

Fisher, S. 1979. "Anticipations and the Non-neutrality of Money." *Journal of Political Economy* 86: 553–70.

Flora, P. 1981. "Solution or Source of Crises? The Welfare State in Historical Perspective." *The Emergence of the Welfare State in Great Britain and Germany.* (W. Mommsen, Ed.). Croom Helm, London, p. 379.

Forte, F. 1979. "Lo scandalo fiscale: i costi dell'economia sommersa." *Mondo Operaio* 32: 67–8.

Foudi, R., F. Stankiewicz, and N. Vaneecloo. 1981. *Les Chomeurs et l'Économie Informelle.* Laboratoire d'Analyse des Systèmes et du Travail (LAST), Lille.

Frey, B. S. 1978. *Modern Political Economy.* Martin Robertson, Oxford.

1981. "Wie gross ist die Schattenwirtschaft." *Wirtschaft u. Recht*, H. 3/4, Jg. 33, pp. 143–52.

1983. *Democratic Economic Policy. A Theoretical Approach.* Martin Robertson, Oxford.

Frey, B. S. and F. Schneider. 1978a. "An Empirical Study of Political-Economic Interaction in the United States." *Review of Economics and Statistics* 60: 174–83.

1978b. "A Politico-Economic Model of the United Kingdom." *Economic Journal* 88: 243–53.

1981. "Recent Research on Empirical Politico-economic Models." *Contemporary Political Economy* (D. A. Hibbs and F. Fassbinder, Eds.). North-Holland, Amsterdam.

Frey, B. S. and W. W. Pommerehne. 1982. "Measuring the Hidden

Economy: Though this be Madness, There is Method in it." *The Underground Economy in the United States and Abroad.* (V. Tanzi, V. Ed.). Heath, Lexington.

Frey, L. 1975a. "Stato e prospecttive delle ricerche sul mercato del lavoro in Italia di fronte ai problemi di disoccupazione e sottoccupazione." *Quaderni di Economia del Lavoro*, pp. 1–28.

1975b. *Lavoro a Domicilio, Decentrmento e Attività Produttiva.* Angeli, Milan.

1979. "Dal lavoro nero alla misurazione del reddito sommerso." *Economia del Lavoro* 10: 120–36.

Frey, L., G. de Santis, and L. Livraghi, R. (Eds.). 1975. *Lavoro a Domicilio e Decentramento dell'Attività Produttiva nei Settori Tessile e dell'Abbigliamento in Italia.* Angeli, Milan.

Gábor, R. I. 1979a. "A második (másodlagos) gazdaság." *Valéoság* 1: 22–36. English translation, Gábor, R. I. 1979. "The Second (Secondary) Economy." *Acta Oeconomica* 3–4: 291–311.

1979b. "Második gazdaság és a háztáji gazdálkodás." *Valéoság* 7: 101–3.

1979c. "Relativ bérszinvonal – ösztönzés – munkaerökinálat." *Pénzugyi Szemle* 8–9, 11: 663–74, 856–72.

Galasi, P. 1982. "Second Economy and Utilization of Labor Power in Hungary." Paper Presented at the Conference on the Hidden Economy: Social Conflicts and the Future of Industrial Society, Rome-Frascati, Italy, November 25–28.

Gallino, L. 1975. "Politiche dell'occupazione e seconda professione." *Economia e Lavoro* 1: 81–95.

1980. *Lavorare due Volte.* Stamppatori, Torino.

Garcia, G. 1978. "The Currency Ratio and the Subterranean Economy." *Financial Analysts Journal*, November–December, pp. 64–9.

Garcia, G. and S. Pak. 1979. "Some Clues in the Case of the Missing Money." *American Economic Review* 69(2): 330–4.

Gershuny, J. I. 1979. "The Informal Economy: Its Role in Post-Industrial Society." *Futures*, February, pp. 3–15.

Gershuny, J. I. and R. E. Pahl. 1980. "Britain in the Decade of the Three Economies." *New Society* 51: 7–9.

Gibbs, J. C. 1979. "The Meaning of Ecologically Oriented Inquiry in Contemporary Psychology." *American Psychologist* 34(2): 127–40.

Ginsburgs, G. and S. Pomorski. 1980. "Enforcement of the Law and the Second Economy." Paper presented for the Research Conference on the Second Economy of the USSR, January, Washington, DC.

Giran, 1981. "Complémentarité et Concurrence entre Marché du

Bibliography

Travail Officiel et Marché du Travail Officieun." G. R. I. F. E., F. E. A., Aix-en-Provence, mimeo.

Gordon, R. J. 1981. "The Consumer Price Index: Measuring Inflation and Causing It." *The Public Interest*, No. 63, Spring.

Gourlay, J. L. 1980. "Tax Abuse – A View from Revenue Canada." *Canadian Journal*, Summer, pp. 82–7.

Greenslade, G. 1980. "Regional Dimensions of the 'Second Economy' in the USSR." Occasional Paper No. 115, Kennan Institute for Advanced Russian Studies, Washington, DC.

Greffe, X. and J. Gaudin. 1980. "Partage du travail et mode de développement." *Droit Social*, 33: 86–99.

Gronau, R. 1977. "Leisure Home Production and Work, the Allocation of Time Revisited." *Journal of Political Economy* 85: 1099–1123.

Grossmann, G. 1977. "The 'Second Economy' of the USSR." *Problems of Communism* 26(5): 25–40.

1981. "La seconde économie et la planification économique soviétique." *Revue d'Études Comparatives Est-Ouest* 12(2): 5–24.

Gutmann, P. M. 1977. "The Subterranean Economy." *Financial Analysts Journal* 33: 24–7, 34.

Haas, R. D. 1978. "Short Note on the Recent Behavior of Currency." Bank of Canada, mimeo.

Hamer, E. 1978. "Schwarzarbeit und Marktwirtschaft." *Frankfurter Allgemeine Zeitung*, November 27, 1978.

1979. *Das Handwerk und sein Markt: Probleme mit Industrie, Heimwerk, Schwarzarbeit.* Hannover, Schlüter.

Hansson, I. 1980. "Beräkning av totala marginaleffekter." Nationalekonomiska Institutionen, Lunds Universitet, Sweden, mimeo.

1981. "Beräkning av skatteundandragandet i Sverige." Riksskatteverket, Stockholm, mimeo.

Hansson, I. and C. Stuart. 1982. "Laffer Curves and the Marginal Cost of Public Funds in Sweden." Department of Economics, University of Lund.

Heckmann, J. J. 1979. "Sample Selection Bias as a Specification Error." *Econometrica* 47: 153–69.

Heertje, A. and H. Cohen. 1980. *Het officieuze circuit: een witboek over zwart en grijs geld.* Het Spectrum, Utrecht, Antwerpen.

Heertje, A., M., Allen, and H. Cohen. 1982. *The Black Economy.* Pan Books, London.

Henry, S. 1978. *The Hidden Economy.* Martin Robinson, Oxford.

Henry, S. (Ed). 1981. *Can I Have It in Cash?* Astragal, London.

Héthy, L. 1980. "A 'második gazdaság' – a gazdaság és a társadalom." *Társadalmi Szemle* 11: 40–7.

369

1983. *Gazdaságpolitika és érdekeltség*. Kossuth, Budapest.

Hibbs, D. A. and H. Fassbinder (Eds.). 1981. *Contemporary Political Economy*. North-Holland, Amsterdam.

Holzman, F. D. 1981. "The Second Economy in CMEA: A Terminological Note." *The ACES Bulletin* 1: 22–35.

Hood, C. and A. Dunsire. 1982. *Bureaumetrics. The Quantitative Comparison of British Central Government Agencies*. Gower, London, pp. 28–36. *International Herald Tribune*, March 3, 1982.

House of Commons. 1979. *Evidence of Sir William Pile to the Public Accounts Committee, 26 March 1979*. Her Majesty's Stationery Office, London.

1980. *Public Accounts Committee*. Nineteenth Report, Session 1979/80, House of Commons Paper 778. Her Majesty's Stationery Office, London.

1981. *Public Accounts Committee*. Twelfth Report, Session 1980/81, House of Commons Paper 318. Her Majesty's Stationery Office, London.

1982. *Public Accounts Committee*. Twenty-Second Report, Session 1981/82, House of Commons Paper 339. Her Majesty's Stationery Office, London.

Institute National de la Statistique et des Etudes Economiques. 1981a. *Le Mouvement Economique en France 1949–1979*. INSEE, Paris.

1981b. *Annuaire Statistique de la France 1981*. INSEE, Paris.

Internal Revenue Service. 1979. *Estimates of Income Unreported on Individual Tax Returns*. Department of the Treasury Publication 1104 (9–79), IRS, Washington, DC.

1983. *Income Tax Compliance Research*, Department of the Treasury, Washington, DC, July.

Ioffe, O.S. 1982. "Law and Economy in the USSR." *Harvard Law Review* 95: 1591–1625.

Isachsen, A. J. and S. Strom. 1980a. "Den skjulte ekonomi og det svarte arbeidsmarked." Oslo Universitet, Sweden, mimeo.

(1980b). "The Hidden Economy: The Labor Market and Tax Evasion." *Scandinavian Journal of Economics* 82: 304–11.

1981. *Skattefritt: Svart Sektor i Vekst*. Universitetsforlaget, Oslo.

Jong, E. de 1976. "Statute on Handicraft-Artisan Trade." *Review of Socialist Law* 4: 266–7.

Judd, J. and J. Scadding, 1982. "The Search for a Stable Money Demand Function: A Survey of the Post-1973 Literature." *Journal of Economic Literature*, 20(3): 993–1023.

Juhász, P. 1978. "A mezogazdasági szövetkezetek és a falu társadalma: négy esszé." Mimeo.

Bibliography

Juhász, P. and T. Prugberger. 1980. "Szocialista kisvállalatok létrehozása – egyéni kezdeményezés alapján ," *Közgazdasági Szemle* 3: 338–47.

Juster, F. T. 1966. *Household Capital Formation and Financing, 1877–1962.* NBER, New York.

Katsenelinboigen, A. 1977. "Coloured Markets in the Soviet Union." *Soviet Studies* 29: 62–85.

Kendrick, J. W. 1979. "Expanding Imputed Values in the National Income and Product Accounts." *Review of Income and Wealth*, Series 25, No. 4, December, pp. 349–63.

Key, V. O., Jr. 1961. *Public Opinion and American Democracy.* Knopf, New York.

Klovland, J. T. 1980. "In Search of the Hidden Economy: Tax Evasion and the Demand for Currency in Norway and Sweden." Discussion Paper 18/80, Norwegian School of Economics and Business Administration, Bergen.

Kolm, S.-C. 1973. "A Note on Optimum Tax Evasion." *Journal of Public Economics* 2: 265–70.

Kornai, J. 1980. *Economics of Shortage.* North-Holland, Amsterdam.
    1982. "A magyar gazdasági reform jelenlegi helyzetéröl és kilátásairéol." *Gazdaság* 3: 5–34.

Kovács, G. 1981. "A magánkisipar szabályozásának közgazdasági eszközei, különös tekintettel a penzugyi szabályozásra." Mimeo.

Kramer, G. H. 1973. "On a Class of Equilibrium Conditions for Majority Rule." *Econometrica* 41: 285–97.

Laki, T. 1983. *Vállalkozások és a társadalmi-gazdasági környezet.* Institute of Labour Affairs, Budapest.

Langfeldt, E. 1982. "The Unobserved Economy in the Federal Republic of Germany: A Preliminary Assessment." Paper Prepared for the International Conference on the Unobserved Sector. NIAS, Wassenaar, June 3–6, 1982.

Langfeldt, E. and H. Lehment. 1980. "Welche Bedeutung haben Sonderfaktoren für die Erklärung der Geldnachfrage in der Bundesrepublik Deutschland?" *Weltwirtschaftliches Archiv.*, Bd. 116, Heft 4, pp. 669–84.

Laurent, R. 1970. "Currency Transfers by Denomination." Ph.D. Thesis, University of Chicago.

Lindbeck, 1980. "Tax Effects versus Budget Effects on Labor Supply." Seminar Paper No. 148, Stockholm Institute for International Economic Studies, University of Stockholm.

Lipset, S. M. and W. Schneider. 1983. *The Confidence Gap.* Free Press, New York, pp 402, 407.

Lowery, D. and L. Sigelmann. 1981. "Understanding the Tax Revolt: Eight Explanations." *American Political Science Review* 75: 963–74.

Lukács, O. 1980, "A kiegészitö gazdaságréol." Mimeo.

Macafee, K. 1980. "A Glimpse of the Hidden Economy in the National Accounts." *Economic Trends (London)*, February, No. 316, pp. 81–7.

McCracken, P. W. 1973. "The Practice of Political Economy." *The American Economic Review*, May, 168–171.

McCrohan, K. F. 1982. "The Use of Survey Research to Estimate Trends in Non-Compliance with Federal Income Taxes." *Journal of Economic Psychology* 2(2): 231–40.

McGee, R. 1983. "The Non-Neutrality of Money and Employment Rates: Tobin and Taxation Effects." *Journal of Macroeconomics* 4: 215–23.

McGee, R. and E. L. Feige 1982a. "Policy Illusion, Macroeconomic Instability and the Unobserved Economy." Netherlands Institute for Advanced Study, April 1982. See also Chapter 3, this volume.

McGee, R. and E. L. Feige. 1982b. "The Unobserved Economy and the UK Laffer Curve." *Journal of Economic Affairs* 2: 36–43.

Magnusson, D. 1980. "Omfattningen av den ekonomiska brottsligheten." *Brottsutvecklingen* (L. Johansson, Ed.). Brotsförebygande Rådet, Stockholm.

Majone, G. 1981/82. "Modes of Control and Institutional Learning. Research Group on Guidance, Control and Performance Evaluation in the Public Sector." Discussion Paper No. 17, Bielefeld Center for Interdisciplinary Research, University of Bielefeld.

Marrese, M. 1980. "The Role of the Second Economy: Lessons from Hungary." Paper Presented at the Fifth Meeting of American and Hungarian Economists, Cambridge, MA, May 7–9.

Martino, A. 1980. "Another Italian Economic Miracle." Mont Pelerin Society, Stanford Conference, mimeo.

Matthews, K. 1981. "The Demand for Currency and the Rise of the Black Economy: 1973–1979." Liverpool Research Group Economic Bulletin 25, University of Liverpool, mimeo.

Matthews, M. 1978. *Privilege in the Soviet Union: A Study of Elite-Life-Style under Communism*. George Allen & Unwin, London.

Maurach, R. 1955. *Handbuch der Sowjetverfassung*. Isar Verlag, Munich.

Mirus, R. and R. S. Smith. 1981. "Canada's Irregular Economy." *Canadian Public Policy*, pp. 444–53. Also reprinted in V. Tanzi (Ed.). *The Underground Economy in the United States and Abroad*,

Bibliography

D. C. Heath, Lexington, MA, 1982.

Morgenstern, O. 1963. *On the Accuracy of Economic Observations*, 2nd ed. Princeton University Press, Princeton, NJ.

Mueller, D. C. 1979. *Public Choice.* Cambridge University Press, Cambridge.

Murphy, M. 1978. "The Value of Non-Market Household Production: Opportunity Cost Versus Market Cost Estimates." *Review of Income and Wealth*, vol. 24, 3 September, pp. 243–55.

1982. "Comparative Estimates of the Value of Household Work in the United States for 1976." *Review of Income and Wealth*, vol. 28, 1 March, pp. 29–43.

Myrdal, G. 1978. "Dags för ett bättre skattesystem." *Ekonomisk Debatt* 7: 403–506.

Myrsten, K. 1980. "Det illegala bygghantverket." *Brottsutvecklingen* (L. Johansson, Ed.), Brottsförebyggande Rådet, Stockholm.

Neldner, M. 1977. "The Determinants of the Currency Ratio, the Time Deposit Ratio, and the Savings Ratio: An Econometric Analysis for the West-German Economy." *Weltwirtschaftliches Archiv*, Bd. 113, Heft. 4.

Niskanen, W. A. 1971. *Bureaucracy and Representative Government.* Aldine-Atherton, Chicago.

Nordhaus, W. and I. Tobin. 1973. "Is Growth Obsolete?" *Economic Growth, Fiftieth Anniversary Colloquium V*. NBER, New York, pp. 343–7.

O'Hearn, D. 1980. "The Consumer Second Economy: Size and Effects." *Soviet Studies* 32: 218–34.

O'Higgins, M. 1980. *Measuring the Hidden Economy: A Review of Evidence and Methodologies.* Outer Circle Policy Unit, London.

1981a. "Aggregate Measures of Tax Evasion: An Assessment." *British Tax Review* 26: 286–302.

1981b. "Tax Evasion and the Self-Employed: An Examination of the Evidence." *British Tax Review* 26: 367–78.

Ofer, G. and A. Vinokur. 1980. "Private Sources of Income in the Soviet Urban Household." Paper prepared for the Research Conference on the Second Economy of the USSR, Washington, DC, January.

Outer Circle Policy Unit. 1979. *Policing the Hidden Economy.* Outer Circle Policy Unit, London.

Parker, R. P., 1984. "Improved Adjustments for Misreporting of Tax Return Information Used to Estimate the National Income and Product Accounts, 1977." *Survey of Current Business*, 64(6): 17–25, United States Department of Commerce, Bureau of Economic

Analysis.

Peacock, A. and G. Shaw. 1982. "Is Tax Revenue Loss Overstated?" *Journal of Economic Affairs* 2:161–3.

Pencavel, J. 1979. "A Note on Income Tax Evasion, Labor Supply and Nonlinear Tax Schedules." *Journal of Public Economics* 12: 115–24.

Persson, L. 1979. "Myter om ekonomiska brott." *Ekonomisk Brottslighet* (L. Johansson, Ed.) Brottsförebyggande Rådet, Stockholm.

Petersen, H.-G. 1981. "Size of the Public Sector, Economic Growth and the Informal Economy." Paper Prepared for the Seventeenth General Conference of the International Association for Research in Income and Wealth, Gouvieux, Frankreich, June 1981.

Pipes, S. and M. Walker (with D. Gill). 1982. *Tax Facts 3: The Canadian Consumer Tax Index and You.* Fraser Institute, Vancouver.

Plott, C. R. 1976. "A Notion of Equilibrium and its Possibility Under Majority Rule." *American Economic Review* 57: 787–806.

Pomorski, S. 1978. "Crimes against the Central Planner: 'Ochkovtiratel'-stvo'." *Soviet Law after Stalin: Social Engineering through Law*, (D. Barry, G. Ginsburgs and P. Maggs, Eds.), *Law in Eastern Europe* 20 (II). Sijthoff and Noordhoff, Alphen aan den Rijn.

Porter, P., T. Simpson, and E. Mauskopf, 1979. "Financial Innovations and the Monetary Aggregates." *Brookings Papers on Economic Activity*. 1: 213–29.

Porter, R. and E. Offenbacher. 1984. "Financial Innovations and Measurement of Monetary Aggregates." *Financial Innovations*. Federal Reserve Bank of St. Louis, Kluwer-Nijhoff, St. Louis, MO, pp. 49–98.

Porter R. and S. Thurman. 1979. "The Currency Ratio and the Subterranean Economy: Additional Comments." Board of Governors of the Federal Reserve System, processed, January 26, 1979.

Radnéoti, H. 1979. "Háztáji gazdálkodás és a második gazdaság." *Valéoság* 4: 9–24.

Ragot, M. 1983. *Le Travail Clandestin*. Avis Adopté par le Conseil Economique et Social. Conseil Economique et Social, Paris.

Ramsay. F. R. 1927. "A Contribution to the Theory of Taxation." *Economic Journal* 37: 47–61.

Rázus, Cs. 1975. "A lakosság részére térítésért vagy ellenszolgáltatásért engedély nélkul végzett szolgáltatási tevékenység, illetve a barkács je munkák volumenének megállapitása." Mimeo.

Rikspolisstyrelsen. 1977. "Organiserad och ekonomisk brottslighet i Sverige: ett åtgärsförslag." Report from Arbetsgruppen mot organiserad brottslighet, Rikspolisstyrelsen, Stockholm, mimeo.

Bibliography

Rosanvallon, P. 1980. "Le développement de l'économie souterraine et l'avenir des sociétés industrielles." *Le Débat* 2: 15–27.

Ross, I. 1978. "Why the Underground Economy is Booming." *Fortune* 9: 92–8.

Royal Commission on the Distribution of Income and Wealth. 1979. *Report No. 8 – Fourth Report on the Standing Reference.* Her Majesty's Stationery Office, London, Table 10.16.

Rumer, B. 1981. "The 'Second' Agriculture in the USSR." *Soviet Studies* 33: 560–72.

Saba, A. 1980. *L'Industria Sommersa. Il Nuovo Modello di Svilluppo.* Marsilio, Padua.

Sachverständigenrat zur Begutachtung der gesamtwirtschaftlichen Entwicklung: Jahresgutachten 1980/81, 1981/82, Bonn.

Sandmo, A. 1976. "Optimal Taxation. An Introduction to the Literature." *Journal of Public Economics* 6: 37–54.

1981. "Income Tax Evasion, Labour Supply, and the Equity-Efficiency Tradeoff." *Journal of Public Economics* 16: 265–88.

Schoemaker, P. J. H. 1982. "The Expected Utility Model: Its Variants, Purposes, Evidence and Limitation." *Journal of Economic Literature* 20: 529–63.

Scott, W. and H. Grasnick. 1981. "Deterrence and Income Tax Cheating: Testing Interaction Hypotheses in Utilitarian Theories." *Journal of Applied Behavioural Science* 17: 395–408.

Seguin, Ph. 1979. *Rapport Fait au Nom de la Commission d'Enquete sur la Situation de l'Emploi et le Chomage.* Documents de l'Assemblée Nationale, No. 1180. Journal Officiel de la République Francaise, Paris.

Sen, 1970. *Collective Choice and Social Welfare.* Holden, San Francisco.

Sen, A. and B. Williams. 1982. "Introduction." *Utilitarianism and Beyond* (A. Sen and B. Williams, Eds.). Cambridge University Press, Cambridge.

Shankland, G. 1980. *Our Secret Economy – The Response of the Informal Economy to the Rise of Mass Unemployment.* London.

SIFO. 1966. "Deklarationsfuskarna." SIFO, Stockholm, mimeo.

1978. "Den sjunkande deklarationsmoralen." SIFO, Stockholm, mimeo.

1979. "En nation av fifflare." SIFO, Stockholm, mimeo.

1980a. "Svartbetalare och svartjobbare." SIFO, Stockholm, mimeo.

1980b. "Småforetagarna och svartjobben." SIFO, Stockholm, mimeo.

1981. "Få uppger för låga inkomster i självdeklarationen." SIFO, Stockholm, mimeo.

Simes, D. 1975. "The Soviet Parallel Market." *Survey* 21(3): 42–52.

Simis, K. 1977. "The Machinery of Corruption in the Soviet Union." *Survey* 23(4): 35–55.

Simon, C. P. and A. D. Witte. 1981. *The Underground Economy: What Is It and What Should We Do?* The Osprey Company, Tallahassee, FL.

Simon, H. A. 1978. "Rationality as Process and Product of Thought." *American Economic Review, Papers and Proceedings* 68: 1–16.

Simpson, T. and R. Porter, 1980. "Some Issues Involving the Definition and Interpretation of the Monetary Aggregates." *Controlling Monetary Aggregates III*, Federal Reserve Bank of Boston Conference Series No. 22.

Singh, B. 1973. "Making Honesty the Best Policy." *Journal of Public Economics* 2: 257–63.

Skolka, J. 1985. "The Parallel Economy in Austria." *The Economics of the Shadow Economy* (W. Gaertner and A. Wenig, Eds.). Springer-Verlag, Berlin, pp. 60–75.

Skolnick, J. H. 1966. *Justice without Trial: Law Enforcement in Democratic Society*. Wiley, New York, Chapter 8.

Smith, A. 1981a. "A Review of the Informal Economy in the European Community." *Economic Papers* 3. Commission of the European Communities, Brussels.

1981b. "The Informal Economy." *Lloyds Bank Review* 141: 45–61.

Smith, H. 1976. *The Russians*. Quadrangle, New York.

Smith, J. D., T. E. Moyer, and E. Trzcinski, 1982. "The Measurement of Selected Income Flows in Informal Markets." Prepared for the Internal Revenue Service, December 1982.

SOU. 1970. *Aspirationer, Möjligheter och Skattermoral*. Liber, Stockholm.

Spicer, M. and S. Lundstedt. 1976. "Understanding Tax Evasion." *Public Finance* 2: 295–305.

Srinivasan, T. N. 1973. "Tax Evasion: A Model." *Journal of Public Economics* 2: 339–46.

Stuart, C. E. 1981. "Swedish Tax Rates, Labor Supply and Tax Revenues." *Journal of Political Economy* 89: 1020–38.

SSRC Working Group. 1981. "Report of the Working Group on the Hidden Economy and the Tax Base." Social Science Research Council, London, mimeo.

Staats, S. 1972. "Corruption in the Soviet System." *Problems of Communism* 21(1): 40–6.

Tahar, G. 1980. "Le marche du travail marginal et clandestin en France, au Royaume-Uni et en Italie," Study No. 79/42, Commission of the

Bibliography

European Communities, Brussels.

Tanzi, V. 1980. "The Underground Economy in the United States: Estimates and Implications." *Banco Nazionale del Lavoro Quarterly Review* 135: 427–53.

1982. "Underground Economy and Tax Evasion in the United States: Estimates and Implications." *The Underground Economy in the United States and Abroad.* (V. Tanzi, Ed.). DC Heath, Lexington, pp. 69–92.

1983. "The Underground Economy in the United States: Annual Estimates, 1930–80." *International Monetary Fund Staff Papers,* pp. 283–305.

Theil, H. 1968. *Optimal Decision Rules for Government and Industry.* North-Holland, Amsterdam.

Thomas, J. J. 1986. "The Underground Economy in the United States: A Comment on Tanzi." *Staff Papers, International Monetary Fund,* Vol. 33, No. 4, December 1986, pp. 782–8.

Tinbergen, J. 1952. *On the Theory of Economic Policy.* North-Holland, Amsterdam.

Tittle, C. and A. Rowe, 1973. "Moral Appeal, Sanction Threat, and Deviance: An Experimental Test." *Social Problems* 20: 488–98.

Treml, V. 1975. "Alcohol in the USSR: a Fiscal Dilemma." *Soviet Studies* 27: 161–77.

United Nations, Department of Economic and Social Affairs, Statistical Office. 1953. *A System of National Accounts and Supporting Tables.* Studies in Methods, Series F, No. 2. United Nations, New York.

University of Michigan, *American National Election Studies Sourcebook 1952–78.* University of Michigan Survey Research Center, Ann Arbor, MI.

Van Eck, R. 1983. "Secundaire activiteiten en de Nationale rekeningen." *CBS-Select II,* CBS, The Hague.

Vanous, J. 1980. "Private Foreign Exchange Markets in Eastern Europe and the USSR." Paper Prepared for the Research Conference on the Second Economy of the USSR, Washington DC, January.

Van Tuinen, H. K. 1980. "Verwarring over officieuze geldcircuits nog groter." NRC/Handelsblad, December 1, 1980.

1981. Lecture presented at the meeting of the Union of Public Finance (Vereniging voor Openbare Financien), *Openbare Uitgaven,* August 1981.

Varga, Gy. 1980. "A mezögazdasagi kistermelés jelentösége, szabályozottságe és a fejlesztés föbb kérdései." *Közgazdasági Szemle* 7–8:

908–22.

Volensky, M. 1980. *Nomenklatura: Die Herschende Klasse in der Sowjetunion.* Fritz Molden, Munich.

Wadekin, K. 1973. *The Private Sector in the Soviet Agriculture.* University of California Press, Berkeley.

Warneryd, K. E. and B. Walerud. 1981. "Taxes and Economic Behavior: Some Interview Data on Tax Evasion in Sweden." The Economic Research Institute of Stockholm, School of Economics, mimeo.

Weber, M. 1964. *Wirtschaft und Gesellschaft. Grundriss der verstehenden Soziologie.* Kiepenhauer und Witsch, Cologne-Berlin.

Weck, H. and B. S. Frey. 1982. "Tax Finance and the Shadow Economy." International Institute of Public Finance, Copenhagen Congress, mimeo, August.

Weiss, L. 1976. "The Desirability of Cheating Incentives and Randomness in the Optimal Income Tax." *Journal of Political Economy* 84: 1343–52.

Wicksell, K. 1896. *Finanztheoretische Untersuchungen.* Gustav Fischer, Jena.

Wildavsky, A. 1964. *The Politics of the Budgetary Process.* Little Brown, Boston.

Wilensky, H. L. 1981. "Family Life Cycle, Work, and the Quality of Life: Reflections on the Roots of Happiness, Despair and Indifference in Modern Society." *Working Life: A Social Science Contribution to Work Reform* (B. Gardell and G. Johansson, Eds.), Wiley, London.

Wiles, P. 1981. *Die Parallelwirtschaft: Eine Einschatzung des systemwidrigen Verhaltens (SWV) im Bereich der Wirtschaft unter besonderer Berucksichtigung der USSR.* Bundesinstitut für Ostwissentschaftliche und Internationale Studien, Cologne.

Wong, F. and D. Rose, 1980. "The Subterranean Economy: A Survey of the Literature and Applications to the Canadian Economy." RM-80-107, Bank of Canada, unpublished research memorandum.

Zemtsov, I. 1976. *Partiia ili Mafiia? Resvorovannaia Respublika.* Les Editeurs Réunies, Paris.

1979. "The Ruling Class in the USSR." *Crossroads* 2: 5–60.